The PRESIDENT WE DESERVE

The PRESIDENT WE DESERVE

★★★★★★★★★★★★★★★★★★★★★★

BILL CLINTON: HIS RISE, FALLS, AND COMEBACKS

Martin Walker

CROWN PUBLISHERS, INC.
NEW YORK

For my daughters.

Published by Crown Publishers, Inc., 201 East 50th Street, New York, New York 10022. Member of the Crown Publishing Group.

Random House, Inc. New York, Toronto, London, Sydney, Auckland
CROWN is a trademark of Crown Publishers, Inc.
http://www.randomhouse.com/
Printed in the United States of America

Design by Deborah Kerner

Library of Congress Cataloging-in-Publication Data is available upon request.

ISBN 0-517-59871-X
10 9 8 7 6 5 4 3 2 1
First Edition

CONTENTS

ACKNOWLEDGMENTS

This is a traditional political biography, written by a citizen of another country who lacks the right to vote for or against Bill Clinton. It seeks to narrate the public life so far of an important historic figure and place that life within the context of his times. It is not an attempt to report, word for word and expletive for expletive and thought for thought, what took place behind closed doors at important moments. This account does not claim to penetrate the psychology of its characters, nor to peel back curtains and bedclothes in order to confide intimacies. Without such presumptive intrusions, the political career of Bill Clinton is already shot through with drama and risk, with achievement and disillusion, and with significance. His administration charted America's new international role in the aftermath of the cold war, as the linchpin of a free-trading global economy.

This is in no sense an authorized biography of Clinton, nor of his administration. No privileged access was sought, nor extended, beyond the courtesies afforded a member of the White House press corps, with the right to travel with the president and access to background briefings. This book is written by an Acquaintance, rather than by a Friend of Bill. It is, however, an acquaintance that goes back nearly thirty years to Oxford, which was renewed in Little Rock long before the presidential campaign began, renewed again on the campaign trail and in office. It is extended by a large number of mutual friends, in the administration and beyond it, in Britain and Germany as well as the United States. It is thus based on casual conversations and interviews, on formal reporting and more impressionistic observation, on the diplomatic and social circuit as well as the seminar and the press conference and the campaign trail. The main feature of my professional life since the end of 1991 has been Clinton-watching, and there has seldom been a dull moment.

This book also rests heavily on published sources, from my colleagues in the United States and international media, and from fellow authors. The starting point has been the work of the extremely impressive Arkansas media, their journalism as well as their books. Meredith Oakley's *On the Make* is an exhaustive and cold-eyed account of a modern governor. *The Clintons of Arkansas* edited by Ernest Dumas is a more sympathetic assembly of portraits by one of the state's most celebrated liberal journalists. John Brummett's *High Wire* tells the haunting story of an entire Arkansan tribe unhappily transplanted to a hostile Washington. Over the past decade and more, the columns of John Robert Starr and Paul Greenberg have proved prescient in defining that cynical and grudging admiration which Clinton has inspired in Little Rock and Washington alike.

No understanding of Clinton's youth and life is possible without David Maraniss's ground-breaking biography *First in His Class.* It is a modern classic. Bob Woodward's *The Agenda* is an extraordinarily clear window on a brief period and one tightly defined issue in the first months of the administration. Elizabeth Drew is indispensable; her accounts of Clinton's first year, *On the Edge,* and of his confrontation with the Republican Congress, *Showdown,* are models of dogged research and clear exposition. Of all the Whitewater books, James Stewart's *Blood Sport* is the most useful, the least intemperate, and by far the saddest. I have relied on all of these books and made use of many more, including the various so far unsatisfactory biographies of Hillary Clinton and the delightful memoirs of Clinton's mother, Virginia Kelley.

I owe a particular debt to my friend Sidney Blumenthal of the *New Yorker* for his invaluable articles and also for his conversation. A host of friends in the Washington media informed and entertained me and advanced my political education, from Mary McGrory to Diane Rehm, Tony Snow to Paul Gigot, Rod MacLeish to Finlay Lewis, David Ignatius to Jodie Allen, William Schneider to E. J. Dionne, Steve Roberts to Howard Fineman. C-SPAN, CNN's *Capital Gang, Washington Week in Review, Inside Washington,* National Public Radio, and Monitor Radio have on occasion asked me to discuss American politics with the best-informed commentators in the business. My colleagues at the World Policy Institute at the New School for Social Research in New York have welcomed me to the most agreeable and collegial of think tanks in international affairs. Thanks to Alan Freed's Washington Workshops, I have enjoyed seminars with a stunningly wide range of military and civilian officials.

This book is published in my eighth year in Washington as the correspondent for Britain's *Guardian,* whose editors and staff have my deepest affection and appreciation. It was a great pleasure to return to a city I first came to know in 1971 as a Congressional Fellow of the American Political Science Association, when I worked on the staff of the estimable Senator Edmund Muskie. Eight years of daily reporting mean that I have no more excuse for my ignorance about America, so all the mistakes and infelicities in this book are my own.

MARTIN WALKER
Washington, D.C.

INTRODUCTION

At the height of the Vietnam War in 1968, the young German revolutionary Rudi Dutschke appealed to the raging students of West Berlin to "commit yourselves like Mao's Chinese comrades to a Long March through the institutions of the state." A generation later, and an Atlantic Ocean away, Dutschke's call was to find a curious echo whenever the FOBs gathered, the Friends of Bill. "FOB" was how they were described on flight manifests on the chartered aircraft of the Clinton campaign. Seen up close, much of the Clinton campaign was the 1960s anti-Vietnam movement grown older and wiser and incomparably more ambitious. The institution of the state that beckoned from the end of this Long March was the White House itself.

Few of the FOBs had been wild-eyed radicals. They embodied the respectable wing of the movement. The man who became Clinton's national security adviser, Tony Lake, was a professor at Mount Holyoke College in Massachusetts when he was asked to manage foreign policy for the Clinton campaign, commissioning working papers from the Democratic experts who had aged in their think-tank wilderness for the previous twelve years of Republican rule. In 1970, Lake had been one of the bright young State Department highfliers recruited by Henry Kissinger to work in President Nixon's National Security Council. Lake resigned in disgust at the invasion of Cambodia, and went on to work for Senator Edmund Muskie, the Democratic front-runner to challenge Nixon in 1972. Lake's deputy in the Clinton White House was to be Sandy Berger, a veteran of the McGovern campaign that rallied the antiwar movement to push Muskie aside and win the nomination.

The FOBs gathered for the endless celebrations of the campaign trail. On the eighth-floor corridor of Clinton's Chicago hotel on the night in March 1992 when he won the Illinois primary, Kevin O'Keefe savored the triumph. He had organized the state for Clinton and delivered the Daley operation in Chicago, the last big-city political machine in America, to the candidate from the Deep South. O'Keefe had first met Clinton's wife, Hillary, in Senator Eugene McCarthy's antiwar crusade in New Hampshire in 1968, when students cut their hair and shaved their beards to be "clean for Gene." O'Keefe went into the White House as presidential assistant for intergovernmental affairs, an obscure but heavyweight job in the political boiler room.

Beside O'Keefe, grinning in victory, stood Eli Segal, who had made his fortune as the publisher of *Games* magazine and was now the Clinton campaign's budget chief. Back in 1968, he had been Harvard organizer for the McCarthy campaign and then a deputy campaign manager for McGovern. Segal was to be charged with implementing one of the ideas closest to Clinton's heart, the Americorps plan for national service, a domestic echo of Kennedy's Peace Corps. Alongside Segal at that Chicago primary celebration stood Derek Shearer, who in 1968 helped run the antiwar movement at Yale and joined up with Clinton at Oxford, where the young Rhodes scholar was putting together one of a series of personal networks, which were maturing over the years into an unstoppable political force. Shearer was in Oxford to visit his sister Brooke, who was staying with the man she was to marry, Strobe Talbott. A fellow Rhodes scholar and Clinton's roommate at Oxford, Talbott was to become deputy secretary of state.

The night Clinton swept the 1992 Texas primary, Garry Mauro reminisced. The man who organized Texas for Clinton, and hoped he could win the state from President Bush in November, Mauro first met the Clintons in 1972 on McGovern's presidential campaign in Texas. It is a legend the FOBs loved to tell, how the awesome couple took off from Yale, worked like dogs in Texas, barely attended a class, and went back to sail through their law school finals.

Sam Browne, another of the Vietnam Solidarity campaign leaders, began to organize the Clinton West Coast campaign with a meeting in Berkeley of Northern California elected officials. "It has the feel of the antiwar movement twenty-five years ago, the way campaigns tend to get captured by the first people in the door. And now we have the party establishment clamoring to get in when the best seats are taken," Browne said. Browne, nominated to be ambassador to the United Nations Disarmament Agency in Vienna, was one of the few to fall foul of his prominence on opposing the Vietnam War, as conservative senators blocked his confirmation.

Harold Ickes organized Clinton's New York campaign, just as he organized the Jesse Jackson primary in 1988. He had been an FOB since he and Clinton worked together on Project Pursestrings in the summer of 1970, an attempt to stop the war by lobbying Congress to starve it of funds. At the time, Ickes had been dating Susan Thomases, another New York lawyer who had gone on to become one of Hillary's closest friends and allies. She served with Hillary on the board of the Children's Defense Fund, and brought order to the campaign's chaotic scheduling system. Carl Wagner, another Project Pursestrings veteran who went on to organize Michigan for the McGovern campaign, had then joined Senator Kennedy's staff. Wagner stood with Robert Reich, one of the main student organizers for McCarthy in 1968, on the lawn before the old state house in Little Rock on that October day in 1991 when Clinton announced his presidential bid.

In this generation of activists against the Vietnam War who were now inheriting the Democratic Party, Bill Clinton knew everybody. To follow the Clinton campaign from New Hampshire to Colorado and Georgia and Florida and Chicago and California was constantly to run into the FOBs, all of them now old friends and veterans of reunions in Clinton's home, the governor's mansion in Little Rock. In their loyalty to him, the FOBs had the feel of a *comitatus,* the devoted bodyguard around some tribal chieftain. In retrospect, there was something that recalled Kennedy in this process—Clinton's deliberate skill at rallying the best and brightest of his generation.

At Clinton's darkest hour in his campaign, when the allegation of dodging the Vietnam draft joined the tabloid scandal about marital infidelity, his Oxbridge friends rallied to his defense. Michael Mandelbaum, of the Council on Foreign Relations and the School of Advanced International Studies, published a stout defense of his old chum in the *New York Times.* Strobe Talbott, then the foreign policy heavyweight at *Time* magazine, wrote a haunting column to explain to his colleagues in the press that Clinton was no draft dodger. Like all the rest of that Oxford generation of Americans, along with the third man who shared their flat on

Leckford Road, Frank Aller, Clinton agonized endlessly and honorably about how to oppose the misbegotten war. Aller, who decided to become a draft resister and was arrested on his eventual return to the United States, was to commit suicide in 1971.

Among the FOBs at Oxford was Robert Reich, a star economics lecturer at Harvard, the source of much of Clinton's policy of economic renewal, and Clinton's future secretary of labor. The anti-Vietnam movement at Oxford was organized tirelessly by Ira Magaziner, who went on to become a wealthy business consultant whose ideas on how to regenerate the sagging U.S. manufacturing base might have made him a White House economic adviser, except that Hillary poached him first, for the health reform task force. There was fellow Rhodes scholar Douglas S. Eakeley, who organized a fund-raising party of Clinton's old college friends that garnered $100,000 even before the campaign began. When they met on the ocean voyage to England, Eakeley had thought Clinton "a classic southern glad-handing politician." Over the next two years, they became staunch friends.

Richard Stearns, another Oxford friend, had brought Clinton into the nerve center of the McGovern campaign at the Democratic Party convention in Miami in 1972. Even before that, in the summer of 1969, Stearns had taken Clinton to a gathering of antiwar student campaigners, veterans of the 1968 McCarthy and Robert Kennedy presidential efforts, where he met David Mixner, who would become Clinton's leading organizer among gay organizations in 1992. Deputy to the McGovern campaign manager Gary Hart, Stearns put Clinton into the trailer outside the convention hall where the voting strategy was plotted and the orders passed on to the whips in the hall. Stearns, who had become a judge in Massachusetts, stepped forth to join the team of spin doctors who took the sting out of the accusation that Clinton had dodged the draft. Stearns found himself explaining patiently to a different generation of journalists how it had been to watch the Vietnam War on a TV set in an Oxford common room. On one awful day, one of the Americans at Balliol saw a college roommate shot in battle on the BBC-TV evening news. By 1993 a judge in Massachusetts, Stearns was Clinton's own preference to become FBI director in 1993, until White House counsel Bernard Nussbaum dissuaded him from elevating an FOB to such a sensitive post.

There were at least seven clearly definable roots in the remarkable agglomeration of talent and ambition that gathered as the FOBs around Clinton. First came the Arkansas network, starting with Thomas Franklin McLarty III, who went to Miss Mary's kindergarten with Bill Clinton forty years earlier, and was in 1992 now chairman of Arkla Inc.—Arkansas-Louisiana, one of the biggest natural gas conglomerates. Mack McLarty's fund-raising campaign among the big corporations was awesomely efficient, and his reward was to be appointed White House chief of staff.

Bruce Lindsey was the campaign director, an Arkansas lawyer who gave Clinton a job when he briefly lost the state governorship in 1980. A self-effacing man, he spent the campaign with a mobile phone glued to his ear. Lindsey's wife, Bev, had run scheduling for the Fritz Mondale presidential campaign in 1984. Along with Hillary Rodham Clinton's partners in the Rose Law Firm of Little Rock, Bev helped organize the Arkansas Travelers, a group of over four hundred volunteers who flew and bused themselves to wherever the campaign was hardest. In New Hampshire, the Travelers helped Clinton overcome the taint of scandal, canvassing the state door-to-door and distributing the Clinton biography videotapes that helped turn the tide.

The Travelers threw themselves a celebration party on the night Clinton won Illinois that was unlike any other political event on the campaign trail. Along the hotel corridor, it was a street party of friends and neighbors, full of talk of home and anecdotes about Clinton, their governor for the past decade. And the "Sooo-eee!" hog call of Arkansas, the supporters' cheer for the Razorback football team of the University of Arkansas, split the Chicago night. Another of the Arkansas gang, who flew into New Hampshire at 3 A.M. just after the draft evasion story broke, was Harry Thomason, the very rich Hollywood TV producer behind *Designing Women*. Thomason came to offer support, cash, and media skills. His wife, Linda Bloodworth, helped swell Clinton's Hollywood network with former Columbia Pictures chief Dawn Steel and TriStar's Mike Medavoy.

Bruce Lindsey got into politics the same way Clinton did, by working for the legendary senator from Arkansas J. William Fulbright, father of the Fulbright scholarships. Fulbright hired the bright young Bill Clinton to work on his Senate Foreign Relations Committee staff back in 1966, when Fulbright began organizing the first critical Senate hearings on the Vietnam War. Fulbright helped put Clinton through Georgetown University, by giving him a part-time job, and later backed Clinton for his Rhodes scholarship to Oxford.

So the Arkansas base led to a Georgetown base, which led in turn to the Oxford FOBs. Clinton's roommate at Georgetown was Thomas Mark Caplan, a delightful Anglophile and novelist who had not the slightest political or governmental ambition, but a boundless affection for his old friend. The only job that might have tempted him was to don the purple as an English bishop of his favorite cathedral, at the diocese of Bath and Wells, which would not be in President Clinton's gift. But whenever Clinton was depressed or under acute fire, Tommy Caplan was called to cheer him up, to talk about books and reminisce.

Another Georgetown friend, Roger C. Altman of the Blackstone Group investment firm, became deputy secretary of the U.S. Treasury. Altman served in Carter's Treasury the last time the Democrats were in office, and his Blackstone Group helped negotiate the sale of Columbia Pictures to Sony. Blackstone, which was also to produce Jeffrey Garten, Clinton's undersecretary of commerce and a top trade strategist, was partly owned by Japan's Nikko Securities. Clinton's firm opposition to protectionism provoked some mutterings on the left about the ways the FOBs were linked to Japanese finance. Robert E. Rubin and Kenneth Brody of the Goldman, Sachs financial firm were Clinton's two main fund-raisers on Wall Street. Goldman, Sachs is partly owned by Sumitomo. Rubin went on to become economic adviser, and then secretary of the Treasury. One of the main Washington fund-raisers for Clinton was the lawyer-lobbyist Tommy Boggs, son of the veteran congressman Hale Boggs, whose firm represented Toshiba, Sony, and Sansui. One of Boggs's law partners was Ron Brown, chairman of the Democratic National Committee during the campaign, and then Clinton's secretary of commerce.

The Clinton campaign embodied in an acute and highly visible way the coming together of a new American establishment. The people who went to elite universities a generation earlier had graduated into politics and business and money and the law, and were now claiming the inheritance that first beckoned when the Long March began in the 1960s.

The third of the Clinton networks, the Oxford mafia of Rhodes scholars, was to British observers the most obvious common factor in this elite. To Americans, it was the fourth network of Yale Law School, where Clin-

ton went after Oxford, that seemed to tie the FOBs' new establis
gether. It was there that he met Hillary Rodham, who added her
midable network to his. Although she too had worked for th
McCarthy campaign, Hillary's contacts went far beyond the anti-Vie
movement. Not just a practicing lawyer, she was a legal theorist of so
distinction, a pioneer in defining the new law of children's rights. Knowing she was unlikely to play the traditional First Lady role, some of the FOBs would muse privately that she might one day be nominated to the Supreme Court, or repeat the role Bobby Kennedy played in the Kennedy administration as attorney general.

Hillary Clinton's legal weight put her on the board of the Legal Services Corporation and the Children's Defense Fund: more networks. The former introduced her to Mickey Kantor, the veteran California lawyer who helped set up the 1960s "War on Poverty" and who became Clinton's U.S. trade representative. The latter network brought her back to Marian Wright Edelman, for whom Hillary had worked after Yale Law School. It was through Marian Wright Edelman, who invited her to a League of Women Voters conference, that Hillary met Vernon Jordan, the civil rights lawyer who was to chair Clinton's transition team after Clinton won the presidency. Marian was married to Peter Edelman, dean of the Georgetown University Law Center and former Bobby Kennedy aide. After working for Edelman, Hillary joined the staff recruited by John Doar to work in the impeachment process of President Nixon as the House Judiciary Committee probed the Watergate affair. Her immediate boss was Bernard Nussbaum, later a corporate lawyer with Wachtell, Lipton, Rosen and Katz, the leading law firm for corporate takeovers in the 1980s, and a main fund-raiser for Clinton. And when Hillary needed a chief of staff in the White House, she hired Margaret Williams, communications director of Edelman's Children's Defense Fund.

The connections intertwined and cross-fertilized, as the new establishment spread its influence into the law and politics, into diplomacy and the think tanks, into the world of money and the media. On the campaign trail, and later to run the Voice of America in the Clinton administration, was Geoffrey Cowan. He had known the Clintons since Yale Law School, and had then taught communications law in California and won an Emmy for his film *Mark Twain and Me*. Cowan founded legal advice centers in Los Angeles and joined the board of Public Broadcasting. Hollywood was filled with FOBs and fund-raisers, from Harry Thomason to Barbra Streisand, Richard Dreyfuss, and TV producer Norman Lear, who had once tried to recruit Clinton to run his liberal lobbying group, People for the American Way.

Clinton's tenure as governor of Arkansas from 1978 to 1980, and then again for the ten years after 1982, brought him the fifth network: the fraternity of state governors. His connection to Massachusetts governor Michael Dukakis in the 1980s won him the invitation to nominate Dukakis as Democratic presidential candidate in 1988. The friendships with the governors and their local political organizations helped him win state after state in the primaries. Governor Zell Miller delivered Georgia, the old Governor Blanchard machine helped win Michigan. Ex-Governor Richard Riley brought in South Carolina, and Colorado's Roy R. Romer did Herculean service in the Rocky Mountain states.

The network of governors, who in 1991 elected Clinton "most effective" of their number, led him into the established power network of the Democratic Leadership Council. Founded in 1985 by defense-minded Southern Democrats to haul the party back to the center after Mondale's defeat and Ronald Reagan's reelection, the DLC was dismissed by Jesse Jackson as "a group of southern boys in suits." In fact, it was to be Clinton's springboard, and his recruiting tours in 1990–1991 to found DLC chapters in state after state became the basis for his national network in the primary campaigns. The DLC also brought Clinton its think tank, the Progressive Policy Institute, which helped prepare his first policy statements and covered his right flank as he began campaigning from the left against the pro-business Paul Tsongas. The DLC was to provide White House domestic policy aides Bruce Reed, another Rhodes scholar, and William A. Galston, who introduced Clinton to the communitarian ideas of Amitai Etzioni.

The final Clinton network was called the Renaissance Group. It began as a holiday, a few days of golfing and policy seminars and networking at the plush Hilton Head resort in South Carolina every New Year's. The Clintons became regulars, along with Supreme Court Justice Harry Blackmun, Kennedy loyalist Theodore Sorensen, and high-powered Washington lawyers like Clinton's general counsel David M. Ifshin, a pro-Israel activist who helped with the Jewish vote in Florida. Philip Lader, who was to become Clinton's deputy chief of staff at the White House, founded and ran the Renaissance weekends with his wife, Linda.

Clinton's skill was to weld all seven of these networks into a political alliance whose common factor was himself and Hillary, and then to use his own personal warmth to deepen and deliberately nurture acquaintance into a vast web of friendships. The group stayed at one another's houses, as Sam Browne stayed at Eli Segal's place on the Vail ski slopes, as the Clintons stayed with Strobe Talbott in Washington and with Derek Shearer when they visited California. Shearer, a professor at Occidental University in Los Angeles and married to the radical mayor of Santa Monica, advised on foreign and economic policy, and served briefly in the Commerce Department before becoming ambassador to Finland.

More than a social round, the endless talks and dinners and reunion weekends of the FOBs had also seen a constant debate about how to reinvent the Democratic Party, to restore the old coalition of the South, the black and working-class vote, and the progressive middle class. This endless conversation, which could be tracked in the books of his Oxford chums Robert Reich and Ira Magaziner, centered on the strategic role of activist government to guide the invisible hand of the free market. Fiscally cautious and socially liberal, it depended deeply on the inspirational role of Clinton himself. Late at night, they could all hark back to the lost leader of their youth, to John Kennedy and the challenge he posed to their generation: "Ask not what your country can do for you . . ."

The echo of Kennedy's challenge was distinct in speech after speech. In South Carolina one campaign evening, Clinton ended with words that brought a long stillness to the hall: "I desperately want to be your president. But *you*"—and he paused after stressing the word—"have to be Americans again."

Over the years, Clinton brought the FOBs together, to reunions at the governor's mansion in Little Rock, to meetings in New York and California and at his old college of Georgetown in Washington. In September of 1991 he summoned them all to the Washington Court Hotel on Capitol Hill to discuss whether this was to be the year for the assault on the presidency.

This gathering of the devoted Clinton clans brought together the nucleus of what was to become the next American government. In September, they declared themselves almost ready, but wanted to see who else might join the race, and whether the rest of the Democratic Party would be receptive. They held off a final decision until Clinton's appearance at a meeting of the Democratic National Committee in Los Angeles, where he reworked the old Democratic slogans into a new and challenging context.

"National security begins at home. The Soviet empire did not ever lose to us on the field of battle. It rotted from the inside out, from economic failure, from political failure," he told the DLC in a speech that rehearsed his campaign manifesto. "You don't have to be an isolationist or protectionist to know that if you're not strong enough to take care of your own folks, you can't do the first thing for anybody else. . . . It is a long, long way in this country from me at the age of six holding my great-granddaddy's hand to a condition where children on the streets of this city don't know who their grandparents are and have to worry about their own parents' drug abuse. I tell you, my friends, if we cannot make common cause with those kids, we cannot keep the American dream alive for any of us."

The speech was a triumph, and the buzz went around the Democrats that Clinton was running, and he was hot. The next day, the FOBs in California gathered at Derek Shearer's house in Santa Monica and talked about campaign finances. At that meeting, the FOBs reckoned that they could come up with a million dollars by the end of October. Then they went out to play basketball in Shearer's backyard. His closest gay friend, Dave Mixner, brought him together with a group of rich Californians, who called themselves ANGLE (Access Now for Gay and Lesbian Equality). Clinton told them he supported full and equal rights for gays, including the right to join the military. They promised his campaign $100,000 on the spot, and $1 million if he got the paty's presidential nomination. They did even better than that. ANGLE had its own list of 1,000 donors, and also sent out a newsletter to another 120,000 well-heeled gays in California. In February 1992, when Clinton was almost sunk by scandal, ANGLE came through with an unexpected $400,000. A week later, Clinton called the FOBs to Little Rock for his formal declaration for the presidency. The Long March had begun.

In retrospect, all political victories appear to have been inevitable from the beginning. But the twenty-year campaign of the FOBs was an extraordinarily quixotic venture. Bill Clinton should never have won the 1992 presidential election. He faced a respected and experienced incumbent in George Bush, who had rallied and led an unlikely international coalition in a victorious military campaign with remarkably little loss of allied lives.

This, ironically, was to be the source of Clinton's success. Better-known and more conventional Democrats, who would normally have been jostling for the 1992 nomination, weighed President Bush's heady triumph in the opinion polls in the spring and summer of 1991 and ducked the opportunity. Governor Mario Cuomo of New York, Congressman Dick Gephardt of Missouri, and Senators Sam Nunn of Georgia and Al Gore of Tennessee would each have dominated the expectations and the fund-raising and the institutions of the national and state Democratic parties, had they summoned the nerve to run. They did not. Clinton had the daring to seize the moment, the political insight to realize that George Bush was vulnerable on the economy, and the reserves of character to battle on through a debilitating series of assaults on the checkered past of his private life.

Clinton had one distinctive asset, the conviction that the old Democratic Party could no longer gather a coalition of voters large enough to win the White House, but that a different kind of Democrat with a plausibly different ideology could do so. Like a handful of his contemporaries in the social democratic parties of Europe, Clinton perceived that the fundamental problem of this political tendency was that it had won. The old Democrats had broadly achieved what they set out to do, and had for a generation suffered from a general bafflement about what to do next.

In Roosevelt's New Deal of the 1930s, in the British Labour government of 1945–1951, and among the Christian Democrats of Germany and Italy in the 1950s, a new model of the liberal-capitalist state emerged. Its main characteristics were old-age pensions, unemployment insurance, heavy investment in public education, and everywhere except the United States, some form of national health insurance. Its underlying principle was that the state had the right and the duty to intervene in the economy, to manage demand and public investment with the broad goal of establishing opportunity for all. In the process, the unfortunate would be cushioned, the wealthy would be taxed, and the inherent class tensions of prewar capitalism would be eased as the state operated on the conviction that the rich and the poor, the intelligent and the slow, the artisan and the professional, were all one nation.

By the end of the 1960s, this new model state had become the norm throughout the Western world. Its ambitions widened. Devised originally to meet the requirements of an industrial working class, it had, through GI bills and tax incentives for home ownership, begun to create a mass middle class whose concerns were subtly different. In Britain in the 1960s, the Labour government saw its new task as civilizing the state, legalizing abortion, abolishing the death penalty, easing the rules on divorce and on homosexuality. In the United States, President Johnson's ambitious vision of the Great Society delivered the rudiments of a national health system for the poor and aged. But the civilizing pattern followed, with the legalization of abortion and the (temporary) abolition of the death penalty in the 1970s.

The economic readjustments of the 1970s, starting with the abandonment of the Bretton Woods international financial system by President Nixon in 1971 and the subsequent inflation, put the fiscal structure of this model under growing strain. But having built and civilized the new model state, throughout the West, the reformist parties of the moderate left were bereft of the main reason for their existence. The job was done. Henceforth, their task would be defensive, to cling to the achievements of the past.

The fulfillment of the original social democratic agenda provoked a reinvigorated conservatism. Led with passionate conviction by Ronald Reagan and Margaret Thatcher, the new conservatives hammered relentlessly at the fiscal crises, the inflationary forces, and the social dislocations that followed the social democratic reforms. Their targets were not simply the faltering economies, but what they saw as the social failures of liberalism. In an Anglo-American chorus, Reagan and Thatcher cited the rise in crime and drug abuse, the growing number of divorces, and the perception of a dangerous challenge to the family structure. They also defined a decline in entrepreneurial vigor, blamed squarely on high taxes and an overmighty state.

Throughout the 1980s, conservatives dominated governments in Britain, the United States, and even in Germany, where the social democratic model had been particularly successful. By the 1990s, the tide was ready to turn again. Free markets and tax cuts and privatizations brought their own social dislocations and their own economic strains as the intense competition of the global marketplace squeezed the incomes of the traditional industrial work force. Nor had there been any signal improvement in the stability of families or the fight against crime.

It was not that the new conservatism had lost steam, but as Thatcher gave way to John Major and Reagan gave way to George Bush, it had lost its inspirational leadership, just as the economic boom of the 1980s turned sour. Ronald Reagan left office with the U.S. national debt just topping $3,000 billion, three times higher than when he had first been inaugurated. The costs of financing the renewed climb in unemployment in Britain after 1989 meant that when Mrs. Thatcher left office in 1990, the share of British GDP consumed by the state was exactly where it had been when she was first elected in 1979, at 43 percent. The conservative decade could claim victory in the cold war, rather than any economic or social triumphs at home. There was thus a political opportunity for the parties of the moderate left, but there was no new program to rally and define it.

Bill Clinton stepped into this gap. His claim to be a New Democrat was not empty electoral rhetoric. It was based on a political grouping he had helped to build and lead, the Democratic Leadership Council, on the new thinking about the priorities of liberal reforms that were emerging from the DLC's think tank, the Progressive Policy Institute, and on "The Conversation." Clinton, from the friends and connections he had made at Georgetown University, at Oxford, and at Yale Law School, had built something unique for a politician, a private and informal think tank. In their gatherings at the governor's mansion in Little Rock, in his return visits to Britain and Germany, his forays to Harvard and Washington, Clinton's friends made The Conversation into an ideological pilgrimage, a search for the Holy Grail of a postmodern social democracy.

Its themes have now become broadly familiar, even though one of the most striking features of the Clinton presidency is how few of them were enacted. An embrace of free markets and free enterprise comes with a commitment to an activist government that sees its mission in providing the lifelong education and job training that can equip people to compete in an intensely global economy. That competition is welcomed, through an active diplomacy to achieve a global free trading system. The large bureaucracies of the old welfare state have to be slimmed down; welfare becomes "workfare" and training; urban policy becomes the encouragement of banks to finance inner-city entrepreneurs. Crime must be fought sternly, with more police and more prisons. Above all, government is not a source of gifts to be parceled out, but an actor in a constant social contract. Government delivers in return for civic responsibility: a college grant in return for two years of public service; a welfare stipend in return for training to get a job.

Clinton called this the "New Covenant," a phrase that signally failed to stick in the national memory in the way that Roosevelt's New Deal and Kennedy's New Frontier or even Woodrow Wilson's New Freedom had. But the insistence that the voters should not expect something for nothing, that the old Democratic paternalism was becoming more fraternal, and that this was refreshingly different was as central to Clinton's appeal as his clear renunciation of traditional liberalism.

Almost unnoticed in the United States, Clinton's ability to recast the Democratic appeal and to set out a reform agenda for America in the post–cold war world had a powerful effect on similar parties overseas. In the week before Clinton's inauguration, his campaign strategists and advisers flew to Britain to pass on the message to an eager Labour Party at a "Clintonomics" conference. Labour in Britain, the New Party in Japan, the Social Democrats in Germany, and Professor Romano Prodi's new center-left coalition in Italy all explicitly sought to echo Clinton's conviction that the party had changed. Perhaps the best single summary of Clinton's ability to straddle old and new Democrats came from Labour Party leader Tony Blair, who nullified the Conservatives' traditional dominance on the law and order theme with the classically Clintonian slogan "Tough on crime, tough on the causes of crime."

This was not simply an American project. Clinton's intellectual curiosity was far more wide-ranging. He had an extraordinary familiarity with European politics, particularly among the social democrats. In April 1992, he had eagerly anticipated the defeat of the Conservative government in the British general election, hoping that the same transatlantic current that had swept Reagan to office in 1980 in the wake of Margaret Thatcher's electoral victory in 1979 would be repeated. A Labour victory in April would augur a Democratic victory in November. When Labour lost, Clinton put his finger on the reason: "It's the difference between Brighton and Bad Godesberg," he told me. Brighton is the comfortable seaside town where the Labour Party had claimed that it had shed the old ideological baggage of the class-conscious past. Bad Godesberg was the spa on the Rhine where Germany's Social Democrats had not just said they were changing, but proved it with a formal renunciation of Marxism.

Clinton's visit to Prague in 1969, after the crushing of the Dubcek government's experiment with "socialism with a human face," had begun his fascination with the politics of the European left. In the 1970s, he read avidly about the phenomenon of Euro-Communism, the historic shift of the Italian Communist Party from slavish devotion to the Moscow line. He admired the Scandinavian model, which seemed to combine vibrant and advanced technological economies with social justice. In 1990, he said that the Western European politician who most interested him was Spain's Felipe Gonzalez—for his ability to consolidate the transition to democracy after the long years of Franco and his ability to swing his party of the left behind a free market economic strategy.

One important focus of Clinton's interest was Germany. Its ability to combine export-led economic growth with a generous welfare state and the world's most advanced system of industrial work-force training became a particular study. He visited Germany four times, on trade missions as governor of Arkansas and to an informal annual conference held by the Bilderberg Group to bring European and American politicians together. He badgered German friends for material on the apprenticeship system and the mixed public-private health insurance scheme. His youthful admiration for Willy Brandt gave way to a mature appreciation of Helmut Schmidt, and after the fall of the Berlin Wall in 1989, he became convinced that a reunified Germany would lead the way to full European integration.

Clinton was also unusually familiar with the politics and economic prospects of Asia. He made four visits to Asia on trade missions before he became president, to Taiwan and Japan. What struck Clinton most forcefully about the fast-growing Asian economies was the powerful role of government in charting industrial and trade strategy—at a time when the prevailing orthodoxy in the United States and Europe was the need to diminish the government's economic role. His old friend Derek Shearer, who had lectured in Japan and served in the Carnegie Endowment's study groups on United States–Japan relations and the Pacific Rim, inspired Clinton with the idea that the United States needed its own version of Japan's MITI, the Ministry of International Trade and Investment.

Shearer also argued that the changes in Japanese politics bore striking similarities to Europe and Japan. The old cold war dispensations of politics were changing. The one-party systems of Japan and Italy, developed under U.S. tutelage in the early years of the cold war, were crumbling with its end. For Shearer, Morihiro Hosokawa, the leader of Japan's New Party, was trying to define a new kind of reform politics, beyond the moribund Socialist and discredited Liberal Democratic parties, in the way that Clinton hoped to do.

By the late 1980s, The Conversation had focused on a broad new principle: that the cold war was over and the global economy had won. In the process, it had transformed the United States from being the world's dominant economy, with 50 percent of global GDP in 1950, to the first among equals, with 25 percent of global GDP in 1990, roughly the same proportion as that of the European Community. It had also transformed the United States from being one of the world's most self-reliant economies, in which trade amounted to around 6 percent of GDP, into an increasingly integrated and dependent part of a global economy, in which trade accounted for over 25 percent of GDP.

America could no longer dominate the world, nor could it afford to retreat from it. Isolation was simply not an option. But not all Americans were benefiting from the growth in trade and global prosperity. The Conversation participant who did most to stress this theme was Robert Reich, who had carved out for himself a curiously Victorian role as a man of public letters and as a political economist at the Kennedy School at Harvard. Reich's interests were too broad to fit easily into the conventional academic structures of economics or politics or business or public policy. He straddled all these fields and more.

Reich argued that the class and party ideologies of the past no longer fit the new economy. There was little point in defending the hard-won earnings and benefits and working conditions of the old trade unions when the pace of industrial and corporate change was changing the nature of work, of ownership, and of employment. There would be few more jobs for life, and few more industrial skills than would endure throughout the traditional working lifetime. Transnational corporations could no longer be seen as American assets, committed to one geographic entity in their investment plans or their taxes or their loyalties. Only the work force would remain as a national asset, and the work force had to be the focus of government action. In the old industrial economy, the United States had performed well because its public school system had produced the best-educated and most productive industrial work force in the world. To compete in the future, a nation would have to devise a system of lifetime education and training to improve and extend the skills of its people. This was a broad national strategy that only an activist government could lead.

What the government should not do was to intervene in the old, bureaucratic way. The good intentions of the Great Society had created a series of bureaucratic establishments that were cumbersome, expensive, woefully ineffective, and politically damaging for the Democrats. The welfare system was the outstanding example, but there were a host of others, from the Department of Education to the Bureau of Indian Affairs, from Agriculture to Housing and Urban Development. Collectively, the performance of the bureaucracy was giving government a bad name.

This was one aspect of the real purpose of The Conversation, which was to define why the Democrats were becoming presidentially unelectable, and chart a different kind of politics to bring New Democrats to office. This debate ranged far beyond Clinton's circle. It consumed the party throughout the twelve years in the wilderness as Reagan and Bush celebrated the Republican ascendancy. It was the staple of Clinton's meetings with other Democratic governors, at the Democratic National Committee, and particularly among Democratic senators from the South, who feared that the Republican tide could wash them away.

The defeat of Walter Mondale in 1984, running on a traditional Democratic platform of an activist government that would levy taxes to create jobs, inspired the formation of the DLC. Al From, a burly fireplug of a man who had worked in the Carter White House, was the organizing force. The political weight came from southern senators—Sam Nunn, Chuck Robb, and John Breaux—from a handful of congressmen who included Dick Gephardt and Dave McCurdy, and from southern governors like Clinton.

They argued that the Democrats had shifted to the left since 1972, and become too influenced by interest groups like organized labor, the urban poor, the peace movement, the women's movement, and ethnic minorities. In the process, the Democrats had lost touch with their old base of the white working and lower middle class, and had simply failed to adapt to the demographic shift of voters to the new suburbs. The Democrats had surrendered to the Republicans the mantle of the patriotic party, and appeared soft on communism, soft on defense, soft on crime, soft on welfare, soft on values.

The irony was rich. The core of the DLC analysis was that the Democratic Party had been captured during the Vietnam War by a radical wing that made the party steadily less electable for most American voters. And yet the first Democratic presidential candidate the DLC could claim as their own was himself an emblematic figure of that antiwar and liberal current. In 1970, while at Yale, Clinton had helped run the Senate campaign of Joseph D. Duffey in Connecticut, the first of the "new politics" crusades to revitalize the Democrats as the party of peace and youth and liberation, after the invasion of Cambodia and the killings of four students at Kent State University in Ohio. Joe Duffey was to be appointed director of the U.S. Information Agency by Clinton, and his campaign was a seedbed for the McGovern crusade to win the Democratic nomination in 1972. Clinton organized Texas for McGovern, and if the DLC was right to say that the antiwar generation had crippled the Democrats politically, then Clinton had helped bring that about.

Time passes, views change, and the politicians move on, retuning their concerns and their antennae to the new themes that move the voters. The most successful among them are those who understand best the currents of the immediate time, and this was to prove a Clinton hallmark. In the 1960s, the single political issue that gripped him most was civil rights, the segregation he saw in his native Arkansas, the cause that inspired the marches of Martin Luther King, Jr., and which burned city after city as Clinton grew to adulthood. By 1970, he had become politically consumed by the Vietnam War, as had most of the rest of his generation, whether drafted to fight it, or finding ways to avoid it, or challenging it in the streets and on the campuses of America. By 1974, when Clinton first ran for Congress, the issue was Watergate and Nixon's slow coup against the Constitution and the need for honest new men to clean up the tired old deal-makers of Congress.

In 1976, when Clinton ran for attorney general in his home state, the theme was reconciliation and a gentle introspection, a mood cultivated by Jimmy Carter's "I will never lie to you" presidential campaign and his promise for an American government "as good as its people." In the aftermath of Vietnam, the task was to cultivate America's own garden, and Clinton caught the mood as he turned his back on Washington and concentrated on Arkansas. In the 1980s, as Ronald Reagan promised to unleash the energies of America's entrepreneurs, the Clintons set out to make some honest money, investing in cattle futures and in a speculative property venture on the banks of the White River in Arkansas. They became partners of an old friend who was running a fast-growing local bank, and called the investment plan to build a small holiday resort "Whitewater."

In 1984, the Democrats were challenging Ronald Reagan's neglect of the country's infrastructure. They condemned his deficits for consuming the seed corn of the future as America's industries rocked under the challenge of flooding imports and America's schools faltered at the task of equipping a new generation for the fierce new world of global competition. In Little Rock, the Clintons turned to education as the dominant theme of his governorship.

But at the same time, the antiwar Clinton of 1972 had also responded to the patriotic notes that Ronald Reagan was sounding from the White House in the 1980s. Almost alone among Democratic governors, he authorized the Arkansas National Guard to train in Honduras, the base from which the Reagan administration was waging a none-too-covert war against the Sandinista regime of Nicaragua. The Clinton who had argued passionately against the death penalty at Oxford and at Yale, since it presumed an impossible infallibility in human justice to maintain that the innocent were never executed, now changed his mind. He vowed to be tough on crime, and came to support the death penalty, while hating it and agonizing on the night of executions as he weighed the last appeal to a governor's mercy. In February 1992, in mid-campaign, Clinton returned to Little Rock to authorize the execution of Ricky Ray Rector, who had killed a policeman after a robbery. But Rector had then tried to kill himself, shooting a part of his brain away. He survived, but almost as a vegetable, barely understanding what was being done to him. After his last meal, Rector put a piece of pie to one side, saying he would have it later, as he was strapped down to the stretcher for the lethal injection that would kill him.

Clinton's admirers would say that his sensitivity to the country's changing concerns was uncannily acute. His critics might retort that this was a professional politician who followed, rather than led. Critic and admirer: each was correct, because Clinton was to a striking degree a palimpsest of a man; what one saw in him depended on the angle of vision. He was a man of instinctive warmth, deeply sentimental and easily moved, and for a sympathetic audience, few other people in public life could match his gift for empathy. At haunting national moments, like the service of mourning for the victims of the terrorist bomb in Oklahoma City, he was able to bring a sense of healing. At the fiftieth anniversary of the D-Day invasion, he was able to convince the hard-bitten veterans lined up on Omaha Beach that he meant the words of admiration and gratitude that he offered to their generation. But while Clinton could catch the tone of a great national occasion, he did not have Ronald Reagan's extraordinary gift to sustain the mood, to keep the memory of the public emotion as fresh and as durable as the moment itself.

Clinton's presidency suffered one dreadful burden, which only slowly became apparent. He initially came to national attention through two hugely controversial events—the allegation of adultery by Gennifer Flowers and the allegation of devious and unpatriotic slipperiness in avoiding the Vietnam draft. For many, perhaps most voters, the first they heard of Bill Clinton was that he was a two-timing draft-dodger with rather too many glib explanations. It was a perception that he could never wholly shed, even as people decided to vote for him. On November 1, the week he was elected, the Battleground 92 tracking poll recorded that Clinton had 51 percent favorable, and 43 percent unfavorable, ratings. A year later, at the end of his first year in office, the Times-Mirror survey found the country divided, with 42 percent saying that he was a man who did not keep his promises, and 41 percent saying he did.

His phrase "I feel your pain" and his habit of biting his lower lip were swiftly caricatured by his critics, who were irritated or disturbed by other Clinton habits. Like many of his generation, Clinton found it easy and natural to hug his friends of either sex. He thought it sensible to hire professional facilitators to make staff meetings go more easily and to build team spirit. In neither his gestures nor his appetites for food nor his way of chairing meetings did Clinton embody that military model of aloof and disciplined masculinity that was, to offer one memorable example, as fresh in the public memory as the bemedaled Colonel Oliver North testifying before Congress. Clinton was simply not familiar with the military model of leadership, rooted in hierarchy and authority. He had not been brought up in that kind of home. He had been educated in an era and in universities where he was encouraged to speak back to his teachers and question authority. And he had learned to govern as a way to rally consensus, as part of a generation whose first models of public action were the teach-in and the seminar. In this too, as in so much else, he was utterly characteristic as a man of his times.

Clinton's sympathies were genuine while they lasted, but they could flare and die as quickly as his anger, and he always hated to give offense. He found it very difficult to fire people. He could never give as much of himself as he liked to promise. And yet there was never any doubt about the power of his personal charm. Successive interlocutors, from John Major to Boris Yeltsin to Helmut Kohl to Newt Gingrich, confessed themselves beguiled by it. Speaker Gingrich told his fellow Republican congressmen during the budget talks in the winter of 1995–1996 that Clinton's charm was so potent that he "had to go through detox" afterward. Clinton came to rely too much on this gift, convinced that he could always talk an opponent around. Some proved immune, from the Republican majority leader in the House, Congressman Richard K. Armey, to his Democratic rival in the 1992 campaign, Senator Bob Kerrey.

The combination of the relaxed social rules of his generation and his personal charm made him highly attractive to women. This was not simply a matter of sensuality. He had been brought up by women, and far more than most of his contemporaries accepted women as intellectual equals. He genuinely enjoyed the company of women, and was able at Oxford and later in Little Rock to make lasting and platonic friendships with them.

There was a sexual revolution under way, and as a student he took joyous part in that brief window of sensuality between the coming of the Pill and what seemed to be the almost vengeful onslaught of AIDS. In the years after his wedding, he later admitted to having "caused pain in my marriage."

The politician in him took a long, hard look at the prospects for a Democratic victory when Reagan was due to step down. A host of considerations were then weighed, but he told friends that as a family man with a young daughter, he decided not to run. "A long, long time ago, I promised myself that if I was ever lucky enough to have a kid, my child would never grow up wondering who her father was," he told a press conference in Little Rock, as Hillary brushed a tear from her cheek. Mockery was stilled by the knowledge that Clinton had grown up without ever knowing his father. But again, one senses the tug of a generational tide, of a sensitivity to a social movement back to family, as the Republicans campaigned hard on family values. This was the time when "parenting" became a verb, when the biological clock began ticking audibly for women of the baby-boom generation.

Clinton's uncanny ability to be thinking and acting in perfect tune and timing with the bulk of his generation was one of his greatest political gifts. He was able to echo the American mood of 1991–1992, campaigning hard on the national sense of economic gloom that President Bush could never comprehend. "The economy, stupid" became the hallmark of Clinton's challenge, placed in a deeper historical context that recognized there was a more profound and darker concern running through the electorate, that they might indeed be "raising the first generation to grow up doing worse than their parents did."

That rang true for Bill Clinton, whose life had been shaped by that extraordinary twenty-five-year period after 1947, when the median incomes of American families doubled, when a generation that had been raised in the Great Depression and gone on to win a world war had come home to forge the great revolution of twentieth-century America, the making of a mass middle class. That steady accretion of wealth had taken the Clinton family from a foreclosed Arkansan farm in 1936 to prosperity for them all and unimaginable opportunity for Bill, the first member of his family to win a college education. For that prospect of growth and ever-widening promise to go into reverse was not just the denial of what America represented to Bill Clinton's generation; it was an affront to the experience of his own life. "The economy, stupid" brought him to the White House, where he was to find that his Democratic allegiance and his vaguely Keynesian principles and his grand plans for investment all rang dully hollow.

Clinton came into office in January 1993 to be caught by two deep fiscal traps, which made it almost impossible to finance the reform measures on which he had campaigned. The first, and the underlying cause of his difficulties, had been set twelve years earlier, in the first year of the Reagan administration. Reagan's budget director, David Stockman, set out deliberately to destroy the welfare state by plunging the budget into fiscal crisis. The strategy was for the White House to cut taxes, and if the Democratic Congress would not then cut spending, the result would be a mounting deficit that would in the long run constrain any more growth in public spending and eventually force spending cuts. Stockman was extraordinarily frank about this: "The success of the Reagan revolution depended upon the willingness of the politicians to turn against their own handiwork—the bloated budget of the American welfare state. Why would they do this? Because they had to! In the final analysis, I had made fiscal necessity the mother of political invention."

It worked. In 1980, when Reagan was elected, the national debt was just over $1,000 billion. Twelve years later, when Clinton entered the White House, it had ballooned to over $4,000 billion, a debt on which interest had to be paid. In Clinton's 1996 budget, $257 billion was allocated for interest, rather more than the entire U.S. defense budget of $247 billion for the year. The debt burden and the annual deficit had become precisely the fiscal restraint Stockman had planned, a straitjacket into which Clinton's reform ambitions had to fit.

The second trap had been set in 1990, when President Bush had been caught up in Stockman's ingenious lure. In the budget conference with Democratic leaders in Congress, Bush had agreed to cap all discretionary spending in the future at the current funding levels. If any new money was to be spent, it had to come out of existing programs. For the Democratic chairman of the House and Senate budget committees, those caps held good for President Clinton, too. And affected by the 1992 campaign in which Ross Perot had made the deficit into his overwhelming issue, the new Democratic members pressed on their committee chairmen the need to be even tougher. Less than two months after Clinton's inauguration, the House and Senate budget committees cut $63 billion from President Clinton's first spending proposals in order to meet the caps. The House committee went even further, imposing a "hard freeze," which did not even allow for the caps to be recalculated upward to allow for inflation.

This was the contradiction that was to define the Clinton presidency. He had won the election with a plausible new definition of what the Democratic Party would stand for, investing in the skills and opportunities of the people. Once in office, he found himself simply unable to deliver on the bulk of those promises because of the budgetary crisis Stockman had plotted in 1981. Like an actor suddenly bereft of a script, a movie director without film, he was condemned to failure in the terms under which he had campaigned. "Putting people first" had been the promise of his election manifesto; putting the deficit first was to be his grim reality.

There was one further and fundamental constraint upon the ambitious new presidency. The nature of the office, and the power it had wielded for sixty years, was changing subtly but decisively in response to a changing international environment. Clinton was to be the first president to grapple with the twilight of what Arthur Schlesinger called the "Imperial Presidency."

One of the most distinctive rhythms of American political history has been the tidal flow of power from White House to Congress and back again. If the usual business of government was shared in creative but often uneasy tension between the two, crisis always strengthened the presidential hand. From the presidencies of Jackson and Lincoln and Teddy Roosevelt and Woodrow Wilson, a clear pattern emerges of the military or economic or political crisis becoming the occasion of a shift in the balance of power from the Capitol to the White House. But the power subsequently shifted back again. The successors to the four crisis presidents—Martin Van Buren and Andrew Johnson, William Howard Taft and Warren Harding—are not names associated with any great assertion of presidential power.

The striking feature of the last six decades, the era that saw the emergence of the Imperial Presidency, was that the crisis never stopped. For over five decades the tide of power did not wash back again up Pennsylvania Avenue to the Capitol. The Great Depression led into World War Two, which led in turn to the cold war. These were three challenges, each threatening the very existence and character of the American state, which flowed almost seamlessly from one to the next. The clear and present danger to the American state embodied in each of these crises was in itself a justification of big and activist government, in which all of the resources of the nation-state had to be rallied, led, and directed by the president.

Until 1939, the White House staff had meant little more than the household servants, and the American head of state had to make do with a singularly truncated court. The president had authority to hire only four staff aides above the clerical rank. That was already an advance—Herbert Hoover had to make do with two. In creating the executive office of the presidency in 1939, Roosevelt won congressional authority to employ six administrative assistants, a special counsel (Sam Rosenman), and a special assistant (Harry Hopkins).

From these humble beginnings, a giant bureaucratic edifice was to grow, the privy court of the Imperial Presidency. By 1942, with the appointment of Admiral William D. Leahy, the White House office had spawned its first chief of staff. By 1945, Roosevelt had 11 administrative assistants. Truman had 13. Eisenhower had 37. By 1972, Nixon had 48. The executive office staff, swollen to 1,175 during Eisenhower's first term, grew to 5,395 under President Nixon. This mass of political courtiers was but the most intimate layer of a growing federal bureaucracy, the machinery of big government.

Beyond these raw numbers, the balance of political power was shifted toward the White House by the strategic nature of the new institutions that were devised to help the presidency meet the challenges of the cold war. The establishment in 1947 by President Truman of the National Security Council and the Central Intelligence Agency brought two unprecedented new tools of executive authority under the president's own hand. In a cold war environment in which information was power, the CIA reported to the president. And the NSC created for the White House the kind of strategic and coordinating power that Von Moltke's general staff had created for the Prussian army. Truman went further, creating the Council of Economic Advisers as an independent source of economic advice, and the Atomic Energy Commission, to keep the awesome new power of the atom under the president's hand.

These four new institutions, along with the executive office of the president, sharply increased the powers, the dedicated resources, and the reach of the White House incumbent. But each of them stemmed not just from presidential ambition, but from a series of fundamentally transformed situations the presidency had to face.

Of these, the most immediately dramatic was the development of the atomic bomb. Not only did it revolutionize the concept and the costs of warfare, it also imposed a new technological imperative upon the traditional responsibilities of the president, as commander-in-chief, and the Congress, as the body with the constitutional authority to declare war. Memories of the sneak attack on Pearl Harbor were still fresh, and the prospect of a surprise nuclear strike on U.S. targets was immeasurably more dreadful. Consequently, the decision-making process became more urgent. As the nuclear balance developed in the 1950s and thereafter, the presidency required the powers to wage instant, retaliatory war, without the time for the constitutional niceties. The most potent symbol of presidential power became the omnipresent football, the deceptively sporty name for the briefcase that contained the nuclear codes.

In order to deal with nonnuclear military threats, the United States accepted the need to change the habits of over 160 years and maintain a large standing armed force in peacetime, based on conscription. By 1960, it comprised some 3 million troops, airmen, and sailors. They were deployed in far-flung garrisons, some 200 overseas bases by the time of the Kennedy administration, all locked into a series of alliances and treaty commitments and local political issues that often conflicted with the overriding strategy of containing the Soviet threat.

This in turn transformed the public finances. The defense budget took roughly one-third of government spending in the late 1940s, and the Korean War rearmament and the cold war almost doubled defense's share. (In 1955, defense spending was $42.7 billion in a federal budget of $68.4 billion.) The share of defense spending in the federal budget has declined steadily ever since, to just over half in 1969, to 40 percent in 1970, to 25 percent in 1980, and 20 percent in 1993. To put it another way, defense took a 3.6 percent share of America's GNP in 1940, the year before Pearl Harbor, and leapt to 15 percent with the Korean War. It was not to sink to such lowly prewar proportions again until 1996.

The size of cold war defense budgets hugely increased the presidential role in the overall economy, and went hand in hand with the prevailing Keynesian theories of the day to become a flywheel by which the activities of the broader economy could be slowed or speeded almost at will. Kennedy's rearmament program after 1961 was financed on annual budget deficits of $6 billion. By the 1980s, the Reagan rearmament boom represented an almost pure form of military Keynesianism. In the twelve years of the Reagan–Bush presidencies, the U.S. national debt quadrupled from $1 trillion to $4 trillion. The difference, $3,000 billion, is strikingly close to the accumulated defense budgets of those years.

A military establishment of this size and dependence on constant technological updating forced the World War Two and postwar American economies into a degree of centralized planning that was dramatic for a broadly capitalist and free market system. The cold war challenge of the space race intensified this penetration of government institutions and targets into the overall economy. The presidential target of 1961, to put an American on the moon by the end of the decade, was triumphantly achieved.

The president's powers over the economy were far from absolute. Congress had the power of the purse; the Federal Reserve controlled interest rates. But federal government expenditure as a proportion of gross national product, which had been but 2 percent in 1930, grew inexorably to around 20 percent in 1965. The president also had the right of emergency intervention in time of economic crisis. The most draconian peacetime controls over the U.S. economy were imposed, ironically, by the Republican president Richard Nixon, on August 15, 1971. A gold crisis provoked by a British request to turn $3 billion in cash into gold led Nixon to overrule Arthur F. Burns, chairman of the Federal Reserve, and impose an executive order that froze all wages and prices, placed an emergency tax on all imports, and took the United States off the gold standard.

All this could be justified in the name of national security. The threat was immediate, and so the president must have the right to engage in instant controls over the economy, just as he required the power to embark on instant nuclear war.

The threat was everywhere, so the president must have the latitude to deploy troops to threatened areas abroad at his will, as President Truman had with Korea. He must also have the right to engage in international agreements, such as those which established U.S. nuclear bases in Morocco and Spain, without a formal treaty, which would require Senate ratification. The threat was insidious, and so the president must have the power to meet fire with fire, to meet subversion with covert operations, to overthrow hostile regimes with secret armies. The threat was strategic as much as military, so the secret arm of presidential policy must be empowered to overthrow elected governments abroad, like the Mossadeq administration of Iran, which had nationalized the oil industry, if they were deemed to challenge the strategic interests of the United States.

Only one nation in the West had the resources to sustain that struggle, and the only American institution that could provide that strategic will was the presidency, required to become "imperial" by the mortal danger of the threat. The cold war defined the modern presidency, and recast the job into the role of commander-in-chief of the free world. And the rest of the world, in consequence, was to be almost as fascinated by the dramas of presidential elections as the Americans themselves. Self-interest reinforced the fascination, as crises in Berlin and in Cuba reminded non-Americans that their existence, and indeed the survival of organized life on the planet, hung on the president's judgment at the nuclear brink.

The great encounters of international life became those graced by the Imperial President, usually at summits with his only parallel, the master of the Kremlin. The president, newly enabled to travel far and fast by jet airliners, newly intimate to millions overseas through television, outgrew the United States, just as the dominance of the American economy determined whether the rest of the world would enjoy boom or endure recession. Perhaps the most telling anecdote of the period comes from President Johnson's visit to South Vietnam in 1966. Arriving at Tan Son Nhut airfield with its vast array of American air power, he was greeted by a young air force officer who said, "Your helicopter is this way, Mr. President." Johnson stopped, gazed at the endless flight lines and replied, "Son, they are all my helicopters."

American citizens and America's allies and its former enemies alike all grew so accustomed to this presidential greatness that its enfeeblement was not immediately apparent. But in the aftermath of the cold war, it was clear that the existence of the United States was no longer threatened. In the 1990s, there was no Great Depression to require emergency powers. There was no world war, and no cold war substitute, and no nuclear missiles poised and targeted at American cities. And in the absence of mortal threat, the question posed itself, what was the need for Big Government, or for an Imperial President to rule it?

The irony was precise. The tidal flow of American power was at the turn, about to ebb away from White House toward Congress, just as the White House was to be entered by the first president of the Vietnam generation. Clinton did so supported and surrounded by his vast and loyal band of contemporaries, whose youth had been spent mounting the sharpest domestic challenge the Imperial Presidents had ever known.

One

Getting There

☆ 1 ☆

THE MAKING OF A CANDIDATE

The eleven white men who have occupied the White House since the United States took up the lead of the Western democracies with World War Two have had little in common save their political ambition. Their social and geographical origins and the career paths they took to the presidency were extraordinarily varied. Five had been vice presidents, but otherwise there is no pattern, no obvious route to the presidency of this most open and haphazardly selective of democracies. If there be any advisable career choice for an ambitious young man with an eye on the White House, it would certainly include military service.

The preferred choice would be the U.S. Navy, which is the nearest to a common factor in presidential biographies. Truman went from the National Guard to the artillery in the First World War, Eisenhower was a career soldier, and Ronald Reagan wore an army uniform when he made military films during World War Two. All the rest could claim a naval home. Roosevelt had made his name as assistant secretary for the navy from 1913 through the First World War. Kennedy served with distinction as commander of a patrol boat in the Pacific. Lyndon Johnson joined the navy after Pearl Harbor, until President Roosevelt summoned the congressman back to Washington. Nixon and Ford served as naval officers during the war, and Jimmy Carter was a Naval Academy graduate who went on to develop nuclear submarines. George Bush was a navy pilot, on the aircraft carrier *San Jacinto.*

It is striking, therefore, that one of the most determined career politicians of them all should have put so much effort into avoiding military experience. The U.S. Navy, the only American institution that can claim to be a cradle for modern presidents, hardly even crossed his mind. But at the age of twenty-three, William Jefferson Clinton was certain of his future career. "For years I have worked to prepare myself for a political life characterized by both practical and political ability and concern for rapid social progress," he wrote, in what was to become a famous letter to the commander of the Reserve Officers' Training Corps at the University of Arkansas.

"I came to believe that the draft system itself is illegitimate," that letter said. "No government really rooted in limited, parliamentary democracy should have the power to make its citizens fight and die in a war they may oppose, a war which even possibly may be wrong, a war which, in any case, does not involve immediately the peace and freedom of the nation."

This was a striking departure from the customary path for a young man bent on political life. And yet, by the time he was elected the forty-second president, Clinton could look back on a career almost perfectly crafted to build toward the ultimate goal of the White House. Clinton's luck played a part, in arranging matters so that the only postwar president without military credentials of any kind would be elected in the first election after the end of the cold war and the fall of the Berlin Wall.

This shift to an essentially civilian political establishment was inevitable, reflecting a generation whose college-educated elite had often been able to avoid the military, despite conscription. The Republican administration that Clinton defeated contained a secretary of defense, Richard Cheney, who had also avoided military service, through student and marriage deferments. The emerging Republican leaders, from Congressman Newt Gingrich to Senator Phil Gramm, were equally innocent of military experience. The end of the military draft in 1971 had suggested that this would be increasingly common, despite the national reflexes that bestow political allure on outstanding military leaders like General Colin Powell.

When Clinton made his decisions as a young man to avoid the draft by joining an ROTC program, and then to abandon the ROTC program and take refuge in his luckily low number in the draft lottery, it was already becoming clear that a politician of his generation need not suffer from escaping military service. A very large proportion of his age and educational cohort had similarly escaped, and the Vietnam War was widely unpopular among them. This was a period when the usual rules of political ambition no longer applied. Military service in wartime was no longer a prerequisite for a political career, and for ambitious Democrats of this generation, support for the war might even have been deemed a hindrance.

Two of his peers, each to be brought into the Clinton administration, illustrate the prevailing mood. Robert Reich, to become his secretary of labor, joined the 1967 march on the Pentagon and was student coordinator for Senator Eugene McCarthy's antiwar campaign in five states. Strobe Talbott, to become deputy secretary of state, led the petition of his Yale class of 1968 to refuse conscription. "Many of us simply could not, if ordered, pledge ourselves to kill or be killed on behalf of a policy which offends our deepest sense of what is wise and right."

Opposition to the war was already politically respectable. Clinton's first political mentor, Senator William Fulbright of Arkansas, led the criticism from his seat as chairman of the Senate Foreign Relations Committee. But raucous demonstrations and breaking the law by refusing the draft were, in Fulbright's view, the wrong way to proceed: "The most effective dissent is dissent expressed in an orderly, which is to say a conservative manner. The student, like the politician, must consider not only how to say what he means but how to say it persuasively."

Clinton took Fulbright's advice. He did not join the 1967 march on the Pentagon, nor did he join Senator McCarthy's 1968 campaign. The first antiwar demonstrations he attended were in Britain, but he played only a modest role in organizing the more polite protests—the delivery of a petition of Rhodes scholars and a religious vigil. On his return to the United States in the summer of 1970, he joined Project Pursestrings, an attempt to work within the system by persuading Congress to starve the war effort of funds. Once at Yale, he volunteered for the antiwar campaign of Joe Duffey, the Democratic candidate for the U.S. Senate in Connecticut. In 1972, Clinton worked for the McGovern campaign. In sum, Clinton's rebellion was a tame one for those times, neither radical nor violent, and located squarely within the political mainstream.

In avoiding the Vietnam War, Clinton was with the majority. Between 1965 and 1972, a total of almost 27 million young Americans were of draft age. The great majority of those who joined the armed forces in this period, 8.7 million, chose to enlist. Only 2.2 million were drafted. Nearly 16 million avoided military service, through deferments, unfitness, alternative service, resistance, or luck. The number of those accused of dodging the draft—209,000—was four times higher than the number of Americans who were to be killed in Vietnam.

In this sense, Clinton was not only the first member of the postwar generation to be elected president, but also the first of the post-conscription generation. While he was still at his studies in 1971, the United States made the fundamental shift to a professional military service. This ended what had been the closest to a unifying experience of American nationhood, in which young black men learned to live alongside young whites, while rich and poor, country and city boys, were all ruled by a common discipline.

The five main Democratic candidates for the presidency in 1992 reflected the changing pattern. The first to declare, Senator Paul Tsongas, had no military experience, but volunteered for the Peace Corps instead. Senator Tom Harkin of Iowa spent five years in the navy, from 1962 to 1967, and then became a strong critic of the war, leading an investigation into the infamous "tiger cages" where the South Vietnamese kept some of their prisoners. Former California governor Jerry Brown had studied for the priesthood. Senator Bob Kerrey had been a war hero in Vietnam, in the Navy Special Forces, and won America's highest award for gallantry, the Congressional Medal of Honor. He lost a leg, and came home to give speeches against the war.

The Vietnam War, whether they fought in it, opposed it, or avoided it, was but one of the defining characteristics of Clinton's generation. There were three others that took shape during the Vietnam era, and between them they amounted to a social revolution, which in retrospect divides the five decades of post-1945 America into two startlingly distinct periods. The baby-boomers, that sudden demographic bulge born to the returning veterans of World War Two, grew up in one kind of America and then matured in another. The civil rights movement, the transformation of the role of women, and the great shift away from the traditional industrial economy were to reshape the social, political, and the economic contours of the country.

Change is constant. But in the decade from 1964, when Bill Clinton went to college, to 1974, when he ran his first political campaign as a candidate for the U.S. Congress, it became tumultuous. For a politically ambitious young man from a southern state, the impact of the civil rights movement was unmistakable. In 1952, 1956, 1960, and 1964, the state of Arkansas had loyally cast its electoral college votes for the Democratic presidential candidate, twice rejecting the national hero, Dwight Eisenhower. In 1968, Arkansas cast its votes for Governor George Wallace of Alabama, and in 1972, for the Republican Richard Nixon. Arkansas voted Democrat again in 1976 for a fellow southerner, Jimmy Carter, but then voted twice for Reagan and once for George Bush.

Since its Civil War defeat at the hands of the Republican president Abraham Lincoln, who emancipated the slaves, the Old South had been steadfastly loyal to the Democrats. Its vote had been overwhelmingly white, and its institutions, from schools to parks to drinking fountains, had been largely segregated. Civil rights ended the segregation, and opened the polling booths to black Americans. In the process, it jarred loose one of the foundation stones of the political system, the southern white vote.

No instant landslide resulted, rather the slow jolting movements of a tectonic plate. In 1964, Georgia and South Carolina, Alabama and Mississippi and Louisiana voted for Barry Goldwater, the Republican candidate. In 1968, Georgia, Alabama, Mississippi, Louisiana, and Arkansas went to George Wallace. In 1972, they all went to Nixon. The Democratic vote stayed more loyal in state and congressional elections, but by 1994, the Republicans had a majority of the congressmen, senators, and governors of the Old Confederacy.

The black vote was a solid compensation, close to 90 percent Democratic, but those numbers were relatively modest. Black Americans in this period amounted to roughly 10 percent of the voting age population. But while roughly 60 percent of eligible whites voted, on average only 50 percent of eligible blacks went to the polls. Beyond the voting figures, it became increasingly plain that if the civil rights movement had made black Americans equal in law, equality in incomes and educational prospects were to prove desperately slow and difficult to achieve.

To a modest degree, the Democrats' loss of the white southern vote was compensated by their ability to take increasing advantage of the second great change of the period, the transformed role of women. In 1960, just over 21 million women were fully employed outside the home. By 1970, the numbers had risen to 30 million, and by 1980 to 42 million, almost exactly the number of men who had been fully employed in 1960. This was a revolution, not only for women but also for the American work force—and it still shows few signs of slackening. By 1990, 53 million women were working outside the home.

This was the real sexual revolution of the period, an economic transformation rather than an erotic one. Women's march into the workplace was accompanied and probably reinforced by cultural factors, from improved contraceptive techniques like the Pill, to the political importance of the Supreme Court's legalization of abortion in 1973. But the political implications of the changing role were striking. In 1960, women were slightly less likely to vote than men. By 1976, they were more likely to vote, and from 1980, they were clearly voting with a Democratic bias.

PERCENTAGE VOTING DEMOCRATIC

YEAR	MALES	FEMALES
1976	52	52
1980	38	46
1984	38	42
1988	42	49
1992	41	45

(*American Enterprise,* Demographic Report, Jan–Feb 93, pp. 90–91.)

The women's vote was clearly affected by their economic status. In 1992, Clinton won strong majorities among women who were employed full- or part-time and who declared themselves unemployed. He lost only among women who declared themselves "homemakers," winning 36 percent of their vote, while Bush won 45 percent. Married women voted 41 percent for Clinton, 40 percent for Bush. But single women preferred Clinton over Bush by a stunning margin of 55–29 percent, and divorced or separated women preferred Clinton by 49–32 percent.

The female invasion of the workplace was part of a deeper economic shift, which can be dated with some precision to 1973. In the twenty-five years between 1947 and 1973, median family income in the United States more than doubled. In constant (1993) dollars, it rose from $18,099 to $36,893. The U.S. economy was growing faster than it had ever done before. From 1869 to 1948, annual GNP per capita grew at rate of 1.7 percent a year. From 1947 to 1973, the growth rate jumped to 2.2 percent a year, sufficient to sustain the massive military investments of the cold war, to offer college education to a majority of high school graduates, and to enable most American households to buy cars and homes. There was even sufficient wealth to pay off the huge level of national debt accumulated to finance World War Two.

But then the extraordinary growth machine ran, not into a brick wall, but into a draining patch of mud. From 1973 to 1980, the annual per capita GNP growth fell back to 1.1 percent. In the 1980s, it improved to average 1.7 percent, the same as in the eighty years before 1947. This prolonged period of slow growth, accompanied by sharp rises in inflation and interest rates, was not sufficient to finance both government and private consumption.

Far less was the slow-growth economy able to afford the demographic change that took the numbers receiving Social Security benefits from 26 million in 1970 to over 40 million in 1991. The aging population required ever more health care. The 20 million Americans enrolled in Medicare in 1970 received just over $7 billion in benefit payments. The 35 million elderly enrolled in Medicare in 1991 received $118 billion in benefits. The effort to finance simultaneously the care of an aging population, to sustain military primacy, and to maintain living standards was straining the American system. Since 1980, the federal budget deficit has never been less than $100 billion a year, and usually much more.

Beyond the demographics, the economic structure was also changing. In 1950, the number of blue-collar and white-collar workers in the United States had been roughly even. By 1973, 47 percent were white collar and 35 percent were blue collar. This signaled the shift from a traditional industrial economy with muscles of steel and fueled by coal, which required a large working class, to a service and knowledge economy, whose characteristic materials were plastics and silicon chips, which required a more educated work force. The nature of the change is best illustrated by the famous 1961 promise of the Soviet leader Nikita Khrushchev that within twenty years, the Soviet Union would exceed the United States in the production of coal and iron, steel and cement. Mocked at the time, Khrushchev was right. In 1981, the Soviet Union outproduced the United States in each of those materials, but the United States had by then become a different kind of economy altogether. The Soviet Union exhausted itself to win a race already condemned to industrial history.

Khrushchev might have made a more potent propaganda point if he had warned the American work force what lay in store for them, in this postindustrial revolution. In the twenty years since 1973, U.S. median family income barely rose at all. It grew by just 4 percent in two decades, from $36,893 to $38,364. Despite the floods of working women adding their salaries to the family income, most families did little more than keep their incomes stable. For individual male workers, 1973 saw the beginning of a sharp decline in real wages, and the less qualified suffered the most. Between 1973 and 1993, the real hourly wage of high school dropouts fell by 22 percent. High school graduates suffered a fall of 14.7 percent. Workers with some college education saw a fall of 11.6 percent. College graduates suffered a fall of 7.5 percent.

The year 1973 represents another important shift in the long-term trends of the U.S. economy. It was the pivotal year in which the relative share of the wealth of the richest 5 percent of U.S. households stopped falling, as it had done steadily since 1947, and began to rise again, as it has done steadily ever since. The fast-growth decades of the U.S. economy were marked by steep and progressive taxation, which redistributed the national income from the wealthy to the poor. The slow-growth decades have been marked by lower tax burdens on the wealthy.

Race, women, and the economy: the three revolutions transformed the American political landscape between Bill Clinton's decision to seek a political career and the culmination in his announcement of his presidential candidacy in October 1991. The three revolutions defined the issues that politicians were required to address, from affirmative action to abortion, from jobs to health care, from taxes to the deficit.

But these were issues that ran more deeply than the grim parade of statistics and were hardly to be answered by some new government program or political promise. There was a disturbing psychological dimension to the politics of the 1990s, a fear that astute politicians could voice in a phrase. "The cold war is over. Japan won" was the pungent expression of Paul Tsongas. "We risk raising the first generation of Americans who will be worse off than their parents" was Clinton's phrase. After decades of being convinced that theirs was the richest and most productive nation on earth and the most rewarding to live in, Americans in the slow-growth years felt themselves poorer than their main international competitors, felt themselves less safe, and far more fearful for their future.

This was hardly a new phenomenon of American unease. A similar mood of foreboding had last dominated political debate in the Vietnam era, when the sense of being entrapped in a losing war abroad swept home to an America that was seeing another kind of war in its own cities, from riots in the inner cities to riots on college campuses. The political odyssey of Bill Clinton saw this wheel turn full circle, from the origins of his ambition in the 1960s to its realization, twenty-five years later.

The ambition began in Arkansas, one of the poorest states in the Union. When Bill Clinton was born in 1946, a majority of the state's counties lacked paved roads. It had the reputation of being a southern state, and a one-party system. Neither charge was entirely true. It was the state where the South began to merge into the West. The vast forests and swamp that originally composed Arkansas had nominally belonged to France, then to Spain, and then to France again until it was bought for the United States as part of the Louisiana Purchase in 1803.

Granted statehood in 1836, when it had just reached the minimum population threshold of 50,000 people, it was late to join the Confederacy in the Civil War. The commander of the Federal arsenal in Little Rock was invited to depart with his men unhindered. He accepted, and marched out to the cheers of the populace, hailed for sparing the state the evils of civil war. But the war came, and brought to Arkansas the spirited battle of Pea Ridge, and for a while the state had two state capitals, one Federal and the other Confederate.

Blacks amounted to less than a fifth of the population, which meant Arkansas was never a typical southern state, except in the east. There the grand plantations and cotton fields filled the Delta, the low-lying and fertile land along the Mississippi River, where the politics were almost feudal. In 1948, the *Arkansas Gazette* reported routinely that "plantation owners in the Delta usually control the votes of their tenants, who cast their ballots in boxes set up in the owners' commissaries." In the 1930s, more than half of all the white farmers in the state were tenants, many of them sharecroppers.

This Delta, not the one by the sea in New Orleans, was the sultry flatland that gave the world the blues. At the old river town of Helena, they still commemorate their local giants Robert Johnson and Sonny Boy Williamson and Big Bill Broonzy with an annual blues festival by the levee, the big earth bank that restrains the mighty river. From the Arkansas town of Helena came the fabled radio show "King Biscuit Time," which brought Sonny Boy Williamson to a wider audience. It was the show that taught local young white boys like Conway Twitty and Johnny Cash all they knew. "Nothing in the world was so important to me as hearing those songs on the radio," recalled Johnny Cash. "The music carried me up above the mud, the work and the hot sun."

But the state's southwestern plain was dominated by endless pine forests, which still covered more than half the state's acreage in the 1980s. The Ozark and Ouachita Mountains of the north and west were hillbilly country, where slavery was rare, and the politics were colorful, and whole counties had voted solidly Republican since the Civil War. Arkansas politics could also be innovative. Hattie Caraway became the first woman elected to a full term in the U.S. Senate in 1932, after Louisiana's populist Huey Long came to stump for "this little woman."

Long's brand of southern populism was one of the several political strains that jostled repeatedly through Arkansan history, reflecting its varied identity as a mountain state, a southern state, and even a part of the Farm Belt. In the 1880s and 1890s, it was the base of the Agricultural Wheel, a radical, farm-based movement which enjoyed a brief vogue in the Plains states. Arkansas even briefly spawned a People's Party, which dedicated itself to the improvement of "the downtrodden, regardless of race."

The first governor of this century to win election three times was "Old Jeff" Davis, a populist who tried to bar from the state any company that ever, anywhere, operated a price control agreement. "A carrot-headed, red-faced, loud-mouthed, strong-limbed, ox-driving mountaineer lawyer, and a friend of the fellow who brews forty-rod bug-juice back in the mountains," Old Jeff campaigned against "the high-collared roosters and silk-stocking crowd" of Little Rock. But the businessmen of Little Rock and the wealthy planters of the Delta combined to defeat him, another battle in the long duel between the hills and the plains, which was equally a struggle between poor whites and the wealthy.

Arkansas took its rustic traditions seriously, to the point of welcoming the hillbilly image when the Dogpatch USA amusement park, modeled on the comic strip, opened in the Ozark hills. Orval Faubus, the most famous of the state governors until Clinton, became its president. Clinton still tells the story of Faubus being visited by an elderly farmer in overalls, whose son had just been sent to jail on a minor charge, while the harvest was rotting in the field. Could the governor let him out? Faubus pondered, and the old man turned to go. Faubus stopped him. "I'm just trying to decide whether I should send for him now, or take you home to the mansion with me for the night, and we'll both go for him in the morning." The old farmer stayed the night.

The Oxford-educated William Fulbright doffed his suits when he came home from being an international statesman in Washington, and went out campaigning in his suspenders as just plain Bill. Prepared to challenge his own party's president over Vietnam, Fulbright followed his constituents over segregation. Along with the state's entire congressional delegation, he signed the Southern Manifesto of 1957, which denounced the Supreme Court's desegregation law as "naked judicial power." (Senator Lyndon Johnson of Texas pointedly refused to sign it, which helped to explain why Kennedy chose Johnson as his running mate in 1960 rather than Fulbright.)

But Arkansas politics were already changing. The process began with the end of World War Two, as the veterans came home to establish a GI movement. They first took on the corrupt city government of Hot Springs, a gambling resort where Al Capone used to stay. Sid McMath, a Marine Corps colonel, was elected prosecuting attorney and the casinos were at least temporarily closed. McMath won the governorship in 1948, and brought into his administration a liberal and reformist local newspaper publisher, Orval Faubus from the Ozarks.

Faubus was a southern populist in the tradition of Lyndon Johnson. Born in a two-room cabin in Greasy Creek, son of a poor farmer who roamed his county preaching socialism, Faubus was a New Deal supporter who began his governorship in 1954 by adding for the first time six black men to the Democratic State Committee. He forced through a $22 million tax increase for education. Education was still laboring under the tradition of 1930s Governor Marion Futrell, who said that Arkansas was a farming state that had no need of high schools. Primary education was quite enough.

Faubus was accused of being soft on race in his 1956 reelection campaign, after forcing the state college campuses to admit the first black students. In 1957, determined to be reelected for a third term, Faubus decided to play the race card, choosing as his issue the desegregation of Central High School in Little Rock. The process had been two years in the planning, since the Supreme Court ruling that segregation was unconstitutional. But Governor Faubus called out 270 members of the state's National Guard, claiming the need to "maintain order" against rumored white mobs. He could never produce any evidence that violence had been threatened, and the effect of mobilizing the guard was to block the access to the school of the first nine black pupils.

After deep hesitation, President Eisenhower sent U.S. paratroopers of the 101st Airborne into the city to enforce the desegregation law, and prevent the ugly mobs from intimidating black children. He did so in part because of the international and cold war implications of what his speechwriter, Emmett John Hughes, described in his memoirs as "the crude practice of racism in the self-styled sanctuary of freedom. . . . The tale carried faster than drum signals across black Africa. It summoned cold gleams of recognition to the eyes of Asians, quick to see the signs, in the heartland of America, of the racial enmities that had helped to make colonialism through the generations so odious to them . . . to all peoples, in all lands, the trained and instructed voice of Soviet propaganda could relay, in almost affectionately fastidious detail, the news of Little Rock."

The first political crisis to be enacted before the cameras of the new television age, the scene of white racists taunting their own troops and spitting at black children transfixed America. Even when forced to submit, Faubus declared himself a martyr before the attendant cameras, crying, "Now begins the crucifixion." One of the nine students, Ernest Green, went on to become assistant secretary of labor in the Carter administration. The only one who stayed in Arkansas, Elizabeth Eckford, did so under medical supervision. Separated from the other black pupils on that first day, to be the lonely target of the jeering, screaming mob, she never quite recovered.

Faubus was easily reelected, and served a total of twelve years as governor, with increasing support from black electors. Some knew that at least his economic policies were on their side, others were still heavily influenced by the landowners and their employers on the plantations, and also by the patronage-based machine that Faubus assembled. The state was run by a large number of boards, which built and administered the highways, the schools, the sewage systems, the whole infrastructure of the state. With the right to appoint members to these boards, which in turn hired employees and contractors, the governor influenced jobs and contracts, and in the process, ensured a steady supply of campaign funds and party workers. Faubus built what amounted to a self-perpetuating reelection machine.

A Gallup poll of Americans in 1958 found Faubus to be "one of the ten most admired men in the world." If there was any justification for this judgment, it lay in Faubus's choice of Winthrop Rockefeller to run the state's new Arkansas Industrial Development Corporation. One of the richest men in America, who had worked in his youth as a roustabout in the Houston oilfields, Rockefeller came to Arkansas, home of an old army buddy, to recover from what was then the fattest divorce settlement in U.S. history: He paid $6 million to end his marriage to the model Bobo Sears.

At Petit Jean Mountain, 70 miles northwest of Little Rock, Rockefeller built a model farm, and pumped millions into his new state's schools, museums, and health clinics. But the state's population was declining as young people left for their education and never returned. Faubus turned to Rockefeller, who achieved something close to an economic miracle. In ten years, the AIDC brought over 600 new factories and 90,000 jobs to Arkansas. Rockefeller then decided that what Arkansas needed was two-party politics, and took over the moribund Republican Party in 1959. In 1964, he ran against Faubus and lost, largely because Faubus won 84 percent of the black vote, and Rockefeller failed to support the Civil Rights Act. But in 1966 Rockefeller won the governorship, with 71 percent of the black vote, against the implacable segregationist Jim Johnson, founder of the Arkansas White Citizens Councils.

This was the first election that young Bill Clinton took part in, coming home from college to volunteer in the Democratic primary campaign of Judge Frank Holt. He drove the Holt family around the state, and was allowed to address the crowd on Holt's behalf in his hometown of Hope, with his grandmother in the audience. But Holt was beaten in the primary by the segregationist Johnson, who was in turn beaten by Rockefeller. With 54 percent of the vote, he became the first Republican to be elected to high office in Arkansas in ninety years.

The state, Rockefeller later recalled in his farewell address, was "like a beautiful antebellum home, the doors and windows bolted, as though to deny the coming of Change, the curtains drawn in fear, somehow, of discovering what Change might bring with it." Rockefeller claimed, with justice, to have played a part in helping "to open the doors and windows bolted too long, to allow those fresh winds to penetrate our home, and yes, even our minds."

One of those winds was feminist. Paul Van Dalsem of rural Perry County was an old-fashioned politician, an ill-tempered brawler who was constantly reelected to the state legislature, which he saw as a male preserve. Irritated by women who ventured to lobby his colleagues, he unleashed his spleen in a speech to an all-male club in Little Rock in 1963.

"They're frustrated," he began. "We don't have any of these university women in Perry County, but I'll tell you what we do up there when one of our women starts poking around in something she don't know anything about. We get her an extra milk cow. If that don't work, we give her a little more garden to tend to. And then if that's not enough, we get her pregnant and keep her barefoot."

Two years later, Van Dalsem's male preserve of Perry County was redistricted into Pulaski County, which included the city of Little Rock. The women voters, pointedly removing their shoes to go into the polling booths, ended Van Dalsem's political career.

Rockefeller proved to be a strikingly successful reformer, overhauling government, enforcing a minimum wage law, raising teachers' salaries, expanding the state university system, and forcing official meetings to be open to the public. He appointed the first black troopers to the state police, and on the day of Martin Luther King's assassination, led the crowd in singing "We Shall Overcome" from the steps of the state capitol. And he continued the energetic wooing of new investment, boasting that during his governorship, a new 50-job factory was opening every 36 hours.

His money helped. Rockefeller later claimed to have invested $35 million in Arkansas, $10 million of it into the building of the state Republican Party and his four campaigns. Elected along with Rockefeller was the state's first Republican congressman in ninety years, John Paul Hammerschmidt. Clinton was to challenge him for the congressional seat in 1974.

There were other engines of change. In 1962, Arkansas saw the birth of another economic phenomenon when Sam Walton opened the first of his Wal-Mart discount stores at Rogers, in the state's northwest corner. By 1972, there were sixteen Wal-Marts, and by 1988 more than a thousand all across America, with sales of over $12 billion a year. The Tyson family went from a small farm that sold chickens in the 1940s to the largest chicken company in the United States by the 1980s, slaughtering 29 million chickens a week by 1993, with over $5 billion in sales, nosing its way into the top 100 U.S. corporations. Wal-Mart and Tyson Foods needed a reliable delivery system and Arkansas's J B Hunt Transport trucking company grew along with them. All three—Wal-Mart, Tyson Foods, and Hunt—were backed by the biggest U.S. investment group not based on Wall Street, Stephens, Inc.

Worth a modest $7.5 million in 1957, the year the troops were sent to Little Rock, Stephens, Inc., grew at an extraordinary rate in the next thirty-five years. Jackson Stephens was named as one of America's 400 richest men in the *Forbes* list of 1994, with a fortune estimated at $1.2 billion made from various interests in natural gas and oil, property and banking, and in Arkansas's bond markets. Stephens, Inc., was the major stockholder of Little Rock's Worthen Banking Corporation, underwrote Wal-Mart when the company went public, and organized Tyson Foods' $1.5 billion takeover of Holly Farms. Jack Stephens and his brother Witt, who died in 1992, grew up on a small family farm, sons of a state legislator. By 1978, they were helping bring the Bank of Credit and Commerce International, to be notorious after its later collapse as the "Bank of Crooks and Con-men International," into the United States. The Stephens group went global, buying the BCCI Hong Kong branch after the collapse. Their partner in establishing the Worthen Bank was the wealthy Riady family of Indonesia.

Back in Washington, with the power that came from seniority, the state's congressional delegation included the chairman of the Senate Foreign Relations Committee in Fulbright, chairman of the Appropriations Committee in Senator John McClellan, and chairman of the House Ways and Means Committee in Congressman Wilbur Mills. Between them, they brought home vast sums of federal investment, from missile bases to the Strategic Air Command air base. Above all, they secured $1.2 billion in federal funds for the Arkansas River Project, making the river navigable from the Mississippi all the way to Tulsa, Oklahoma, and turning the cities of Pine Bluff and Little Rock into ports.

The Arkansas to which Bill Clinton returned to build his political career was neither typical of the South, nor a one-party state. Moreover, it was a state with a long tradition of electing local boys who had gone away to elite colleges for their education. Fulbright had gone to Oxford as a Rhodes scholar. Wilbur Mills had been to Harvard Law School. The Arkansas electorate tended to be forgiving of personal peccadilloes. After being found in the company of an exotic dancer known variously as Fannie Foxe and the "Argentine Firecracker," wading in the fountains of Washington in the early hours, Mills was still voted back to Congress. His successful reelection slogan was "Never Drink Champagne with a Foreigner."

The most striking political change of all reached Arkansas in 1972, when Clinton was sharing his time between Yale Law School and running the McGovern presidential campaign in Texas. For the first time in the twentieth century, black politicians were elected to the state legislature—three legislators and one state senator. It was the last state in the South to do so.

But by then, the cause of liberal reform in Arkansas had spread beyond Rockefeller's Republicans and reached the small Ouachita Mountains town of Charleston, where Dale Bumpers was the town lawyer, Sunday school teacher, and chairman of the school board. Bumpers, a burly Marine Corps veteran of World War Two, had dabbled in politics once before, in a losing run for the state legislature. But in 1970, Bumpers pulled off a surprising upset to win the governorship, thanks in part to the fund-raising efforts of Senator Fulbright. Rockefeller spent $3 million on his vain race, tarnished by the open secret of his alcoholism. Centrists and liberal Democrats who had voted for Rockefeller in the past now had an alternative.

Bumpers continued the modernization of the state machine that Rockefeller had begun, shrinking 65 state agencies into 13. He was able to reform the tax system, to build health clinics in rural areas. After two terms, Bumpers challenged Fulbright for the Senate, and won, and was replaced in the governor's mansion by another liberal Democrat, a Ouachita newspaper editor who had served three terms in Congress, David Pryor. He served for two terms, ran for the Senate and left the governorship available for Clinton's successful 1978 campaign.

Clinton inherited an Arkansas that was already accustomed to reform, to electing Republicans and black legislators and state officials. Twenty years after Orval Faubus played the race card at Little Rock's Central High, the state had undergone an economic transformation, which had reversed the steady population decline of the 1950s. New jobs and a flood of retirees into the western part of Arkansas had increased the population by 19 percent in the 1970s, making it one of the fastest-growing states in the country. The old Arkansas of small country towns was giving way to half-empty Main Streets and gleaming new Wal-Mart malls on the outskirts. And Arkansas had grown used to politicized women and to clever young men who had come back from fancy colleges to build a political career.

☆ 2 ☆

THE MAKING OF A POLITICAL ANIMAL

There are two ways to tell the story of Bill Clinton's childhood and upbringing. Each is perfectly suited to the making of myth, and each is true enough in its way. On the one hand, he was born poor in a poor and backward state, and his redneck life unfolded to the plaintive rhythms of a country-and-western song. His daddy died in a car wreck before he was born. His mother married five times, twice to the same man, and buried three husbands. He was raised by an alcoholic stepfather, who beat his mother, fired the occasional drunken pistol shot into the house wall to get her attention, and was only deterred when young Bill challenged him. Still, Bill chose to take his stepdaddy's name, and felt the tug of family so strongly that he drove hundreds of miles each weekend to the dying man's sickbed at the cancer hospital at Duke. His younger brother played in rock bands and went to prison for dealing cocaine. Bowling was Clinton's best sport, and he also did a fine imitation of Elvis Presley, whom his mother worshiped. He had an eye for women which "caused pain in my marriage," but the Baptist Church was always there to steer him back into line.

On the other hand, Clinton was the classic scholarship boy, from a modestly comfortable home. He was a perfect symbol of the great American meritocracy that exploded after 1945 into the creation of that profound social revolution, a mass middle class. Even without the mechanism of a G.I. Bill, which raised the hopes and social expectations of a generation of Americans, his mother applied herself to improve her skills and become a nurse anesthetist, and resolved that her elder son should rise even further and faster. He was spoiled by his mother, given the master bedroom in the ranch-style suburban home, and drove to high school in his own car, always ready to give his friends a ride and charge them two bucks for gas money.

Fat as a child, and regularly the teacher's pet, he was often the butt of school jokes and the cruelty of children. He recalled late into adulthood the childish sneers of "Sissy, sissy" when he broke his leg at kindergarten. But adults liked him, and thought he would make a fine preacher, someday. Clever and ambitious, he charted his career from his teenage years, picked out his colleges and jobs as so many springboards to a glittering future. He made friends easily and wisely, carefully listing their names and addresses and interests on cards for future reference. He was adept at winning the favor of powerful men and women who could help him.

The essence of Bill Clinton lay in that contradiction, and in the easy, winning manner that helped him reconcile the ambivalence between the bubba and the brains, between the redneck and Rhodes scholar. *Reconcile* is perhaps too harsh a word. There was no artifice in the way that he rose through an American system that was almost uniquely structured to favor the fortunes of those equipped with talent and drive. Clinton was never in the least ashamed of the small towns and modest circumstances that bred him, and never turned his back on his family. Rather the reverse. Clinton could hardly wait to get back to Arkansas. He went to college in Georgetown, and took his friends home to stay and enjoy the vast plenty of his mother's cholesterol-laden cooking, the sweet potato pie stuffed with marshmallows, the gallon jars of his favorite peach ice cream, always in the refrigerator. He crossed the Atlantic to attend Oxford and boasted of the giant watermelons of Hope, Arkansas. He went to Yale Law School, wooed and won one of the outstanding women students of the time, and took her home to Arkansas, too.

Arkansas was where the home-grown but elitely educated politician could flourish. Nowhere else but his home state could he have aspired to become a credible congressional candidate at the age of 28, attorney general at 30, and governor at the age of 32. But the state of Arkansas, to which Clinton committed his career and his loyalty, remained one of the poorest and least regarded states in the Union. Not the most promising springboard for a political career on the national stage, it was still home, and he loved it.

The gap between origins and ambition is one of the oldest themes of the American presidency. It long predates Abraham Lincoln, who was indeed born in a log cabin in Kentucky and raised in another in Indiana. William Henry Harrison, the Whig candidate in 1840, not only ran on the slogan of "Log cabin and hard cider," he campaigned in a log cabin, constructed on top of a horse-drawn wagon. The ultimate symbol of humble origins, the log cabin birthplace kept its force well into the modern era. John Nance Garner, twice Franklin Roosevelt's vice president, will doubtless be the last to claim the distinction. "That log cabin did me more good in politics than anything I ever said," Garner recalled in retirement.

The mythologized film biography that Clinton crafted for his presidential campaign—the poor boy from a small southern town who made good and fought for his ma against a drunken stepdaddy—probably did Clinton more good than all his speeches. It was not just an American life, recognizable to millions from their experience and echoing the confessional TV talk shows that had become a staple of their entertainment. It was also an American parable, of triumph over adversity, of loyalty to home and family, of small-town values that steered Our Hero to success in the wider world of challenge.

Bill Clinton was born at the Julia Chester Hospital in Hope, Arkansas, on August 19, 1946. It was three months after his father, Billy Blythe, died when driving over 500 miles home to Hope from his salesman's job in Chicago. A front tire blew out on Route 60, just outside the town of Sikeston. He was knocked unconscious, thrown from the wrecked car, and drowned in a shallow ditch. Blythe had married Virginia Cassidy in 1943, just before going to war in Italy with the 125th Ordnance Base Auto Maintenance Battalion. The couple had little time to get to know each other, before and after the war. She did not know that he had been married three times before, and had two children. By the time Blythe returned from the war, Virginia had qualified as a nurse, and, a year after her son was born, she determined to improve her medical qualifications. A woman of great spirit and ambition, raised by parents with a profound respect for education and by a mother who was a devout member of Hope's First Baptist Church, Virginia left her son in capable hands.

The infant Clinton was one year old when his mother left to train as a nurse anesthetist in New Orleans, where she remained for the bulk of the next two years. The former town iceman, his grandfather, had worked in a liquor store and then opened a small grocery on the border of what was then called Hope's "colored" district. A kindly man, Grandpaw Cassidy extended credit and courtesy to his customers, as well as illicit liquor in a county that had voted to go dry. He had been raised on a small cotton farm and left school at the age of ten. Clinton's grandmother was a private nurse, who had qualified through a correspondence course, and was much respected in the town, not least for her willingness to treat patients in the colored district on her days off. His grandparents' white-painted house on Hervey Street was large and comfortable, a two-story building with running water and hardwood floors and a large front porch.

"My grandparents taught me to count and read by the age of three. They didn't have much formal education, but they really helped embed in me a real sense of educational achievement," Clinton later recalled. "It was not John Stuart Mill reading Milton at age five or anything like that, but it was reading." His mother remembered him reading the local paper, the *Hope Star,* at the age of five. Bill lived with his grandparents until 1950, when his mother married Roger Clinton, the local Buick car dealer, a fast-living, hard-drinking gambling man known as "Dude." The two had met at the family grocery store, when Dude was making one of his discreet deliveries of alcohol, which the store sold illicitly on the side. Grandpaw kept the bottles hidden under the soda pop in the big chest refrigerator. The Clintons moved to a house of their own, and Bill went to the local kindergarten, where he met Mack McLarty, whose father also ran a car dealership, which prospered far more than Roger Clinton's. In 1952, his business in some difficulties, Roger Clinton sold it and gambled away much of the money; the family moved to Hot Springs, helped to start again by Roger's elder brother Raymond.

Bill Clinton went to a Catholic parochial school until he was nine, and made some impact. His third-grade teacher, later Monsignor John O'Donnell, recalls teaching him the fall of the Roman Empire: "At the end of the course, little Willy [then eight] stood up and said that if he had been emperor, Rome would never have fallen." A self-confident lad, he went on to the local public primary school, Ramble Elementary. His mother working, and enjoying the horse racing and the nightclubs of Hot Springs, he was largely brought up by a nanny-housekeeper, Mrs. Walters. Another devout Baptist, she pressed Bill's mother to realize that her son was a born preacher. "Have you thought about it, how he could lead people to Christ?" is how his mother recalls Mrs. Walters's constant refrain. "She prayed that he'd be a minister, because she could see his leadership qualities." Mrs. Walters urged Bill to go to church, and to read his family Bible, and every Sunday he put on his best suit and walked alone to the nearby Park Place Baptist Church.

In his grandmother, his mother, and Mrs. Walters, Bill Clinton was raised by three strong women, and he was about to meet another. The Hot Springs High School principal, Johnnie Mae Mackey, saw his talents and drove him on. She ran a proud and impressive school, a solid example of an American public school system that was probably the best in the world. An institution that had absorbed million upon million of immigrants from every country in Europe, and turned out English-speaking and literate Americans within a generation, the American public high schools offered a solid, traditional education. And the best of them, like Mrs. Mackey's Hot Springs High, offered something more.

There was a degree of imagination, which encouraged the Latin class to dress up the students in togas to reenact the speeches of Cicero, the trial of Catiline, to ram home the lesson that the United States was the true heir, in power and in republican principles, to ancient Rome. After enjoying his own defense of Catiline, Clinton told his Latin teacher, Elizabeth Buck, that he intended to study law someday. There were classes in public speaking, mock elections and political debates, and encouragement to public service. Clinton worked as a youth volunteer at Levi Hospital. Bright pupils like him were steered early to go out into the world, to give inspirational addresses to local civic bodies, to meet the local worthies, and to understand the institutions that would one day be theirs to run.

It was not all duty, in the bright high school years of the early 1960s, when America was the richest and most self-confident country in the world, with its dashing young president John Kennedy. And it was a glorious time to be a teenager in America, to have, like Clinton, one's own four-door black Buick with high and flaring fins, in a high-living resort and gambling town perched like a neon oasis in the middle of the Bible Belt. Finer still to be a musician with a saxophone in the backseat, a member of a jazz trio of piano, sax, and drums called Three Blind Mice, to cruise around town singing Elvis Presley's "Love Me Tender."

Despite the threat of nuclear war in the Cuban Missile Crisis of October 1962 and the assassination of President Kennedy in November 1963, announced as Clinton sat in calculus class at school, it was a time of extraordinary promise. Clinton was convinced he would get into Georgetown. Even if he failed, he was assured of a place at the University of Arkansas, knowing that he would be the first member of his family to get a college degree. The economy was booming; there was no fear of unemployment or recession. Like the rest of the South, Arkansas was hauling itself out of the century of hard times it had known since the Civil War, transformed into a region of opportunity by the coming of air conditioning.

Even the worst aspect of America, the denial of civil rights to its black citizens, was changing. Hot Springs High was already an integrated school. It would change further, Clinton insisted in the high school debates when he would cite Martin Luther King's "I have a dream" speech. In his class graduation ceremony, Clinton was asked to give the formal benediction, and he broke convention by introducing a political theme. "Leave within us the youthful idealism and moralism that have made our people strong. Sicken us at the sight of apathy, ignorance, and rejection so that our generation will remove complacency, poverty, and prejudice from the hearts of free men."

One of the distinctive features of American life is the speed and efficiency with which it breeds and selects its provincial elites. The high school yearbooks of America record a unique system of competitive elections, of the students voted Most Likely to Succeed, of class presidents and secretaries. They list the arrays of qualifications and school club memberships and sporting achievements, which are the raw materials of each curriculum vitae to come. In communities across the country, the clever and the athletic and the ambitious are encouraged early to learn the mechanisms of politics, lobbying for votes and forging alliances. The essence of the system is that merit is matched with popularity among the peers, or at least with the ability to garner votes.

Bill Clinton was elected president of his junior class at Hot Springs High School. He was band major in a school where music was taken as seriously as football. He was president of the school version of the Kiwanis civic group, the Key Club, president of the scholarly Beta Club, a member of the National Honor Society, a National Merit Scholarship semifinalist. Nearly a thousand miles to the north at the same time, at Park Ridge High School in the suburbs of Chicago, Hillary Rodham was elected student council representative, junior class vice president, a National Merit Scholarship finalist, and was voted Most Likely to Succeed.

In some states, the process of selection and politicization is encouraged to go beyond the school and test its champions in a larger crucible. In Arkansas of the early 1960s, an institution called Boys State was taken seriously by teachers like Mrs. Mackey, who saw it as their task to groom coming young men. At the end of each summer, the high school faculty would pick the chosen few to attend this gathering of their peers at Camp Robinson, an old U.S. Army training base in North Little Rock, to simulate the political procedures of adulthood. The most competitive election was for governor of Boys State, which in Clinton's year was won by his boyhood friend from the small town of Hope, Thomas "Mack" McLarty. Organized by the American Legion, a nationwide veterans' group, Boys State in Arkansas enjoyed the further patronage of Governor Faubus. Each year, he would mount an old army jeep with the Boys State "governor" to make a formal inspection review of the boys, neatly lined up in their ranks. McLarty would go on to the University of Arkansas and be elected class president, in what was seen as an almost inevitable rise to the real governorship.

The election the young Clinton most wanted to win was to be one of the two Boys State senators. Along with their peers from the other 49 states, the "senators" would be sent to Washington, D.C., to see the sights, to lunch with their states' real senators, and to meet the president in the garden of the White House. The president and senators alike took Boys Nation seriously enough to welcome them and make time for the visit. In one sense, it was no doubt a conventional enough courtesy to promising young voters who had families who voted, and would be pleased at the honor given to their sons. But it was also a part of a deep-rooted national ritual, to select and bring on and reward the next generation of the national elite.

"I don't know if I could win a race like that, because when I was a student politician, I was about as controversial as I have been in my later life," Clinton later recalled. "I was not one of those guys who won all of his races. And I wasn't always universally popular."

Clinton's determined lobbying of his fellow Boys State citizens became a local legend. And although he lost his bid to be elected vice president of Boys Nation, his speed at being the first of the young Boys Nation senators to leap forward after President Kennedy's speech and be photographed shaking his hand became the stuff of national myth. It was to be the high point of the filmed biography at the Democratic Party Convention that nominated him as their presidential candidate, a symbolic laying on of hands by the last Democratic president to have won an enduring place in the nation's affections.

There was never any doubt about Bill Clinton's political allegiance. He became a Democrat through state and family tradition, through ideological conviction, and through personal connection and ambition. The family was Democratic on both sides, partly because of the South's inveterate political loyalties, and to a degree from personal experience. Like many another poor farming family in the Great Depression, Clinton's paternal grandparents had seen their farm foreclosed in 1936. The Clintons, his stepfather's family, were closely involved in state Democratic politics. Ray Clinton, one brother of his stepfather, had been a member of the returning veterans and reformers who tried to clean up the worst of the gambling and corruption in Hot Springs after 1946. Another brother, Roy, who ran a feed store, was to be elected to the Arkansas state legislature, inevitably as a Democrat.

Clinton's own convictions began to form early. The family bought its first TV set in 1956, in time for Bill Clinton to acquire his first taste for national politics, watching the Democratic presidential nomination of Adlai Stevenson and the Republican renomination of President Eisenhower. The following year, his mother recalled him being upset as his home state became a synonym for racial segregation as Governor Faubus defied the courts and U.S. troops deployed in the state capital to enforce the law. At the age of fourteen, he took the part of the Democratic candidate John Kennedy in a high school civics class election debate.

"When he came back from Washington, holding this picture of himself with Jack Kennedy, and the expression on his face, I knew right then that politics was the answer for him," his mother recalled. More practically, through the Boys Nation trip to Washington, he got to know his state's two senators, William Fulbright and John McClellan, over lunch in the Senate dining room. Politics may have been in his plans, but the immediate prospect was to equip himself for a diplomatic career. He applied for Georgetown, a prestigious Catholic university in Washington, celebrated for steering its foreign service school graduates into the State Department. Georgetown meant proximity to Capitol Hill, and the prospect of part-time work that could bring political experience and a modest income.

Clinton had already realized that such a job required politics as well as qualifications. He spent part of the 1966 summer vacation working for the gubernatorial campaign of Judge Jack Holt in the Democratic primary. Holt lost, but Clinton asked for some help in getting a job in Senator Fulbright's office. Holt telephoned Fulbright's chief aide, Lee Williams, to recommend the young Georgetown student who had met Fulbright through Boys Nation. After a jocular phone call, he was hired to work in the documents room of the Senate Foreign Relations Committee, which Fulbright chaired.

College was also something of an escape from a home life of intense strain. Clinton had been brought up by a series of powerful women, but except for his grandfather and Virgil Spurlin, the high school band director, there were few men to admire. He had never known his real father, and Roger Clinton was a poor substitute, an alcoholic of spasmodic violence. Bill had been five the first time that his stepfather, drunkenly refusing to let Virginia take Bill to see her grandmother in the hospital, fired a shot into the wall above her head. She called the police, and he spent a night in the local jail. The fights and arguments, jealous rages and drunken abuse, were a constant part of his boyhood. In 1959, according to the affidavit Virginia filed in support of a divorce action, "He threw me to the floor and began to stomp me, pulled my shoe off and hit me on the head several times." In his own affidavit, Bill said he witnessed that assault. "It was I who called my mother's attorney who in turn had to get the police to come to the house and arrest the defendant." Virginia separated from her husband, but took him back when he promised to stop drinking.

But Roger Clinton could not stop. At a Christmas party in 1961, he drank himself so insensible that Virginia could not haul him into the car. Bill had to help. Two months after that came the famous confrontation, related by Virginia and described in the biographical film made for Clinton's presidential campaign, when the fifteen-year-old youth pulled his stepfather away from his mother, and warned him never to attack her again. In his affidavit for the divorce, he said, "It is impossible in my opinion for them to continue to live together as husband and wife. The last occasion on which I went to my mother's aid when he was abusing my mother he threatened to mash my face in if I took her part."

The divorce was on May 15, 1962, and Virginia took the boys to a new, more modest house. But within two months, after Roger Clinton had sat outside the house in a parked car, day after day, not drinking, she took him back. In August, they were remarried. By then, Bill Clinton had made another gesture of conciliation, an act of family solidarity that he thought would help his little brother, formally changing his name from William Jefferson Blythe to Clinton.

The nightmare of living with an alcoholic was kept a family secret. Clinton's school friends did not know about it. The effects on the adolescent Clinton can be imagined. The only man in his home life was a tragic, violent wreck. His own roles, as his mother's defender and as the family conciliator and the one to comfort his terrified younger half-brother, forced him into an early maturity and responsibility. When the burden seemed to lift with the divorce, he then had to buckle down once more as his mother, against his pleadings, took Roger Clinton back. And despite Clinton's decision to take his name, his stepfather did not return the compliment by making a formal act of adoption.

In September 1964, on the eve of a presidential election that would reelect Lyndon Johnson to enact his Great Society programs, the campus of Georgetown was more than an escape from a difficult home. It was the heart of political promise, the Washington Monument rising sharp and white along the river from the university, the Capitol dome gleaming beyond the Mall where Martin Luther King, Jr., had convened his hundreds of thousands, and on the far bank of the Potomac, the neoclassical pillars of Arlington Cemetery that guarded the fresh grave of President Kennedy.

The grave was one of the first sights Clinton wanted to visit, and he found the perfect guide, three doors down the hall from his room on campus. Tommy Caplan was the son of a prosperous Baltimore family who had interviewed Kennedy for his school paper during the 1960 campaign, then visited the White House to promote his idea of a teenage version of the Peace Corps. He had become something of a young favorite, invited to stay at the Kennedy compound at Hyannis Port. Caplan took Clinton to meet Evelyn Lincoln, Kennedy's secretary, and also helped the political campaign that Clinton launched almost immediately, to be elected president of his freshman class. In a blitz of speeches, leaflets, and handshaking, backed by a makeshift band, Clinton won, on a platform of studied moderation. "The freshman year is not the time for crusading, but the building of a strong unit for the future. You must know the rules before you can change them," the new class president solemnly informed the *Courier,* the college paper.

The most influential teacher of Clinton's time was Professor Carroll Quigley, who taught a class that was required of all new students on the history of Western civilization. A theatrical lecturer who would rip up a copy of Plato's *Republic* as he denounced the ancient Greek philosopher as the father of totalitarianism, Quigley was a legend on the campus. The moral of his course on Western civilization was rammed home into generations of Georgetown students, and like most of them, Clinton never forgot it.

"The thing that got you into this classroom today is belief in the future, belief that the future can be better than the present and that people will and should sacrifice in the present to get to that better future," Quigley's moral began. "That belief has taken man out of the chaos and deprivation that most human beings toiled in for most of history to the point where we are today. One thing will kill our civilization and way of life—when people no longer have the will to undergo the pain required to prefer the future to the present. That's what got your parents to pay this expensive tuition. That's what got us through two wars and the Depression. Future preference. Don't ever forget that."

Clinton recited Quigley's theme repeatedly in the future, even during the speech when he declared his candidacy for president. Quigley's impact may have become even sharper when Clinton became one of only two students in that class to be awarded an A grade. But the four years at Georgetown were to be a testing time for Quigley's passionate faith that the future could be better than the present. Between 1964 and 1968, the bright confidence of America in the early 1960s and the massive legislative achievements in domestic reform that marked Lyndon Johnson's presidency gave way to the double crisis of war abroad in Vietnam, and something that looked like war at home, as city after city burned and flared in racial riots.

Clinton had no doubts about patriotism or about the military when he joined the Reserve Officers' Training Corps in his freshman year at Georgetown. Despite the woeful coordination that wrecked his drill, he wore the uniform, marched, and attended parades. He was by no means a student radical. He lost his coveted class presidency in his final year when he proved rather too moderate in an increasingly radical time. In his campaign, under the uninspiring slogan "A realistic approach to student government," he stressed that he would not pander to "the radical segment of the student body." He was beaten by a rival who had once attended an antiwar prayer vigil. But working in Fulbright's office while the senator was conducting his landmark hearings into Vietnam slowly but surely turned him against the conflict, which was drafting 30,000 young Americans a month by Clinton's final year at Georgetown.

Clinton was never violently against the war. His opposition to it developed from the very heart of the foreign policy establishment, from the Senate Foreign Relations Committee, where Fulbright's hearings were making it increasingly respectable to question the undeclared and fruitless war. The arguments among Clinton's housemates on Potomac Avenue were not strident, although Tom Campbell was heading to join the Marines after graduation. Tommy Caplan, who would volunteer for Robert Kennedy's presidential campaign, was cool about the war, supporting Kennedy's argument for a negotiated peace. Kit Ashby, who was working for the robustly hawkish senator Henry "Scoop" Jackson, thought Vietnam was part of the cold war and had to be won. He too would join the Marines after college. Jim Moore, son of an army family, had access to the post exchange store at nearby Fort Myer and kept the house in subsidized food.

The large and weird antiwar demonstration that descended on the Pentagon in 1967, to chant incantations designed to levitate the building so that the evil spirits could fall out, took place without the support of the Potomac Avenue household. Even the widespread perception of American defeat with the Tet Offensive in 1968, when Viet Cong guerrillas attacked the U.S. embassy in Saigon, did not provoke any rifts or drama.

They were serious young men, "boringly respectable and responsible," in Caplan's memory, intent on their careers and their futures. Clinton, recommended by Senator Fulbright and backed by his college professors, already knew his next step. He had won a Rhodes scholarship to spend two years at Oxford. "How do you think I'll look in English tweeds, Mother?" was his way of breaking the news to his family. Rather than getting stoned on marijuana, his group's idea of a special occasion was to head up to New York and dine at the grand 21 Club for Caplan's twenty-first birthday. When Peter, Paul, and Mary sang their protest songs on the Georgetown campus, Clinton avoided their "Blowing in the Wind," and stayed in to listen to Caplan's record of the soundtrack from *Gone With the Wind.*

For Clinton at Georgetown, student solidarity was not a charge to the barricades but the building of a network. When a group of European students came to Georgetown for an international conference, Clinton was there as class president to greet them, and test his rusty German on young Rudiger Lowe from Munich. When he found that Lowe was interested in U.S. foreign policy, he insisted that the young German meet Senator Fulbright. "He is too great a man," Lowe protested. "When are you free, lunch or breakfast?" Clinton replied, and went off to phone. He took Lowe to breakfast with Fulbright the next day, and stayed in touch constantly thereafter. Lowe would later provide German children's fairy tale books for young Chelsea, arrange meetings with Bavarian industrialists for Governor Clinton's trade missions, and attend Clinton's inauguration as president.

As a campus, Georgetown was concerned far more with the racial antagonisms at home than with Vietnam. There were African students at the college, but no black Americans. As a Catholic college, there were priests who took the civil rights cause with desperate earnestness. Father Richard McSorley organized a group of Georgetown students to join the Freedom Riders in the South after demonstrators were gassed and beaten crossing the bridge at Selma, Alabama. Initially, Clinton questioned McSorley's plea for the student body to help fund the trip, supporting the mission but acknowledging conservatives' objections to the use of their funds. In the end, Clinton supported McSorley, but not before he had been dismissed as "a southern phony" by some of his critics in college politics.

By this time, racial tension was not simply a matter of civil rights marches. The Civil Rights and Voting Rights laws had already been enacted by President Johnson and the overwhelmingly Democratic Congress. But legal reform had not bought racial peace. Harlem had erupted in two days of riots in 1964, and the Watts district of Los Angeles burned in 1965 for six days, with 34 dead, over 1,000 injured, and over 4,000 arrests. In the summer of 1966, with renewed riots killing two more people in Watts, Clinton went home to campaign for Judge Holt in Arkansas. Although he had grown up in segregation, he was startled to see its survival in the poor Delta townships of his own state.

"Now we are campaigning in the heart of cotton country, south and east Arkansas, where Negroes are still niggers—and I couldn't believe my eyes when I saw restrooms and waiting rooms still marked 'Colored' and

'White.' It made me sick to my stomach," he wrote to his girlfriend, Denise Hyland.

The next summer, Detroit exploded, with over sixty deaths in nine days of rage that took 9,000 National Guard troops to quell. Smaller riots followed, in New York, Rochester, and Birmingham, and President Johnson appointed the first black, the legendary civil rights lawyer Thurgood Marshall, to the Supreme Court. In Clinton's final year, Martin Luther King was assassinated in Memphis, and riots erupted in Washington, the flames reaching within six blocks of the White House. National Guard troops were quartered on campus.

Clinton volunteered to help the Red Cross ferry food and medical supplies and blankets to a black church in the city that was sheltering burned-out families. He had a white Buick convertible and pasted a giant red cross on each door, and drove to the airport to pick up an old school friend and neighbor, Carolyn Yeldell. Telling her that she had volunteered, too, he drove into the urban nightmare—city blocks burned and littered with charred cars and broken glass, the smoke still drifting across the American capital. They delivered the relief supplies, drove around the eerily empty streets, and got out to walk around. They turned a corner, saw six black men walking abreast toward them, and left fast. "You will never forget this as long as you live," Clinton told her.

That summer, Clinton sailed for England with the other Rhodes scholars, aboard the grand ocean liner *United States*. The British took the Rhodes scholars seriously, and rarely had the farsighted investment in anglicizing future American elites paid off more handsomely than in the class who came with Clinton in 1968. The Clinton administration was to fulfill Cecil Rhodes's dream. Seldom has any foreign country been run so completely by such a narrowly defined elite. The Rhodes scholar in the Oval Office was joined by three more among senior White House staff—Bruce Reed, George Stephanopoulos, and Ira Magaziner. Another Rhodes, R. James Woolsey, ran the CIA. Strobe Talbott was deputy secretary at the State Department, Walter Slocombe at the Pentagon, Robert Reich and Thomas S. Williamson, Jr., at the Labor Department. David Souter sat on the Supreme Court, James Billington was Librarian of Congress, and there were six Rhodes scholars in the Senate (Sarbanes, Feingold, Boren, Lugar, Pressler, and Bradley).

Yet the Clinton administration was to prove a great disappointment to the British establishment as it casually presided over the twilight of the Anglo-American special relationship. The administration ran roughshod over Britain's attempt to continue testing nuclear weapons in Nevada. They gave a visa to Gerry Adams of Sinn Fein, and Clinton personally pushed the British government to negotiate with what London saw as a terrorist organization. They engaged in a public row over Bosnian policies. They made it clear that Germany and France had become their favored interlocutors in Europe.

Clinton and his fellows felt, on the whole, only limited affection and nostalgia for Britain as a result of their time at Oxford. As much as pellucid May mornings punting on the Isis and sunsets gilding the dreaming spires, they recalled snooty undergraduates, languid dons, cold rooms, and bad food. From the vantage point of an elite enclave, they experienced Britain as a country in palpable decline. The contradiction was acute between the snobbish complacencies of Oxford and the wider realities of shriveling British grandeur. Their memories were colored by strikes in the 1960s and 1970s, by the politics of class war in Mrs. Thatcher's 1980s, all against the background of a simmering counterinsurgency campaign in Northern Ireland, punctuated by terrorist attacks.

Clinton came to an Oxford that was toying with revolution as spectators of the feats of others. The Oxford left-wingers were entranced by the students of Paris who had manned the barricades against the riot police in May 1968. They thrilled to the students of Warsaw who had battled their own police that Easter in support of the reformed socialism of the ill-fated Prague Spring in Czechoslovakia, and were fascinated by the American antiwar movement. The most popular destination for the Rhodes scholars was Balliol, the most self-consciously intellectual and meritocratic of the colleges, where the students' basement bar was luridly decorated in scenes of America's urban riots, with the slogan "The Fire Next Time."

The month after the Rhodes scholars arrived, Oxford's leftist groups descended on Grosvenor Square in London, home of the U.S. embassy, to demonstrate against the Vietnam War. For the British students, the seriousness and left-wing dedication of the antiwar movement also had the flavor of a lark, a modern version of the license to riot that Oxford and Cambridge students had traditionally enjoyed on boat race night. For the Americans, who faced conscription and the prospect of a wretched death on some miserable jungle trail in an unknown country in a cause they opposed, it was all deadly serious. None of that year's new intake of Rhodes scholars attended. It was all too somber for British student follies, dallying in somebody else's cause.

And it was all too exciting to be students at a university where young men had studied for eight centuries and put on white tie and gown and mortarboard for the "Matriculation," the Oxford word for formal acceptance into the body of scholars. Scholarship at Oxford was a gentlemanly business. The method of teaching was wildly different from anything the Americans had known. Attendance at lectures was entirely voluntary. The only required learning event of the week was the hour or two spent sipping sherry with a tutor, reading aloud one's essay for the week, and discussing it in the politest terms. At the end of tuition, the essay theme for the following week would be suggested, a list of useful books and essays suggested, and the student would depart down the worn stone steps of the college staircase into an ancient quadrangle where the lawns were perfect, because they had been kept that way for hundreds of years.

On the one hand lounged the languid Oxford tradition—the festive dinners in Hall on Torpids Night or Bumps Night, as Oxford called its boat races, with the port passing to the left, and dons and undergraduates alike heading out to circle ancient trees and urinate together in the traditional, collegial way. On the other, loomed Vietnam, a distant America in crisis both foreign and domestic, and a sense that in this best-educated and most pampered generation in history, students around the globe had something in common. But what they held in common was unclear. There was much intellectual Marxism, usually of the Trotskyite variant. After Soviet tanks had crushed the Prague Spring there was no more sympathy for that regime than there was for the American Way, at least as expressed in Selma and in Vietnam and at the police riot during the Democratic Party Convention in Chicago in that summer of 1968, which had also seen both Martin Luther King and Robert Kennedy assassinated. In that first term, the Oxford Union, a venerable debating society and breeding ground of British politicians, carried the motion that "American democracy has failed" by 266 ayes to 233 noes.

There was some Maoism, based largely on a blend of romance and ignorance and the hunger for some political model that avoided the twin poles of the cold war. But neither Trotskyism nor Maoism held any appeal for Clinton, who proved wholly resistant to the period fashion for Marxism. More than most among the American students at Oxford, he would stand up for the American system. "In the end, democracy usually makes the right choices," he insisted to a mocking circle in Balliol's Junior Common Room one summer evening in 1969. His example was civil rights, where America had eventually done the right thing. As a southerner, he would talk of the slow force of the courts outlawing segregation, the equally slow process of turning the Voting Rights Act into electoral power. The political figure he cited most often was Martin Luther King, and his argument that civil rights were only half the battle. Having won legal equality, black America now had to reach economic equality.

"Bill was cool. He was easy around black folks, like a lot of southern boys. None of that tensed up nervousness you met in the Ivy Leaguers," recalled Oliver Franklin, an American black at Balliol who knew Clinton well. "He knew what he thought and where he stood, and didn't run off with political fashions. Vietnam was a mistake, and America was a place that learned from its mistakes—that was his line. You could goad him by saying that the slavery mistake had lasted for three centuries and the South had run things its own way for another century after that and a lot of us weren't prepared to wait any longer. You could goad him, but he'd smile. Bill didn't get fazed."

Clinton was not a leader in the antiwar movement at Oxford. He took part in some events, including a prayer vigil, and the presentation of a petition by many of the Rhodes scholars to the U.S. embassy. But then, he was not much of a leader in anything at Oxford. He took almost no part in the Oxford Union, the main debating and political forum. He was not involved in the Labour or Conservative clubs, traditionally the breeding grounds for the ambitious, and a magnet for those fascinated by politics. As Clinton went about his studies, the British chancellor of the exchequer, Roy Jenkins, was a former chairman of the Oxford Labour Club; the leader of the Conservative opposition, Edward Heath (also a former prime minister), had been a chairman of the Oxford University Conservative association; and the minister of defense, Denis Healey, had been a former secretary of the Communist Club on the eve of World War Two. Clinton did not take part in OUDS, the dramatic society, another showcase for the talents of those who liked to perform in public. Even his close friend Robert Reich, who became a legendary dramatic impresario at University College, could not draw him into the theater.

Clinton's was a surprisingly low-key existence at Oxford, for a man of his energies and the relentless political ambition he had shown at school and at Georgetown. He took enthusiastic if clumsy part in the rugby games of University College, where he lived for his first year. He attended many parties, danced a great deal, and struck up an intense friendship with a young woman student, Sara Maitland, who gave tea parties and was to become a distinguished novelist. With her and one of her housemates, Mandy Merck, an American student, he went to a popular lecture by the feminist Germaine Greer, then at the height of her fame as the author of *The Female Eunuch*. The speaker said at one point that she preferred sex with nonintellectual men, inspiring Clinton to ask her to remember him if she ever changed her mind.

Oxford at the end of the 1960s was a place where soft drugs were commonplace and LSD was widely available. But there was little marijuana in Britain. The usual drug was hashish, imported from Lebanon or Afghanistan in the form of solid bricks. The usual procedure was to warm some hashish with a match and crumble it into a hand-rolled cigarette filled with conventional tobacco. This meant that except for hash cakes and brownies, which were occasionally featured in the circles Clinton moved in, the only way to get stoned was to smoke tobacco. Clinton, with his allergies, could not inhale tobacco, although on occasion he tried. He could not abide thick tobacco smoke, sometimes leaving a pub or throwing open a window to put his head out at a party if it became too intense. His Oxford acquaintances were amused at the mockery Clinton inspired for saying "I didn't inhale" during his campaign. Technically, it was true.

Mainly, Clinton read; he later calculated he had devoured three hundred books in his first year. It was a vast range that included westerns and philosophy, history and some economics, Soviet studies and classic novels. He read some Proust and Balzac in translation, and developed a fondness for the *Meditations* of Marcus Aurelius that continued throughout his life. As president, he took a copy on his travels. He read books on Vietnam and on American foreign policy, from George F. Kennan to his former boss, Senator Fulbright. He read the whole of Gibbon's *Decline and Fall of the Roman Empire,* and liked to cite Gibbon's view that the greatest civilization of antiquity had fallen victim to "the triumphs of barbarism and religion." He read Hobbes's *Leviathan* and Locke and Macaulay, rediscovered Charles Dickens, and the metaphysical poetry and sermons of John Donne.

He did not take a degree, which was neither required nor expected of Rhodes scholars. Oxford was for Clinton a time out, to read and think and reassess the hitherto uninterrupted soaring of ambition and achievement that had been his life so far. To such introspections, and to such passionate reading, Oxford may be the most indulgent of universities. He was liked and respected by his tutors, who understood the demons of Vietnam that haunted most of the young Americans, and saw little reason to push a man of such obvious talents beyond the point which he then was in a mood to go.

And he traveled, hitchhiking around England, visiting the Continent, Scandinavia, and Moscow, where he characteristically made friends with two Americans who were on a quixotic mission to persuade the North Vietnamese embassy to help in the release of some American prisoners, missing in Vietnam. From his reading, Clinton knew just enough about the workings of the Soviet system to be useful. Equally characteristically, he impressed them so much they later showed up as volunteers for his future political campaigns. They also could have provided an alibi, although at the time nobody bothered to ask, refuting the bizarre suggestions by the Republicans in 1992 that there had been some sinister purpose to his trip. Moscow was a fairly common destination for curious Oxford students in those years, being cheap to visit and mysterious. He had one acquaintance there, a West Indian girl studying at Moscow University, who was the friend of a friend. She showed Clinton around the city, met his POW-hunting acquaintances, and helped them with some translating.

He went to Spain and read voraciously on its civil war, from George Orwell to Arthur Koestler to Hugh Thomas, and dove deep into Hemingway's luxuriant paean to bullfighting, *The Sun Also Rises*. He went to Germany to stay with his friend Rudy Lowe, and read the novels of Günter Grass, and to Czechoslovakia, fascinating after the Soviet suppression of Prague Spring. Rudy came back to Oxford for Clinton's summer party in that summer of 1969, when Clinton thought the draft might never let him return for his second year of the Rhodes scholarship. He had received his formal notice of induction from his draft board. Under such a cloud, the party was a legendary affair, that lasted on and off for three days, fueled by what Lowe told them had been Bismarck's favorite drink, Black Velvet, of champagne and Guinness. It included an Arkansas-style hog-roast barbecue in the medieval college court that spilled out on the ancient college roof, punting trips up the river at dawn, and the formal presentation of "jungle gear" to Clinton—a walking stick and deerstalker cap to equip him for Vietnam.

He went home to America in the summer of 1969, to work out his tangled draft problems, and after several maneuvers secured another year's deferment from his draft board with a promise to join the ROTC program at the University of Arkansas Law School after a second year at Oxford. It was not clear even to him if he meant it, or if this was a device, like so many others adopted by his contemporaries. He went home and wrote a letter to withdraw his ROTC promise, asking for the draft deferment to be lifted, but never mailed it. By now, the months were punctuated by the news of deaths in Vietnam of boys he had known in high school.

Then he went to Washington to spend a week with Rick Stearns, a friend volunteering with Senator McGovern, and calling in at the Vietnam Moratorium Committee, which was organizing a massive antiwar demonstration in Washington for October 15, 1969. In September, he went with Stearns to a gathering of antiwar campaigners on Martha's Vineyard. Not a part of their intensity and dedication to the cause of organizing, he nonetheless shared their conviction that the war was wrong and wicked and must be stopped. He made more friends—Taylor Branch, whom he was to meet again in the McGovern campaign, and David Mixner, later to become a prominent gay rights activist. He left them his name and number as a contact in Britain, to coordinate whatever international support could be rallied for the October 15 demo.

Back in Oxford for his second year, Clinton led the existence of a visitor, sleeping on other people's floors, arranging no permanent room, living out of a duffel bag, and looking ever more shaggy as his beard and hair grew thick. He did little organizing for the October 15 demonstration, but went to Grosvenor Square, watched from the sidelines, and spent his evening at a church vigil with Father McSorley from Georgetown. By the end of October, he had moved in with Strobe Talbott and Frank Aller, into one of the most extraordinary households in Oxford. Aller was studying Chinese, and Talbott was not just studying Russian, but was plunged into a highly secret job that made the Leckford Road flat a tempting target for one of the world's most ruthless intelligence services.

Fluent in Russian even at Yale, Talbott had also worked as an intern at *Time* magazine. When *Time* got wind of the great scoop that the memoirs of the former Soviet leader Nikita Khrushchev might be available, Talbott, with access to the libraries and scholars of Oxford, was their imaginative choice to translate and edit the vast text in complete discretion. Clinton and Aller knew of the project, and knew the Russian émigré Yasha Zaguskin who came to the flat to help Talbott, and they kept the secret.

By Thanksgiving of 1969, the three Rhodes scholars were preparing a turkey feast while enthralled at the implications of President Nixon's latest pronouncements on the draft. In October, Nixon had allowed graduate students to complete their academic year, which meant that Clinton was now safe at Oxford until the next summer. On the eve of Thanksgiving, Nixon announced a draft lottery, to let chance rather than the whims of draft boards decide which eligible men would be taken. The lottery was based on birth dates. When numbers were drawn on December 1, Clinton's birth date was number 311, so far down the list that it was almost inconceivable he would be called. The cloud lifted. He could see his way ahead, and Clinton sat down to write his December 3 letter to Colonel Holmes at his draft board, the letter that was to become central to the 1992 campaign. Then he wrote to Yale Law School, to apply for the next academic year.

☆ 3 ☆

THE MAKING OF A GOVERNOR

Bill Clinton had become a committed antiwar activist by the time he tried to register twice at Yale Law School in the fall of 1970. The second time was superfluous, an excuse for the opportunity to chat with the young Hillary Rodham while standing in line. They had met briefly but inconclusively in the first week, introduced by Robert Reich, who had known Hillary since a conference of student council leaders at Dartmouth in 1968. Then, in marital legend, they discreetly stalked each other from safe distances. Hillary recalled eavesdropping on his bragging of the giant watermelons of his native Hope. He was intensely aware of the young woman in brown corduroys in his civil liberties class, until one afternoon in the law library she came up and said, "If you're going to keep staring at me and I'm going to keep staring back, we should at least introduce ourselves. I'm Hillary Rodham."

"And I couldn't remember my own name," continues his version, in the oft-recounted tale, now honed into romantic drama by each one. "I was so embarrassed. But that's a true story. It turned out she knew who I was. But I didn't know that at the time, either. But I was real impressed that she did that. And we've been together more or less, ever since."

It was to be the most important meeting of his life, the acquaintance not just of his future wife, but his closest political adviser. From the beginning, his rangy, undisciplined, and endlessly curious intelligence was matched and entranced by her sharply focused and analytical mind. "I remember being genuinely afraid of falling in love with her. She was a star," he recalled. But there was a balance, as if each had some quality the other needed. His vast and affable appeal, which is to say his political gift, was sharpened by her bent for organization. His talents were enthusiasm and an appetite for grand concepts, and hers were for structure and essential detail. From their first joint effort, at the annual Yale event of the Prize Trial, a mock court case, they made a formidable partnership. Her forensic legal rigor buttressed his skills in drawing out witnesses and in charming the jury.

Politically, she was the idealist and Clinton the pragmatist. She was fascinated by children's rights, volunteering to work at Yale's Child Studies Center, staying on an extra year to study children and the law. He could always make her laugh, and she could almost always make him concentrate. They could argue with intensity, sometimes in flares of anger, but also with the dispassion that she could deploy to shape argument into discussion. It was to become an alliance as well as a marriage, and none the worse for it, rooted in the enduring and compelling way they complemented each other.

On their second encounter in the registration line, he was caught out when the clerk noticed he had been there the previous day. "After we finished, we went out for a Coke. We started talking, went for a long walk," she later recalled. "We ended up in front of the Yale University Art Gallery. It was closed. But Bill had been there a week or two before and wanted to show me the Mark Rothko exhibition inside and a Henry Moore exhibition in the sculpture yard. He found a worker who said it had to be closed because of a labor dispute. And so Bill said, 'Well, if we pick up the garbage, will you let us in?" In the version he recounted to friends, on that first date they talked African politics and liberation movements.

Big and now clean-shaven, but his thick bush of curly hair still long enough for Senator Fulbright to tell him to get it cut, Clinton had returned from Oxford to work for the summer at Project Pursestrings in Washington. This was still the respectable wing of the antiwar movement, lobbying Congress to block funds from what was now a different war from the Vietnam of 1968, when the Paris peace talks had begun. By 1970, the bombing of North Vietnam had become relentless. The U.S. war effort had helped South Vietnamese troops attack Cambodia, in an abortive and eventually disastrous effort to raid Vietnamese bases across the border. Cambodia was being battered by wings of B-52 bombers, and President Nixon's policy to Vietnamize the war did not immediately weaken the opposition at home. The mass demonstrations continued, in Washington and on campuses around the country. At Kent State University in Ohio, four students were killed when the National Guard opened fire. U.S. troops were still being shipped across to the war. Just before arriving at Yale, Clinton had attended the wedding of his old Georgetown roommate Kit Ashby, who wore his Marine Corps uniform and was about to depart for Saigon.

Installed at Yale, Clinton at once began working for the quixotic campaign of the antiwar candidate and theology professor Joe Duffey to become U.S. senator for Connecticut. A dress rehearsal for many of the young activists who would staff the McGovern presidential campaign two years later, the Connecticut election was for many of them their first acquaintance with the traditional working class and ethnic Democrats, union members, and deeply patriotic, who still formed the base of the party. Their suspicion of the student activists, spurred by the Nixon White House, which was trying to rally the hard-hat vote, rehearsed the divisions that were to ravage the party for years to come. Fearing the loss of the party's base, Duffey had a rule that the student volunteers could only campaign when accompanied by his loyalists from the neighborhoods. But in the third congressional district, where Clinton was the coordinator, he moved easily through the Irish and Italian communities, and became the informal ambassador to woo the traditional Democratic candidates Duffey had beaten in the primary.

Duffey came second in a three-way race, a quarter of the vote going to the old traditional Democrat, the former incumbent Thomas Dodd. (His son Christopher was to win the Senate seat in 1980, and become Democratic Party chairman alongside President Clinton.) In a perceptive analysis of his own defeat that Duffey later circulated to his campaign team, he defined what was to be the central political dynamic of Clinton's future career, and the way the Democratic Party would have to change. "Many of our policies have been formulated as if the nation were composed of only two major groups, the affluent and the welfare poor. But somewhere between affluence and grinding poverty stand the majority of American families, living on the margins of social and economic insecurity. The new politics has thus far not spoken to the needs and interests of these Americans."

Clinton had to catch up quickly at Yale when the election ended in November, borrowing the notes of friends on the lectures he had missed, reading himself into the law. It was not too formidable a task. He was an extraordinarily fast learner, shone in class discussion, and Yale in 1970 was a relaxed place, without hierarchic grading. On the assumption that the admission process was the real test, courses were graded Pass or Fail. Yale prided itself on being less rigorous than Harvard Law School, with its solid, traditional insistence on statutes and cases. Yale preferred the theory and the social policy of law.

Clinton had won a scholarship, but he still needed money and took a succession of part-time jobs. At the University of New Haven, he taught constitutional law and criminal justice to policemen in a course to educate policemen. He did research for a New Haven lawyer on civil cases, tracking down witnesses: "I wound up going into tenements where people were shooting up heroin, doing stuff like that," he recalled. He stayed in touch with politics by working for a Hartford city councilman. He lived in a rented house at Fort Trumbull Beach on the shore of Long Island Sound with four other law students, including his fellow Rhodes scholar, Doug Eakeley, and Bill Coleman, one of the ten black students in his class.

Clinton and Hillary did not start to live together until the beginning of their second year at Yale, but their relationship blossomed throughout the academic year of 1970–1971. It was an extraordinary time in America: young white radicals resorting to bombs and terror as the Weathermen; the Black Panthers asserting and even glorifying the right to violent resistance; President Nixon's government deploying the FBI in covert operations against them both, and against the wider antiwar movement. At Yale, where the anti-Vietnam demonstration of October 1970 was one of the biggest in the country, radicalism had a romantic, even utopian cast. Yale was the elite campus from which Charles Reich had written his best-selling *The Greening of America* to suggest that the antiwar generation would graduate to humanize American life.

Reich provided a vague, rosy-tinted blueprint for the caring and sensitive society, which would replace individual ambition with communitarian generosity, soften social discipline with spiritual freedom, balance corporate profits with environmental sensitivity. Hillary may have agreed with the goals, but was characteristically practical about the ways to reach them. She helped to found the *Yale Review of Law and Social Action,* a defiant alternative to the *Yale Law Review.* Radical but not untypical of the time, its covers featured cops as hairy-snouted pigs, armed pigs marching in formation, pigs decapitated with the headline "Seize the Time."

The first issue featured an essay, which Hillary edited, titled "Jamestown '70," an echo of the original Jamestown settlement where the first English colony of America had begun in Virginia in 1607. "Experimentation with drugs, sex, individual life-styles or radical rhetoric is an insufficient alternative. Total experimentation is necessary. New ideas and values must be taken out of heads and transformed into reality. . . . What we advocate is the migration of large numbers of people to a single state for the express purpose of effecting the peaceful political takeover of that state through the elective process . . . where alienated or 'deviant' members of society can go to live by their new ideas, providing a living laboratory for social experiment through radical federalism."

This was not just airy theorizing. Such projects were to find practical expression. Clinton's Oxford friend Ira Magaziner would try to establish a modest version of such a radical community at Brockton, Massachusetts, and then try to make the small state of Rhode Island into a test tube for his social democratic reforms. Clinton's first term as governor of Arkansas was to have a faint echo of this ambition. But such ideas were a very long way from the comfortable suburb of Park Ridge, outside Chicago, where Hillary grew up to win every Girl Scout badge that was available and star in school. Her pure and single-minded drive inspired the nickname "Sister Frigidaire," and she wrote off to NASA to apply as an astronaut. She was infuriated when NASA wrote back to say they were not yet considering women in space.

Like her future husband, Hillary grew up in that gigantic social revolution, America's making of the mass middle class. Her father's father, born in England, had come to the United States as a boy and sought work in the Depression-era coalfields of Pennsylvania. Thirty years later, when Hillary's family spent their summers each year at Lake Winia, Pennsylvania, her father took them all to the coalfields to instill his constant lesson: "It's hard out there." He taught that prosperity came through work and thrift, through self-discipline and competition. Hugh Rodham's children were sent to weed the garden, with a copper penny for each dandelion plucked, and taught to read the stock market tables in the newspaper. It was a Republican household, and at fifteen Hillary read Barry Goldwater's *The Conscience of a Conservative* and become a Goldwater Girl in the 1964 election. But when her schoolteacher assigned her to play the part of Lyndon Johnson in a mock-election debate, she did so with conviction, stressing the need for racial justice and the civil rights legislation.

This was the influence of the Reverend Don Jones, the youth leader at her local First United Methodist Church, who held a Thursday evening class called the University of Life. They talked of teen pregnancy and debated the existence of God, and read the poetry of Wallace Stevens. They were assigned theological readings: Paul Tillich and Reinhold Niebuhr, Søren Kierkegaard and Dietrich Bonhoeffer, the anti-Nazi Lutheran who was hanged in a concentration camp. Some of Bonhoeffer's passages stayed in her memory for life: "The weak always have to decide between alternatives that are not their own." She also memorized Martin Niemoller's anguished call for pluralist solidarity against the Nazi state, because if he did not stand with the Jew, with the Communist, with the trade unionist, "When they came for me, I was alone."

They discussed the politics of race, and Jones took his young charges into the Chicago ghetto, to meet and talk with young black Americans, so akin and yet so different from themselves. On one such visit, Jones brought out a large print of Picasso's painting *Guernica,* and asked them to discuss it. The comfortable suburban teenagers spoke of the symbolisms of the horror of war that was unfamiliar to them, and the young blacks related the painting directly to the violence of their immediate experience in the inner city. In 1962, Jones took them to hear the Reverend Martin Luther King, Jr., speak on "Sleeping Through the Revolution," and introduced his entire youth group to Dr. King afterwards.

The echo of Clinton's handshake with President Kennedy, and Hillary's with Dr. King, was later to be charged with the political symbol of inheritance; more immediately, it was for each of them a personal identification with greatness, with the hopes and also the violence and assassinations of the period. Two bright and ambitious children of the 1960s, each maturing from the comforts of the Eisenhower years to the challenges of Kennedy's New Frontier and then the turmoil that consumed the end of the decade, they were making parallel journeys. But the differences were important. Hillary had the longer political trek to make from Goldwater conservatism, and was prepared to be far more open in her confrontations with the established order.

Her speech to her graduating class at Wellesley in 1969, challenging the bland remarks of the black liberal Republican senator Edward Brooke, became legend among her classmates, as she abandoned her prepared remarks to say: "I find myself in a familiar position, that of reacting, which is something that our generation has been doing for quite a while now. . . . We have had lots of empathy, we have had lots of sympathy, but we feel that for too long now our leaders have used politics as the art of the possible. And the challenge now is to practice politics as the art of making what appears to be impossible, possible."

Featured in *Life* magazine as a leading voice of her generation, in striped bell-bottomed pants and long hair and aggressively big glasses, she was at once more prominent and less conventional than Clinton. He had been a student leader, but a moderate, and his political ambition was expressed in orthodox ways for a coming young man who was too sure of succeeding within the system to confront it. From Senator Fulbright's office to Project Pursestrings, from the Duffey campaign of 1970 to the McGovern presidential bid in 1972, Clinton remained firmly within that politics of the possible that Hillary yearned to transcend.

The McGovern challenge for the presidency in 1972 was a little of both, an unlikely bid to topple an entrenched President Nixon with a passionate antiwar campaign that would first capture the machinery of the Democratic Party. The McGovern campaign was inside the system, while hoping to transform it. Clinton had been committed to McGovern from the beginning, even when the vast bulk of the other campaign staff for Joseph Duffey decided to go with the Democratic front-runner Senator Edmund Muskie. But Clinton covered his political base, going to see the Arkansas congressman Wilbur Mills, who had some hopes of emerging as a compromise Democratic nominee, to seek his blessing. That was easy. Then Clinton persuaded Mills to let him canvass his Arkansan delegates on behalf of McGovern, if Mills were to withdraw from the race. The Arkansan delegates composed much of the core of the Democratic Party in the state, and two of them were to become close political friends and allies. James Blair was general counsel to the party, before going on to his career in the Tyson's Food empire and introducing Hillary to the lucrative opportunities of the cattle futures market. The woman Blair was to marry, Diane Kincaid, taught political science at the University of Arkansas in Fayetteville.

Rick Stearns, the fellow Rhodes scholar with whom Clinton had traveled to Germany and Spain and to Wales in search of Dylan Thomas's birthplace, was McGovern's deputy campaign manager. At the Democratic convention in Miami, Stearns put Clinton into the heart of the political operation. This was the trailer outside the convention hall, from which the McGovern delegates inside were guided and instructed through a series of complex and technical voting procedures by Stearns and future senator and presidential candidate Gary Hart. Clinton was the coordinator for the McGovern whips in the southern state delegations. McGovern having secured the nomination, Clinton was dispatched to Texas to coordinate the state campaign. His partner was Taylor Branch, later to win a Pulitzer Prize for *Parting the Waters,* his book on Martin Luther King. Clinton had first met Branch at the Martha's Vineyard retreat for student veterans of the Robert Kennedy and Eugene McCarthy campaigns in the summer of 1968. For Billie Carr, the dowager queen of Texas liberals, "It was sort of a good cop–bad cop routine. Clinton was the good cop. He always thought your idea was good. He was always sweet. Taylor would have to say, 'No, you can't do it, we don't have the money.' "

Texas was a forlorn hope from the beginning, in what was emerging as a national landslide for Nixon. But it was politics at a very high level, and as in the Duffey campaign, Clinton displayed a rare natural talent for it. His great skill was to make the radical appear more mainstream, to persuade suspicious veteran Democrats that the McGovern campaign was still their Democratic Party and still needed their wisdom and support. Not all of them responded. Senator Lloyd Bentsen, later to become Clinton's secretary of the Treasury, declined to become McGovern's state chairman. But Clinton never took a refusal personally, even when former Governor John Connally formed "Democrats for Nixon." The San Antonio Democratic party office would slam the phone down on McGovernites, but Clinton was always able to make himself welcome.

Like the Duffey campaign in Connecticut or the McGovern convention in Miami, Texas in 1972 was a place where Clinton won his spurs as a party activist, made friends and contacts, and learned the arts of politics from the grass roots. There was a liberal base within the party, and Clinton set out to recruit it, reviving the organizations that had supported Ralph Yarborough's senate campaign against Bentsen, and backed Sissy Fahrenthold's bid for the governorship. One key figure in both those campaigns had been Betsey Wright, former president of the Texas Young Democrats, and a firm feminist who thought America needed to be redeemed by a new generation of women politicians. Wright liked Clinton, and joined the McGovern team, but she was really impressed by the young woman from Yale who came to Austin to join him. "I remember thinking she would make a wonderful political candidate, wherever she ended up," Wright noted, wondering if she had met the woman destined to become the first female president. "I was less interested in Bill's political future than in Hillary's. I was obsessed with how far Hillary might go."

The one who left Texas with the most defined ambition was Clinton. "As soon as I get out of school, I'm moving back to Arkansas," he told Billie Carr. "I love Arkansas. I'm going back there to live. I'm going to run for office there. And someday I'm going to be governor. And then one day I'll be calling you, Billie, and telling you I'm running for president and I need your help." There would be endless help in Texas, from the union organizers and Chicano leaders he had befriended to the young activists like Garry Mauro, later to be Texas land commissioner, and even from old opponents like Senator Lloyd Bentsen whose respect he won in 1972, if not his support. Clinton also took away from Texas a clear and pragmatic political lesson, that good causes do not necessarily win elections.

"What was so disturbing to the average American voter was not that McGovern seemed so liberal on the war but that the entire movement seemed unstable, irrational," Clinton recalled a decade later. "The average person watching it on television in Arkansas, the kind of person who is the backbone of my support there, had the unsettling feeling that this campaign and this candidate did not have a core, a center, that was common to a great majority of the country. In Arkansas, there's probably a hard-core thirty percent that is always going to vote for the more conservative of the two candidates. But the election can still be won by a more progressive candidate if you can persuade people you have got a center core they can understand and relate to and trust."

When Clinton graduated from Yale as a freshly minted lawyer in 1973, he and Hillary each took the precaution of passing the Arkansas bar exams to qualify them to practice law in the state. There was an understanding between them. Clinton had already proposed before they left Yale, telling Hillary that she was the only person he could envisage growing old with. He knew his own plan, Arkansas and politics. But no firm decision had been made about her future. Washington was alluring, less for electoral politics than for issues and causes that a talented Yale lawyer could effect quickly. She began with a job as staff attorney for Marian Wright Edelman's Children's Defense Fund, and was then offered a post on the House Judiciary Committee staff, which was considering the prospect of impeaching President Nixon over the Watergate scandal.

Clinton had been offered a similar position by John Doar, the lawyer heading the impeachment staff, who had seen Clinton and Rodham perform at the Yale mock trial the previous year. Clinton recommended Hillary, already on Doar's list. But he had decided to stay in Arkansas, at his new job teaching law at the university in Fayetteville, and was already planning his first political race. Hillary knew his ambition, shared it, and believed in him. She told her immediate boss on the impeachment staff, Bernie Nussbaum, that her boyfriend would be president someday. Nussbaum nodded politely, not knowing that he would become Clinton's first White House counsel. Arkansas was a small and unlikely state as a presidential springboard. The action, Nussbaum knew, was right there in Washington.

Nussbaum's staff, ensconced in an ancient suite in the run-down Congressional Hotel, were touching each day the very stuff of history. Listening to the tapes of the conversations inside Nixon's Oval Office, they transcribed the words that would topple a presidency. "It was surreal, unbelievable," Hillary later recalled. "It was Nixon taping himself while he listened to his tapes, inventing rationales for what he had said. At one point he actually asked Manuel Sanchez [his valet], 'Don't you think I meant this when I said that?' " With the headphones on, trying to decipher Nixon's mumbles, Hillary was a part of an extraordinarily privileged few, the legal team that heard the phrases that would become the smoking gun of Watergate: "I don't give a shit what happens. I want you all to stonewall it, let them plead the Fifth Amendment, cover up or anything else if it'll save it—save the plan. That's the whole point."

Hillary and Bill spoke constantly by phone, an odd symmetry between the presidential history that Hillary was helping to make in Washington and the first steps of presidential ambition Clinton was taking in Arkansas.

He decided to run for Congress in the third district, which covered the north and west of the state, including Fayetteville where he lived and Hot Springs where he had grown up. But it also embraced the region around the military base of Fort Smith, where the retired military were solid for the incumbent Republican, John Paul Hammerschmidt. Clinton began with few hopes of winning, but rather of making his name in state politics and building up the core of supporters he would need for the future.

Running for Congress was a fast-track strategy. The conventional route was followed by his old kindergarten friend Mack McLarty, already elected to the state legislature. Clinton had some advantages, through Senator Fulbright, and through whom he had met the next generation of Arkansas leaders, Dale Bumpers and David Pryor. His work for Judge Holt had introduced him to Paul Fray and some of the state's Young Democrats, and his politicking among the Wilbur Mills delegation at the Miami convention had made him acquainted with many more. One of them, Jim Blair, was now campaign manager for Senator Fulbright's reelection bid. His stepuncle, Raymond Clinton, could help with Democrats of Hot Springs, and launched the campaign with a check for $10,000. His mother bought him a blue and white–striped seersucker suit, claiming no true southern politician could be without one.

Fayetteville would be a strong base for the campaign, the state's university seat, with staunch liberal votes. Among his law school students, Clinton was much liked, an easygoing teacher who gave generous grades and got on with everybody. The black students called him "Wonder Boy," and his lectures were popular. But the main asset in Fayetteville was the card index file belonging to Carl Whillock, the campaign manager for the last Democrat to hold the third district. Whillock knew every Democrat who mattered in the region, the staff at the small county courthouses and crossroads diners that were the backbone of political life in the Ozark hills. In Clinton, Whillock saw the best young political prospect for years, and agreed to introduce him to all the local Democrats, and support the campaign to the hilt.

Clinton was a strikingly effective candidate, a first-rate public speaker who could mingle and glad-hand with the crowd and make winning small talk that managed to produce names and phone numbers and offers of support. He also listened, taking the advice of Billie Schneider at the Hillbilly Hollow country steakhouse to drop the William J. Clinton that appeared on his election papers and run as plain Bill. He was well briefed, stunning the party regulars when he secured the endorsement of the trade union organization, the AFL-CIO, the main source of campaign funds for the $43,000 he was to spend on the Democratic primary. He and the other two primary contestants appeared before the union committee, but Clinton had virtually memorized the AFL-CIO briefing book on the main labor issues pending before Congress. To an essentially local race, based on the courthouses and the handshakes, he brought a national perspective, and won over a party resigned to another Hammerschmidt victory with the prospect of making the race a referendum on President Nixon, Watergate, and Republican corruption. The Democrats, said Clinton, were "protecting the American people from virtual dictatorship." He came first in the Democratic primary, and won the subsequent runoff, and with his friend Mack McLarty as state party chairman, the Democratic machine was fully committed to his side.

"A lot of people had seen that Robert Redford movie *The Candidate,* which had come out the previous year. And here was The Candidate in person, right here in our own backyards," recalled Roy Reed, one of the outstanding journalists of the South in the civil rights years, who went on to teach at Fayetteville. "Young and energetic, brilliant and educated, but with this gift for coming across like Just Plain Folks. And he had this passion, Nixon and Watergate, clean up Washington. He was the Redford of Arkansas, star quality all the way."

Hillary, stuck in Washington until Nixon's resignation on August 9, 1974, made the impeachment job superfluous, sent an advance party of her father and brothers. Some suspected their job was to keep an eye on Clinton's dalliances with the adoring young campaign volunteers. But they drove dutifully around the mountain roads putting up Clinton signs, a rare sight in their Cadillac with the Illinois license plates. But once Nixon resigned, Hillary pondered her future. She had an offer from Edward Bennett Williams, one of Washington's most powerful lawyers and men of political influence, to join his firm.

Instead, she phoned Dean Wylie Davis of the law school in Fayetteville and asked if the job they had once discussed was still open. To the great surprise of her friends, and the dismay of Sara Ehrman, who agreed to drive Hillary and her books and bicycle the 900 miles to Arkansas, Hillary turned her back on a glittering Washington career. She and Ehrman had met on the McGovern campaign in Texas, and Hillary boarded at Ehrman's house in Washington while she worked on the impeachment staff. They arrived in Fayetteville just after the college football game with Texas, and the hot summer night rang with the eerie Arkansan game chant of "Soo-eee, sooo-eeeee, pig, pig, PIG!" To the two young women from Washington, it sounded barbaric, like war cries of a terrifying alien and aggressive culture. "For God's sake, Hillary. Are you crazy? Why are you doing this?" Ehrman gasped. After a long silence, Hillary replied, "I love him." And they began to unpack the car.

Clinton's own furious campaigning energy made the seat look increasingly winnable, and the Hammerschmidt camp became seriously alarmed. In public, Hammerschmidt denounced Clinton for a "radical, left-wing philosophy." In private, his camp spread the rumor that Clinton had been the famous antiwar protester who clambered up a tree with an antiwar sign when Nixon came to a football game at Fayetteville. In fact, Clinton had been in England at the time. Hammerschmidt had reason to panic. Six days before the election, an opinion poll showed him with 46 percent and Clinton with 38 percent. This was not a comfortable lead, with Hammerschmidt dropping like a rock, losing nineteen points of his lead in the course of a month.

"The campaign styles of the two candidates contrast dramatically. Clinton runs—literally, physically runs—from place to place as he strives to personally meet as many of the district's eligible voters as possible," reported the *Arkansas Democrat.* "At one point, Clinton had about twenty minutes to get from Fort Smith to Lavaca [about twenty miles]. Stopped at a traffic light, he spotted some men working on a sewer repair project. Clinton said, 'There's ten votes,' and jumped out of the car to talk to them."

Clinton campaigned as a radical populist, demanding a rollback of gasoline prices, which had risen with the OPEC tripling of the oil price. He demanded the resignation of Earl Butz, secretary of agriculture, for selling grain to the Russians and forcing up the price of poultry food. An appeal to the chicken farmers who supplied the abattoirs of the fast-growing Tyson's chain, it also helped win campaign support from the Tyson family, who financed a telephone bank for Clinton. "He was young and he was impressive. I don't believe we ever talked about his politics. Hell, he was Democrat," Don Tyson recalled years later of the candidate he had first met over chicken-fried steak at Billie Schneider's Hillbilly Hollow. "The Arkansas system had always been to find some good young people and encourage them to work on the local level. The system kind of weeds them out, and out of that comes a United States senator or a governor." That was how Orval Faubus got his start, funded by Don Tyson's father back in 1954. Here came another promising young hopeful. "It's like a horse race. You back three or four, so you always get a winner."

This time, no winner. On election day, Hammerschmidt held his seat with just over 51 percent of the vote. But Clinton had become the party's darling, thrilling the Democrats with an intensely tight race and the conviction that they had a new political star now known across the state. For Clinton, it was something of a relief. Victory would have taken him away from the state, the springboard of his political future. He would have served two years in Congress, then been faced with a desperately difficult battle to hold the seat, and this time without the Watergate factor to help him. This had been a defeat so honorable that it was almost a victory, and gave him an instant claim on the next political nomination he wanted, as state attorney general. Not just a stepping-stone to the governorship, the job of attorney general would give him constant and unrivaled access to the statewide structure of county courthouses that Clinton had learned were the keystones of the Arkansas political system. There already was a bright and popular young Democratic attorney general, Jim Guy Tucker, but he was planning to run for the second congressional district, after Wilbur Mills's expected retirement.

The political way was open. The personal future was still in some doubt. He proposed to Hillary again and again, always diffident about asking her to make a choice that would subordinate her own career to his commitment to Arkansas. They had separate apartments in Fayetteville; the community would have been shocked had they not. But they saw each other constantly, and her brothers had enrolled at the university. Hillary had founded a legal clinic at the university, organizing a federal grant to provide legal advice to the poor. She had joined the campaign trying to pass the Equal Rights Amendment in the state legislature. Diane Kincaid, now Mrs. Diane Blair, had become a close friend. The local commitments were piling up. Finally, as Clinton was driving her to the airport to make a visit to college friends in New York, they passed a small glazed-brick cottage on California Street, which Hillary admired. When Clinton picked her up again at the airport, he had a surprise for her. He had bought the house, bought an antique brass bed, bought some flowered sheets from Wal-Mart, and as he pulled into the driveway, he said, "So you're going to have to marry me."

The wedding was performed in the living room of the cottage on October 11, 1975, by the Reverend Victor Nixon, a Methodist whom Clinton had met while campaigning in the Ozarks. Roger Clinton, now nineteen, was best man. Virginia Kelley's eyes filled with tears when she heard that her daughter-in-law planned to keep her own name. They had made no plans for a honeymoon, but Hillary's mother knew of a cheap package tour to Acapulco, and the whole family went along, Hillary's parents and her brothers. And when they returned, Clinton began campaigning again.

In a way, he had never stopped. Shortly after the 1974 defeat, he had become chairman of the state party's committee on affirmative action. One result of the failed McGovern presidential campaign was that McGovern's supporters took over the party machinery and established new rules for the selection of delegates to the next convention that would pick the presidential nominee for 1976. This took Clinton around the state, to county after county, explaining the new procedures, and building what was to become a formidable network of support among black voters.

Democrats had been weak on law and order, Clinton realized. He began teaching a course in criminal justice for police officers at the Little Rock branch of the state university, which took him to the capital each week, and brought more useful contacts to the future state attorney general. He cultivated police friends, thought long and hard, and dismayed the Methodist minister who had married him by announcing that he was now in favor of the death penalty, so long as the laws were "narrowly drawn and fairly applied." His sense of political balance was acute. He began to work with the Arkansas Housing Development Corporation, which helped low-income families and was a cherished cause on the left. He joined the Fayetteville Jaycees, the Junior Chamber of Commerce, traditionally the haunt of the rising professional men and shopkeepers, which met to lunch and network and help local charities.

It was an easy campaign, on the slogan "Character, Competence, and Concern." He beat two rivals for the Democratic nomination in March, and faced no Republican opponent in November. He spent the intervening time organizing the state for the Democratic presidential candidate, Jimmy Carter, another southerner and the governor of Georgia. There was one sobering incident for Clinton's supporters in the labor movement, who had worked their hearts out for him in 1974. Like most of the South, Arkansas was a right-to-work state where unions' powers to organize a closed shop and to strike were firmly curtailed. The state's AFL-CIO had fought this for over thirty years, and in 1976 they were trying to place a referendum question on the state ballot. They were sure they would have the support of the new attorney general. Two days after getting into the race, with the AFL-CIO endorsement, Clinton wavered. The recession made this "the wrong time," when the state was trying to keep old jobs and attract new ones. "It pissed our people off something tremendous," said J. Bill Becker, the state's AFL-CIO organizer. The United Steel Workers, which had lent the Clinton campaign some furniture for his district office in Fort Smith, angrily turned up with a truck and took it away.

Nor was it easy to make his way with Jimmy Carter. Mack McLarty helped. McLarty had been Democratic state chairman when Carter began his two-year campaign for the White House, had helped him, and set up a meeting for Clinton. He and Hillary flew down to Little Rock, to find Carter had already gone to bed. McLarty pleaded, and Carter got up. Clinton flew twice to Atlanta to maintain the connection and, recalling his work for McGovern, Carter asked him to be Texas coordinator again. Clinton, aware of his own interests, pleaded that he could do more good in Arkansas. Hillary also became Carter's field director in Indiana. For Clinton, the post of Arkansas campaign chairman offered direct access to the political and fund-raising powers of the state. Tyson was one of Carter's main contributors, and whenever Carter visited Arkansas, he stayed at the home of his old Naval Academy classmate, Jackson Stephens, of the Stephens, Inc., investment firm.

When Carter won the presidency, and also became the first Democrat to carry Arkansas since Lyndon Johnson twelve years earlier, Clinton was in a powerful position. A president has jobs to bestow, and for Arkansas, the new attorney general suddenly had the power of patronage, and of White House access. Eighteen months married, not four years out of law school, the Clintons were invited to the state dinner for Canada's Pierre Trudeau. President Carter appointed Hillary to the board of the Legal Services Corporation, where she swiftly became the first chairwoman of the federally backed agency, which provided legal aid for the poor. In Little Rock, she was hired by the Rose Law Firm, the state's most prestigious legal practice, which paid her $26,500 a year. With Clinton's $6,000 a year as attorney general, it was enough to take out a mortgage to buy a small home in the Heights, the best district of the city.

To be a Democrat in the South was to be an heir to the New Deal. As attorney general, Clinton was determinedly populist, challenging the powerful utility corporations, from Arkansas Power and Light and Arkansas-Missouri Power to the telephone companies, when they tried to raise the cost of a pay phone call from a dime to a quarter. He flew constantly to Washington, lobbying for more federal funds for Arkansas, becoming a committee chairman in the National Association of Attorneys General, and testifying before Congress on legal reform. He gathered a bright young team of attorneys to work with him, drove them hard to meet his goal of announcing a new headline-catching initiative each week, and told them, "If you're not having fun, it becomes just work, and it's time to move on to something else."

Clinton had already planned his next move. Always ready to bring national political expertise to his cause, he had used the polling skills of Patrick Caddell in his congressional race and in his campaign to become attorney general. He had met Caddell during the McGovern campaign, and worked with him on southern polls when Caddell became Jimmy Carter's pollster. In 1977, just settling into the job as attorney general, he called Caddell again to talk about his options in 1978, to run for the governorship or for the U.S. Senate. It was one of a constant flow of calls and letters and consultations with the contacts he had made in the past decade. There was never a more assiduous maintainer of acquaintance and friendship than Clinton, and his political network was extraordinary. From the Martha's Vineyard summer camp of the antiwar campaigners, from the Rhodes network and Project Pursestrings, from the 1970 Duffey campaign and the 1972 McGovern campaign, from Miami and from Texas and across Arkansas, his shoeboxes of index cards grew steadily. Names, addresses, phone numbers, and birthdays, weddings, and children, updated with new jobs and the latest publications, new meetings, and family bereavements, they were all cross-referenced, with a note of any campaign contributions they had made. When Betsey Wright began to transfer the shoeboxes onto computer, she found over 10,000 individual files.

In the course of the conversations with Caddell, the name first surfaced of a bright young political consultant from New York called Dick Morris, who had originally been associated with West Side Democratic reformers. But Morris had a further skill, not simply to use polls to tell a politician where he stood with the voters, but where he should stand. It was a matter of identifying which issues to stress and which to skirt, to track and reflect the mood of the electorate rather than pitch a flag and campaign to rally opinion around it.

Clinton asked Steve Smith, his former campaign manager, and chief of staff in his attorney general's office, to get in touch with Morris. The young New Yorker came down to Little Rock, and the big Arkansan and the short, mercurial consultant from Manhattan hit it off at once. Morris ran two polls for Clinton, one to assess his prospects for governor, a job Clinton thought was his for the asking, and the other for the crowded race to succeed Senator John McClellan. Clinton was right about the governorship, Morris reported, but the Senate seat was winnable, too. Ever cautious on polling matters, Clinton had had a secondary poll, from the veteran Arkansan pollster and political consultant Jim Ranchino, which showed him winning 57 percent in a four-man race.

It was not caution that tipped the balance for Clinton, nor even the prospect of a hard fight against Governor David Pryor, who was planning to run for the Senate. It was opportunity, the chance to make the kind of changes in Arkansas as governor that would give him a wider reputation as an administrator. That had been Jimmy Carter's strength as he campaigned for the presidency, his record as a reforming governor in Georgia. There was also an echo of the old arguments at Yale about the chance to take over a single state and make it into a test-tube of reform.

"I really want to be governor," Clinton declared, announcing his candidacy from the steps of the old state house on a cold March day. "A governor can do more for more people in less time than any public official in the country, with the exception of the president—if the president can get along with Congress. . . . If you will let me be your governor, no one will love this state more, care more about our people's problems, or work harder to see that we become what we ought to be."

It was an easy campaign. He led the ballot in the first primary vote, and then won the runoff with 60 percent of the vote against Joe Woodward, a lawyer known in his local Columbia County and in Little Rock from his work for Governor Bumpers. Clinton had budgeted $350,000 for the primary, and spent almost $400,000. He had almost the entire black vote, his old stamping ground of the third district, the consumers' groups he had back as attorney general, and the strong support of the outgoing governor Pryor, with whom he forged a close alliance. But Woodward's link to Bumpers, and the enduring doubts in the labor movement, prevented Clinton from winning the unreserved support of the Democratic Party machine across the state. "The organization that carried him into office had been put together with painstaking care over four years," commented *Arkansas Democrat* managing editor and columnist John Robert Starr. "It was without question the best organization ever put together in Arkansas without machine support."

The Clinton organization was not noticeably rocked when a retired air force lieutenant colonel, Billy G. Geren, called a press conference at the state capitol the month before election day to denounce Clinton as a draft dodger who had demonstrated against his government during the Vietnam War. Such a man was not fit to become governor and command the Arkansas National Guard. Clinton dismissed the allegation, telling local reporters that he had never received a draft deferment, and had offered himself to the local ROTC before being given such a low number in the draft lottery that the matter became irrelevant. This was only partly true. He had received a deferment; hence his anguished letter from Oxford to Colonel Holmes. But the last Clinton knew of the matter had been during his 1974 congressional race, when he secured from old ROTC files what he thought was the only copy of that letter to Colonel Holmes. With Clinton ahead of his Republican rival by thirty points in the polls and poised to become governor, Colonel Holmes held his silence. He could not remember the details, he told the Arkansas reporters. So many draft files had been across his desk since then.

Despite the denunciation by Colonel Geren, and despite his opponent's charge that he was the most liberal candidate Arkansas had yet seen, Clinton won the election overwhelmingly, with 338,684 votes to 195,550. To celebrate the triumph of Clinton's Arkansas organization, the devoted friends of the far-flung network flew in for the inauguration, for one grand triumphal ball and an informal version that was dubbed "Denims and Diamonds." The biggest diamond of all was borrowed from the state museum, the 4.25 carat Kahn diamond mined in the state, which glittered on Hillary's neck.

Betsey Wright came from Washington, where she was working on a campaign to urge the Democrats to field more women candidates. Sara Ehrman came back to Arkansas, despite the threat of "Sooo-eeee" calls, to celebrate with her old lodger. From Georgetown days came Tommy Caplan and David Matter, who had helped manage Clinton's last, failing election to be reelected class president. The two POW campaigners he had met in Moscow flew in from Virginia, and Steven Cohen from the antiwar campaign and Greg Craig from Yale, now working for the Edward Bennett Williams law firm Hillary had refused. Joining them all was one veteran Arkansan politician whose presence they could never have imagined. Clinton had invited the man who had made Little Rock an international synonym for race segregation, the old governor, Orval Faubus.

Clinton's inaugural address was a rhetorical success, but a damp squib as an event, the bitter cold reducing the audience for his speech from the state house steps to a couple of hundred shivering figures. What they heard was a series of pledges wrapped in cadences and topped with an inspiration that Clinton had heard from Steven Cohen at the ball on the previous evening, that he felt at this triumph of his old Yale friend a rare blend of pride and hope.

"For as long as I can remember, I have believed passionately in the cause of equal opportunity, and I will do what I can to advance it. For as long as I can remember, I have deplored the arbitrary and abusive exercise of power by those in authority, and I will do what I can to prevent it. For as long as I can remember, I have loved the land, air, and water of Arkansas, and I will do what I can to protect them. For as long as I can remember, I have wished to ease the burdens of life for those who, through no fault of their own, are old or weak or needy, and I will try to help them. . . . Pride and hope. Pride and hope. With those two qualities, we can go a long way."

Despite the soaring hopes of the moment, he was to go just two short years. But the energy and the ambition set a cracking pace. He promised a new Department of Economic Development and education reform, a new Energy Department and rural health centers and new roads. He imported a team of reforming experts from around the country: Don

Roberts from Virginia to be director of education; John Danner from Berkeley and his wife, Nancy Pietrafesa, who had known the Clintons at Yale, to run long-range planning; Robert Young from West Virginia to run the Health Department; Paul Levy from Massachusetts to run the new Energy Department; Gail Huecker from Kentucky to run Human Services.

"Can't he find anybody from Arkansas smart enough for him?" demanded state senator Knox Nelson. Clinton could, in his old campaign manager Steve Smith and Rudy Moore, who looked after the liaison with the state legislature. Along with Danner, Smith and Moore became known as "the three beards," and the entire Clinton team became the Children's Crusade, symbolized in the press cartoons as the baby-faced governor riding his tricycle. There was a high casualty rate. Danner and his wife left for Washington after a year, officially for a career in the new Department of Education, in fact after a staff revolt and a leaked Danner memo on a public information strategy to sell the administration. Blurring Arkansas law that forbade the use of state employees as campaigners, it had to be disavowed.

Steve Smith left in bruising circumstances after leading the administration's battle against the state's timber industries and their clear-cutting of large tracts of woodland. Unsightly and condemned by the environment lobby, this practice also raised memories of the wholesale looting of the Arkansas forests in the years before the Great Depression, when over three-quarters of the state's 20 million acres of pine forest were cut. Smith accused the worst offender, the giant Weyerhaeuser Company, of "public insensitivity and environmental disregard," and organized a series of public hearings around the state.

Most of the woodland was in the southern half of the state, which Clinton knew less well, otherwise he might have seen the political battle that lay in wait. Some 40,000 people in Arkansas depended directly on the timber industry. More ominously, some 240,000 Arkansans owned land with timber. The vast majority of them were small landholders whose incomes did not depend on their small stocks, but the Forestry Association whipped up a Save-Our-Timber campaign that warned of threats to their property rights. Smith left the governor's staff to join a colleague who had been Clinton's aide for banking and industrial development, James McDougal. They went off to Madison County, to run the small rural Bank of

Kingston, which was to grow into the ill-fated Madison Guaranty Savings and Loan.

Rudy Moore, a friend from the Fayetteville law school days who had become a state legislator and Clinton's 1978 campaign chairman, stayed with his governor throughout the term, battling through a series of setbacks as they scrambled to pass bill after bill in an overambitious agenda of reform. When Clinton took office, he had already promised over 50 separate reforms. The first to fall was the plan to reorganize the state's host of small rural school districts into larger, more manageable structures. The state legislators, knowing the sturdy local determination to control their own school boards, stalled that plan quickly. The one reform that Hillary managed, to establish a network of rural health clinics, had to be scaled back as too costly and offended country doctors and small county hospitals, who saw this as a threat to their livelihood.

There were well-reported administrative scandals, large bills for Paul Levy's energy conferences, including the purchase of fifty corkscrews to open the free bottles of Arkansas wine given to the participants. A rural retreat conference for the Energy Department to discuss energy-saving measures and grand plans for wind and solar power was mocked when the expense claims showed most participants had driven their own cars to the event, even while urging the rest of Arkansas to use car pools. The head of the state's Building Services was accused of directing contracts to his own hardware company. Much of the criticism was petty stuff, but in a state where the per capita income was $6,183 per year, the press thundered at the $450 monthly rental charge for potted plants for the office of the new director of economic development. The best-intentioned schemes became controversial. The SAWER (Special Alternative Wood Energy Resources) project tried to train the unemployed to cut firewood and distribute it as fuel to low-income families. After $62,000 was spent, it had trained six woodcutters and produced three cords of wood, which could have been bought from local woodsmen at less than one percent of the cost.

Clinton's main achievement was to persuade a low-tax state to raise its taxes to increase the public education budget by 40 percent. His Energy Department also won a major battle, a lawsuit against overcharging by the Arkansas Power and Light Company, which forced it to refund $8.5 million to its customers. The administration also battled the big electricity utility over its plans to pass on to Arkansas customers part of the costs of the new Grand Gulf nuclear power plant being built in Mississippi.

Having taken on the timber industry and the big power utility, Clinton then defied the other two main Arkansas business lobbies, the trucking industry and the chicken processors. On the eve of his election, which had been strongly backed by funds from the Tyson family, Clinton assured Don Tyson that he would try to meet one of the chicken emperor's main concerns. In most of the country, trucks could carry up to 80,000 pounds, but in Arkansas, where the roads were underfinanced and in poor repair, they were restricted to 73,000 pounds. This cost Tyson a fortune. To improve the Arkansas roads, the state Highway Commission warned, would cost over $300 million a year for a decade. Clinton had already raised the state budget to unprecedented heights; the *Arkansas Democrat* called him "Billion-Dollar Bill." Clinton proposed a bill to raise road taxes, falling mainly on trucks but also on private cars, to finance a more modest road improvement plan.

The trucking and poultry lobby fought the taxes on them, so Clinton shifted the weight of taxes to car owners. This did not appease Tyson, who still wanted his 80,000-pound limit, but it offended far more voters as they stood in wait each year to get their annual car registration tags and found their charges doubled. The new taxes were based on weight, which penalized rural voters with pickup trucks and older cars. It was a cumbersome procedure to go to the county courthouse, show that the vehicle had been inspected, that the previous year's property tax had been paid, provide an assessment of current property for the next tax, and then pay the higher car registration fees.

The public anger intensified when the *Arkansas Gazette* reported that Hillary had not paid her own car tags for 1977 and 1978. She had an excuse. Her small Fiat had been stolen and wrecked in 1978, but Hillary Rodham's insistence on keeping her own name was already an issue, which became more prominent when she gave birth to Chelsea Victoria in February 1980, Clinton's reelection year. She was the result of a happy summer holiday back in Britain. They had been trying to have a child since the marriage, and were increasingly worried when no pregnancy developed. They had even made an appointment to attend a fertility clinic after their return from England. Clinton confided to some friends that his daughter was named after the Judy Collins song "Chelsea Morning," to others that she was named after the fashionable quarter of London where she had been conceived. The pregnancy entranced them both, and they studied the Lamaze method of natural childbirth. But Chelsea arrived early, and with difficulty, and was finally delivered by caesarean section. She became her father's great delight, and his devotion to the baby, combined with his national political ambitions, served to distract him from his mounting unpopularity across the state.

Clinton was wooed by both Senator Edward Kennedy and by President Carter for his support in the 1980 Democratic nomination. He stuck with Carter and lobbied hard for the chance to offer a nomination speech at the party convention. He dismayed his feminist friends by backing Carter's election platform, which ignored the women's movement demand for federal funding for abortions. He gave a brisk eight-minute speech that warned that the American governing system established by Franklin Roosevelt was starting to break down, that "a dangerous and growing number of people are simply opting out of our system—another dangerous and growing number are opting for special interest and single interest group politics."

It was not until the late summer, with the state and its chicken farmers devastated by an unusual drought, that Clinton began to focus on the reelection campaign. He had raised over $400,000, which he thought would be enough, and was stunned to learn that Tyson, the utilities, and the timber industry had armed his opponent with as big a war chest. The national economy was in grim straits, with high unemployment, high interest rates, and high inflation, and Arkansas had its own woes. There was a resurgence of Ku Klux Klan activity and a sudden spate of calamities. A maintenance man at the Damascus missile base dropped a wrench inside one of the Titan II rockets, causing an explosion that blew the nuclear warhead out of the silo. An understandable alarm about radiation and about the safety of the half-forgotten missiles swept the state, unrelieved by any official explanation. The federal government did not help, saying it could "neither confirm nor deny the existence of a nuclear weapon" at Damascus.

The final straw came from Cuba, where Fidel Castro had opened the port of Mariél to would-be emigrants, and decanted the bulk of his prison population there to join the refugees in the United States. Hunting for places to hold the refugees while they identified the undesirables and tried to ship them back, the Carter administration picked on Fort Chafee, Arkansas, and sent 19,000 Cubans there. Clinton tried desperately to change the decision, but his boasted White House connections were of no avail. In May, the Cubans rioted against their crowded and uncomfortable conditions, demanding to be allowed to go to Florida. Over 300 of them got out of the camp, and the TV news showed them stopped just short of the township of Barling by local police, as U.S. Army guards stood by and watched. Clinton mobilized the National Guard, contained the situation, and secured a promise from the White House that no more Cubans would be sent to Arkansas. In August, that promise was broken, as the White House decided to concentrate all the remaining Cubans in camps around the country at Fort Chaffee. Clinton yelled obscenities through the phone to Washington, but could not get the decision changed.

Clinton had taken on every big lobby in the state. The timber industry worked actively against him. Tyson funded his opponent, Frank White, who shifted allegiance from being a Democrat to Republican on the day before he announced. The utility industries backed the White campaign. As he traveled the familiar back roads of Arkansas, all Clinton heard were complaints about the car tags and the Cubans. He had made too many enemies, and lost too many friends. In the last ten days, as Frank White deployed his lavish funds on a series of harsh TV ads that featured rioting Cubans, Hillary called Dick Morris to come down to Arkansas and save the campaign. It was too late. On a huge turnout of 300,000 more Arkansans going to the polls than in 1978, Clinton was defeated, by 435,684 votes to 403,241. He knew it was coming, but went through the anguish of watching NBC declare him the winner on projected votes. The most brilliant career in American politics had collapsed.

☆ *4* ☆

GOVERNING AND THE MAKING OF A PARTY ANIMAL

Clinton was stunned into gloom by his defeat, seeing the vote as a personal rejection, when it was also a local eddy of the national political tide that swept President Carter out of the White House and elected Ronald Reagan. That tide had been swollen by the Reverend Pat Robertson and other TV evangelicals and fundamentalists, and Clinton's opponent Frank White acknowledged their help when he boasted that his election was "a victory for the Lord." In the first legislative session, the new governor signed into law the Creation Science Act, which required all Arkansan public schools to give equal time to teaching the biblical assertion in the Book of Exodus that God created the world, as well as Darwin's theory of evolution. By the time this was thrown out by the federal courts, Arkansas teachers were distributing bumper stickers that read: "Don't blame me; I voted for Clinton."

At first, this was little compensation for Clinton. "Remember me as one who reached for all he could for Arkansas," he concluded in his farewell speech to the legislature, Hillary beside him with ten-month-old Chelsea in her arms. Her job at the Rose Law Firm was a cushion against financial concerns, and he took an office and a post of "counsel" at the law partnership of his friend Bruce Lindsey. He practiced little law, facing over $50,000 in campaign debts. These were finally settled when Mack McLarty telephoned fifty friends and asked each for $1,000. Clinton searched to explain and understand his rejection by the voters, and in interviews with local reporters consoled himself by suggesting that he had tried too hard.

He also faced a wide surge of gossip and speculation about the state of his marriage, and whether that had explained his lackluster campaigning. "Bill Clinton was not the same person psychologically," recalled Rudy Moore. "It must have been something personal, perhaps in his relationship with Hillary, but he was ambivalent and preoccupied. Those fantastic political insights had abandoned him." John Robert Starr, *Arkansas Democrat* columnist, concluded that "he fell in love with somebody, it was relatively brief, and because he referred to it in the singular when he offered to tell me about 'it,' I don't think there was more than one—I don't think if there had been wholesale infidelity that Hillary would have put up with it."

More than anyone else, Hillary was responsible for reviving his resolve. She had called Dick Morris, the New York campaign consultant, to come down in the last days of the doomed campaign. After the defeat, she called Betsey Wright, the old friend from the Texas McGovern campaign, to come down from her Washington job at the National Women's Education Fund and help put the Clinton political machine back together. She also gave up something on which she had decided at the age of nine, when she vowed to keep her own name in marriage. "We've got to talk about this name deal," she told her husband. "I couldn't bear it if this costs you the election. It's just not that big a deal to me anymore."

"My only request is that if you do this you've got to be completely honest about it. I want you to tell people what you told me—that you're doing it because you think it might bother other people for the First Lady of this state not to have the same name as her husband," Clinton later recalled saying in response. "Do not tell them you've had a change of heart. Do not tell them you decided you were wrong, because that is not true and it won't wash. If you tell them the truth, maybe it will work."

Hillary changed her business cards and her office notepaper and became Mrs. Clinton. She cut her long hair and used contact lenses rather than her glasses, even though they left her eyes red and strained. And she gave a lecture to the political science club of the Little Rock branch of the state university to talk about the defeat. She judged that Frank White's negative TV ads had been devastating, the ominous black and white shots of dark-skinned Cuban rioters against white-faced police and Arkansans had carried a powerful subliminal message.

"A political campaign has come down to a thirty-second war on television," she concluded. They had not fought back hard enough against the ads, and had not energized their more complacent supporters, who had been too sure of a Clinton victory to vote. The lessons were plain: never be outnegatived again, and get out every last vote. She instilled the message in her husband. At a Democratic National Committee meeting in Iowa, part of the party's painful reassessment after Reagan's capture of the White House, Clinton argued that they had to fight back against negative TV ads and unfair attacks. "When someone is beating you over the head with a hammer, don't sit there and take it—take out a meat cleaver and chop off their hand."

Hillary marched Bill to Immanuel Baptist Church on Sunday mornings, whose service was televised across the state, installed him in the choir, and jockeyed him into a spot where the camera angle would feature him behind the minister's shoulder. He went to call on Bill Becker, to explain that he had learned he needed to stick with his friends in the labor movement, and was invited to address the state AFL-CIO convention that summer. The unions helped pay Betsey Wright's wages, and the Democratic Party in Washington hired Clinton as a consultant on the next Arkansas state and local election cycle. Less than a year after his election defeat, Clinton commissioned Morris to run his first poll, which suggested that Governor White was beatable, but the voters were still unsure whether Clinton had learned his lesson. Broadly, they reckoned that he had been too sure of himself, had become arrogant and out of touch with ordinary Arkansans. They respected his brains and his capacity for hard work, and several of them told the pollsters they regretted he had lost.

He began actively campaigning again, raising funds and making speeches. And in February of the new election year of 1982, he bought TV time to make his statement of apology for trying too hard in his first term. That, at least, was how Dick Morris had planned the script that Clinton recorded in a New York TV studio. But Clinton revised the script overnight, never quite apologized, and instead spoke in the homely phrases of Arkansas: "My daddy never had to whip me twice for the same thing." He made mistakes, but learned from them. In order to lead, he knew he had to listen. The voters should give him a second chance.

The same national tide of recession and high unemployment that had helped sweep him out in 1980 now made the comeback in 1982 all the more likely, if he could only win the Democratic primary. But after the TV ad, his polls dropped sharply, and his main rival, former congressman Jim Guy Tucker, tried the same negative campaigns against Clinton that had worked for Frank White. Clinton fought back in the same coin, and drove down Tucker's polls. But his own had already touched bottom, and the televised apology seemed, in Dick Morris's perception, to have inoculated Clinton against further attack. The two men fought desperately for the endorsement of the teachers' union, the Arkansas Education Association. Tucker won it, with promises of a hefty pay rise for teachers, despite what one of the teachers' leaders called Clinton's threat "to tear our heads off and beat our brains out."

As Clinton and Tucker gouged at each other in the gutter, a mild-mannered third candidate, former lieutenant governor Joe Purcell, began to rise in the polls. Clinton won the primary with 41 percent of the vote, but faced a runoff against Purcell, an elderly man vulnerable to Clinton's subtle hints of health problems. Runoff elections meant a low turnout, and the advantage to the better machine. Clinton won the Democratic nomination with 54 percent of the vote. But to beat Governor White he would need more than his revitalized personal network. White's friendship with the utility companies and the corporate interests had fattened his war chest. He had scrapped Clinton's old Energy Department, which won him the devotion of Arkansas Power and Light. "He's got half a million dollars because people who wanted decisions from the governor's office paid for them," charged Clinton.

Clinton brought in an old country banker, W. Maurice Smith, as his finance chairman. Smith had started in politics as an aide to then Congressman Fulbright in 1942, knew everyone in the state, and became informal ambassador to Don Tyson. This time Clinton would raise the truck weight limit to 80,000 pounds, and Smith would be appointed highway commissioner and take care of the roads. Tyson said he would wait and see, but decided not to fund Governor White's campaign again. Maurice Smith raised over $1 million for Clinton's campaign, an Arkansas record at that time.

Clinton wanted to be sure of a strong black vote and hired one of the law school students who had called him Wonder Boy, Carol Willis. Two more young black activists came aboard, Rodney Slater, later to become federal highways administrator in Clinton's presidency, and Bob Nash, who became director of the Arkansas Development Finance Authority, and later undersecretary in the Agriculture Department in Washington. Between them, and with lavish amounts of what political custom called "walking around money" to get out the voters on election day, they delivered an unprecedented black turnout. It provided Clinton's margin as he beat White with 55 percent of the vote.

It was gratifying to be back in the governor's mansion two years after the humiliation of defeat, and to be back with a blueprint of what not to do. He had learned from the first time the need to scale back his ambition from reform on all fronts and concentrate on just one or two. He had learned to tread warily in his dealings with the Tysons and the state's corporate giants, and backed the bill that raised the truck weight limit, just as Tyson had wanted. He had learned from Morris's polling that voters could not even recall any of his achievements in office. He would have to pin his governorship to some grand project that was both popular and memorable. If possible, it should be something that would help reconcile Arkansas to Hillary, and that would require a political fight to keep Clinton in the headlines as the people's champion in a righteous cause.

The choice almost made itself: education. Governors throughout the South, of both parties, were pushing education reform, from the Democrat Richard Riley in South Carolina to the Republican Lamar Alexander in Tennessee. The testing schemes inaugurated in Clinton's first term gave him the ammunition for his second—hard evidence that Arkansas schoolchildren ranked far below the national average in basic skills like reading and mathematics. Clinton's Quality Education Act of 1983 authorized the state's board of education to draft minimum standards of achievement for each grade, which would in effect lead to the first statewide school curriculum. The board launched an education standards committee to produce the draft, and the governor appointed Hillary to chair it. "This guarantees that I will have a person who is closer to me than anyone else overseeing a project that is more important to me than anything else," Clinton said. "I don't know if it's a politically wise move, but it's the right thing to do."

His education reform was given urgency by the state supreme court, which ruled that the prevailing system of delivering state money to local schools was unfair. Determined largely by the tax base of each district, it meant that the wealthier the district, the more the school received. The more, therefore, the school could offer. A high school student in a small district might be limited to 23 course units; at Little Rock High School, students could choose among 182. In 148 of the state high schools, there were no classes in physics, and no foreign languages were taught in 180 schools.

The striking difference between the Clinton reforms of the first term and the hard-driving campaign on education in the second was the intense marketing effort. Hillary took a leave of absence from her law firm and organized a total of seventy-five hearings, at least one in every county in the state, for her standards committee. The names and addresses of those who attended became a mailing list for the extraordinary single-issue movement that was then launched. Clinton and Betsey Wright started the Blue Ribbon Education Committee and urged friends and supporters to join and wear a small blue lapel ribbon, and recruit others to do the same. Clinton raised $130,000 for his special education campaign, some of it in private loans from Maurice Smith's bank, trusting that his political machine would eventually be able to raise the money to repay him. They did. Tyson Foods was to contribute $15,000, and Frank Hickingbotham, the leading shareholder in TCBY Yogurt Corporation, based in Little Rock, gave $25,000. The Union Bank (source of the original $20,000 loan for the down payment on Whitewater) gave $11,500, and Wal-Mart gave $1,000.

"We bought radio ads, newspaper ads, TV ads. We did a lot of direct mail across the state," Betsey Wright recalled. "We had people doing postcards and letters to their legislators. We had people wearing the blue ribbons and rallied meetings across the state, all meant to snowball into the beginning of the legislative session so that by the time these legislators convened, each of them had a constituency in their district begging them to raise their taxes for education. Never has a legislature convened with it being so easy to raise taxes."

It would cost $180 million to fund the reform package Clinton introduced; smaller class sizes, a longer school year, and a basic state curriculum. Usually the strongest lobby in support of the reform would have been the teachers. But partly from conviction and partly from the political calculation that it would gain much wider public and political support, Clinton added the requirement, not recommended by Hillary's committee, that Arkansas teachers would themselves have to pass a test of competence.

There was political calculation here. The Dick Morris polls found this had 75 percent support among Arkansas voters, many of whom suspected that in his first term Clinton had been too close to special interests like the teachers' lobby. The Arkansas Education Association, the 17,000-strong teachers' union, had made the mistake of supporting Clinton's opponent in the primary. And, Clinton insisted, relating the old story about the one who taught "World War Eleven" from ignorance of the Roman numerals of World War Two, some teachers were scandalously bad.

"There will be no tax increase without a testing bill," Clinton insisted. Without the tax increase, there would be no more money for teachers' salaries or school repairs. Convinced he had a winning issue, Clinton was prepared to fight hard, insisting that the overall education reform was "something that's worth putting myself and whatever career I might have on the line for."

To pay for it, the main device was to increase the sales tax from 3 to 4 percent. There were other taxes, on country club memberships, on cable TV, on natural gas extraction and on corporate profits. Clinton had few options. The natural gas lobby managed to defeat that tax, and the increased corporate tax also fell in the legislature. Under Arkansas law, a two-thirds or three-quarters majority of the legislature was required to pass any tax. This was almost impossible to achieve. The only exception was a sales tax, which could be passed with a one-third majority of both houses. By far the biggest contribution would be the annual $160 million that would come from the increased sales tax. This was to invite a collision with Clinton's natural supporters, the consumer, community, and labor lobbies, who loudly complained that a broad sales tax with no exemptions for food or utility bills would hurt the poorest Arkansans.

Clinton decided to cut a complex deal. He wanted support for an emergency bill that would make the new sales tax immediate. To win labor support, he promised Bill Becker of the AFL-CIO and Brownie Ledbetter of the Fairness Council (an umbrella organization for several civic groups) to back a special bill that would give the poor a rebate on their sales taxes. He passed his sales tax emergency legislation, but the rebate plan went down to defeat in the senate, and Clinton did not work hard to save it. When the composite legislation went back to the house, Clinton gave up on the rebate, saying that he had only offered Becker "a 24-hour commitment." Becker never forgave him, later telling the AFL-CIO convention that "Bill Clinton is the kind of man who'll pat you on the back and piss on your leg."

"I love it," Clinton told local reporters when they asked him how he was taking the hurly-burly of the legislative session. There were extraordinary scenes as Clinton begged his loyalists for their vote, stood at the door of the legislative chamber and yelled to his aides, urging them to "run up and down the aisles" to keep the lawmakers in their seats. He brought in the Razorbacks' football coach to help him lobby, rallied his Blue Ribbon supporters to demonstrate at the state capitol. He worked the phones late into the night and his special lobbying fund hired phone banks to work the districts of individual legislators on the day before a crucial vote. The legislator would then get a torrent of phone calls from his own constituents. "We had them just snowed the next day," bragged Betsey Wright, after the legislation passed.

In the event, some 10 percent of the teachers failed each time the test was given. But they could sit and take it again and again, and be retrained at state expense, until they passed. A total of 25,077 teachers and school supervisors and aides took the test in 1985, along with several incognito reporters. They reported that it was, in effect, the equivalent of the eighth-grade graduation test. After the series of tests were completed, and despite the remedial education, 1,315 teachers had failed and had to find other work. Most of the teachers who failed were in the Delta, and most of them were black. To the charge that the tests had been a disguised form of racism, Clinton responded, "Black children and poor white children in our state have no other shot but the public schools to have a decent education and a decent opportunity in life. We're doing this for them."

Clinton's victory in the education struggle was to be the rock on which his political future would be based, and also the model for his political tactics in the White House. He had taken on his friends in the unions, organized an intense lobbying campaign, squeezed out the narrowest of majorities along with every drop of suspense as the public saw him stake everything on a single vote. The rush of adrenaline, the burning of midnight oil, the gambler's thrill at the high-stakes plunge, were all to become characteristic of Clinton's dealing with legislative bodies in Little Rock and Washington alike. The very scale of the risk intensified the rewards, and after his success, Clinton had an achievement to trumpet and a label to sport, "The Education Governor." The result was that he coasted to victory in the Democratic primary in 1984 with 65 percent of the vote, and did almost as well in the general election. He was reelected governor for a third term with 63 percent of the vote.

He spent the reelection year campaigning to extend the terms of the senior elected officials from two years to four. The provision would apply to governor, lieutenant governor, attorney general, secretary of state, auditor, treasurer, and land commissioner. Clinton argued that a two-year term meant six months of work and eighteen months campaigning for the next election. But a four-year term for a governor would also mean a dramatic extension of his power, through the governor's right to appoint members of the range of boards and commissions, from Highways to Game and Fish, from Banking to Insurance. These boards set the rules that governed the daily lives of most Arkansans, and had their own budgets and their own patronage, through the award of contracts. In Arkansas, the boards had not fallen under the control of a single governor in the twentieth century, because only Clinton and Orval Faubus had ever served more than two terms. Clinton with a third term, and then running for another four-year term, would have the right to appoint his loyalists to every board, creating an unprecedented statewide network of day-to-day power and patronage. The new four-year term came into effect in 1986, which also gave Clinton an untrammeled chance for a presidential bid in 1988.

The Democratic presidential campaign of 1984, between former vice president Fritz Mondale and Colorado senator Gary Hart, faced Clinton with a choice. He had known Hart since the McGovern campaign of 1972, and many of his friends across the country were actively working for the first of the antiwar generation to run for the presidency. But the party machine and party elders were for Mondale, and, faced with the choice between the sentiments of his youth and the national politics of his maturity, he cast his ballot for Mondale at the Democratic convention in San Francisco. Clinton's speech to the convention made it clear that he was not enthusiastic about Mondale's traditional Democratic platform, nor by the barnstorming speech by New York's Mario Cuomo, which celebrated all the New Deal virtues.

"Harry Truman would tell us to forget about 1948 and stand for what America needs in 1984," Clinton declared, in a speech to the convention about education and productivity and the threat of global competition, which prefigured most of what would become the DLC platform after Mondale's defeat. "That's the way to attract the millions of Americans who feel locked out and won't vote because they think we're irrelevant. That's the way to attract millions more, mostly young and well-educated, who intend to vote against us because they think we have no program for the future."

When Clinton made that speech, he had only half his mind on national politics. He and Hillary and Betsey Wright had spent three months keeping the secret that his half-brother Roger was the target of an undercover police investigation for trafficking in cocaine, and would almost certainly be arrested and charged before Clinton's next election. Clinton had managed to ease Roger out of trouble before, arranging for him to be bailed out of the Little Rock city jail during his first term, after his arrest for speeding. Roger had called the governor's mansion from jail, and Clinton arranged for him to be bailed into the custody of Sam Tatum, a half-cousin who was also chairman of the state crime commission. In March 1982, before the election that brought Clinton back into office, Roger was arrested for driving while drunk and possessing drug paraphernalia. The charges hung fire until after Clinton was elected, and were then dropped.

This new threat was incomparably more serious. Roger was involved in serious cocaine dealing, with a direct connection to a Colombian wholesaler named Manuel Rodriguez, who was shipping the drug by the kilo from New York to Little Rock and Hot Springs. Roger was part of a distribution chain that spread the cocaine into the flashy world of the Arkansas new rich, the lawyers and bond traders and glitzy nightclubs of Hot Springs. Hidden cameras and tape recordings recorded Roger boasting that his big brother made him untouchable. Clinton was stunned to be told of the undercover operation in May, but behaved with strict propriety. He told the police to continue the investigation in the usual way, and asked only that he be given some notice of the public release of the charges. He could tell neither his brother nor his mother, and had to behave normally with them. The grand jury sent down its indictment in July, and Roger was arrested, charged, pleaded not guilty on all six charges, and was released on $5,000 bail. Immediately after Clinton was reelected in November, Roger went back to court and changed his plea to guilty.

It was not clear why he had pleaded not guilty in the first place. Given two hours' notice of the indictment being made public, Clinton had issued a brief public statement to hastily summoned reporters: "My brother has apparently become involved with drugs, a curse which has reached epidemic proportions and has plagued the lives of millions of families in our nation, including many in our state. I ask for the prayers of our people at this difficult time for my brother, for my family, and for me. I love my brother very much and will try to be of comfort to him, but I want his case to be handled as any other case would be. Because this matter is now in court, I will have no further comment."

Clinton then drove to Hot Springs for a grueling family meeting with his mother and his brother, who arrived talking wildly of suicide. In his mother's account, Clinton became enraged, strode across and grabbed his brother by the shoulder, shook him and shouted, "How dare you think that way." Roger had tried to deny to the police that he was involved with drugs, until they revealed the videotapes. He then tried to deny to his family that he was addicted. "You don't understand," Clinton said. "You have been putting cocaine into the bodies of others for money. I want you to go to prison for ten years. You're my brother, and I love you, but I want you to go away for a long, long time."

He arranged for his brother to be enrolled in an addiction treatment program, and he and his mother then joined in the counseling sessions. They became anguished when Roger confessed that he had still used cocaine after his arrest. For the first time, Clinton and his mother began to talk openly of their life with Roger's alcoholic father, the denial and the accommodations that had become part of the constant pattern of their family life. Clinton's mother, Virginia, explained that she had built a mental "white room" in her head, where she could retreat to block out anything negative or unpleasant, a way to deny reality, or to reshape it in her own perception so that she could continue to function. Clinton, who read a series of books on addiction and on the ways that families of addicts would respond, recognized himself in one of the classic patterns: the child of the addict who becomes a conciliator, desperate to make peace and fend off confrontations.

The Clinton family responded admirably to Roger's disaster. They supported him, found treatment for him, tried to understand the roots of his plight and of their own. They did all that the police had asked, and were even grateful. "It was a nightmare, but it was the right thing to do," Clinton said. "He had a four gram a day habit. They said if he hadn't been in incredible physical shape, he would have died." But it was a time of intense strain, which saw some furious and public rows between Clinton and Hillary, and a renewal of the gossip about other women. Again, the local press investigated, and again nothing was established. But the tension between them was palpable. On one reported occasion, the fight started in his office in the state capitol, and continued out onto the landing, with Clinton shouting after Hillary as she stormed down the stairs, "I'm still the governor here, bitch, and don't you forget it."

In February 1985, Roger Clinton was sentenced to two years in prison, after agreeing to testify against others. His evidence resulted in the convictions of Sam Anderson, Jr., a lawyer and a friend since his Hot Springs boyhood, and of Dan Lasater, a multimillionaire businessman who was one of Clinton's campaign contributors. In 1984, panicking as he so often did in the closing weeks of the campaign, Clinton had suddenly felt he needed money for a final blitz of TV ads.

His campaign donors for that year are known, in records filed with the Pulaski County Courthouse. They included the usual corporate donors, from Coca-Cola to Union Pacific Railroad. He had made his peace with the timber interests, so Weyerhaeuser contributed, along with the Worthen Bank of the Stephens family. Three members of Lasater's family each gave $1,000, the legal maximum. There were other donations from beyond Arkansas, from the Democratic Party's godmother, Pamela Harriman; from Hillary's old boss on the impeachment staff, Bernard Nussbaum; from John Gutfreund, head of Salomon Brothers in New York. But the biggest single donor was Clinton himself, who borrowed $50,000 from Maurice Smith's Cherry Valley Bank to pay for the last round of TV commercials. It was to help repay this loan that James McDougal of the Madison Guaranty Bank held a portentous fund-raising party in April 1985, which raised $30,000.

Clinton's easy reelection victory in 1984 probably meant that the final round of TV ads, and the sudden need for campaign funds, had been unnecessary. The voters had not been offended by his brother's arrest, nor even by the trial testimony that he had taken cocaine and weighed out his packages in his upstairs room at the governor's mansion. Secure in Arkansas, and with the opinion polls suggesting that he would have an easy reelection to a four-year term in 1986, Clinton turned his attention to national politics, building on the important connections he had made in his two years out of power. Other jobs had been dangled before Clinton after his defeat, including the chance to be national chairman of the Democratic National Committee, to become chief of staff to Governor Jerry Brown of California, to administer the liberal lobby People for the American Way, or to manage the University of Kentucky. One part-time post he did accept at the end of 1980, a first sign that the depression was lifting and that he was determined to remain in politics.

The offer had come from Pamela Harriman, wife of the former ambassador and New York governor and multimillionaire Averell Harriman, to join the board of her fund-raising political action committee, Democrats for the '80s. Raising $1.2 million for the 1982 midterm elections, it became known as PamPAC. It was also a political salon, based at Mrs. Harriman's Georgetown home, its sitting room graced with Van Gogh's *White Lilies,* Matisse's *Blue Hat,* and Picasso's *Mother and Child.*

Her home on N Street and the Harriman farm at Willow Oaks in Virginia were alluring showcases for the Democratic senators and powerbrokers who came to raise campaign funds and flesh out the PamPAC network to which Clinton had now been given constant access. He was not the only rising young Democrat taken under her wing. Al Gore of Tennessee and Bob Kerrey of Nebraska, Jay Rockefeller of West Virginia and Chuck Robb of Virginia were also her protégés for the future. But Clinton's Rhodes scholarship was a recommendation to Pamela Harriman, born the daughter of the 11th Baron Digby and daughter-in-law to Winston Churchill. In 1979, in Clinton's first term as governor of Arkansas, he first met and impressed the Harrimans at one of their regular political evenings. When he lost in 1980, he was an early choice to serve on the board of her new organization, Democrats for the '80s. The first time she was invited to talk about it on national TV, Clinton was her escort to the studio and her TV coach.

A month after he was reelected in 1982, Clinton was back at the Harrimans' home for one of her PamPAC seminars on the '82 elections, "A View from the States." When the other guests left, Clinton and another young rising Democratic star, Governor (now Senator) Bob Kerrey of Nebraska, stayed on, asking Harriman about Stalin and Churchill until 1:30 A.M. Harriman went to bed, but Pamela stayed up, and they talked on about the war and Churchill and the Atlantic Alliance for another hour.

She liked his brains, his readiness to work at her project, and above all, his resilience in defeat, and determination to come back.

When Harriman died in 1986, his gift to Pamela was a legacy of $75 million and his paintings. In the 1980s, PamPAC raised a total of $12 million for the party, culminating in a glittering evening at the Kennedy Center in 1990, when 45 senators and 2,700 other guests attended her "Democrats—Party of the Decade." That night alone raised $1.5 million for the Democratic congressional and Senate campaign committees. She was to do better still. The party chairman Ron Brown was to gather the PamPAC team down at her farm in the Middleburg countryside in 1991, to get them to pledge to raise $3 million for whichever Democratic candidate would be going into dubious battle against George Bush in 1992. Not only was Pamela one of the few who insisted that Bush could be beaten, she went on to raise $3.2 million in a single evening.

Pamela Harriman's original idea had been not simply to raise money, but to use it to bypass a cumbersome Democratic National Committee and start a new activist group within the party, reinforced with a small policy think tank, to push the Democrats back to the electable center. In the wake of Reagan's reelection landslide in 1984, winning 49 states against Walter Mondale, the Democratic Leadership Council was formed. Its executive director and main fount of energy was Al From, who started in Democratic politics working for Lyndon Johnson's War on Poverty. From spent a frustrating four years in Jimmy Carter's White House as part of the anti-inflation task force, and then ran the House Democratic Caucus.

"What we tried to do was to say that this party has to understand that if we are going to win, we have to unite our core constituency, those who are aspiring to get into the middle class and those who are struggling to stay there," From argued. He took as his text the speech made by Mondale's challenger, Senator Gary Hart, on the night of the Iowa Caucuses in January 1984, in which he said that the Democratic Party faced a choice between its past, the moribund and no longer sufficient coalition that Roosevelt had put together, and its future, which would have to appeal to the suburbs as well as the inner city, to the mass middle class as well as the dwindling working class. From had learned from Carter's 1976 victory that the Democratic Party could not afford to abandon the South to the Republicans, and southerners became the core of the DLC. Other than Congressman Dick Gephardt of the border state of Missouri, the first chairmen were all southerners: Senators Chuck Robb of Virginia, Sam Nunn of Georgia, John Breaux of Louisiana, and Governor Clinton from Arkansas.

Their immediate goal was to give the South an institutional force in presidential politics with an early southern primary in the election year. The fourteen southern and border states held 207 votes in the Electoral College, three-quarters of the way toward a presidential majority. A Super Tuesday simultaneous primary across the South would create a built-in advantage for a southern candidate and force all the others to address southern concerns. As a regional block, the South could outweigh the special interests of labor and minorities and women, which they feared were dominating the national party.

Under From's relentless urging, the DLC assumed an ideological as well as a regional identity. "Even a heavy Democratic vote in the cities can no longer carry a Democrat to the White House. So Democrats need to make inroads into the suburban vote without turning their backs on the cities. That will require radical new approaches that transcend the old urban-suburban divide. Putting new dollars into old programs won't do. To sell in the suburbs, these new approaches must meet three criteria. They must be entrepreneurial, non-bureaucratic, cost-effective and results-oriented. They must inspire responsibility and self-sufficiency among the beneficiaries. And finally, they must be universal, available not just to inner-city residents but to anyone."

From's ideal was the old G.I. Bill that had educated the servicemen who returned from World War Two. In the context of the 1980s, he favored a revived system of national service, not necessarily aimed at the military, but at community service in the police or the schools, in care of children or the elderly, which would be rewarded by grants for a college education. The association of the Democratic Party with a costly, ineffective, and unpopular welfare system was a major concern. From worked with Clinton, the most policy-conscious of the DLC founding politicians, on ways to reform welfare and the poverty environment that sustained it. The broad theme was the need to reward work, with tax rebates to ensure that nobody who worked a 40-hour week should fall below the poverty line, with training and child-care projects to help welfare recipients into work.

Clinton pursued a further route to national prominence, through the National Governors' Association. In 1986, he was elected vice chairman for the following year, and at the conference in Boise, he made his mark and established a reputation as a centrist by brokering a political deal. There were 34 Democratic governors and only 16 Republicans, and President Reagan issued a fund-raising appeal that said, "The lopsided Democratic majority in our statehouses is the most dangerous threat facing the conservative agendas. . . . Many Democratic governors turned right around and increased state sales taxes and income taxes, wiping out the tax cuts given to you by our administration."

The Democrats were outraged. Their new taxes were to pay for the extra responsibilities Reagan had loaded onto the states. They immediately moved to block the expected election of Tennessee's Republican governor, Lamar Alexander, to be NGA chairman. Clinton brokered the compromise, insisting that the NGA had to remain a bipartisan body. At one heated moment, when Massachusetts governor Michael Dukakis and New Hampshire's John Sununu almost came to blows, Clinton stepped in to separate them. Then he persuaded Alexander to back a joint resolution that stressed the new burdens the Reagan administration was imposing on the states.

Easily reelected governor of Arkansas in 1986, Clinton shrugged off a primary challenge by old Orval Faubus and defeated Frank White, in their third encounter, with 64 percent of the vote. It was not an edifying election. A live TV debate became a verbal brawl, and White's two prepared ambushes each backfired. He demanded that Clinton submit to a drug test. Clinton coolly said he already had, and so had his campaign manager Betsey Wright, and the results would be made public. White then raised Clinton's connection to Dan Lasater, who had just been formally indicted for drug trafficking. Clinton responded with figures showing that White's main sponsors, the Stephens family, had done far more bond business with the state. Lasater himself then gave a press conference to assert that he had contributed to White's 1980 campaign, and then produced a recent letter from White asking him to contribute again in 1986, after the drug indictment had been filed.

Now chairman of the National Governors' Association, Clinton had a series of opportunities to prepare the ground for the 1988 presidential campaign. His reelection had made him a contender, said *Newsweek. Time* listed him as one of the nation's fifty leaders, and a hearing by the governors' association in Iowa gave him the perfect excuse to sound out support in the state with the first caucus of the 1988 campaign. Gloria Cabe, a former state representative for Little Rock who was field director for his reelection campaign, was sent to the first primary in the state of New Hampshire on a scouting trip. Clinton began to sound out donors. Jerry L. Maulden, president of Clinton's old foe, Arkansas Power and Light, declared that he would be proud to support a run for the White House. Taking trip after trip out of state, Clinton was dogged by a posse of Arkansas reporters, demanding if his home state would be "the last to know" of his election plans.

One of the striking features of Clinton's career in Arkansas was that the journalists who knew him best were the most dubious about him. "Bill Clinton is not ready to be President of the United States," declared the *Arkansas Gazette.* "He has strong potential, to be sure, and it could suddenly blossom into prospects for strong national leadership. While we are waiting for that to happen, the memory of the early Clinton comes to mind." The *Gazette* could be dismissed, but the *Arkansas Democrat* usually supported him, but one story kept nagging at its political reporter, John Brummett.

It took place in 1985, when Clinton decided to veto a bill that allowed donations to private and public colleges in the state to be tax deductible. In principle, this was an admirable idea. In practice, there were already so many tax exemptions granted in Arkansas that it cost the state budget over $200 million a year, and nobody dared estimate what this new one might cost. Clinton hesitated, and finally stamped "Disapproved" on the bill, the state version of the veto, and asked an aide to take it to the Clerk's office. He had dithered so long that the Clerk had gone home, and the envelope was slid under the door. Then Clinton went home and began calling college presidents to tell them of his decision. Slowly, they talked him around. So Clinton ordered a state trooper to drive to the capitol and retrieve the bill. The state trooper, finding the door locked, scoured the building for a wire coat hanger, and used it to scoop the envelope back under the door. Back at his mansion, Clinton scratched out the letters "Dis," and the bill was approved. Telling the story, Brummett wondered whether "this man is equipped to deal with, as an example, the Soviets on questions that have to do with the very security of the world."

Clinton's interest in the presidency quickened in May 1987, when Gary Hart withdrew from the race after the *Miami Herald* took up his challenge to catch him committing adultery. Clinton knew all the other contenders.

Mario Cuomo and Michael Dukakis were familiar from the National Governors' Association. He knew Al Gore and Dick Gephardt and Bruce Babbitt through the DLC. None of them intimidated him. But Gary Hart's fate was a concern. He consulted his usual advisers, and spoke to Gary Hart at length. Would infidelities in the past be a concern? The broad conclusion was that it would be a problem, but not fatal to a campaign so long as the marriage was visibly strong.

The Arkansas State Democratic Committee adopted a formal resolution urging him to run. His mail was running three to one in favor. He had lined up $2 million in commitments, and a speech to the New Hampshire Democrats had been a success. Tradition suggested that a presidential bid never succeeded at the first attempt; a candidate should lay down a marker with a spirited campaign, learn the ropes, and become nationally known, then come back to the fray four or eight years later. Clinton was still just forty in that early summer of 1987, and all his instincts said that was the time. Reagan, bruised by the Iran-Contra affair, was about to step down after his second term. With Gorbachev in the Kremlin, the cold war was evidently winding down, sufficient at least to make foreign policy experience and national security far less of an issue.

The Excelsior Hotel's ballroom in Little Rock was booked for Clinton's announcement on July 15. His friends began to fly in from Washington and Texas and Cambridge and California for the long-awaited event. Robert Reich had told the readers of the *American Oxonian,* "Rumor has it that Bill will be the Democratic candidate for president in 1988. I just made up that rumor, but by the time you read this, the rumor will have spread to the ends of the nation."

On the day before the announcement, Clinton decided not to run, apologizing to the friends gathered at his lunch table. His family was the main consideration. Chelsea was seven, and when he had told her he might not be joining the family holiday so he could run for the presidency, she had said that she and her mother would just go without him. That was the reason he gave to friends in private and in public the next day. In one subsequent interview, Betsey Wright hinted at another factor. She had forced him to sit down and go through the list of women with whom he was rumored to have had affairs, demanding he tell her the truth, and then assess whether the women would keep silence. At the end of the process, Wright concluded that for the sake of his family, he should reconsider. After Gary

Hart, the media—and the Republicans—would be relentless in pursuing sexual gossip about any candidate.

Clinton withdrew, and watched the other Democratic rivals, dubbed the Seven Dwarfs, go through the ritual of the primaries, interrupted by the sudden forlorn attempt by Gary Hart to get back into the race. But there was still the opportunity for Clinton to put down his marker for the future. He had prepared a schedule of campaign speeches across the nation, many of which he decided to keep. The local press kept track, reporting that in the 96 days between stepping down from the presidential race and October 27, he had spent 50 of them outside Arkansas. In private, he committed early to Dukakis, but did not make his public endorsement while the Super Tuesday primary was pending, an event tailor-made for his DLC colleague, Senator Al Gore. The eclipse of Gore in the New York primary opened the way for Clinton and the other Democratic governors to come out for Dukakis, and Clinton began speaking and campaigning hard, and trying to mediate between Dukakis and a prickly Jesse Jackson.

Clinton's reward was to give the nomination speech at the Democratic convention in Atlanta. It was a coveted showcase to stamp his abilities on the national TV audience, just as Governor Cuomo had achieved with his nomination speech for Mondale four years earlier. Clinton's speech had been crafted and approved by the Dukakis team. Dukakis read it and said, "Whatever happens, give the speech." Clinton had been asked to speak for twenty minutes, in prime time. He timed the speech at fifteen, leaving some minutes for applause. It was a disaster. The house lights were not turned down. The Dukakis floor whips began chants of "We want Mike." The speech droned on, amid shouts of "Give him the hook," until Clinton, after 32 minutes, evoked a cheer with the words "In closing . . ."

The recovery was better than the speech. Harry Thomason quickly began to make arrangements in Hollywood. Clinton went on the Johnny Carson show, made some self-deprecatory jokes about giving a similar speech for Bush to make Dukakis look good, and finally promised "a short number" when he picked up his saxophone to play "Summertime." "We got lemons, and we made lemonade," Clinton told the party the Thomasons threw for him that night, his eye on the big sign on the garden wall. It carried a picture of the White House, with the caption "On the Road Again—Clinton '96." One person could not quite forgive him, however. He had told Carson that he had decided not to run because of his seven-year-old daughter. The next day, he called Chelsea, who told him bluntly "I am eight."

The humiliation in Atlanta was one low point in a prolonged period of gloom. Clinton was uncertain of his political future, or whether he had one. He had told the voters in 1986 that he could not envisage running for a fourth consecutive term in 1990. But out of office and out of politics, there might be no springboard to the White House. He had mused about challenging Dale Bumpers in the Senate primary, but the first polls suggested it would be a difficult race. George Bush's victory over Dukakis, and the ruthless way Bush's campaign strategist Lee Atwater had fought the Massachusetts Democrat and even managed to bring up his wife's depression was a warning of what Clinton might face in the future. But the deeper crisis was a personal one, as he entered his forties nagged by the fear that his political opportunity was ebbing. He felt bereft of some of his closest friends. In 1989, an infuriated and clinically depressed Betsey Wright took a long leave of absence, and Clinton's personal minister at Immanuel Baptist Church, Worley Vaught, died on Christmas Day, shortly after Clinton had carried the Christmas tree into the sickroom so his old minister could see it.

Above all, his marriage was in serious trouble. The rumors of his infidelities were constant, and ever more public, fueled by two personal crusades. One was run by a black businessman who ran a janitor service company and made locally celebrated sweet potato pies. Known as the "Black Santa," he was an indefatigable organizer of charities and an extraordinary publicist, who dumped garbage on the City Hall steps and roped himself to a cross facing the state capitol to further his causes. One of them was the claim, repeated in handbills he circulated in the city, that Clinton was the father of a black child. The second personal assault on Clinton came from Larry Nichols, a functionary in the Arkansas Development Finance Authority who was sacked in 1988 for making 642 unauthorized phone calls, 202 to leaders of the Nicaraguan Contras, and another 392 to Darrell Glascock, a former aide to Congressman Tommy Robinson, who had become a public relations assistant to the Contras. Nichols claimed, and later repeated the charges in a lawsuit, that he had been fired because of his knowledge that Clinton had used state resources, including his state trooper bodyguards, to facilitate his infidelities.

Hillary turned to her church, not just for comfort, but for practical help. A devout Methodist who gave unpaid legal assistance to her church, she went to see the Reverend Ed Matthews, who offered counseling. Hillary's biographer suggested that her decision was provoked by a question from a weeping Chelsea, "Mommy, why doesn't Daddy love you anymore?" In December 1989, Hillary confronted her husband, who waved away the rumors. She would not be denied. She would not tolerate the situation any further. "Unless you're ready to change, we're getting a divorce."

Just before Christmas, they began meeting Reverend Matthews in his study. Hillary said she wanted to make the marriage work. Clinton said that he loved his wife and daughter more than anything in the world. Under Reverend Matthews's direction, they held hands and knelt to pray together, and Clinton promised to change his ways, to work harder at being a better husband and father, and to devote more time to his family. There were repeated sessions in the pastor's study, and Hillary too pledged to change. She went on a ferocious diet and lost twenty pounds, changed her hairstyle and began to dye her hair blond. She bought a new wardrobe, spending what friends estimated at $10,000, including $2,400 for a cashmere jacket, and went to a beauty salon for advice on cosmetics. The marriage had been through a severe crisis, and their friends were heartened to see it restored in the course of 1990.

They had reaffirmed their marriage vows before Reverend Matthews, and it was barely in time for the 1990 reelection campaign, at which the Republican campaign behind Sheffield Nelson tried to use the allegations of Larry Nichols against Clinton. It was a difficult election, battling against the widespread perception that after eight straight years as governor, and two years in his first term, Clinton had been there too long. His negative ratings in the state were well above 30 percent. He faced a primary challenge from Tom McRae, a liberal who voiced the widespread resentment on the left that Clinton was no longer much of a Democrat. McRae was backed by Bill Becker, who tried to persuade the rest of the AFL-CIO to endorse him, after Clinton's Industrial Development Corporation guaranteed a loan to the (minority-owned) Morrilton Plastics Company as it fought a strike by the autoworkers union.

Hillary came to her husband's rescue again, in a prepared interruption of a McRae press conference, heckling, "Get off it, Tom." She then read earlier endorsements of Clinton that McRae had made. The effect of this was mixed. McRae said it helped his campaign, but with Betsey Wright installed as chair of the state party, the machine was on Clinton's side. He won the primary, albeit with an unimpressive 54.8 percent of the vote. But the real battle loomed in the November general election against Sheffield Nelson, a former Democrat and former head of the Stephens-owned Arkla gas corporation. A formidable candidate, he was strongly backed by the Republican Party in Washington.

Lee Atwater, the architect of President Bush's victory in 1988, had a double agenda. The first was to recruit conservative Democrats across the South into the Republican Party and the second was to bleed Clinton, whom he feared as a potent challenger to Bush in 1992. Atwater's first target was former Pulaski County sheriff and Democratic congressman Tommy Robinson, whose Republican opponent in 1988 exemplified the difficulty Atwater faced in finding good candidates. Robinson's opponent had claimed that his trailer in North Little Rock was under assault by radiation waves, all part of a conspiracy that led to the Reagan White House. Robinson, who once boasted of his campaign contributors, "I can be hired, but I can't be bought," was a colorful figure who had chained convicts to the prison's outer fence, and yet had also cast his ballot for Jesse Jackson at the 1988 Democratic convention because "he touched my soul."

Robinson announced his conversion to the Republican Party in July 1989, after Atwater had promised that President Bush would make it a national event with a White House ceremony. Robinson was a serious threat to Clinton, but Clinton and Betsey Wright manipulated the Republicans' open primary, sending in their supporters to vote against Robinson and for Sheffield Nelson. In Washington, Lee Atwater would have recognized Clinton's response as the challenge of another smart southern politician, but had collapsed in February with the brain tumor that would kill him. Atwater had, however, already explained his strategy to Sheffield Nelson. "Taken alone, I don't give a damn who the governor of Arkansas is," Atwater told him. "We know how to beat a liberal from the Northeast. We proved that with Dukakis. I ain't worried about Mario Cuomo. But Bill Clinton does worry me."

Atwater went on to tell Nelson that the strategy in the 1990 gubernatorial election against Clinton would be "to tar him up and down" and make him unelectable as president. "There was an excellent chance that womanizing would have been used if Atwater had lived," Nelson said later. "He did not like Bill Clinton. I'm not saying Clinton would have lost, but if Atwater had lived, it would have been a much, much different race in 1992."

Nelson came dangerously close to success, with a last-week TV ad that took one of Clinton's earlier speeches against Reagan's insistence that the states spend their own money on education. "Unlike our friends in Washington, we cannot write a check on an account that is not funded. We either raise and spend, or we don't spend." Nelson's campaign took the videotape and doctored it. A tape loop of Clinton saying "Raise and spend, raise and spend, raise and spend" dominated the Arkansas airwaves from the Friday evening before the election, assuming it would be too late for Clinton to respond.

Clinton, as so often in the final days of a campaign, panicked. Dick Morris ran a final tracking poll that showed him slumping ten points in three days, down to 46 percent. Clinton's other polls still showed him fifteen points ahead. Nonetheless, he took out another personal loan from a small Arkansan bank, taped a counterattack, and dispatched his supporters by light plane and car around the state's TV and radio stations to get it on the air by Sunday night. Clinton also called John Robert Starr at the *Arkansas Democrat,* warned him that defeat loomed, and that the one thing they both believed in, education reform, would crumble if Nelson won. Starr was persuaded, and later recalled, "I came down to the office, pulled out a column I already had in the paper for Monday, and I wrote a column endorsing him, and then wrote another for Tuesday."

Tuesday was election day, and Clinton won with 59 percent. Perhaps Morris's final poll had been an aberration. Certainly he was never paid for it by the Clinton campaign. John Robert Starr was not pleased with the result of his promise to back Clinton if the education reforms ever looked to be in peril. "I kept my part of the bargain and he began almost immediately to break his," Starr later grumbled. The Nichols allegations of womanizing had sunk with little trace. Clinton was back in the governor's mansion for four more years. But his target date was 1992. Despite the Gulf War, Clinton's closest political adviser was convinced that Bush could be beaten.

"She always thought that the right kind of Democrat would have an opportunity to be elected in '92, always, I mean from the beginning of his [Bush's] term, when he took office, she told me that. And when he got up to 70 percent or 90 percent or whatever in the polls after the Gulf War, she never wavered in her conviction," Clinton later recalled. His adviser, in whose judgment he had complete faith, was Hillary. "It was amazing. And I've got to give her credit for that. That's one where her instinct was right, and I didn't feel that way for the longest time. She thought that in '88 we still had a reasonably good economy and that the adverse consequences of Reaganomics were not fully apparent to most voters and that by '92 they would be. And she always believed that. And she never changed her opinion."

☆ 5 ☆

THE 1992 CAMPAIGN: THE PRIMARIES

The calls went out to the FOBs to gather in Washington for a final conference at the Washington Court Hotel in September 1991. Mickey Kantor and Derek Shearer and the Thomasons flew in from California, Robert Reich and Eli Segal from Massachusetts, Stanley Greenberg from Connecticut, Bill and Hillary, the Lindseys, and McLarty from Little Rock. For Frank Greer and Vernon Jordan, and former air force officer John Holum, Washington was already the hometown. They talked campaign staff, money, and the campaign timetable. There was just over $1 million in the war chest. And Kantor finally ran through Hillary's role, as a campaigner in her own right, with her own network of support through the Bar Association, the Children's Defense Fund, and her corporate connections.

"All of you are nice not to bring it up, but I know all of you are concerned," Clinton said finally. They had to talk about the sexual rumors. Gary Hart's campaign had been destroyed by it, and the whole issue was ripe for hypocrisy and the kind of negative campaign to be expected from the Republicans. It was a strange world, where a politician could avoid trouble if he divorced, but court it if a couple stuck by their marriage and worked through their problems. It was, mused Clinton, the kind of pettiness that reminded him of decadent, declining Rome.

Jordan was for saying nothing. Greer said there was so much gossip that it had to be addressed. Greer had already arranged for Clinton to attend an off-the-record breakfast with Washington's top political journalists, convened regularly by Godfrey Sperling of the *Christian Science Monitor.* It was the perfect chance to lance the boil, and Greer had already urged several of the reporters to raise the question. At the breakfast, they proved curiously reluctant to do so. Finally it came up, and Clinton came out with the prepared phrases: "Like any couple who have been together for twenty years, our relationship has not been perfect or free from difficulties. But we feel good about where we are, and we believe in our obligations to each other. And we intend to be together thirty or forty years from now whether I run for president or not."

The formal declaration came on October 3, at the old state house in Little Rock, amid Harry Thomason's carefully staged theatrics, and the ear-splitting sounds of the chosen campaign song, Fleetwood Mac's "Don't Stop Thinking About Tomorrow." It was to be, Clinton said, in the phrase that became his mantra, "a campaign about the forgotten middle class." The local press corps counted the words "middle class" 132 times, "responsibility" 12 times, and "opportunity" 10 times, along with the requisite promise to "restore the American dream." It was a conventional start, significant enough to be broadcast live on CNN, and a joyous day for the FOBs, who gathered that night to sing together around the piano in the governor's mansion.

But October was a grim month. George Bush's foreign policy credentials looked even stronger, as Boris Yeltsin dispatched the Communist Party and the Soviet Union to oblivion, and Palestinians and Israelis gathered at the Madrid peace conference. Up in Albany, New York's governor Mario Cuomo was hinting that the Democratic nomination was his for the taking. The campaign funds of the AFL-CIO were committed to Tom Harkin, and Democrats looking for the representative of the new generation were thrilling to the Vietnam War heroics of Senator Bob Kerrey. Worst of all, Clinton's fund-raising was a catastrophe.

Money was a problem Clinton assumed he had solved, when Robert Farmer, the star fund-raiser for the Dukakis campaign in 1988, agreed to join the campaign. Clinton had begun in September with just over $1 million, raised from the FOBs. He was sure that another $1 million would come with the formal announcement in October, and he would begin the election year with $4 million in the bank by January 1. But Farmer, preoccupied with a new job in Boston, could only work part-time. Not a single fund-raising event was scheduled for November, and the campaign was starting to bleed to death.

Clinton's embryonic campaign was saved by three unexpected factors.

The first was a U.S. Senate off-year election in Pennsylvania, where a respected former state governor, Richard Thornburgh, lost a thirty-point lead in the opinion polls to a little-known college administrator, Harris Wofford. Thornburgh had been President Bush's attorney general, and his defeat was the first hard sign the Republicans might not sweep to victory on clouds of Gulf War glory. Wofford's campaign was run by James Carville and Paul Begala, who crafted a populist message that the recession was hurting and a national health service was desperately required. The Pennsylvania election galvanized Democrats with the conviction that they could win in 1992, that health reform was the issue, and that Carville and Begala were the campaign strategists to hire.

Thanks to his friend, Georgia governor Zell Miller, whom Carville and Begala had helped elect the previous year, Clinton had already started to sound them out. But Senators Bob Kerrey and Tom Harkin were also calling Carville at The Batcave, the chaotic basement flat on Capitol Hill where he worked and slept. Begala liked Harkin's populism. Carville thought Kerrey had star quality. But Carville from Louisiana and Begala from Texas decided to go with their fellow southerner. "Hell, I just liked the man, and if you're gonna be in the foxhole together for the next year, close enough that you smell each other's breath, that's a lot of it," Carville explained. "And he liked his food. He had good appetites. A good heart. He was in this thing to win, and I thought he could do it."

Signing Carville and Begala was a vote of confidence that gave Clinton both momentum and credibility among party professionals. And in hiring George Stephanopoulos, the bright young floor manager for House minority leader Dick Gephardt, Clinton was winning the staff primary. Kerrey had also tried to hire Stephanopoulos, but the son of a Greek Orthodox priest warmed to his fellow Rhodes scholar at his interview in Little Rock. "After five minutes, I felt like I was walking on air. We had a Democrat who could win," Stephanopoulos said later. Bruce Lindsey was firm, telling Clinton, "You have to hire this guy."

But Clinton still desperately needed money, and Chicago came to the rescue. Clinton's crucial ally was Kevin O'Keefe, who had grown up with Hillary in the suburb of Park Ridge; they had worked together in Eugene McCarthy's anti-Vietnam campaign in 1968. The Democratic Party in Chicago was no longer the legendary vote machine the elder Mayor Daley had controlled in the 1960s. But his son had rebuilt much of it, and

O'Keefe was closely connected. His uncle Jimmy had been the Kennedy family's man in the city. His law partner, Thomas Lyons, was chairman of the Cook County Democratic Party. O'Keefe introduced Clinton to the Daley brothers.

The Chicago machine had had a saying when they turned away interlopers who were not vouched for, "We don't take nobody nobody sent." O'Keefe was Clinton's first credential. He had to earn the second, in a toe-to-toe debate in October with Senator Bob Kerrey before a party audience on Chicago's North Pier. Clinton was in extraordinary form, hammering away at "the eight-year fraud of Reaganomics" and insisting that the Democrats could only win by winning back the middle class who were sick of both parties. Kerrey, in Chicago a nobody whom nobody had sent, was unfocused. "I kicked his butt," Clinton bragged afterwards.

David Wilhelm, who had managed two mayoral campaigns for Richard Daley, and the Senate reelection campaign for Paul Simon, agreed to do the same for Clinton. With Daley's blessing, Wilhelm brought along a slim young former ballet dancer, Rahm Emmanuel, who was very much tougher than he looked, and had run Mayor Daley's fund-raising operation. Passionately pro-Israel, Emmanuel had volunteered to grease Israeli army trucks when the Scud missiles began landing on Tel Aviv in the Gulf War. Clinton was to conclude that "Emmanuel was to fund-raising what Moshe Dayan was to war."

The 1991 recession was hurting the cash flow of all the Democratic campaigns, and the month before Christmas was always dreadful for raising money. Emmanuel said Christmas didn't count in his religion, and threw himself and his candidate into the desperate hunt for cash. He scheduled 27 fund-raising events in twenty days, set a target of $2.2 million by December 31, and raised the money. His "never take prisoners, never take no for an answer" style was effective, if abrasive. After the 1988 campaign, he sent a note to Democratic pollster Alan Secrest that said: "It's been awful working with you. Love, Rahm." The note was taped on a rotting fish.

Even before the money began to come in, Clinton ordered $50,000 to be invested in Michael Whouley, who was organizing the Clinton effort at the Florida state Democratic convention in Orlando. In a southern state, the most prominent southern candidate had to be seen to win convincingly in the straw poll of delegates. But Florida, with its strong proportion of retired people from the Northeast, was not a typical southern state. Tom Harkin's trade union supporters were a formidable obstacle.

When Whouley arrived in Orlando, he was sure of just 50 of the 2,200 delegates. But by getting to the convention hotel well in advance, booking the hotel's audiovisual control room and its walkie-talkies, and grabbing the prime sites for the Clinton campaign, Whouley began to make up for lost ground. Clinton, croaking from a cold, gave a lackluster speech while Harkin won cheers for a barnstorming attack on Bush, and Senator Kerrey held the crowd spellbound. But then Kerrey left town, while Bill and Hillary worked the convention tirelessly. Clinton won the straw poll with 54 percent, against 31 percent for Harkin and just 10 percent for Kerrey.

The Florida straw poll, although neither a popular election nor the considered choice of party professionals weighing odds in a smoke-filled room, was highly important for the party across the country. It draped Clinton in the perception, not just of success, but of a skillful and well-honed political operation. The delegates found themselves in Clinton country, pitched by Clinton staffers who were plugged into the only effective communications system in the hotel. It felt like an efficient machine, and more than just the news that he had won, the word went out in the party around the country that Clinton had by far the best organization, one of those subjective judgments that can become a self-fulfilling prophecy.

And by the end of the year, everything had changed. On December 20, Mario Cuomo ducked his last opportunity to run in the New Hampshire primary. Overnight, Clinton became the front-runner because, with an unusually serious and even old-fashioned combination of campaign speeches and policies, and that reputation as the man with the organization, he had begun drawing ahead of the Democratic pack.

As election year began, the New Hampshire polls showed Clinton with 23 percent of the vote, breathing hard down the neck of the local candidate Paul Tsongas, who had invested most of the last six months in New Hampshire. Money that was being reserved for Cuomo became free, and Clinton, who once noted sardonically that "the first primary is money," steadily caught up with the funds from organized labor that had already gone to his populist and protectionist rival, Senator Tom Harkin of Iowa.

But New Hampshire was traditionally unhappy terrain for front-runners. The state's proud tradition of being first in the nation to judge each new crop of presidential candidates came with a curious pride in being the giant killer, the first chance that real people had to puncture the airy predictions of the polls and pundits. They had sunk Lyndon Johnson in 1968, deflated Ed Muskie in 1972, and destroyed Bob Dole in 1988. Clinton was nervous about entering New Hampshire as the front-runner and thus the fattest target, because he found the place very hard to read.

New Hampshire had become a schizoid state, at once high-tech and deeply rural, a culture of moose and microchip. The biggest employer was Digital Equipment, and yet its biggest city had fewer than 100,000 people, and over 200 of the state's drivers collided with straying moose on the roads each winter. Hardly any blacks, no inner-city nightmare, no state income taxes, and the best school results in the country, New Hampshire was a most untypical place in which to hold the election that defined America's presidential year. But the state's record of picking White House winners was remarkable. Since 1952, every American president had won his party's New Hampshire primary.

This unusual state played a talismanic role in the American political process, a rite of presidential passage that must be undergone. It required a ritual baptism by town meeting, factory gate, local store, and front parlor before sending the survivors into the nationwide electronic campaign of press conference and sound-bite.

"We get to watch the candidates' eyes as they answer our questions, and the rest of the country watches us watching," said the local poet Donald Hall. Every four years, the northern state of New Hampshire played its cruel and unusual trick upon the modern American political system. It forced all presidential candidates into a pre-television time warp of old-fashioned politics, meeting the voters, looking them in the eye, and explaining why they want to get elected. The tarmac-to-tarmac campaign of airport press conferences was held in abeyance as the state's 511,000 registered voters asserted their traditional right to hold America's only intimate election. In 1992, only 150,360 of them were registered Democrats, being wooed by five Democratic hopefuls, and usually only half of them were likely to vote in the primary.

To persuade a plurality of those 75,000 likely voters, Bill Clinton bought two hours and two minutes of TV time on WMUR, the state's only TV station. It charged $1,000 for thirty seconds in prime time, but only $10 between midnight and 5 A.M. Much of Clinton's TV buy was prime time, and Republican challenger Pat Buchanan had bought over three hours. The other two leading Democrats, Paul Tsongas and Bob Kerrey, each bought over an hour.

The 1992 New Hampshire primary was an extraordinary event, which set the course not only for the election year to come, but for the new political environment that was brewing. First in importance was the striking success of Pat Buchanan in challenging and bleeding his incumbent president. Bush, having been televised throwing up over the trousers of the Japanese prime minister in Tokyo, was dismally unable to reassure the stricken New Hampshire voters that he understood how bad the recession felt. Buchanan won only 37 percent of the Republican primary vote, but he inflicted a mortal wound, not only on the president, but on the pragmatic and traditional wing of the Republican Party, which Bush represented. Without Buchanan's New Hampshire challenge, the Christian Coalition and the fundamentalists would never have been able to capture the party convention in Houston. The way would not have been opened for the fiercely combative and uncompromising new Republican leadership that would emerge in Congress.

The second extraordinary feature of the New Hampshire campaign was that Clinton survived it. His campaign was torpedoed twice, by Gennifer Flowers and her taped phone conversations with Clinton, and then by the *Wall Street Journal*'s revelation of Clinton's equivocation over the military draft. Her tapes probably did less damage than his own letter. Two phrases stood out from the letter he had written in December 1969 to Colonel Holmes, who had directed the ROTC program at the University of Arkansas. Clinton described himself as part of a generation that found themselves "loving the country, but loathing the military." And he said that his motives in trying to escape the draft by joining ROTC were "to maintain my political viability within the system. For years I have worked to prepare myself for a political life."

Had there been a competent and well-funded Democratic alternative to Clinton, his campaign would have ended in New Hampshire. But Tom Harkin had been unable to rise above his prairie populism, the traditional Democratic appeal that had failed with Mondale and Dukakis. Douglas Wilder barely bothered to campaign. Jerry Brown, without funds or an organization, had made little impact. The man Clinton most feared was Senator Bob Kerrey of Nebraska. One of the few clear phrases from Clinton in the transcripts of his taped calls to Ms. Flowers said: "I might lose the nomination to Bob Kerrey—because he's got all the Gary Hart–Hollywood money, and because he's single, looks like a movie star, won the Medal of Honor, and since he's single, nobody cares if he's screwing."

But Kerrey ran a wretchedly half-hearted campaign, that simply failed to build on his personal merits and his serious health reform plan. He did not take to New Hampshire, and it showed. Worse still, he did not take to the constant glad-handing and telephonic supplications of fund-raising. When chaotic accounting meant that he entered the last week of New Hampshire with the sudden knowledge that he had just $200,000, rather than the $1 million he had assumed, that showed, too.

But the third portent of New Hampshire lay in the odd success of Paul Tsongas, whose most memorable slogan was "I'm no Santa Claus." Initially dismissed as "another Greek liberal from Massachusetts," a former senator who had resigned to fight cancer and make a full recovery, he was little known outside the region. But his hometown of Lowell was just across the New Hampshire border. Fighting on his home turf, Tsongas made a virtue of the grimly serious remedies of belt-tightening and sacrifice he prescribed for America in his 86-page pamphlet, "A Call to Economic Arms." He distributed over 200,000 copies around the state.

"The cold war is over, and Japan won," Tsongas intoned. America was wasting its victory and its future by failing to invest and by consuming too much. The federal budget was heading for disaster and had to be frozen, with no new spending. "We're going to get this budget in balance. So no tax credits for having children. No middle-class tax cuts. No drain on the Treasury. You cap expenditures." There was no room for tax cuts, except possibly cuts to provide incentives for investment. There had to be a sharp increase in gasoline taxes.

This all ran so contrary to the conventional wisdom of political candidacies that the substance was as refreshing as Tsongas's solemn, almost sanctimonious style. There could not have been a sharper contrast with the successful election theme song of 1988, "Don't Worry, Be Happy," and although the Tsongas campaign was to falter, his message was to prevail. His argument that the deficit was out of control was hard to refute. His questioning of Clinton's promised middle-class tax cut was cogent, and it lingered on to haunt Clinton in office, when even his own party's congressmen abandoned his economic stimulus package and donned the Tsongas hair shirt to insist on expenditure caps. The fiscal climate in Congress after the 1992 election was Paul Tsongas's legacy.

Clinton survived New Hampshire against all odds because he was an inveterate and indomitable politician. He never stopped campaigning, never ceased to fight back, and it was later calculated that he had met personally every fifth voter, over 20,000 New Hampshire citizens. His campaign team, of Carville and Begala, Stephanopoulos and Greer, and his young assistant Mandy Grunwald, proved their worth. Grunwald came up with the line about "a woman I never slept with and a draft I never dodged." She also blunted the first shock of the Gennifer Flowers scandal with a fiery challenge to Ted Koppel on *Nightline*, accusing him of sleazily following the tabloid press into the gutter.

Begala came up with the phrase "the Comeback Kid," which was to make Clinton's second-place showing, with 25 percent of the vote against Tsongas's 36 percent, into a kind of moral victory. It was deserved, in that Bill and Hillary Clinton never gave up. One virtue of the long, exhausting running of the gauntlet that is the American primary system was that it became a ruthless test of character. The flaws of self-indulgence that Flowers gushingly described were visibly balanced by the grim determination Clinton showed as he battled through his crisis.

Hounded by the press, battered by the polls, Clinton also had to contend with a demoralized staff. There were extraordinary moments: an ashen-faced Greenberg clutching the phone as he got the latest poll result and muttering, "Meltdown"; Carville taking to his bed and rolling up into a fetal position; Begala banging his head against his desk and mumbling, "I don't believe this is happening to me"; Mickey Kantor assuring Clinton that he was a young man, he could run again; Bruce Lindsey saying it would just take one word from Hillary, and Clinton would withdraw.

But that was the word Hillary never said. She became raw steel in New Hampshire, determined not to give up, holding the entire campaign together by pure force of will. The reporters who stayed closest to the campaign shared an abiding image of her, gray with fatigue, face bereft of makeup and smudged with printer's ink, limping back through plates of cold pizza to hand out yet another document that might just change the spin: a photocopy of an ancient UPI wire report of Barbara Bush saying how she had been prepared to stand by her son when he told her and George he was going to refuse the draft.

The comeback would not have been possible without Hillary, and her steadfast support on *60 Minutes,* the episode after the Superbowl, the most watched event of the year. But that was simply the most public of an endless round of public rallies in New Hampshire, in which she stood by her husband. In Bedford, two days after the Flowers affair surfaced, she was cheered to the rafters when she said, "Is anything about our marriage as important to the people of New Hampshire as whether or not they will have a chance to keep their own families together?" And in the Elks' hall in Dover, a moment of pure electricity, only possible in the tiny state of New Hampshire where intimacy and person-to-person campaigning were the core of politics, Clinton roared his defiance. Like some Shakespearean figure challenging the very elements, Clinton vowed he would fight on against it all, and if New Hampshire stuck by him, "I'll be with you till the last dog dies."

The synergetic stories of draft and womanizing were still covered thoroughly, were still the prime questions that the reporters fanned out to ask of the departing rally crowds. But another story was beginning to emerge, of a candidate and, more intriguingly, of a husband and wife team whose marriage had been terribly strained, keeping their nerve and fighting back under an intense bombardment. It was this that enabled Clinton's cool effrontery, in claiming that coming in a poor second in New Hampshire made him "the Comeback Kid," to prevail and to dominate the final reporting of the election result.

Beyond Clinton himself, his wife, and his staff, there was a further outflowing of support that helped turn the tide. The Arkansas Travelers were his volunteers, over 600 people coming up to New Hampshire at their own expense by the coachload, canvassing homes, handing out videotapes of the Clinton message, providing warmth and cheers at his rallies. They were ordinary folk, even if their accents sounded a touch exotic in the New England winter, whose devoted support for the governor spoke powerfully to the local voters. Not since the students of 1968 had turned out in their hundreds to canvass for Eugene McCarthy had a New Hampshire primary seen such a flood of sincere and committed strangers. The Arkansas Travelers got little attention in a press and TV that was obsessed by scandal and Clinton's gyrating opinion polls, but they were his secret weapon.

Clinton had survived New Hampshire, and had virtually disposed of Tom Harkin and Bob Kerrey. But in the process, the Clinton controversies had left him looking unelectable in November, and many Democrats flailed around almost desperately looking for an alternative. There was a brief attempt by party leaders like Arthur Schlesinger, Jr., to draft Cuomo back into the race. Others, rallied by the pollster Paul Maslin, went to see Congressman Dick Gephardt, the House majority leader, who showed them the results of a report written by his 1988 campaign manager Bill Carrick, explaining why it was unrealistic to jump into the primaries so late. Gephardt called it his "Why This Is Impossible" memo.

Maslin's A.B.C. movement—Anybody But Clinton—had a life of its own. Senators Bill Bradley, Sam Nunn, and Lloyd Bentsen were all approached to jump in and save the party. When they each declined, the searchers were left with the candidates still in the race, and still listed on the primary ballots. But these were candidates Clinton had already worked out how to beat. The only one who could have benefited, Senator Kerrey, had palpably lost interest. Even Tsongas looked promising after New Hampshire, but his puritan calls for tax increases allowed Clinton to run against him from the left. The improbable Jerry Brown then mounted an incoherent but fiery challenge from terrain that was partly Old Left and partly New Age. Clinton could run against Brown from the right.

"Going home," Clinton sang as he left New Hampshire for the South. Confident that his campaign was about to soar with the Junior Tuesday primary in Georgia and Maryland, and then Super Tuesday when the rest of the South voted, he was stunned when he landed in Georgia. "We're not just bleeding, we're hemorrhaging," said his friend and crucial ally, Governor Zell Miller. Senator Sam Nunn, Clinton's colleague from the DLC, was barely campaigning. The *Atlanta Constitution* had endorsed Tsongas. The polls showed Tsongas at 30 percent and rising. Stanley Greenberg's private polls had even more bad news—Clinton's natural constituency, college-educated and affluent whites, were turning to Tsongas in droves. The overwhelming problem, Greenberg reported, was that the voters did not trust Clinton.

"The only way we can survive this is if we convince people that Paul Tsongas is not a Democrat. This is still a Democratic primary," Stephanopoulos told Clinton. New TV ads were shot, on the theme of People First versus Business First. An extraordinary effort was put into the black vote, relying on the proven party machines of Governor Miller and Atlanta's Mayor Maynard Jackson. In the end—and in Clinton's view it was because people in the Bible Belt believed in both sin and redemption and were prepared to forgive—it was enough. Clinton won Georgia by 57 percent to Tsongas's 24 percent. But Tsongas won Maryland, Utah, and Washington on the same day. Jerry Brown had won Colorado, despite the feverish effort for Clinton by Governor Roy Romer. Again Clinton had done enough for his campaign to remain credible, but no more. And yet, with his home ground of Super Tuesday looming, credible was all Clinton had to be.

Clinton's campaign became ruthless in its determination to crush Tsongas. Clinton battered him in working-class districts as a watered-down Republican, espousing the discredited "trickle-down" economics of Reagan and Bush. They shot a new ad, written by Mandy Grunwald, which thumbed through the Tsongas manifesto. "Page 22—he proposes a capital gains tax cuts for the rich. . . . Page 21—cuts in cost of living increases for older Americans." At the end, the Tsongas pamphlet was tossed on the table, and the voiceover said, "Isn't it time we closed the book on the '80s?" Clinton's relentless campaign machine ground Tsongas hardest in Florida, with leaflets that warned pensioners that Tsongas would cut their Social Security checks, and claiming unfairly to Jews that Tsongas was no friend to Israel.

"Super Tuesday was designed to eliminate guys like me," Tsongas said, with some bitterness, as the results of the eleven primaries and caucuses came in. Clinton predictably swept the South in the Super Tuesday primaries. In Florida, the most demographically "northern" of the southern states, he brushed aside Tsongas's best chance of an upset, winning by a margin of 51–34. In the rest of the South, Clinton won an average 70 percent of the vote, gaining the same overwhelming share of the black vote that Jesse Jackson had managed four years earlier. But this was far less of an enthusiastic mandate than it appeared. Of a total of 18 million people eligible to vote in six southern Democratic primaries, only about 4 million actually did. In Florida, for example, the Democratic turnout was well below 40 percent. In contrast to 1988, when Jesse Jackson whipped up a strong following, turnout among blacks fell to about one in four.

The race was not quite over, because Tsongas comfortably won his home state of Massachusetts. And the quixotic but strongly ecological campaign of Jerry Brown of California was beginning to look threatening. Brown denounced the corrupt political finance system and started to rouse a wave of campus enthusiasm not seen since the 1960s. Brown also won the endorsement of the United Auto Workers branch in Willow Run, whose closure had just been announced by General Motors.

Victory in the South allowed Clinton to advance on the next big primary of Illinois and Michigan with confidence. The Daley machine was with him in Chicago, and money was pouring into the campaign as Greenberg reported that Clinton had 30-point poll leads in both states. The campaign spent it all in a TV blitz that left them broke and unable to buy TV time for the next primary in Connecticut. Tsongas fought back with his own attack ads that said, "He's no Bill Clinton, that's for sure. He's the exact opposite. Paul Tsongas. He's not afraid of the truth." But Tsongas was facing war on two fronts, as Jerry Brown's populist appeal among the car workers and unions of Michigan pushed Tsongas down into third place in the polls.

It was Jerry Brown who gave Clinton the opportunity he needed to seal the race, in the last TV debate. The question had been asked, inevitably, about electability. Tsongas, rattled by plummeting polls, decided not to attack the issue of public trust in Clinton and talked vaguely about mandates to govern. Brown, on the basis of a faxed copy of that day's *Washington Post,* went for the jugular.

"I think he's got a big electability problem," Brown began. "It was right on the front page of the *Washington Post* today. He is funneling money to his wife's law firm for state business. That's number one. Number two, his wife's law firm is representing clients before the state of Arkansas agencies—his appointees. And one of the keys is the poultry industry, which his wife's law firm represents. It's not only corruption, it's an environmental disaster."

Clinton exploded. His face went red, and his finger began jabbing at Brown. It looked as though Clinton was gearing up to hit him. "Let me tell you something, Jerry. I don't care what you say about me, but you oughta be ashamed of yourself for jumping on my wife. You're not worth being on the same platform with my wife."

It was a raw moment, a genuine emotion, a gallant anger on behalf of his wife that became the perfect film clip as it was constantly repeated on the TV news. On Stan Greenberg's polls, Clinton's negative ratings among women nose-dived, and so did the numbers of working-class voters who said they were worried about trusting Clinton. They felt they had seen something of the man behind the politician, standing up for his wife, looking like a brawler.

"We just carried Macomb County," said Greenberg. A blue-collar suburb of Detroit, Macomb County was where Greenberg had defined the phenomenon of the Reagan Democrat, the patriotic white working class, union members and natural Democrats who had turned to Reagan's promise of tax cuts, his sneers at welfare, and his unabashed Americanism. Any Democrat who could win back Macomb County would win the White House, Greenberg had argued. Clinton's honest aggression had just connected with his most important constituency. Greenberg was right. Clinton got 47 percent of the vote in Macomb County, as much as Tsongas and Brown together.

But Brown had put his finger presciently on the issue that was to haunt Clinton in office; the casual ethics of Arkansas, the role of his wife in the Rose Law Firm, whose influence and clients snaked back and forth between politics and business, law and money. For the moment, Clinton had squashed the story, but the Hillary issue was to bounce back within 24 hours, at a coffee shop called the Busy Bee. A local TV reporter asked her about doing work as a lawyer for firms that dealt with the Arkansas government.

"I suppose I could have stayed home and baked cookies and had teas," she said firmly. "But what I decided to do was to fulfill my profession, which I entered before my husband was in public life."

It was the sound-bite that was to define her as the Yuppie Princess who patronized mothers who stayed at home, at least until she turned the tables by publishing her own cookie recipe and having hundreds of them baked for the Democratic convention. It was a sign of that other potent factor beginning to stir in this year's campaign—the female vote. A little-known Chicago politician, Carol Moseley-Braun, unseated a twelve-year Senate veteran to win her Democratic primary in Illinois, promising to become the first black woman senator. She ran on abortion rights and against Bush's appointment of the controversial Clarence Thomas to the Supreme

Court, despite the widely publicized allegations of sexual harassment against him in stormy Senate hearings. A remarkable 62 percent of white women, including many Republicans, voted for her. If the women voted that way again in November, George Bush would lose the election. But all the cookies in Chicago could not dull the triumph of the primary vote. Clinton won both states overwhelmingly, and knocked Tsongas out of the race.

"Money is the mother's milk of politics, and our mothers did not show up until late January," he explained in an emotional, but graceful withdrawal statement to his staff. "The alternative was clear, to play the role of spoiler. That is not worthy. I did not espouse my ideals to be the agent of the reelection of George Bush."

His eclipse was a victory for the old-style politics of big money, which Tsongas was never able to raise, and the gritty business of organizing a grass-roots voting machine, which he never mastered. Ironically, 1992 was the most hopeful year for underfunded candidates, as the late start to the campaign and the recession combined to lower the financial threshold. By the end of January 1988, George Bush had raised $25 million. In 1992, even with the attributes of presidential office, he had raised only $11 million. Four years earlier, Dukakis had raised $15 million by January 31, compared to Clinton's $5 million. All told, the 18 candidates of 1988 had raised $149 million by the end of January; in 1992, the thirteen candidates raised only $32 million among them.

Only Jerry Brown of California now remained to challenge Clinton. Brown himself was not popular. His "negatives," as the pollsters described public doubts about his reliability and character, were even worse than Clinton's. His background as a leading fund-raiser for the Democrats in California, as a lobbyist for the junk bond industry, and as the son of Governor Pat Brown, one of that state's most consummate political insiders, made Jerry Brown's populist rhetoric ring hollow. But he became the Democratic Party's version of Pat Buchanan, the repository of the angry electorate's cry of rage, which could relieve its sense of political impotence with a protest vote. It had become increasingly evident throughout the election year that American voters were in a grim mood, ready to take out their resentment on anybody they deemed to be a professional politician. They turned with enthusiasm to outsiders, whether Ross Perot as an independent, or to any underdog, a Pat Buchanan or a Jerry Brown, who seemed to offer something other than politics as usual. President Bush faced a consistent 30 percent protest vote from his own Republicans in the primaries. This tendency to political iconoclasm dealt a salutary jolt to Clinton, and removed some of the smugness, which was beginning to afflict his campaign.

Clinton narrowly lost Connecticut to Jerry Brown, and 33 percent of Republicans voted against President Bush, even though his right-wing opponent Pat Buchanan had barely bothered to campaign. Brown's victory by 37–36 over Clinton was based around a new coalition of trade union voters, environmentalists, and liberals, and marked by the first primary campaign where he was able to outspend Clinton in TV advertising. The Connecticut result was a powerful springboard for Brown as he swiftly redeployed his shoestring campaign for the important New York and Wisconsin primaries on April 7.

"The people of this country have had enough. They want to take their government back. I'm just the vehicle," Brown said, after his second victory in a full-scale primary (although he had also won three of the less formal state caucus elections). "I don't think Bill Clinton owns it. I don't think you [in the media] own it. It belongs to the people."

The electorate's discontent was apparent in the low turnout, one-third below the 1988 primary. American voters are not enthusiastic at the best of times; in the 1988 presidential election, just one in two bothered to exercise the right to vote. But with the exception of the city of Chicago, the 1992 primaries plumbed new depths of voter turnout. The voters' unhappiness was also plain in the way 55 percent of Democrats told exit pollsters they wanted another candidate in the race. And 71 percent of them said they broadly agreed with Brown's angry campaign against what he dubbed "the new one-party system where the incumbent party always wins."

Mathematically, Clinton was virtually assured of the nomination, but he led a restive and unhappy army of delegates and party chieftains. And overconfident, he had taken a weekend off before the Connecticut vote to play a round of golf at a Little Rock club that had no black members. The outraged press and black comment made it, for Carville, "the most expensive fucking golf game ever played in American history." Brown responded with the obvious TV ad about race in Arkansas, denouncing Clinton as slick, shrinking his head to the size of a golf ball, and driving it away. Tired, depressed, and prey to self-pity, Clinton snapped and shouted at his staff. Then he went on TV and admitted that he had tried marijuana as a student, "but I didn't inhale." Friends from his Oxford days, who knew that marijuana was rare and most students smoked hashish crumbled into a conventional cigarette, knew it was true. He was allergic to tobacco smoke. But it hardly sounded convincing.

The psychological dynamics of a presidential campaign are extraordinary. The campaign staff become manic-depressives, veering from euphoria to despair. In a sense, that is their job, just as the candidate must try to stay above their moods, to be the focus of calm. Clinton, fascinated by polls and the minutiae of campaigning, was incapable of this. At times, he was the most manic-depressive of them all, and in the days before the New York primary, he was at his best and his worst.

Harold Ickes, Clinton's manager in New York State, was seriously frightened that Brown would win it. His innovative telephone fundraising was bringing in $100,000 a day. The polls showed him ahead in Wisconsin, and rising fast in New York, a state that greeted Clinton with characteristic pugnacity. "Bubba Stinks," said the placard at a Brooklyn rally for Clinton on the Sunday before the poll. That was the quietest protest Bubba Clinton had met so far. His New York campaigning schedule was ambushed by black activists protesting his golf game at the all-white club; by gay activists demanding he lead the fight for AIDS research; by Italians protesting his incautious remark about Mario Cuomo "acting like a Mafioso"; and by the tabloid *New York Post* trumpeting its "Most New Yorkers Believe Clinton Can't Be Trusted" poll.

"Governor Moonbeam and Slick Willie" was the welcome given to the White House hopefuls by the *Daily News.* The brashest voice in the city, *Newsday* columnist Jimmy Breslin, gave Clinton his own inimitable endorsement, writing: "He is described as being slick, scheming, shameless and slimy; that he has the self-control of a tomcat; that he is a fraud and a fake, and a man who long ago metabolized simple ambition into desperate greed. He is also vulgar, garish and, of course, a liar."

New York, called "the Lebanon of American politics" by Jerry Brown, had never been kind to southern politicians. Jimmy Carter lost in the primaries of 1976 and 1980; and in 1988, Tennessee's senator Albert Gore virtually took out Israeli citizenship but was still flattened by the New York vote. New York was a confusing place to campaign in, as Clinton's advance team found when they got to the Williamsburg section of Brooklyn to prepare the ground for the candidate's major policy speech on the Middle East. "Isn't Williamsburg mostly Jewish? This whole place looks Italian," muttered Clinton's man. Clinton arrived, junked his speech on helping Israel, and delivered his standard "Bring Us Together" speech instead.

That was the third sighting of Clinton's conversion to born-again Zionism. In Miami, he donned a yarmulke. In Florida, it worked. But in cynical New York, even the massed elders of the Conference of Presidents of Major American Jewish Organizations pronounced themselves baffled when he promised to open a "glatt kosher" kitchen in the White House. Then Clinton went to a rigidly Orthodox Brooklyn synagogue, where the women were sequestered behind a screen, and began, "This is a wonderful occasion for me, just like every Sunday night at an Arkansas barbecue." The campaign turned to David Ifshin, a director of the America-Israel Public Affairs committee, the main organization of the pro-Israel lobby. Ifshin, another veteran of the antiwar movement, had gone to Hanoi and broadcast anti-American rantings. He had undergone a conversion to the usefulness of American arms in the Yom Kippur War of 1973, when as a young volunteer on an Israeli air base he had helped unload American ammunition and resupplies. Ifshin helped persuade Clinton to make the key pledges on Jerusalem being indivisible, and then lent Clinton the mantle of his own potent credibility with the Jewish community. Ifshin was to die, tragically young, of cancer in 1996.

Clinton took the advice of Mandy Grunwald to ignore the conventional media and reach ordinary people on the nonpolitical shows. He went on the Don Imus morning-drive radio show, and joked about being a southern bubba. He went on the Phil Donahue show, which usually dealt with sexual oddities and confessional confrontations, and bluntly refused to answer Donahue's question, whether he had had sex with Gennifer Flowers.

"We're gonna sit here a long time in silence, Phil," Clinton snapped. "I'm not gonna answer any more of these questions. I've answered them until I'm blue in the face. You are responsible for the cynicism in this country. You don't want to talk about the real issues."

The studio audience cheered him, the rest of the media took up the story of Clinton's defiance, and the campaign staff suddenly realized that there was a way out from the relentless theme of Slick Willy and his girls. There was a greater hunger for reform, for political change, than there was for scandal and gossip. "We bottomed out on the sleaze," Grunwald recalled. "People really wanted something more—answers, directions, ideas. Change."

Clinton won New York easily with 41 percent of the vote, Kansas with 51 percent, and Wisconsin with 38 percent. That triple success gave him 1,279 delegates of the 2,145 needed to win. Brown came in third in New York, three points behind the write-ins for Paul Tsongas, who was not even campaigning. Clinton won Wisconsin by three points, and in Kansas, Brown finished fourth in a two-man race. Brown was trounced again in Pennsylvania, and with only California to go, Clinton was assured of the nomination.

It threatened to be an empty success. The party was not enthusiastic about him, and the opinion polls showed Clinton a poor third in a three-way race with Ross Perot and George Bush. Even registered Democrats were showing so little interest in the primaries that Clinton's victories rang hollow. Only 27 percent of New York's registered Democrats voted in the April primary, sharply down on the 45 percent turnout in 1988 and the 39 percent turnout of 1984, years when Jesse Jackson was on the ballot to inspire black voters.

Party elders like Mario Cuomo suggested that this was the time to rally the Democratic base, that the 40 percent of voters who almost always voted Democrat would be enough to win in a three-way race. Cuomo might have done it, inspiring them again with a new passion for the old religion of the New Deal and Great Society. This was not Clinton; it ran against everything he claimed to stand for as a New Democrat. But he was no longer sure, after so many months on the defensive, what he was campaigning on. His reserves of adrenaline were exhausted, after so long living for each new moment of press conference and speech and media appearance, without time to sit back and reflect and think about the way ahead.

His oldest friends realized they had to do more than cheer him up. Robert Reich wrote him a long letter, warning him against sinking into his own sense of personal grievance. Greenberg accused him of self-pity. Derek Shearer picked out some new detective novels, and told him to take time off and read them. The primaries were won, but with the candidate in a shape like this, they were heading for disaster in the real fight, against Bush.

Unknown to Clinton, the Bush campaign felt it was in similar shape. Fred Steeper, Bush's pollster, had been in despair since the disastrous New

Hampshire primary. On Super Tuesday, he warned the president that in a thirty-day campaign against Clinton, Bush would lose. On March 11, he sent a memo to the Bush campaign managers, which said bluntly: "We face a 20-month recession, a 78 percent 'wrong track' number, and a Southern Conservative Democrat. In my mind, this is our worst political nightmare."

It is at this point that campaign staffs earn their fees. Awed by the presidency, Bush's team was unable to force him to adjust. Clinton's staff drew up a plan to reinvent their candidate, persuaded him to agree, and then rallied coherently behind the new strategy. They called it the Manhattan Project, and Greer, Greenberg, and Carville delivered it on April 27, as South Central Los Angeles was going up in flames and riot.

"This report of the 'general election project' recommends a fundamental rethinking of your campaign to reflect the new political realities and new phase of the campaign, and most important, to address the debilitating image that is dragging us down," it began. "The core problem of the Clinton candidacy is Clinton's essential 'political' nature."

The report went on to list the six main conclusions from a series of focus groups:

1) Clinton is not real. He is packaged.
2) Clinton is privileged, like the Kennedys.
3) Clinton can't stand up to the special interests.
4) Clinton cannot be the candidate of change.
5) Clinton's for himself, not for people.
6) Clinton's message-ideas are discounted.

"The campaign has to take radical steps to depoliticize Bill Clinton," the report concluded, and went on to explain how and why. Greenberg and Greer had spent days poring over the gloomy and often contradictory reports of focus groups, trying to understand why Clinton was not connecting. Greenberg had a hunch that while the political class knew about Clinton even before the primaries began, the public's first view of Clinton was in mid-scandal in New Hampshire. That was their image of him, a man constantly weaving to talk his way out of trouble. And in the absence of any countermessage, that image was taking firm hold. Greenberg tried an experiment, making a brief biography of Clinton with a few key facts.

Born into a poor home, widowed mother, public schools, standing up to a drunken stepfather, scholarships to Oxford and Yale, but then came back home to be a reformist governor who created jobs, built schools, and balanced his budgets.

Greenberg first ran a quick poll, asking the focus groups to list Bush, Perot, and Clinton in order of preference. Clinton ran last. Then he offered the biography, and afterwards ran his standard tests of Clinton's views and speeches. His first group was ten middle-aged, middle-class women from Pennsylvania. He polled them again. Clinton had gone from last to top in their preferences. Greenberg ran the same test on middle-aged men, blue-collar workers, elderly couples, and got the same result every time.

"Bingo," said Greer. "It's the magic bullet. They didn't know this guy. All we gotta do is tie down the American people and beat them over the head with his biography."

The Manhattan Project report went on to explain how to do just that. Two-minute film clips and a 30-minute Infomercial to introduce "the real Bill Clinton." It concluded: "We must begin immediately and aggressively scheduling the popular talk shows to introduce the real Bill Clinton. That includes the national popular culture shows and the regional radio interview and call-in shows. We should start with Johnny Carson, and move to Barbara Walters, Oprah and Donahue, Larry King and Rush Limbaugh. These shows must introduce these elements of biography, our principal 'change' message and the human side of Bill Clinton (e.g., humor, sax and inhaling). Our goal is to break the political mold."

In effect, Clinton's campaign strategists judged that they could not win with the candidate the public thought they had. The public had to be introduced to a new Bill Clinton altogether.

☆ 6 ☆

THE 1992 CAMPAIGN: THE GENERAL ELECTION

Bush and Clinton were winning primaries, raising funds, producing policies, building coalitions, and following all the other conventional ways to the White House. But they suddenly took on the bemused look of dinosaurs just after the big meteorite hit. The ecosystem had changed, and they were slow to adapt. The meteorite was the Larry King TV talk show just after the New Hampshire primary. Aired on the CNN cable network, it was seen by fewer than two million people, heard by rather more on radio, and it began with Ross Perot saying that he did not want to run for president.

Then came the challenge; if the people wanted him to run, then they would have to organize themselves to get him on the ballot in all fifty states, and he would answer the people's call. It was not till March 19 that Ross Perot made a conventional campaign appearance, a speech to the National Press Club. But by then, the bandwagon was rolling, with over a million telephone calls of support logged to a 100-line phone bank installed in his Dallas HQ.

On the single day of Wednesday, March 18, the phone company logged 257,139 calls. This followed Perot's appearance the previous day on the Phil Donahue show. This was the politics of narrow-casting. Perot was the first candidate to ignore the big news shows, to shun the classic 30-second campaign ad, to understand the fragmented new media and cruise for free through the myriad channels' hunger for product.

By the first week in May, Texan billionaire Ross Perot was ahead of President Bush and Bill Clinton in the opinion polls. This was not just because Perot was rich enough to purchase all the TV time he wanted in a political system that had become the best democracy money could buy. Perot hardly needed to buy TV time at all. He was a news phenomenon in himself, and something deeper was at work. Clinton won the Oregon Democratic primary with a comfortable 52 percent of the vote, but 45 percent of his electors told exit pollsters they would vote for Perot in November. President Bush swept Oregon's Republican primary with 76 percent, but 41 percent of his voters said that they would back Perot in the presidential election.

Perot seemed to be inventing a new politics of a postmodern media age. He fed the hunger of the endless channels of cable TV and radio talk shows; played the free airtime into the free publicity of news coverage, and turned the public interest into recruitment through his array of telephone banks. Surfing above the traditional political process of parties and interest groups and broadcast TV, he reached the voters direct at an extraordinarily vulnerable time.

All year, American voters had been yearning for a savior who was also a departure from politics-as-usual. They flirted with Paul Tsongas and Pat Buchanan and had a longer dalliance with Jerry Brown. "Take it back, America" was Brown's slogan, tapping the sense of national desolation that something precious had been lost. The process was psychological, as if Americans were dredging their nation's archetypes to find the new Lone Ranger, the honest stranger in the white hat who rides into town and cleans out the bad guys. The sense of national disillusion was acute. Even before the savage shock of the Los Angeles riots, a poll by the American Viewpoint Survey, held in the last three days of March, asked 1,000 voters if they agreed with the statement: "The entire political system is broken. It is run by insiders who do not listen to working people and are incapable of solving our problems." In a stunning vote of no confidence, 73 percent of them said that reflected their views. So did Perot.

Perot, whose personal fortune was estimated at $2 billion, give or take $500 million, had talked grandly of investing $100 million in his campaign—which was less than his wealth would earn in interest between the 1992 springtime and the November election. In the spring and early summer of election year, the fascination with Perot dominated the political agenda. In retrospect, much of the reason for this was the sheer lack of enthusiasm for either the incumbent president or for Clinton, who by the end of April had become secure as the Democratic challenger. Perot, rather like the Los Angeles riots, temporarily filled a political vacuum.

But his very success made him a target, and Perot had to strain to fight back against the Bush campaign's skill at painting him as an unstable conspiracy theorist. "Perot's paranoia knows no bounds," sniffed the White House spokesman Marlin Fitzwater, after revelations that Perot unleashed his private intelligence force of lawyers and investigators on George Bush and his family, as well as against Perot's more customary targets of business rivals, errant employees, and anyone who disputed his conspiratorial views on the fate of American prisoners of war in Vietnam.

The private war between Bush and Perot was a great relief for Clinton. But the assaults on Perot illuminated two intriguing new aspects of American politics. The first, the new role of a factor called "the negatives," followed logically from the way that the American electorate had become the most comprehensively polled and studied and analyzed in the world. Political professionals no longer paid much attention to the raw opinion poll data about the candidate the public would vote for on a particular day; they increasingly scrutinized the small print of poll data for the response to the question of whether the voter viewed a candidate favorably or negatively.

In April, when Perot was first seen leading Bush and Clinton in opinion polls in Texas and California, his negative ratings were in single figures. By early June, the CBS–*New York Times* poll gave him a negative of 20, and a CNN-*Time* poll showed his negatives at thirty. Private tracking polls conducted by both the Republicans and the Clinton campaign showed Perot's negatives around 35 percent, even before the bombshell about his private investigations of President Bush. Among the focus groups of selected voters, whom the campaigns studied with the assiduous attention of an intensive care team, this information sent Perot's negatives above 40 percent, the level that Lee Atwater had called "sudden death." Negatives above 30 were serious, above 35 were mortal wounds, and above 40, "time to look for a new job," Atwater used to say.

The problem was that both Bush and Clinton had also been hovering around this doom level. But why were all three candidates so unpopular? The answer lay in the second new factor, which promised to haunt American politics for elections to come. It was called "Oppo," which is short for Opposition Research, and there was an entire floor of the Republican National Committee building in Washington devoted to little else. It had on compact disc the text of every public speech Bill Clinton had ever made, a videotape library of every TV appearance, a computerized index of all known friends and acquaintances, with a special section marked simply "Oxford" and another marked "Anti-Vietnam Campaign."

Perot's own fondness for private intelligence networks suggested that he was well equipped to fight back. And the Clinton campaign had a similar, but smaller unit, beefed up by some sympathetic journalists who made available, for example, the names of six women they suspected had been romantically involved with George Bush. Neither circulated nor used, this was defensive Oppo, a political version of the nuclear deterrent, and the Clinton campaign kept this stuff in its missile silos as a warning for the Bush campaign not to go nuclear over Clinton's marital embarrassments.

But this kind of politically motivated gossip and rumor did tend to leak out in nasty ways. Journalists were assured, when Clinton was fighting for his life in the New York primary in April, that a national magazine was about to publish explicit photos of him kissing a young woman in a most intimate way. Among the choicer items floating down this Washington sewer were ridiculous tales of Hillary Clinton's lesbian experiments; Clinton's role in covering up the use of a private airport at Mena in Arkansas for cocaine shipments; George Bush's romantic tryst with a New York socialite during the 1980 campaign; and his alleged protection of another former mistress when U.S. Customs detained the British-born woman trying to smuggle in some expensive fur coats.

For the first time in thirty years of public life, President George Bush was formally confronted on live TV about allegations that he had committed adultery. He denied it. But with the election only 84 days away, what Bush's sons called the issue of "the A-word" was out in the open in a campaign that Mr. Bush wanted to center on family values. "I am not going to take any sleazy questions like that from CNN," Bush snapped at the TV reporter who was asking for his comment on a front-page splash story in the *New York Post*.

The Bush-Quayle campaign's deputy manager, Mary Matalin, said the *Post* story was "beyond a flat-out lie. It is total trash." She sought to pin the blame on the Democrats, whom she accused of running a "negative, trashy, sleazy campaign." The Clinton campaign smiled quietly to itself and said nothing. Once the respectable press like the *New York Times* and CNN became ready to pick up on the stories that used to run alongside the two-headed Martians in the supermarket tabloids, this scurrilous gossip spread into the serious public domain. It was helped along by the new phenomenon of talk-radio, call-in shows where literally anything could be said and often was.

For all this skullduggery, the next important shifts in the politics of the campaign summer were entirely orthodox initiatives from Clinton. Or rather, from his war room in Little Rock, where James Carville had been installed. Carville had four priorities. The first was to seize the political initiative, to make Clinton, rather than Perot, the focus of the media. Perot's use of unconventional media was an inspiration of Mandy Grunwald's, who sealed her rise from Frank Greer's associate to top media adviser by arguing that "in tandem with our high-road, serious speech effort, we ought to design a parallel track of pop culture national and local media efforts. . . . Moments of passion, personal reflection, and humor do more for us than any six-second sound-bite on the national news." Her wildest suggestion, an appearance on Rush Limbaugh's right-wing radio show, was turned down. But Clinton's sax-playing appearances on the Arsenio Hall late-night TV show and his courting of the MTV rock music channel energized his campaign and stressed the age difference with the grand-paternal Bush.

Carville's second priority was to impose a single grip upon the campaign, to coordinate the great randomness of Clinton's own mind and the blizzard of faxed policy advice coming from the FOBs. The third was to speed up the reflexes of the campaign, to ensure that no charge went unanswered in a single news cycle. An attack made on morning TV must be challenged by the midday news, and squashed by the evening network news. The final task was to ram home Bush's weakest point, the economy. This was not hard to do, because both Pat Buchanan from the right and Ross Perot from his new third-party perch were hammering at Bush on the same theme.

Carville plotted with great precision the weeks leading up to the party convention in New York in July. It would be the greatest chance to reintroduce their candidate as a new kind of Democrat, leading a newly revitalized party. This was not just a matter of political puffery. Now that all the votes had been counted from the primaries, Clinton had emerged, in spite of his personal problems, as a campaigner of unprecedented skill. He scored 32 primary victories, more than any other Democrat ever had. He won 52 percent of the total primary vote, the highest share since the primary process became competitive back in the 1960s. And despite a generally low and unenthusiastic turnout, Clinton had accumulated 10.5 million primary votes. By running everywhere, Clinton had piled up more votes than any previous candidate, Republican or Democrat, in the history of primaries.

Carville's first ploy, planned with Stephanopoulos, was a carefully plotted public snub of Jesse Jackson. His second was to extract maximum publicity from his search for a running mate. But given the potentially explosive factor of race in the United States and Democratic politics, and the edgy way that the Democratic candidates of 1984 and 1988 had dealt with the man, Clinton's ambush of Jesse Jackson was the more startling. Clinton publicly defied Jackson and the remnants of the party's left wing, denouncing black extremism as "filled with hatred," and the mirror image of the racism of former Ku Klux Klan leader David Duke.

As Jackson sat grimly silent at his side, Clinton condemned the "kill the whites" lyrics of a black woman rap singer called Sister Souljah, who had been an invited speaker at Jackson's three-day Rainbow Coalition conference at a Washington hotel. Clinton planned the confrontation as a defining moment of his campaign, insisting that the future of the Democratic Party could not be left in the hands of the minority vote of the inner cities. Clinton went on to challenge the "new political math" of Jesse Jackson, who claimed that the Democrats could win the White House in a three-way race with only 38 percent of the vote. This would have strengthened Jackson as the man who could deliver a big minority turnout at the polls. Clinton explicitly rejected this view, making it clear that he was going to campaign for the center.

"Pointing the finger at one another across racial lines—if we do that we're dead, and they [Republicans] will beat us, even in Reverend Jackson's new math of this election. It's hard to get a 34 percent solution or a 40 percent solution if the American people can be divided," Clinton said. He then contentedly watched his poll ratings rise by 10 percent over the next two weeks, as he pondered his choice for vice president. The polls and the choice came together, as pollster Stan Greenberg became the main lobbyist for the man who had once loomed as Clinton's rival, Senator Al Gore.

Clinton chose Gore while spending the July 4 holiday weekend in Little Rock, but held back the name for maximum publicity on the eve of the Democratic convention in New York. The Southern-Yuppie-Democratic ticket of Bill Clinton and Tennessee senator Albert Gore was entirely characteristic of the Arkansas governor, being both bold and safe at the same time. It was bold, in that Clinton nailed the Democratic colors to the mast of the new generation, the postwar baby-boomers whose formative political experience was the Vietnam War. It was bold also in ignoring the traditional rules, which call for a vice president from a different wing of the party and different part of the country, in order to widen the ticket.

The Gore appointment highlighted the remarkable new political power of the South. Perot came from Texas, and President Bush claimed to do so, although he was born a New England patrician. So all four could call a tiny patch of the old Confederacy their home, far from the traditional centers of gravity of American politics in the Northeast and California. All four liked to portray themselves as products of small-town, rural virtues. Gore's acceptance speech stressed that both he and Clinton came from towns where "they know about when you are born, and care about it when you die."

But the choice of Al Gore was also safe and politically conventional. A product of a Tennessee political dynasty, who went to private schools and Harvard, Gore was in 1992 a respected senator and political centrist, with sixteen years' experience in Congress, eight of them in the Senate. A tested campaigner, Gore served in the U.S. Army in the Vietnam War, and was one of ten Democratic senators who broke with the party line to support President Bush in the Gulf War. Hawkish on rearmament in the 1980s, and staunchly pro-Israel, Gore hailed back to the cold war liberals who dominated the Democrats' foreign policies until the Vietnam War.

Gore had announced that he would not run for the 1992 presidency, citing family reasons. He had every right to do so. In April 1989, his six-year-old son was hit by a car as the family left a baseball game, knocked thirty feet through the air, and spent weeks in intensive care, forcing his father to reevaluate his own life and career.

"The single horrifying event triggered a big change in the way I thought about my relationship to life itself," Gore later recalled. "He was motionless, limp and still, without breath or pulse. His eyes were open with the nothingness stare of death, and we prayed, the two of us, there in the gutter, with only my voice. Slowly, painfully, he fought through his shock and fear and latched onto the words as a beacon to find his way back."

That experience persuaded Gore to take up once more the cause of the environment, which he had dropped when the media simply failed to report it in his 1988 campaign. Gore put aside his presidential hankerings to research and write *Earth in the Balance,* an impressive book on the environment that nudged into the best-seller lists. Gore went to Antarctica to study the hole in the ozone layer, to the Aral Sea in the old Soviet Union to study desertification, and to the Amazon to watch the destruction of the rain forest. He even spent twelve days floating on a slab of the Arctic ice pack and living in a tent, after helping persuade the U.S. Navy to share its top secret sonar soundings from under the Arctic ice with the scientists. Clinton called the book "magnificent," and it weighed heavily in his choice.

Gore met his wife, Tipper, while working as a reporter on the *Daily Tennessean,* after his return from Vietnam. She was then a news photographer, and by the time of the campaign was best known as a spokeswoman for family values. The mother of four, she had led a campaign to require record companies to put warning labels on records with "explicit sexual or violent lyrics."

All three campaigns, Bush with his opposition to abortion, Perot with his refusal to appoint gays to his cabinet, and the Clinton-Gore ticket, were playing different themes of the politics of social conservatism. But Clinton and Gore were playing them better, and brandishing his new vice-presidential candidate for the voters, Clinton headed for his party's convention in New York with an explosive new power. The week before Clinton picked Gore, he was level with Bush and Perot. The day he arrived in New York, ABC-TV was collating a poll with a stunning result: Clinton-Gore at 45 percent, Bush at 28 percent, Perot at 20 percent. With the huge success of the convention, capped by Perot's decision to withdraw from the race, Clinton's lead was to grow even further.

The astonishing ascents and plunges of the opinion polls over the previous two years were highly unusual. The polling electorate had traditionally been far more stable, as one might expect from a political system that had no by-elections to register spasms of protest and warning. But that had begun to change, as if the straitjacket of polling caution had been sliced open by the soaring popularity that took President Bush up to a dizzily unprecedented 90 percent approval just after the Gulf War. This was unsustainable, and began to droop in the summer as the recession returned.

The volatility then became a constant. Bill Clinton plunged to 17 percent approval in February, when the scandals broke around him and rose to 61 percent approval in July. In the two short weeks that saw his choice of Senator Al Gore as running mate, the Democratic convention in New York, and the withdrawal of Ross Perot, the number of people who told pollsters they would vote for Clinton more than doubled from 29 to 62 percent. The poll gyrations were intensified by the new wild card of Ross Perot. Between February 18, when he first spoke of running and his peak in June when he led both Bush and Clinton in the polls, Perot went from nowhere to 40 percent, and then plunged back to 20 percent in July before pulling out of the race. The main reason, he said, was that Clinton's performance at the New York convention had finally persuaded him the Democrats had "revitalized" themselves.

Clinton's new Democratic manifesto contained a quiet revolution. The 1988 (Dukakis) Democratic platform had been based on the old religion: "We believe the strength of our families is enhanced by [government] programs to prevent abuse and malnutrition among children, crime, dropouts and pregnancy among teenagers." Clinton's 1992 manifesto rejected "the old notion that there is a program for every problem. . . . People who bring children into this world have a responsibility to care for them, and give them values, motivation and discipline."

There was a sharp difference between the two defense policies. In 1988, the Dukakis Democrats said: "We believe our national defense has been sapped by a defense establishment wasting money on duplicative and dubious new weapons." Clinton's 1992 manifesto said: "[Our] military structure for the 1990s must maintain the two qualities that make America's military the best in the world—the superiority of our military personnel and of our technology."

Clinton's 1992 version on wealth and power could have been written by Mrs. Thatcher: "We honor business as a noble endeavor. . . . An expanding, entrepreneurial economy of high-skill, high-wage jobs is the most important family policy, urban policy, labor policy, minority policy, and foreign policy America can have."

It was clear why Brown and his radicals and Jesse Jackson were so reluctant to rally to Clinton's New Covenant. But there were other reasons, and one of them was the stretched limousine hired for the New York convention by Tommy Boggs, of the Washington law and lobbying firm of which the Democratic Party chairman, Ron Brown, was also a partner. On convention eve it was parked outside an expensive place called Tatou, where Boggs was hosting a lavish affair for Brown. The next night the limo was outside the River Cafe, to honor Senator John Breaux of Louisiana, Clinton's successor as chairman of the Democratic Leadership Council. The banners of 21 major lobbyists, all sponsors of this party to celebrate the recapture of the Democrats by electable pro-business types, hung like feudal emblems from the roof.

On the Sunday before the convention, all the congressmen at the Democratic convention were invited to the country by Commodity Exchange, Inc., to play golf or tennis. Then Speaker Tom Foley, the Democrats' leader in Congress, had a party thrown in his honor by AT&T, Pepsi, and the Anheuser-Busch brewery, and then went to another celebration, courtesy of the Partnership for Plastics Progress. This put a slightly different complexion on the new Clinton platform's statement that "workers must also accept added responsibilities in the new economy. In return for an increased voice and a greater stake in the success of the enterprise, workers should be prepared to join in cooperative efforts to increase productivity, flexibility, and quality."

Evidently there were compromises to be made for Clinton's New Democrats. But Jackson finally came around and so did the custodians of the New Deal tradition, in Senator Edward Kennedy and Governor Mario Cuomo, because Clinton offered them an agenda that liberals as well as businessmen could applaud. Clinton's New Covenant contained the most ambitious program of public investment and expanded state services that the United States had seen for a generation: free college education or an industrial training apprenticeship for any American. The liberals duly rallied to the cause. Mario Cuomo gave the keynote speech. And with a tear-jerking tribute to the Kennedy dynasty, after an equally emotional reception for Jimmy Carter, the last man to lead them to the White House, sixteen years ago, the newly centrist Democratic Party sought the credentials of continuity and tradition. In a shamelessly sentimental display, the party feasted on the Kennedy myth. The children of the assassinated brothers, President John Kennedy and Senator Robert Kennedy, introduced a film of the two lost leaders. And then the newly wed Senator Edward Kennedy, aged sixty, cast the mantle of that former greatness over the party's new candidate, whose proudest possession was a photograph of himself as a teenager shaking hands with JFK.

As President Kennedy put it in his own inaugural speech in 1961: "The torch has been passed to a new generation of Americans." It was a scriptwriter's challenge to blend convincingly the stories of the super-rich Irish Catholic with the young Southern Baptist son of a single mother who depended on scholarships. But thanks to the skills of Harry Thomason, the old Arkansas friend who had become the successful producer of the *Designing Women* series, the myths were stitched together. The Democrats' skilled manipulation of emotions and images was plain in the irony that had this real, live convention of real, live people sitting back to watch a film. On the first convention night it was ten minutes of Kennedyana, and on the last it was twenty minutes of Clinton, as the television cameras filmed the delegates contentedly watching the movies. Free popcorn was on hand, as the delegates became just another audience, and politics blurred into entertainment.

Heartstrings were tugged, wallets were tapped, loyalties were commanded and dissidents squashed in the most disciplined convention the Democrats had staged in living memory. And it was all capped by the carefully crafted new myth of the candidate, humbly born and hard-striving, a meritocrat who remembered his roots and revered the values they had taught him. It was time to unveil the party's new champion, the reinvention that Clinton's strategists had demanded in April. He did them proud.

"I have news for the forces of greed and the defenders of the status quo: your time has come and gone. It's time for a change. This election is about putting power back in your hands and putting government back on your side. It's about putting people first," he began, in a speech that blended old Democratic sentiment with his crisp new message of tough love, in which there would be no more something for nothing. In an intensely personal film and speech about his own life, the trials of his widowed mother, his stepfather's alcoholism, his brother's drug addiction, and his own troubled marriage, Clinton offered himself anew to the American people as one of them. And in a calculated statement that the baby-boom generation was taking over, the convention ended with Clinton and Gore, their wives and children and party barons all dancing onstage to Fleetwood Mac's campaign song "Don't Stop Thinking About Tomorrow." And the old and the new were wrapped together in the phrase that called on the town of his birth to capture the promise he offered: "Tonight, I want to tell you as plainly as I can who I am, what I believe in, and where I want to lead America . . . but I end tonight where it all began for me: I still believe in a place called Hope."

Clinton and Gore charged from New York into an eight-state campaign bus tour to consolidate their 23-point lead over President Bush in the opinion polls, as the first reaction of most of Ross Perot's abandoned supporters was to turn to Clinton's promise of change. At the same time, the Clinton-Gore coach tour through the heartlands of America seemed to reinvent the art of campaigning, the first genuinely innovation in election tactics since the demise of the old whistle-stop train trips.

All this served to demoralize the Republicans. The *Orange County Register,* usually the most loyally conservative newspaper in the most loyally Republican suburb of California, ran an editorial titled "Stand Down, Mr. Bush." Published in the usually rock-solid Republican Orange County, where Bill Clinton suddenly led Bush by an unprecedented 18 percent in the polls, the *Register* twisted the knife, saying, "George Bush has failed every bit as much as that last notable failure, Jimmy Carter."

Bush had so few defenders, none of that core conservative support that sustained Reagan in the depths of the Iran-Contra scandal. It was not just the broken pledge on taxes, relentlessly exploited by Pat Buchanan, that turned them away. "It is conservatives and Perot voters who are the swing votes this year, and they just don't believe in him," said Paul Weyrich, who devised the mass-mailing fund-raising techniques that built up the conservative movement in the 1980s.

New York Republican senator Al D'Amato publicly raised the stunning question whether Bush should decline reelection for the good of the party. Then came the Field poll in California, showing the president lagging Clinton by the widest margins in California's polling history. The poll showed Clinton ahead by 62 to 28 points, and four out of every five former Ross Perot supporters moving to the Democrats. It also showed the Republican heartland of Orange County, which proudly named its airport after the patriot actor John Wayne, voting for Clinton by ten clear points. This was the stuff of earthquakes.

"There is no question in my mind that if the bland approach we have seen this summer continues, we are going to lose," warned Congressman Newt Gingrich, then Republican whip in the House of Representatives, a conservative who was sticking by his president. "If this White House and campaign don't change their approach, we are going to lose this election."

This panic on the right led to a new if understandable disaster, as President Bush decided to use his own party convention in Houston to win back the conservatives. Despite his vicious attacks throughout the primaries, Pat Buchanan was wooed back with the promise of an uncensored prime-time speech. In Houston, where the Republicans were drafting their campaign manifesto, President Bush mollified the restive conservatives by endorsing the party's sharp move to the right. The Republican platform opposed on principle any recognition of homosexuality, pledging to fight "any legislation or law that recognizes same-sex marriages," including the right to adopt children.

President Bush also gave his support to a new alliance with the Christian Coalition, as the Republican Party rallied behind a platform that called for a constitutional amendment to ban abortion. The Christian Coalition, the vehicle of TV evangelist Pat Robertson, controlled 28 votes on the party's 107-strong drafting committee. "The language on AIDS, education, abortion, homosexual rights, prayer in schools, and taxes is all being strengthened so we can telegraph a message to the core constituency that this is their party and that we want their votes in November," explained Ralph Reed, executive director of the Christian Coalition. Its views were, on some issues, bizarre. Pat Robertson's letter to his supporters in Iowa, explaining his opposition to the Equal Rights Amendment was a classic example: "The feminist agenda is about a socialist anti-family political movement that encourages women to leave their husbands, kill their children, practice witchcraft, destroy capitalism, and become lesbians," Robertson proclaimed.

The resulting convention in Houston may have rallied the conservatives, but it did little to redeem Bush for voters in the center. The very fervor of the conservative rhetoric probably offended them. Buchanan's speech proclaimed "a cultural war," evoking the Los Angeles riots to make it sound like the Battle of Stalingrad: "As the troopers of the Eighteenth Cavalry took back Los Angeles, street by street and block by block, so we must take back our cities, take back our culture and take back our country." Bush got a very modest "bounce" of around 6 percent in the opinion polls with the intense media coverage, and in the first week after the convention even that bounce seemed to erode.

In effect, the Republicans abandoned the center ground to Clinton, allowing him to purloin some of what had been their better lines. Bush's implosion was perfectly tailored for Clinton to exploit. Clinton's politics had been inspired by the old Democratic vision of John Kennedy, but he got his real political education in the Reagan years, learning painfully just how responsive American voters could be to the patriotic and feel-good nostrums that Reagan peddled with simplistic genius. This produced a fundamental and unsettling ambiguity in which Clinton instinctively thought like a 1960s liberal but felt driven to campaign like a 1980s conservative. It made for a difficult progress through the primaries, but an easier final run against President Bush. The more vulnerable the recession made George Bush look, the less Clinton had to cover his right flank.

The Bush campaign also proved, despite its Oppo research, too squeamish or perhaps too decent to go for Clinton's jugular. Bush personally squashed plans to make a 30-second TV ad using extracts from Clinton's tape-recorded conversations with Gennifer Flowers. James Baker prepared some hard-hitting attacks on Clinton for the TV debates, including one that said, "Governor Clinton has a problem. He's a programmed politician with a pathological pattern of prevarication." Fearing that it was as much tongue twister as slogan, Bush decided not to use the line.

The Bush camp had repeated opportunities to take the low road. Campaign manager Charles Black was advised that a group of former Arkansas state troopers were prepared to talk publicly of Clinton's sexual trysts as governor of Arkansas. "Nobody in this campaign can pursue this. You have to go to the press," Black replied. The troopers' story emerged in the conservative magazine, the *American Spectator,* but not until the end of Clinton's first year in office.

Campaign managers from Britain's Conservative Party, fresh from their unexpected general election victory in April, came to Washington to offer their help. In general, their advice to stress the issue of taxes was followed, but not the daring suggestion of a campaign poster to feature Miss Flowers, with the slogan "And now he wants to screw the whole country." The embarrassment, it was explained, would come with the legally required subtitle "Paid for by the Bush-Quayle Reelection Committee." The British assistance also backfired, once it emerged that officials at Britain's Home Office had gone through its files from 1968–1970 to see if any damaging material emerged from Clinton's Oxford years. Unofficially, the Bush campaign paid an American student volunteer at Oxford, Gary Maloney, $8,000 in fees and expenses to try to track down photographic evidence of Clinton in antiwar demonstrations. Maloney found some inconclusive footage. A campaign ad was made, but then Bush scrapped it.

The Bush campaign counted instead on the power of its twin advertising themes against Clinton: Trust (too little) and Taxes (too much), and on the return to politics of James Baker. A legendarily successful campaign manager for Reagan and Bush in the past, Baker had performed with distinction as White House chief of staff, U.S. Treasury secretary, and secretary of state. The resuscitation of the Bush campaign proved beyond his powers, however, even as the race inevitably tightened in the closing weeks.

But the relentless question of whether the voters could trust Clinton got steadily under the candidate's skin. Usually Little Rock or Hillary could talk him down. Not always. In the closing lap of the campaign, Clinton finally exploded one night in Louisville. "Every time Bush talks about trust, chills run up and down my spine," he rasped, his voice cracking from overuse. "The very idea that the word 'trust' could come out of Mr. Bush's mouth, after what he has done to this country and the way he has trampled on the truth, is a travesty of the American political system."

Despite the constant assurances of his pollsters that his core lead was holding in all the target states, and that he had simply to hammer away at Bush's economic record, Clinton repeatedly came close to panic. On the rumor that Bush was about to attack him on the Vietnam draft at the National Guard Association conference in Salt Lake City, Clinton diverted his campaign plane to Utah and prepared a counterblast for an attack that did not come. It was based on a formal affidavit from Colonel Holmes, the officer in charge of ROTC at the University of Arkansas. He charged that he had been deliberately deceived by Clinton. "There is an imminent danger of a draft-dodger becoming commander-in-chief," the colonel said, explaining his decision to break his long silence. Despite a complex operation to secure this affidavit, involving Republican congressman John Hammerschmidt of Arkansas and Wes Pruden, editor of the *Washington*

Times, Bush decided not to unveil this before the National Guard, and its later release fizzled.

The Clinton campaign had been alerted to the plan for the Holmes affidavit by a source inside the Bush-Quayle team. When trouble loomed, the Clinton team were always ready for it, even when the threat suddenly seemed to come from overseas. The prospect of Britain's Conservatives helping Bush do to Clinton what they had done to defeat Britain's Labour Party was taken very seriously indeed. Only one formal toast was drunk at the Clinton campaign staff party on the night Clinton won. It was to Philip Gould, and the Labour Party. The act of recognition was testimony to a political connection that became a key part of the last month of the Clinton campaign. At Clinton headquarters at the old *Arkansas Gazette* building in Little Rock, it was called the British Operation. It was activated in September after the chairman and deputy chairman of the Conservative Party campaign flew to Washington with videotapes and newspaper and billboard ads to show George Bush's campaign how John Major—despite recession and disenchantment with the long Tory hold on government—had pulled off his victory in the British general election in April.

To ram home the point, the Heritage Foundation, a conservative political think tank based in Washington, imported Sir John Lacy and Mark Fulbrook, director and deputy director of campaigning for the Tories. They went on to give seminars to the Bush-Quayle campaign staff and the Republican National Committee, and set off the first alarm bells in the Clinton campaign. Carville called in a volunteer who was taking time off from a lobbying job with General Electric's Washington office, Bennett Freeman, who had studied at Oxford. Carville wanted a study of both sides' tactics in the British campaign. Freeman wrote a nine-page memo, which was taken seriously but not given priority. Then Bush television ads began running, showing snapshots of families, individuals, and elderly couples, assigning to each a sum, ranging into thousands of dollars, which was allegedly what Clinton's tax plans would cost them. It was a direct copy of the Conservative ads in the British tabloids in April.

In Little Rock, Carville hit the panic button. Freeman was told to update his memo and get anything new he could from Oxford friends. They put him in touch with Philip Gould, communications and polling director in the Labor campaign. Gould flew the same day to Little Rock. By the time he landed, the Anglo-American parallels had become even more uncanny, with the sudden attempt to create a scandal over Clinton's student trip to Moscow in 1969. Gould's office then sent everything they could on a parallel smear over Neil Kinnock's visits to the Soviet embassy in London that had appeared in the British *Sunday Times.*

Gould's arrival sent the British Operation into high gear, warning that the new Conservative Party communications director, Tim Collins, had just been in Washington advising the Bush campaign, and that the Tory communications chief during the campaign, Shaun Woodward, had sent everything in his archives to Washington. Gould's first priority was to write the kind of attack plan that the Conservatives had used, and that the Republicans would use, and suggest ways to counter it.

"It is the last week that counts" was the first warning point. "Forget the plaudits, concentrate on the smears. . . . The Republicans are slowly building a reservoir of fear. Fear builds slowly, is hidden and only shows in the vote—it is a strategy of victory by stealth. Tax and trust are the only issues that matter," he insisted, and warned that the Bush campaign would borrow four more tactics from the Tories. They would say the recession was not their fault, but a global economic downturn. They would use the third party of Ross Perot as a Trojan horse, claiming that a vote for Perot was a vote for Clinton. They would say that Clinton would make the economy worse and, finally, they would bring back memories of President Jimmy Carter.

Gould recommended holding back advertising resources to cope. Forewarned and forearmed, with another special team set up to devise instant rebuttals to the wave of local radio ads that Bush began to air, the campaign felt in reasonable shape. That was, until the final week when Gould's memo of October 29 arrived on the Clinton plane. It said Clinton had to fight fire with fire. "The line that struck home was: 'Reawaken anger about Bush's record and maximize fear about a Bush second term.' Do to them what they were trying to do to us," said Paul Begala, who was with Clinton when the memo came through. Clinton launched his counterattack, with a barrage of TV ads that asked the voters if they really wanted "four more years," and the slide in the polls stopped.

The British Operation was an illuminating sideshow in that part of the campaign in which, in Carville's phrase, the two campaign teams "messed with each other's minds." Despite the serious investment of time and effort that went into this British affair, it was tangential to the event that transformed the dynamics of the race. With just 33 days to go before the election, Ross Perot decided to reenter the race. The extraordinary timing had one merit; it enabled him to take part in the candidates' national TV debates. And it rocked the nerves of both Bush and Clinton, whose always delicate voice had strained itself hoarse on the campaign trail. Hillary was reduced to spoon-feeding him slices of lemon coated in honey. In the end, despite a Bush campaign ad that showed a vulture looking out over the wastelands of Arkansas, and despite the inevitable narrowing of the opinion poll leads toward election day, the debates finally settled matters.

The second debate had a format, chosen by Clinton, which echoed the popular daytime TV talk shows—a single moderator roaming a large studio audience and offering them the microphone to pose their own questions. The interesting result was that this carefully chosen audience of uncommitted voters was impatient of the negative character attacks on which Bush had relied, and were not much interested in foreign policy, which Bush saw as his strength. Instead, these voters wanted to talk about health care, education reform, crime, the deficit, and the economy.

The instant after-polls conducted by the ABC and CBS networks concluded that Clinton, whose campaign had stressed these domestic issues, had emerged the clear winner. The CBS poll of 1,145 voters found 53 percent saying Clinton had "won" the debate, 25 percent gave the verdict to Bush, and 21 percent to Perot.

Alternately perching on his stool and then strolling down toward the audience to engage his questioner directly, Clinton appeared the most relaxed and most focused. Bush had one dreadful moment, which summed up his failure since the New Hampshire primary in February to convince the American people that he understood the pain being inflicted by the recession, or had any plan to end it. A young black woman asked: "How has the national debt personally affected each of your lives? And if it hasn't, how can you honestly find a cure for the economic problems of the common people if you have no experience in what's ailing them?"

The Texan billionaire quickly stepped in to reply: "It caused me to disrupt my private life and my business to get involved in this activity. That's how much I care about it."

Then it was President Bush's turn, and he began: "Well, I think the national debt affects everybody."

MODERATOR: You personally.

BUSH: Obviously it has a lot to do with interest rates.

MODERATOR: She's saying you personally. You, on a personal basis. How has it affected you?

BUSH: I'm sure it has. I love my grandchildren.

MODERATOR: How?

BUSH: I want to think that they're going to be able to afford an education. I think that that's an important part of being a parent. If the question . . . maybe I . . . get it wrong. Are you suggesting that if somebody has means that the national debt doesn't affect them?

QUESTIONER: What I'm saying is—

BUSH: I'm not sure I get—help me with the question and I'll try to answer it.

QUESTIONER: Well, I've had friends that have been laid off from jobs.

BUSH: Yeah.

MODERATOR: I know people who cannot afford to pay the mortgage on their homes, their car payment. I have personal problems with the national debt. But how has it affected you, and if you have no experience in it, how can you help us, if you don't know what we're feeling?

BUSH: Well, listen, you ought to be in the White House for a day and hear what I hear and see what I see and read the mail I read and touch the people that I touch from time to time.

Bush finally went on to try to answer the question: "I talk to parents. I mean, you've got to care. Everybody cares if people aren't doing well. But I don't think it's fair to say, you haven't had cancer, therefore, you don't know what it's like."

By contrast, when Clinton came to answer, he looked the woman in the eye, and said: "I've been governor of a small state for twelve years. I'll tell you how it's affected me. In my state, when people lose their jobs there's a good chance I'll know them by their names. When a factory closes, I'll know the people who ran it. When the businesses go bankrupt, I know them. And I've been out here for thirteen months meeting in meetings just like this ever since October, with people like you all over America, people that have lost their jobs, lost their livelihood, lost their health insurance. What I want you to understand is the national debt is not the only cause of that. It is because America has not invested in its people. It is because we have not grown. It is because we have had twelve years of trickle-down economics."

That was not quite the seal on the campaign that restored a Democrat to the White House for the first time in twelve years. On the Friday before the election, Lawrence Walsh, independent counsel running the unending Iran-Contra inquiry, filed an indictment against former defense secretary Caspar Weinberger. The accompanying documents, Weinberger's own notes, cited Bush as present at the meetings that had approved the secret transfer to Iran of U.S. arms in return for hostages. It was not a mortal blow, but sufficient to stop in its tracks Bush's slow rise in the polls. Dan Quayle, desperate to counterattack, tried on his own to say that Clinton's womanizing made him unfit for the job. Then Quayle called Baker to urge Bush to join the offensive. Again Bush refused to bend his own rules of acceptable politics, the final decision in a campaign that was shaped as much by Bush's feeble grip on power, as by Clinton's determined grasp for it.

George Bush became the first Republican president who failed to be reelected since Herbert Hoover in 1932, in another and far deeper recession. But that election had kept the Democrats in power for twenty years. In their rout, confronted by a New Democrat who seemed to have learned how to skirt accusations of liberalism, and with the end of the cold war devaluing the patriotic card that had served them so well, Republicans feared they could be heading back into that long barren wilderness of political impotence. And the jubilant Democrats felt that at last they had a leader who knew the art of winning once again. But in a three-way race, Clinton had won with only 43 percent of the electoral vote, against 37 percent for Bush and 19 percent for Perot. The New Democrat had won no more votes than the old ones, Mondale and Dukakis. A majority of the electorate had voted against a Clinton presidency.

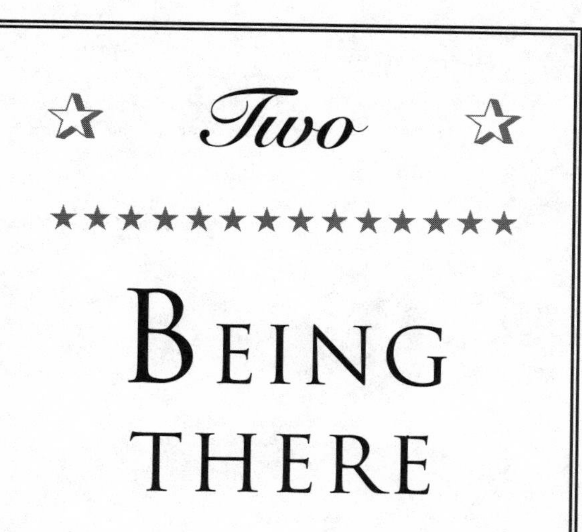

Two

Being There

☆ 7 ☆

TRANSITION

On the morning after the triumphant election night in Bill Clinton's governor's mansion in Little Rock, all was quiet. Clinton had got to bed just after 4 A.M. Staff and aides were tiptoeing to let him get some sleep and fielding the flood of phone calls. Then the phone in the private quarters, not the mansion switchboard, suddenly rang. A young staffer for Al Gore picked up the phone and heard the Kremlin's international operator say, "Will you hold please for President Boris Yeltsin."

The aide checked with Bruce Lindsey, Clinton's campaign manager and former law partner, who said, "No, let him sleep." John Major, prime minister of Britain, got the same answer, and so did Helmut Kohl of Germany. The next President of the United States was not available—call back tomorrow.

Clinton was delighted when he heard this before he went off for a morning of relaxed porch visits to old friends around town. The message that he wanted to send, to the American people more than to foreign leaders, had been delivered. This would be a president who would give foreign affairs a lesser priority than George Bush, who had loved nothing so much as his telephone diplomacy with his fellow heads of state.

But then Clinton told Lindsey to get his foreign affairs advisers to draft swift briefs on three looming crises which could distract him from the immediate concern of restarting the American economy and pushing his reform agenda through Congress. The issues were the threat of a trade war with the European Community, where the Bush administration was about to impose $300 million in punitive tariffs on European imports. The second was how to keep the Middle East peace talks going. The third was the faltering of democracy and economic reform in Russia.

The main task of the transition was to select the new administration. There was one transition office in Little Rock, and another in a nondescript modern office block on Washington's Vermont Avenue, where the thousands of resumés and job applications were processed, while Clinton's advisers simultaneously tried to thrash out the policies and the priorities they would adopt in office. Nothing quite as ambitious and far-reaching as this takes place in any other democracy, where the career civil servants hold a much tighter grip on the executive branch than they do in the United States. Indeed, the only parallel was the wholesale restocking of the Soviet state bureaucracy after the Moscow coup of 1991. The Americans do it with each new incoming administration.

Choices and options, the juggling of what Hillary Clinton called her EGG rule (standing for the criteria of ethnicity, gender, and geography), patronage and policy meetings—these were some of the delights of the presidency that Clinton most relished. But they were to cause him considerable and damaging early distress. This was not new. In 1989, President George Bush failed to win the nomination of Senator John Tower of Texas to be his secretary of defense. But George Bush faced a Democratic majority in the House and Senate. Clinton, having promised an end to gridlock with both the executive and legislative branches of government in Democratic hands, anticipated no such difficulty.

But the initial signs from Little Rock were disturbing. A very swift and serious tension emerged within 24 hours of the polls closing, between the Young Turks and the FOBs, who believed they had won the campaign, and the old Democratic Party hierarchy, whose private jets began filling the Little Rock airport even as California was still voting. The appointments that would define the Clinton administration were White House chief of staff, the secretaries of state, defense, and Treasury, attorney general, chairman of the Council of Economic Advisers, national security adviser, and U.S. trade representative. There was a new creation, a new White House office called the National Economic Council, intended to reflect Clinton's insistence that economics were just as important as the old National Security Council, which had been established in 1947 as a form of general staff to manage the cold war. These were the commanding heights of the administration, despite the time and effort taken to pick the secretaries of humbler departments, like Housing, Transportation, Education, Energy, and Health and Human Services.

The New Guard of the campaign staff reckoned they would have won if the names of the FOBs and campaign advisers Bruce Lindsey, Eli Segal, Mack McLarty, Robert Reich, Derek Shearer, Ira Magaziner, Robert E. Rubin, and Roger Altman appeared on those commanding heights. They all got jobs, but mostly at rather lower levels in the hierarchy. The appointment, by contrast, of Warren Christopher or Zbigniew Brzezinski or Robert Hormats, would signal a Clinton administration that would look comfortingly familiar, but depressingly like Carter retreads. Clinton being Clinton, most of the New Guard expected a compromise.

Despite the euphoria of their success, the campaign staff and the New Guard were right to expect such balance. Clinton had not won the Democratic nomination by avoiding the party's veterans. Warren Christopher had become invaluable after running the search process for a vice-presidential candidate. Tony Lake was Old Guard in the sense that he had worked in the Carter administration, but counted almost as a campaign hand from his devoted work as a foreign policy adviser. But the selection of a cabinet and top administration posts had to range beyond FOBs and campaign staff and the veterans of previous Democratic administrations. The loyalists of Arkansas deserved their reward, like Hillary Clinton's partners from the Rose Law Firm. Politicians had to be part of the mix, from the DLC staff who had provided Clinton his springboard, to governors who had delivered their states, and to the party's proud barons in Congress.

Apart from Georgia's governor Zell Miller and Colorado governor Roy Romer, who had played crucial roles in the primary campaigns, the only member of the party's political hierarchy to whom Clinton was really indebted was Democratic National Committee chairman Ron Brown. A former aide to Jesse Jackson and law student of Mario Cuomo, Brown was a splendid campaigner, fund-raiser, and organizer, and once Mario Cuomo dropped out of contention, increasingly devoted to Clinton. Brown wanted to become secretary of state, but had to settle for commerce secretary, even though the prospect of this corporate lawyer defending his firm's lobbying for Japanese firms like Toshiba before his Senate confirmation hearings rang warning bells in Little Rock.

Senator Sam Nunn of Georgia was also interested in the State Department, but he was very late to come on board the campaign, and lukewarm in the crucial Georgia primary in March. Nunn and the chairman of the House Armed Services Committee, Les Aspin, were each leading contenders for the Pentagon. The tension in Little Rock was widespread, but its immediate focus was between campaign chief of staff Eli Segal and campaign chairman Mickey Kantor. Although they were both frustrated when Clinton chose his friend Mack McLarty, each man had hoped to become White House chief of staff. Kantor, a Los Angeles lawyer who got to know the Clintons through service on the Children's Defense Fund with Hillary, was kicked upstairs during the campaign to run the transition preparation team while Segal really took over.

"My cabinet will look more like America than any previous administration," Clinton promised. He was by nature a coalition builder. Indeed, he half-offered a role in his administration to Ross Perot in the last week of the campaign. There was serious talk of inviting Bush's secretary of state James Baker to take some role in maintaining the progress in the Middle East peace talks, which he began after the Gulf War. And wisely, Baker's key Middle East aide Dennis Ross was kept on in the job. President Clinton had over 3,000 senior administration posts to hand out and was too astute a politician not to find some way of satisfying most candidates—FOBs, Old Guard, Young Turks, and Arkansans alike.

Clinton's mandate was not quite as sweeping at the Little Rock loyalists assumed. With just over 43 percent of the popular vote, it was a minority presidency, winning with only one million more votes than the unlamented Michael Dukakis four years earlier, even though the total number of voters jumped from 90 million to 100 million. The mandate was a touch tarnished, the world impatient, the economy fragile. The last thing Clinton needed was a row over the transition that got out of hand.

The crucial moment for the Clinton presidency came on November 15, two months before the inauguration, when he invited the three Democratic leaders in Congress—Speaker Tom Foley, Senate leader George Mitchell, and House majority leader Dick Gephardt—to dinner in Little Rock. This was Clinton's first opportunity to define his initial planning for the first Democratic administration in twelve years.

These were men who had been national names when Clinton was still an obscure governor, the great barons of the entrenched Democratic majority in Congress. By forcing George Bush to reverse his campaign pledge of "Read my lips—no new taxes," they could claim a major role in his electoral defeat. Powerful men, and at ease with their power over the legislative branch, they came to Clinton not only as political equals, but as party elders, wise in the arcane ways of Washington.

They also arrived claiming a unique knowledge of the new Congress, and in particular, of the 64 newly elected Democratic congressmen. This was, Foley explained, a different political generation, honed in the crucible of what had been in an important way the year of the Perot phenomenon, when the size and the menace of the federal budget deficit had become an overwhelming political fact. The new congressmen wanted deficit reduction, Foley explained, and so did he and Gephardt and Mitchell, although for a different reason. They had lived through the Reagan ascendancy of the 1980s, watched the national debt quadruple from $1 trillion in 1980 to over $4 trillion. From the time of Reagan's 1981 tax cuts, they had known the reckoning was coming. This was the time to prove to the nation that the Democrats were the responsible party, not the tax-and-spenders of Republican myth.

"We all know what '81 did to this country, and this is the first chance we have had as a party to fix this problem," Gephardt explained over the beef fillet. "We all believe in the micro things you have talked about, training, education, infrastructure, health care reform, government backing of high-tech research. But we'll never get to those things unless we tackle the larger economic problems. Difficult as it is, nasty as it is, we have to do it."

Clinton replied that they all knew that everything would depend on the state of the economy, and that this had to mean deficit reduction. But there had to be balance, between cutting spending on some items, making the rich pay their fair share of taxes, and investing in the future. The Democrats had to convince the voters that they were on their side, that they knew their priorities and could chart a sure course for the future. That meant offering hope as well as financial discipline, as he had done to win the election.

To Gephardt, this sounded like a campaign speech, and he suggested that Clinton had to understand the nature of the Washington process. The key post would be the director of the White House Office of Management and Budget, Gephardt said, the boiler room where the deals between Congress and White House were finally struck as the budget made its alchemical transition from promises into words and real numbers. It was vital to have the OMB run by someone with clout in Congress. Gephardt had just the man: Congressman Leon Panetta.

Success also meant, Foley said, using the extraordinary asset of Democratic majorities in both houses of Congress. This was the real promise of an end to gridlock. The core of Clinton's reform agenda would be safe in the hands of Congress, so long as Clinton remembered that Congress was the essential ally. The last Democratic president, Jimmy Carter, had forgotten that at times and wasted the asset. He was sure Clinton would not make the same mistake.

"There are people who will tell you to take on the Congress," Foley went on. That would be folly. Tension between Clinton and the Democratic Congress could only hurt the party at the midterm elections, and a reduced majority could only hurt Clinton and his agenda. Reform procedures by all means, Foley said, from campaign finance to the lobbying system. The new congressmen in particular wanted to do all that. But work with them, not against them. "You can trust us. We all want to make this administration succeed."

Clinton made one key concession that night, dropping his insistence on a line-item veto for the president, which had been a core commitment of his campaign. It would give the president the right to veto individual words and phrases and clauses of bills, rather than vote the whole bill up or down. Faced with Republican presidents, the Democratic Congress had become masters at the art of tacking controversial or even self-serving items onto bills that the president broadly accepted. Clinton, like Bush and Reagan before him, wanted that veto right. Faced with his party elders, he backed away. It was the first and perhaps the decisive concession to congressional leaders who were to prove unable, in test after test, to deliver the Democratic votes and majorities that they had airily promised in the dining room at the governor's mansion in Little Rock.

In retrospect, that first post-election dinner of celebration with his congressional leaders foreshadowed the disaster that would befall the Democratic Party in 1994. The end to gridlock, a Congress and president of the same party working in harness, had been a constant theme of Clinton's campaign. It was to prove the hollowness of his presidency, and the ruin of his ambitious program of domestic reform. The problem was not that the congressional barons were self-serving, or no more than politics required. It was that they were promising something they could not deliver. Foley was an impressive man, craggy in face, huge in frame. But he was not the leader to rally the 258 Democratic congressmen behind Clinton's program, to whip them through the committees and the votes, to cajole them past the blandishments of lobbyists and hometown constituents. Not one of the congressmen reckoned that he owed his election to Bill Clinton's coattails. Mathematically they were right. They did not have to face a third-party candidate, and so congressmen by definition came to Washington with over 50 percent of the vote. Clinton's 43 percent did not impress them.

At the time, amid the bustle of the transition and amid the interventions of Hillary Clinton, who wanted to impress these men that she too was going to be part of the policy-making team, in an evening of long and self-indulgent discussions over a round table in the small family room, the importance of Clinton's concessions to the barons of Congress passed with little remark.

There was too much to do. And with all the choices to be made about selecting his administration, there was also one other figure with whom Clinton had to deal, whose decisive role in his economic calculations was already fixed. Alan Greenspan, the chairman of the Federal Reserve Board, was America's central banker. The Fed set short-term interest rates and governed the money supply. Its constitutional role was designed to spare the Fed the day-to-day political pressures from the White House or from Congress. Greenspan's term would last most of Clinton's first term, and there was nothing Clinton could do about that.

His economic advisers told Clinton in November that they did not know whether in January they would inherit the usual recovery from the recession, coming six months too late for George Bush, or whether they would inherit a global depression. They were glumly persuaded that it could go one way or the other, which explained the nail-biting in Little Rock about trade rows with the European Community and the prospects for a successful conclusion to the Uruguay round of the GATT world trade talks. According to the airy estimates of "up to $200 billion in extra world trade," tossed around by the Commerce Department and the U.S. Trade Representative's Office, success at GATT could tip the balance against a global recession. And that in turn would tip the balance in favor of the Clinton administration having some chance of enacting its social reforms while convincing the voters and the markets that the Democrats were to be trusted with the economy.

Greenspan was invited to Little Rock on December 3. The two men had never had a serious conversation before. Clinton knew Greenspan was a conservative, who in his youth had been a devoted follower of Ayn Rand, a Russian-born novelist who believed passionately in completely free markets and in a currency based on gold. Greenspan had been appointed to chair President Ford's Council of Economic Advisers as a sympathetic Republican. Appointed to the Fed by President Reagan, Greenspan hated inflation, and was notoriously unsympathetic to the Keynesian views that Clinton instinctively upheld. Clinton could expect little help from the Fed in his plan to stimulate the economy.

Clinton's briefing paper on Greenspan contained two nuggets that intrigued the president-elect. The first was that while Greenspan might look like a dried-up academic, his escort around Washington was the tough and stylish NBC-TV reporter Andrea Mitchell, the journalist who had opened the door to Clinton's problem with gays in the military by asking him if he would keep his election pledge to end discrimination. The paper also noted that Greenspan may have been the single figure most responsible for George Bush's defeat. In 1989 and 1990, Greenspan had promised to secure a "soft landing" for an overheated economy by delicately manipulating interest rates upwards. He had failed. The soft landing had bumped hard to become the Bush recession.

The conversation between the two men had been expected to last for two hours or so, but it extended far longer and through lunch, as Greenspan explained the predicament that he and the new president now faced. Something unusual was happening to interest rates, Greenspan said. The recession was ending, and recovery was well under way, thanks to the Fed's steady reduction of short-term interest rates from 7 to 3 percent. But long-term interest rates for ten to thirty years ahead were not following the short-term rates down. They were stuck much higher, at around 7 percent, which meant that the markets feared future inflation. The markets were dominated by the scale of a federal budget deficit of over $200 billion a year, which had now become a structural fixture of the American system. That amount of regular government borrowing left less money available for investment in the real economy. This was a crisis of confidence; the markets did not trust the politicians. The only way to bring down the long-term rate was to convince the markets that the era of budget deficits would end. Once convinced, the market would deliver lower interest rates

Other children "used to come round to watch him think," went the local legend. The adults of Hope thought Mack McLarty would become the politician, and that Billy Blithe would grow up to be a golden-tongued preacher.

Arkansas Post Card Company

All photos courtesy of AP/Wide World Photos, except as noted.

Reuters/Family/Jeff Mitchell/ARCHIVE PHOTOS

The first dysfunctional family in 1959: Bill at age 13 with his mother, Virginia, and half-brother, Roger.

Senator George McGovern's 1972 presidential campaign: a touchdown at Little Rock airport by the Democratic candidate and face time for the young volunteer Bill Clinton. On the right, Joe Purcell, chairman of the state Democratic party.

Arkansas Democrat Gazette

Sharing the good news: Bill Clinton and Hillary at the church service preceding his inauguration as governor, Little Rock, January 1979.

The future First Couple make their entrance to President Carter's White House dinner for the nation's governors in 1979. Clinton is the youngest of them all.

A much younger Tom Brokaw interviews a much younger Governor Clinton on the *Today* show in 1980. Robert Redford had just released the film *Brubaker,* which was highly critical of Arkansas prison conditions.

The comeback campaign of 1982: a carefully casual Bill Clinton challenges the Republican incumbent, Governor Frank White, to a debate.

Reelection and vindication, 1982: Bill's triumph and Hillary's palpable transformation.

Clinton in uniform as commander in chief of the Arkansas National Guard, observing missile firing by Troop E of the 151st Cavalry at Fort Chaffee, 1983.

A toe in the Washington water: testifying before the Senate Subcommittee on Taxation and Debt Management, May 1983.

Just another Democratic primary voter: Governor Clinton and his daughter, Chelsea, then 6, at a polling booth in Little Rock, May 1986.

The two most prominent Arkansans, Sam Walton of Wal-Mart and Governor Clinton, as Walton presents the pledge by the Arkansas Business Council to support higher taxes to finance education reforms, 1988.

Preparing for takeoff: a rare portrait of a double jogging just before Governor Clinton began his hugely successful bus trip through the Midwest, July 1992

The candidate makes a pass in public: a carefully staged moment on the campaign trail, October 1992. Receiver Al Gore proved fit enough to run and make the catch, but as usual is out of the picture.

Walk on the wild side: Bill and Boris at their first summit in Vancouver, April 1993. Yeltsin spoke no English, and Clinton no Russian. They exchanged some words in broken German.

It's communication, stupid. George Stephanopoulos feeds the beast, painfully learning the difference between spinning the press during a campaign briefing for the hungry White House press corps.

Vince Foster of Hope, Arkansas, partner in the Rose law firm and deputy counsel at the White House, from January 1993 until his suicide six months later.

The president at 47, a figure who suggests a classic Clintonian compromise between the duties of jogging and the lifelong temptations of food, which date back to his childhood addiction to peanut butter and banana sandwiches.

The handshake that remains the keystone of Bill Clinton's claim to be the world's peacemaker: Israel and Palestine finally achieve peace on the White House lawn, September 13, 1993.

Camouflage Bill: the president as duck hunter, Taylor Island, Maryland, December 27, 1993.

Aw shucks! The Arkansas country boy convenes the first Pacific Rim summit, Blake Island, Washington, November 1993.

Mobbed in Moscow: President Clinton in a Russian *shapka* in his triumphant return to Red Square in January 1994. He had last seen it as a student in 1969.

(Top row, left to right)
Harold Ickes, deputy White House chief of staff;
Bruce Lindsey, presidential counsel;
Bernard Nussbaum, White House counsel.

(Middle row, left to right)
Mark Gearan, White House director
of communications;
Lisa Caputo, press secretary to the First Lady;
Roger Altman, deputy secretary
of the U.S. Treasury.

(Right)
Maggie Williams, chief of staff to the First Lady.

Washington Times

At bay: The shadows advance upon the First Lady in what could be a still from a German expressionist movie of the 1920s. She has just emerged from nearly four hours of questioning by the Whitewater grand jury, January 1996.

The McDougals—Jim and his ex-wife, Susan—once the golden couple of Arkansas, now tarnished and on trial in Little Rock, March 1996.

and thus improve the prospects for the U.S. economy incomparably more than any short-term stimulus could possibly do.

"We can do business," Clinton told Gore after the meeting, which had left him fascinated and impressed, and optimistic. Clinton had referred to his campaign pledge to halve the budget deficit by growing the economy. If that could be credibly put in motion, Greenspan had told him, the long-term rates would drop and the economy would grow at a strong sustainable rate. If not, then any short-term stimulus could result in a renewed recession in 1995 or so. Greenspan did not have to spell out the key date in Clinton's head, of his reelection challenge in 1996. The message was clear enough, and Clinton filed away the crucial implication for his economic plans: deficit reduction would do the economy—and him—more good than the immediate stimulus package he had been planning.

Then it was back to the transition process, whose personalities turned out to be very different from the administration itself. Al From was appointed head of domestic policy for the Clinton transition team. This was taken as a signal that Clinton would govern in the centrist spirit of the Democratic Leadership Council. Two days after the election, Al From was in Bill Clinton's office in Little Rock with a strange request. "Just walk out the hallway with me so the photographers catch us—it's worth a million bucks in fund-raising to me," From said. "I'll do better than that, Al," said Clinton, putting his arm around the burly director of the DLC as they posed for the cameras.

From's deputy in the transition team was Bruce Reed, yet another of the Rhodes scholars around Clinton, another DLC staffer who was Al Gore's speechwriter and the issues director of the Clinton campaign. From and Reed were widely expected to move smoothly from the transition office into the domestic policy office at the White House in what would amount to a DLC takeover of Clinton's domestic agenda. This did not happen. From did not move on from the transition team to the administration itself, but remained at the DLC. Reed became a deputy in the domestic policy staff at the White House, where he was joined by the DLC's favorite academic sociologist, Dr. William A. Galston. Elaine Kamarck, a welfare reform expert at the DLC, joined Vice President Gore's staff. But overall, the DLC was not prominently represented in Clinton's administration.

The first round of senior appointments to the new Clinton administration contained excellent news for Wall Street, but disappointment for those who voted for Clinton because of his promise of a swift stimulus to revitalize the economy. The Greenspan influence was already at work. Clinton announced a markedly conservative economic team, led by Senator Lloyd Bentsen of Texas as Treasury secretary, which was expected to focus on reducing the budget deficit. The congressional barons had their way. The new White House budget director was House Budget Committee chairman Leon Panetta, and his deputy was the former director of the Congressional Budget Office, Alice Rivlin.

Bentsen had caught the national imagination in his spirited campaign as Democratic vice-presidential candidate with Governor Michael Dukakis in 1988. His retort to Vice President Dan Quayle, "I knew Jack Kennedy. You're no Jack Kennedy," entered American folklore. Wealthy and elegant, with the look of a more worldly Duke of Windsor, Bentsen was skilled in the ways of Congress. But he had also won Clinton's gratitude in the campaign by using all his Texan connections to try to dissuade Ross Perot from getting back into the presidential race. Bentsen failed, but Clinton never forgot the effort, nor Bentsen's tireless service as a "surrogate," ever ready to do another satellite interview for some remote local TV station on the campaign's behalf.

Two Wall Street investment bankers, both Clinton friends and fundraisers, were also appointed to key posts. Robert Rubin of Goldman, Sachs, a respected Wall Street figure of discreetly liberal views, was named special assistant for economic policy, a role Clinton said was comparable to that of the national security adviser. Roger Altman, a Georgetown college classmate of the president-elect and a member of the Blackstone Group investment firm, was nominated to be the deputy secretary of the Treasury. The appointments were calculated to reassure the markets, and to send a powerful signal that the Clinton administration would focus on the long-term structural problems of the deficit, rather than on any quick fix to spur job growth.

"If, come January, employment is substantially on the rebound, then obviously there is less need—there may be no need—to take immediate action," said Reich, FOB from Oxford days, head of the Clinton economic transition team, and named secretary of labor. It was the first warning that Clinton's economic stimulus package might not live up to the pre-election rhetoric. But the appointments made that even more clear. Expansionist and Keynesian policies could not be expected from Bentsen, Panetta, and Rivlin. During the election campaign, Congressman Panetta had criticized the Clinton economic plan for not adding up, and for failing to address the budget deficit.

"The first priority is to bring about a long-term deficit reduction plan," Congressman Panetta said in December. "And not from the point of view of a stimulus, but from the point of view of fairness, we will be developing a more progressive income tax structure in this country." Alice Rivlin, the deputy head of the OMB office in the White House, had also shown little sign so far of being in tune with the kind of economic thinking Clinton had voiced during the campaign. In a recent book, she had suggested that responsibility for some of the strategic economic stimulants like public works and job training should be transferred from Washington to the individual states.

It was all a question of balance. Clinton's old chum Robert Reich was given the Labor Department in order to realize Clinton's job-training promises. Reich was a great believer in government intervention in the economy to set strategic priorities and provide that infrastructure that the states and private industry often neglect. Laura D'Andrea Tyson, a Berkeley trade economist, became the first woman to chair the Council of Economic Advisers. Known as a "managed trader" who believed commerce was too important to be left to the free markets, Ms. Tyson won her spurs during the transition when she gave a very public lecture to the Institute of International Economics to assert that she was not a managed trader, but "a cautious activist" on trade disputes. "The United States is not the unparalleled technological leader anymore, so I suggest we think more like our competitors [in planning trade strategies] and they think more like us and take responsibility for developing multinational rules," Ms. Tyson said then.

The new year started badly for the president-elect, and not only because of the controversy aroused by his decision to spend $10,700 a year for his daughter to attend an exclusive private school in Washington. The most sobering news came from the outgoing Office of Management and Budget in what was still for the moment the George Bush administration. Their revised estimates of the budget deficit suggested that the structural problem was very much worse even than Clinton thought it would be. The OMB report found that even after the bailout of the savings and loan industry, which had swollen the budget deficit over the last four years, this deficit was going to be $20 billion higher than Clinton thought. Without new taxes, and even assuming optimistic assumptions for growth and employment, the deficit would be $60 million higher than envisaged by 1997, and would exceed $400 billion by the end of the decade.

"This sounds the final warning bell. This endless pattern of rising deficits must stop," Clinton commented. "It is long past time we replace this legacy of debt with a new era of investment and fiscal responsibility." These grim forecasts should have come as no surprise. On the campaign trail, Clinton had accused the Bush White House of massaging the statistics to make the deficit projection look better than it really was. But on the eve of the election, Bush's Commerce Department had released figures showing the economy growing at 2.7 percent in the third quarter. Clinton had begun to reckon that he was inheriting an economy in promising shape, finally emerging from the recession that helped put him into the White House.

The budget news also implied difficult times for Clinton's new cabinet. There was already an inbuilt tension between the fiscally cautious men Clinton chose for the Treasury who hold the purse strings and the new appointments to the domestic departments, where the money was spent. It was Clinton's job to adjudicate that process. Moreover, Clinton had promised in the campaign to pass an economic stimulus bill in his first hundred days in office. That was but the beginning. Clinton decided that he wanted an overall economic plan for his entire first term. He convened the first planning meeting on January 7.

That meeting was dominated by two statistics. The first was offered by Leon Panetta, who said the deficit was heading out of control and by fiscal 1997 (the target date of the end of Clinton's first term) would be $360 billion a year. The second was from Gene Sperling, thirty-four, a Yale Law School and Wharton Business School graduate who had worked for Governor Cuomo in New York and then joined the Clinton team to help draft the economic plans in Clinton's campaign manifesto "Putting People First." Now a deputy to Rubin in the National Economic Council, Sperling was a workaholic, and certified by Stephanopoulos as "a genius." Sperling, who knew them better than anyone else, had costed the economic stimulus plans set out in "Putting People First." They would cost $88.8 billion in the first year.

For Clinton, the meeting contained only bad news. Laura Tyson said that she did not expect robust growth from the current recovery, no more than 3 percent a year. Her new deputy, the Princeton economist Alan S. Blinder, warned that deficit reduction might sound politically popular and reassure the markets, but it would reduce the rate of economic growth. To cut the deficit by 1 percent of GDP, roughly $60 billion, meant taking that much money out of the economy, and would cut the year's growth rate by 1.5 percent. A crash program to balance the budget would take 4 percent of GDP out of the economy. This would cause obvious hardship for the pensioners, welfare recipients, defense industries, and others whose access to federal funds would be cut. The reward for this virtue would come much later, Blinder went on. It could come faster if the markets believed that the deficit cuts were genuine and the Fed visibly shared that confidence, and lowered long-term interest rates. But the markets, after the roller-coaster years of the 1980s and the accumulation of deficits, would be extraordinarily hard to convince.

"You mean to tell me that the success of the program and my reelection hinges on the Federal Reserve and a bunch of international bond traders?" said Clinton. Precisely so. Or as Clinton said later in the meeting, "So we have to pick up the tab for the Reagan-Bush deficits. They got elected by wrecking the economy and I lose reelection by fixing it." Again, Clinton was correct. The presidency he had fought so hard to win from George Bush was a poisoned chalice. Unless—and this was to be the essential perception that shaped all the forthcoming battles over his stimulus package and his budgets—unless he could take advantage of the one way out. It meant relying on Alan Greenspan, the Republican economist he had to live with, rather than Alan Blinder, the Democrat he had chosen. Blinder thought the markets would take years to drop interest rates. Greenspan had suggested, rather than promised, that their reward might in certain circumstances come much sooner.

Bentsen then intervened with a politician's cunning. Whatever battle Clinton chose to fight first, whether to stimulate the economy immediately or to raise some taxes, to carry out the investment plans of "Putting People First" or to attack the deficit, he absolutely had to win it. Washington was a city that gave respect only to people and institutions it feared. Panetta then chimed in with two more warnings. The first was that the Fed could hurt the administration badly by raising short-term interest rates, if it feared that the budget deficit was going to continue rising. The second was that Clinton had to understand the new mood of Congress after the Perot campaign. If Clinton did not show results fast, this was a Congress that could pass a constitutional amendment to require a balanced budget. The Democratic votes were there to do that, Panetta insisted.

The meeting had begun shortly after 9 A.M. It ended just before 4 P.M. And despite all the disorganization and endless discussion and lack of control that was to mark White House economic meetings over the next few months, this one ended in a decision. Clinton decided to stick by his campaign plan to halve the federal budget deficit by 1997. But he did not accept as a target Panetta's figure of an expected deficit for that year of $360 billion. When he had promised to halve the deficit, Clinton had thought it would be $290 billion. His target was therefore $145 billion in cuts by 1997. That would mean subtracting $145 billion from $360 billion, aiming for a deficit of $215 billion in 1997. Round out the numbers, Clinton went on, and say $200 billion. The economic plan for the first term now had its firm baseline. By fiscal 1997, with the budget on which he would fight the 1996 election, the federal deficit had to be kept below $200 billion.

This was the first and most enduring decision of the Clinton presidency. It represented a victory for Greenspan, for Bentsen, for the congressional leaders Foley and Gephardt, and for the man they had recommended to run the OMB, Leon Panetta. It was also a victory for that shadowy force whose disembodied power had loomed over the January 7 meeting, the bond markets. And when the word of the decision seeped out to the campaign advisers, they concluded that the election victory they had worked so hard to secure was being stolen.

James Carville, Paul Begala, Mandy Grunwald, and Stan Greenberg had been the heart of the Clinton campaign. They had believed in him, bonded with him, suffered his rages, and engineered his triumph. They were people of remarkable skills and of passionate convictions. Broadly populist, Democrats because they genuinely believed that Republicans were selfish and that politics should be fair and filled with hope, they agonized over the new markets-oriented orthodoxy that was enclosing Clinton in its grip. Sidelined away from the prize seats that they deserved at Clinton's inauguration, Begala felt humiliated and Carville watched it from TV at home.

They were not isolated. Hillary ensured they were brought back into the inner circle, inviting them to the first Camp David policy weekend. Stephanopoulos encouraged them to remain part of the policy-making group, and to write scorching memoranda on the need for Clinton to stick to his campaigning guns. They were also well rewarded. Begala and Carville had a consulting contract from the DNC for $300,000 a year; Greenberg had $25,000 a month, with further payments for polling expenses; and Grunwald, charged with devising the media strategy to sell health reform, had $15,000 a month. But they were not people to be bought off, even if Clinton had wanted to exclude them, and he had far too much respect for their skills to do so.

The Clintons tried to reconcile the populist passion of the campaigners with the hard-edged realism of the economic team. The first Camp David session, in the last weekend of January, with two professional "facilitators" to smooth the way, saw a reconciliation. One of their ploys, to get everyone to relate some private or embarrassing event, inspired Clinton to recall that he had been plump and unpopular as a boy. Warren Christopher shyly confessed that he had a fondness for piano bars. There was much talk of the need for vision, of the twenty-first century, of big ideas and "the little people." It was all quite genuine, and widely mocked when news of the "touchy-feely" event leaked out to a media avid for insights into the nature of this new presidency. But a team spirit had to be built among the forty people gathered at the presidential retreat, the cabinet officials and White House staff and campaign team, and it had to be done quickly, even as they all grappled with the new jobs and responsibilities thrust upon them.

Greenberg was assured by Clinton, in a brief aside, that he would not "lose track of why we ran." Hillary spoke of the lessons of governing Arkansas, the need to focus on one well-defined and achievable goal, and the duty, on occasion, to be seen to challenge one's friends. Arkansas only took their education reforms seriously when they took on the teachers' union, she recalled. The problem they were facing now was different, and much bigger, but it had to be faced in the same way; people would accept the hard implications for change if they were inspired by a story to put it all into context. The story was that the Clinton administration was for ordinary people. Her "open day" for the public after the inauguration in the new White House had been a start. Reform of the health system and education opportunity and the new promise of a college education in return for public service would continue the process.

Begala was inspired all over again. "The Story" was being taken from them piecemeal by press leaks that portrayed great policy decisions as a tax increase here, an attack on Social Security there, airy sums of billions that had little meaning to the people who had elected Clinton. The Story had to be crafted, and Begala went off to write it, a memo stressing that "every day between now and the address to the Joint Session [of Congress], the president should be in the media with an economic event stressing cuts in government and taxes on the rich."

It had been a disorienting first ten days in office. The Clinton team arrived in the White House to find aged computer terminals with their memories wiped clean, the filing cabinets empty, and the telephone system archaic. The operators still used cables plugged manually into sockets on a giant switchboard to run the communications of the world's most powerful state. There was no phone on which Clinton could hold a conference call.

But the twin themes that were to shape the administration were in place. The deficit had to be cut. But the domestic reform program had to be preserved, reshaped into a single inspirational goal, and marketed as a Story. Almost without being aware of it, the administration's resolve was hardening into two approaches so different that they amounted to a bad-cop, good-cop strategy. The tough measure was deficit reduction; the kindly one was the reform of the health system, Hillary's particular interest.

☆ 8 ☆

THE DREADFUL START

The vast goodwill that America generates for each new administration enfolded Clinton's inaugural day and welcomed the shortest and most succinct speech of his orotund career. He spoke of sacrifice and renewal, of the years of drift and the urgency of repair. It was a sound, rather than memorable speech, filled with the pride of a new generation coming of political age, and thick with devotion to the American idea. The forty-second president was introduced to the music of *Monty Python,* which had been his favorite TV comedy show. There were eleven official and a host of more unofficial balls on inauguration night. The new president played the saxophone, and his fellow Arkansans filled the Washington night with their pig-hunter's call of triumph.

As he took his oath of office, Clinton inherited the supreme command of American marines still engaged in Somalia, an air force pounding Iraq, and a navy mounting a blockade of Haiti and cruising watchfully off the coast of what used to be Yugoslavia. "There is no clear division today between what is foreign and what is domestic—the world economy, the world environment, the world AIDS crisis, the world arms race affect us all. . . . Today, as an old order passes, the new world is more free, but less stable." Clinton set a reforming theme for a presidency already heavily laden with symbolism, of a new generation for the new world after the cold war. He promised to maintain "American leadership of a world we did so much to make," with a plainly moralistic tone whose intellectual lineage traced back clearly to Woodrow Wilson. "When our vital interests are challenged, or the will and conscience of the international community are defied, we will act—with peaceful diplomacy whenever possible, with force whenever necessary."

The inaugural day at least gave Clinton some relief from a trying transitional period, which was to make his presidential honeymoon the shortest on record. There was controversy over his nominee for the Commerce Department, Ron Brown, a lawyer-lobbyist who may have been too close to his corporate clients for comfort. And there was real anguish over Zoe Baird, the nominee for attorney general, who informed the Clinton transition team that she might be embarrassed by her technical crime of employing illegal immigrants to care for her child as she earned $500,000 a year as a corporate lawyer. The transition team said this problem could be managed. They were thumpingly wrong, and her nomination was duly and embarrassingly withdrawn.

Then Clinton got into a dreadful mess over his promise to end discrimination against homosexuals in the military. This had begun immediately after the election, at a Veterans Day parade in Little Rock, when the president-elect was asked about his campaign pledge to end official discrimination against gays. "Yes, I want to," Clinton replied, adding that he would consult with the Joint Chiefs on how and when to do this. He thought he could get away with a quick executive order, and ran into two formidable hurdles. The first was Senator Sam Nunn, chairman of the Armed Services Committee, who had some reason to feel aggrieved that he was not appointed to the Clinton cabinet, as secretary of state or defense. The second was General Colin Powell, chairman of the Joint Chiefs of Staff, who opposed lifting the ban as a matter of personal conviction, and took his opposition to the open admittance of gays into the armed forces to the brink of insubordination.

In a democracy, the elected politicians tell the generals what to do, and if the generals disagree, they may resign. Indeed, in an address to the Naval Academy in Annapolis on January 12, Clinton hinted at this, telling the midshipmen that if his policy was "completely unacceptable and strikes the heart of your moral beliefs, then I think you have to resign." But with his Vietnam baggage, Clinton was on weak ground in any confrontation with the military. With the support of his party in Congress, this would not have mattered. But Clinton was then given a brisk Washington lesson in the degree of respect required by a well-placed congressional baron. Senator Nunn made public his pique at not being consulted by the White House, and vowed to hold public hearings on it. This would give national prominence to what might have been a fairly minor readjustment.

Senator Nunn's attitude licensed a kind of congressional revolt against his party's president, quickly exploited by the Republicans. Senator Dole, the Republican leader, made snide remarks about Bill Clinton never having been in a foxhole and therefore not understanding the potential damage to military morale. The Republican whip, Congressman Newt Gingrich, seized upon the issue as a way to weaken Clinton's new coalition, using homophobia to steal back those blue-collar Reagan Democrats and conservative southerners whose votes decided the election. And the Republicans had a powerful new ally to hammer at the new administration as a new element in American democracy took over: the radio call-in shows.

In 1989, when the U.S. Congress discreetly passed itself a thumping pay raise in the early hours of the morning, talk-radio came of age, orchestrating a barrage of public fury. Politicians had since made a point of monitoring the outrage-meter of their local talk-radio shows, as a better way to judge what the constituents were mad about than any number of opinion polls or letters to the editor. The outrage bounced off the scale for Zoe Baird. And the outrage-meter soared again over the question of gays in the military. For a man who showed himself in the election to be good at reading the popular pulse, Clinton took an oddly long time to realize that he was affronting the popular mood.

"This is our time," Clinton declared in his inaugural address, to announce the arrival in power of the new baby-boomer generation born after World War Two. But the baby-boomers were also the yuppie generation. Zoe Baird earned $507,000 a year as chief corporate lawyer for Aetna Insurance. Her husband, Yale law professor Paul Gewirtz, earned over $100,000. They were rich enough to have bought qualified and legal child care. Instead, they paid the Peruvian couple whom they hired as nanny and chauffeur just $250 a week plus board—well below minimum wage. They did not pay Social Security or taxes for their employees, until a belated check was hurriedly forwarded on the eve of the public fuss. Zoe Baird and her husband were not members of that "forgotten middle class who work hard and play the rules," to whom the Clinton campaign had appealed. They were the overpaid yuppies and ubiquitous lawyers whom American voters had come to resent.

Zoe Baird looked troublingly typical of the Clinton cabinet, fourteen of whose eighteen members were lawyers. Hillary Clinton, who had earned some $200,000 a year with the Rose Law Firm, was another member of the breed. So was the new secretary of commerce, the black lawyer-lobbyist Ron Brown who earned over $750,000 from his law partnership in 1992, and was given a $1 million farewell gift by his firm. Vernon Jordan, the corporate lawyer who chaired the Clinton transition team, and new secretary of state Warren Christopher, and Zoe Baird's main supporter, were corporate lawyers who had earned over $1 million a year each. Robert Reich, Clinton's Oxford chum who was now labor secretary, was no lawyer, but earned over $500,000 in 1992 from the lecture circuit. Robert Rubin at the National Economic Council and Roger Altman, deputy Treasury secretary, were multimillionaires and helped to make Clinton's cabinet one of the wealthiest in history.

This level of Democratic wealth helped explain the corporate culture inside the Clinton transition team, which knew of Zoe Baird's potential embarrassment, yet reckoned that it would not be a political problem. Having withdrawn Zoe Baird's nomination, the transition office unveiled a new candidate. The name of Judge Kimba Wood was floated, confirmed to the press, and then suddenly withdrawn as it emerged that she too had employed an illegal alien and neglected to pay her Social Security.

The subsequent embarrassment not only overwhelmed Clinton's signing of the Family Leave bill, it threw up disturbing questions of yuppie arrogance inside the Clinton camp, which assumed that they could get away with a double standard toward the law. And it suggested that Clinton's yuppies were out of touch with the plight of millions of ordinary Americans who have to juggle jobs and children with far less money. It was a Republican kind of mistake, blotting the early days of the first Democratic administration for twelve years.

The result was reflected in a Gallup poll in *Newsweek* on February 9, which found Clinton suffering the highest disapproval at such an early stage of a presidency since polling began, with 34 percent giving him a negative rating. (His approval rating was 51 percent.) The only other president whose disapproval ratings reached double figures so soon was Ronald

Reagan, who scored 13 percent disapproval in 1981. It was a sharp change from the Gallup poll of inauguration week, which gave Clinton 58 percent approval, 20 percent disapproval. But then the president delivered his economic message to the joint session of Congress, a masterful performance that was widely praised, and his approval rating jumped to 63 percent in the ABC News poll. His disapproval dropped to less than 30 percent in the polls of Gallup (29), Times-Mirror (25), and ABC (26). The poll volatility of the campaign months had returned with a vengeance, rising and falling week by week, performance by presidential performance, reflecting mood swings among the voters that were taken extremely seriously by the White House.

Some of Clinton's performances were very good indeed. The speech to the joint session of Congress, much of it ad-libbed as Clinton took the risk of abandoning his written text, was extraordinary, given that its message was inherently depressing. It was a speech to explain and justify the decision to attack the budget deficit, promising a total of $490 billion in spending reductions over the next five years, balanced by $165 billion in tax relief for the working poor and in new spending on education and job creation and industrial and infrastructure investment. The deficit was to be reduced by raising taxes on the wealthy, and raising energy taxes for everyone, to reduce the federal bureaucracy by 100,000 jobs, starting with a 25 percent cut in the White House staff. It offered a much-shrunken stimulus package of $30 billion in job-creation schemes, barely a third of the ambitious plan laid out in Clinton's election manifesto.

And yet there were moments when his rhetoric seemed to soar, at least to Stan Greenberg, who kept a phone line open to a focus groups of voters in Dayton, Ohio, monitoring their approval line by line as they twirled little knobs that became hard numbers on the computer screen. "We need to break the old habits of both political parties and say there can be no more something for nothing, and admit frankly that we are all in this together" sent the meters racing up above 65. "We must believe in rewarding work" hit a 63. "We must scale the walls of the people's skepticism" touched 65 again. "The test of this plan cannot be what is in it for me; it has got to be what is in it for us" nudged the figure 70. Already the most intensively self-regarding White House, obsessed with its own weekly polling, it was now measuring itself from moment to moment.

The most important sensor of all was about to come into play, with unexpected speed. Hillary Clinton had chosen the two guests who would sit behind her on the congressional balcony to hear the speech with great political cunning. One side was John Sculley, the head of Apple Computer, one of the new generation of high-tech business leaders whose support the Clintons courted. On the other was Alan Greenspan, chairman of the Fed. Common courtesy required that he rise to join a standing ovation whenever the First Lady did, and a great deal of courtesy was required of him. The bond market rose the next day. The day after that, Greenspan appeared before a congressional committee to praise the Clinton plan as "serious and plausible," an endorsement widely reported. The following week, the interest rate on 30-year bonds dropped below 7 percent for the first time since they had been issued, fulfilling Greenspan's promise at Little Rock that stringent economic virtue could bring its own reward with some speed.

To reach this process had required prolonged meetings and arguments and late-night and chaotic sessions in the White House, free-floating seminars that lived in plates of fruit and cookies and take-out pizza. "This is fun," Clinton would murmur as the staff buckled down to another long night, churning through files to answer sudden questions about the numbers of people affected by a change in COLA (the cost-of-living allowance) or the effect of an energy tax on slowing growth.

Engaged in the numbers, Clinton often seemed to step back from the core political arguments. At times, it was left to Gene Sperling to challenge Secretary Bentsen on the need to remember Clinton's election pledges. One crucial promise had been to change the tax code so that the working poor did not pay income tax, but instead received a tax credit that would take them above the poverty line. The need to reward honest work had been a central theme of the campaign. But the "earned income tax credit," as it was called, would cost $27 billion a year, Bentsen objected. Sperling stressed the campaign pledge. Clinton let the argument unfold, and only later took Sperling aside and told him to stick to his guns.

Bentsen kept his eyes on the numbers, and was the first to understand that much of the debate was shadowboxing, or perhaps an educational process, for the president as much as for his staff. Clinton wanted to take this first opportunity to watch his team at work, arguing and trying to reach deals, as he assessed their performances and noted the issues for which they were prepared to fight. Bentsen noted that after all the late nights and the argument, the bottom line had remained rock solid. The goal from which Clinton never wavered was exactly the one that had been set on January 7 in Little Rock, a deficit in 1997 that would be less than $200 billion, a control of the deficit monster that would sway Alan Greenspan and the bond market.

The money ruled every part of the process. On the campaign trail, it had sounded so easy. Health reform would be a way to save money, to pare back the 14 percent of GDP the United States spent on health toward the far smaller sums spent by similar countries. They could afford to deliver health insurance and services to all their citizens far more cheaply, like the 7 percent of GDP spent in Britain, the 9 percent in Germany, the 10 percent in Canada. But whatever savings reform might bring in the future, to provide health insurance to the 35 million Americans without it would cost money in the short run.

Similarly with welfare reform, to move welfare recipients into work would require training programs, public service jobs, day care facilities for their children. "There must be a certain time beyond which people don't draw a check for doing nothing when they can do something," Clinton told a conference of state governors in February. "We must begin now to plan for a time when people will ultimately be able to work for the check they get, whether the check comes from a private employer or the U.S. taxpayer."

After years of recession, there were at least 30 million Americans dependent on various forms of welfare, although different definitions in different states made the national statistics unreliable. Of these, roughly half used welfare for less than a year, and then found another job. Half of the remainder stayed on welfare for over eight years. This core of 7 million people were the long-term dependents, the prime targets of Clinton's plan to offer job training, and child care while they trained, then requiring them to take whatever job was offered.

The scale of the problem was spelled out by Senator Patrick Moynihan of New York, chairman of the Finance Committee. He surveyed the children born in 1980 to point out that 22.2 percent of all white children and 82.9 percent of all black children would have been at some point dependent on welfare by the time they entered the work force. Clinton's plan of forcing welfare recipients into public employment would involve increasing public employment by at least 1.5 million jobs, Senator Moynihan warned.

This might be excellent social policy, but it complicated an economic policy that was already committed to deficit reduction. This was one of a series of wrenching choices that repeatedly confronted Clinton, forcing him to adjudicate between two unanswerable cases. The choices were hardest when his Democratic leaders in Congress were on one side and his own staff on the other. Panetta had proposed to delay raising the COLAs, which allowed benefits to keep pace with inflation, by three months. Over five years, this would save $20 billion. But in an Oval Office meeting where the plan was proposed on January 27, Senator George Mitchell said simply, "It's wrong." He spoke of old ladies living alone with no other income but Social Security. Democrats could not do this. The Senate would not pass it. Senator Moynihan went on TV to denounce the plan as "a death wish—let's get it out of the way and forget it right now."

Complicating the raw choice between saving money and squeezing poor old ladies were the personalities involved. Clinton needed the support of his Senate majority leader George Mitchell and his finance chairman, Senator Moynihan, to enact anything. But Moynihan had been one of the strongest supporters of Clinton's rival in the Democratic primaries, Senator Bob Kerrey. That put an edge on their relations, made worse when an anonymous staffer was quoted in the press during the transition as saying that if Moynihan got in the way "we'll roll right over him." Clinton had to call Moynihan to apologize and promise retribution on the aide (who was never identified).

And then Clinton was stuck with his pledge "to reform welfare as we know it," although the current welfare system probably owed more to Senator Moynihan than to any other individual politician. He would be the central figure in Congress on a reform close to Clinton's heart. But Panetta and Bentsen were firm. One major and costly social reform could be launched in the first year, but not two. It was health or welfare. A choice had to be made, and with Hillary's health reform task force being assembled, the choice made itself. Welfare reform was delayed.

To the experienced Bentsen, the grueling and jumbled process concealed a core of Clinton order, at least when he was present. For much of the time, the new president was on the road, still in campaign mode, running TV town meetings and talk shows. There was one in Detroit that was beamed by satellite to Miami and Seattle, with the populist message that the government's fleet of limousines would be slashed by half, and there would be no more subsidized executive dining rooms in government offices. This was followed by a Saturday morning call-in show for children from the White House. At the same time, Hillary began her road tour for health reform with TV town meetings in Pennsylvania.

These events were all crammed into the week before Clinton unveiled his economic plan to Congress. At the same time, the health reform task force was being hastily assembled. There was little time to focus. In the same period, there was a speech to the National Governors' Association on "the end of welfare as we know it," and another to pledge "a new deal for the environment" to the eco lobby. There was a trip to Seattle to promise the Boeing workers a tough trade policy of "No more Mr. Nice Guy—for the last several years, we have stood by while Europe invested $26 billion in the airbus to push American people out of work." Punitive tariffs were imposed on European steel imports, symbols of toughness announced on the eve of a planned visit by the British prime minister.

The Bosnian war imposed its own new and distracting flurry, as Cyrus Vance and Lord David Owen delivered their ill-fated plan to divide Bosnia into ten autonomous cantons. The prime minister of Turkey was told over the phone that Clinton "did not like it." Secretary of State Warren Christopher said that if it worked, "we are prepared to use our military power to enforce a peace agreement if necessary." But wary of any agreement that appeared to endorse a victory for the Serbian strategy of ethnic cleansing, the Clinton administration refused to support the Vance-Owen plan. Instead, in what proved to be the start down a slippery slope of increasing U.S. involvement, Clinton agreed to start dropping food and medical supplies to beleaguered Bosnian enclaves.

In the same week, Clinton announced his national service plan, unveiled his "reinventing government" initiative with Vice President Gore, and North Korea announced that it would no longer observe the nuclear nonproliferation treaty. President Clinton simultaneously tried to mend his fences with the military, visiting the aircraft carrier *Theodore Roosevelt* in what became a public relations disaster. Sailors donned wigs to mince and dance on the flight deck, and tell accompanying reporters of their disdain for a president who had avoided the Vietnam draft and wanted to impose gays on the military. "Regardless of the president's politics, we need to show support for the president," Captain Stanley Bryant told his crew over the loudspeaker system, serving only to highlight the president's discomfiture.

The day after those dismaying reports appeared in the Washington press, the president received a delegation of senators from western states. They wanted to talk about the administration's plans to raise the grazing fees charged to ranchers using federal land, and to sound some warnings about new interior secretary Bruce Babbitt and the environmentalists on his staff. These were issues the western senators had to raise. The ranchers were their constituents and this was their job. What they had not expected was that the president would agree so fast to "do something about this." Senator Max Baucus, a Democrat from Montana, was stunned at the ease of the victory, and after he reported back to colleagues on Capitol Hill, the word passed that "this guy can be rolled." After other meetings, Senator David L. Boren of Oklahoma, a fellow Rhodes scholar and initially a warm admirer of Clinton, confided to colleagues, "He just doesn't look like the president," and worried at the lack of deference that Clinton seemed to inspire in the loose and rambling meetings he favored.

These perceptions of a disorganized White House and a less than forceful president were swiftly spread in the media. When there were attempts at presidential firmness, they backfired. A conservative southern Democrat, Senator Richard C. Shelby, was singled out for punishment when he condemned the president's budget package as "high on taxes and low on cuts." Suddenly there were no special passes to the White House tours for his favored constituents. A NASA office, with a budget of $380 million, was deliberately moved from his state to the Houston Space Center. In a Senate where the Democracts had 57 votes and the Republicans had 43, and where the Republicans could delay legislation almost indefinitely by filibusters if they could keep 40 solid votes, the White House could not afford to affront many Democrats. Indeed, to maintain their legislative program and schedule, they had to be able to win over four Republicans at crucial moments.

And the Republicans were showing little sign of breaking ranks. Clinton passed the budget resolution, the agreement in principle to support his economic package, by 235 to 190 in the House, and 54 to 45 in the

Senate, where the Republicans voted as a block, with the support of Senator Shelby. This was ominous. Clinton had come into office with the Republicans demoralized by their defeat. Under Senator Dole's leadership, they had begun to recover. They had already won an extra seat, in the Senate runoff election in Georgia, and were poised to win another, for Lloyd Bentsen's old seat in Texas. And the Democrats were showing signs of crumbling. The energy tax was a great concern for Southern Democrats from the oil and gas states. Senator John Breaux of Louisiana had already warned that he might have to oppose it, and Senator David Boren was publicly fretting. The new White House chief of staff, Mack McLarty, had run the giant Arkla natural gas company, knew the senators, and sympathized with their objections.

But McLarty, like Clinton, had little experience of Washington politics, and the degree to which the White House lost control of legislation and policies as soon as the bills went to the Hill. An entirely different set of political dynamics then came into play, in one of the world's least disciplined legislative bodies. In most parliamentary systems, party loyalties were firm, held in place by the potent threat of expulsion or the removal of the party label, which would make it far harder for the rebellious member to be reelected. In the British system, this was called the withdrawal of the party whip, and it had no parallel in an American Congress where each senator and congressman was supplied a paid staff whose main job was to ensure the member's reelection, whatever the party might say.

Party discipline in the United States was maintained by patronage, the power of the congressional leaders to bestow powerful committee posts, or useful federal contracts from new roads and bridges to military bases. And the authority of the ruling party in Congress could also be applied through adroit manipulation of the rules of procedure. Senator Robert C. Byrd of West Virginia was master of both patronage and procedure. As chairman of the Appropriations Committee, he ruled the entire process of government expenditure. So when Byrd promised Clinton that he would enact the stimulus package, Clinton relaxed. This was to prove a mistake.

Politicians work fastest, if not best, at times of obvious crisis. But immediately after the president's speech on his economic plan, the GDP statistics for the last quarter of 1992 suggested that the crisis was over. At 4.7 percent growth, the economy was starting to recover very fast indeed. The argument for a stimulus package eroded in proportion. And the package Clinton devised, a ragbag of spending schemes that had already been half-planned, or were on the wish lists of Democratic mayors in the bigger cities, could hardly be called a well-crafted model of expansionist ideas. A parking lot in Florida, $250 million for new computers for the Treasury, a cemetery in Puerto Rico, funds for the National Library of Medicine, public golf courses, swimming pools, and rural sewage projects and an atlas of fisheries all jostled with $4 billion to extend the time the unemployed could receive their benefits.

Clinton had already scaled back its scope, from the $88.5 billion of his campaign plan to the $30 billion he announced to Congress, and now to $16.5 billion. This was a puny sum, not much more than a quarter of 1 percent of GDP, the equivalent of what America spent each year on video rentals. Its economic merits were questionable, even to Democrats in Congress; its moral importance to the White House, as a symbol of being seen to act on election promises and push its policies through Congress, remained as intense as ever. It assumed a new force, as the Black Caucus in Congress objected that the cuts in the overall budget would hit their constituents hardest of all. The stimulus package thus also became a way to compensate them for the pain in the budget, which gave the Republican critics another line of attack.

Senator Byrd, true to his word to the president, devised a complex procedure called an amendment tree to prevent changes to the package as it went through the legislative process. In effect, it tried to sidestep the usual amendments by locking a series of measures into a sequence of single votes that would forestall debate. Had the Democrats voted as a block, this would have worked. But Senators John Breaux and David Boren refused to cooperate, and disrupted the tree by proposing amendments of their own, insisting that they were carrying out the real objective of the president by controlling spending in order to reduce the deficit.

The set-piece events, like the first summit with Yeltsin at Vancouver, were competently handled. The two men got on, staged amicable walks for the cameras, and agreed on the broad outlines of an aid package as Clinton stressed his support for Yeltsin's bid to win a further democratic mandate through a referendum to widen his presidential powers. "Win, Boris, win," Clinton urged him as they parted. But Clinton hardly seemed to give the summit his full attention. Yeltsin spent one afternoon on a pointless boat trip around the harbor, drinking tumbler after tumbler of Glenfiddich single-malt scotch, while Clinton lounged in his suite, watching college basketball games and eating popcorn. After the truncated formal dinner, Clinton went up to his rooms for coffee with Sharon Stone and other members of a film company shooting nearby. One crucial message that Yeltsin delivered was simply not comprehended: that Yeltsin was under such pressure at home from Slav nationalists that he had reached the limit of his support for further sanctions or action against the Serbs in the Bosnian conflict.

The warning was well-timed. Bosnia was waiting for Clinton to fulfill his campaign rhetoric of air strikes against the Serbs and an arms lift for the embattled and outnumbered Bosnians. Fearing an eventual U.S. intervention, the Serbs accelerated their offensive, tightening the siege around Srebrenica and demanding the town's surrender. Clinton's attention was spasmodic, and his own top aides were quarreling furiously. Ambassador to the UN Madeleine Albright stressed that the war was a moral issue in which the United States must take a stand, a view quietly supported by Vice President Gore and by National Security Adviser Tony Lake, but bitterly opposed by the Pentagon. General Colin Powell was firmly against the risk of any military involvement without clear public and congressional support, a well-defined political objective, and a quick and obvious way out.

There was little time to focus on this looming problem. Others were clamoring for Clinton's attention. Howard Paster, the White House liaison man with Congress, began to sound the alarm over the fate of Clinton's economic stimulus package. The pace of events, tumbling over one another as the president's new team struggled to adapt, intensified yet further. Hillary's father suffered a stroke, and she flew down to Little Rock. The Congressional Budget Office announced that Clinton's budget estimates did not add up, to the tune of $60 billion. To balance the books, the congressional committees started to cut away at the president's planned "investments."

The ghost of George Bush then came back to haunt his successor. In his 1990 budget deal with Congress, when he had broken the pledge of "Read my lips—no new taxes," Bush had agreed to a new rule to cap discretionary spending in the future. For Clinton, that future was now, and the caps would prevent his spending any new money on his investment program unless he could find parallel savings elsewhere in that fraction dubbed discretionary spending, about a third of the overall budget. This was to distinguish it from mandatory chunks of spending, like interest payments on the national debt, Social Security, and entitlement programs like health benefits. The caps had been put into law as part of the 1990 budget. To raise these caps would require a new law, which would have to get past the Senate, where the Republicans wielded the constant threat of filibuster.

This was not complex. Nor did it come as news to the White House team. Leon Panetta had been a key player in the 1990 negotiations and understood the rules well. But Clinton and Rubin, and Labor Secretary Robert Reich and Gene Sperling, the strongest advocates of the investment strategy, came new to these Washington ways. On April 7, just back from his first summit with Boris Yeltsin, Clinton was staggered when Sperling described the effect of the caps on his spending plans. They would limit him to $1 billion of investments in his 1994 budget, $6 billion in the next year.

Clinton erupted. The whole point of his economic strategy was to make room for these investments in human resources, education, and job training. They were what his entire campaign had been about, to use the power of activist government to reconcile ordinary people to economic change by giving them the tools to meet its challenges. That message of hope was what had won him the election, what defined him as a Democrat who went beyond the arid numbers.

"We've just gone too far. We are losing our soul," he said, echoing the written memos that kept coming to him from Paul Begala. His anger was genuine, but it came spiced with political calculation. Without investments, he would have little to campaign on in 1996 except the memory of hollow promises. The anger stayed with him throughout the day. Having learned of the impact of the caps on his spending plans, he went to another meeting in the Roosevelt Room on health reform. There was already a dispute about the costs of the plan, with Panetta and Bentsen openly questioning the numbers coming from the task force run by Mrs. Clinton and Ira Magaziner. Al Gore was worried about the timing of unveiling the health plan, fearing a deeper logjam if it collided with the economic legislation on the Hill. Maybe it would be better to delay.

"Where are all the Democrats," Clinton exploded again, but this time with a colder, sarcastic fury. "I hope you're all aware that we're all Eisenhower Republicans. We're Eisenhower Republicans here and we're fighting Reagan Republicans. We stand for lower deficits and free trade and the bond market. Isn't that great?"

Then former prime minister Margaret Thatcher energized the campaign to help Bosnia with a blitz of TV appearances, insisting that the Serbs had to be stopped from committing genocide, and Senate and House leaders chimed their agreement. Then Clinton was hit by an internal revolt, a well-leaked letter from almost the entire Balkan staff at the State Department demanding U.S. military intervention, alone if necessary. The pressure on Clinton was intense, and then the long-standing siege of the Branch Davidian compound at Waco, Texas, ended horribly, as the FBI's planned assault became a funeral pyre in a fire that killed over eighty of the men, women, and children inside.

The holocaust by fire on the plains of Texas took place on April 19, and Clinton appeared to duck any blame for the FBI's assault with tanks that pumped hundreds of rounds of tear gas into the cult compound before the fire began. His new attorney general, Janet Reno, stepped up to take responsibility on April 20, and the next day Clinton hosted what became a diplomatic disaster, the formal opening of the museum to the real Holocaust—that of the Jews butchered in Hitler's Germany. Half the leaders of Europe were there as Nobel laureate Elie Wiesel publicly called on Clinton to stop the new genocide in Bosnia. And then through an extraordinary excess of security and lapse in protocol, many of them were left outside the White House in drenching rain, refused admittance by the guards. Finally British ambassador Sir Robin Renwick used his car phone to alert Tony Lake, and the reception proceeded, damply and sobered by the hideous coincidence of the commemoration of the victims of Nazism with the resumption of European tribal savagery in Bosnia.

On the next day, Clinton's economic stimulus package went down to defeat in the Senate. His first real test with Congress, and he had failed it, despite Democratic majorities in both houses. It was a dreadful way to mark the first hundred days of the administration that had begun with such high hopes. One most remarkable feature of those first hundred days was the degree to which the president had begun to resemble the man he replaced in the White House, George Bush. Clinton won his election because his campaign cleaved to the slogan "It's the economy, stupid" and was able to portray George Bush as a foreign policy president, out of touch with the country's domestic concerns at a time when the end of the cold war had reduced the rest of the world to a second-order problem. But distracted by Bosnia and by the fate of Boris Yeltsin's reforms in Russia, by trade rows with Japan and the European Union, Bill Clinton let slip that tight focus on the causes and the remedies and the political compulsions of the American introspection.

He paid too little attention to Democratic moderates in the Senate, and permitted marginal questions like ending the ban on gays in uniform to balloon into a damaging controversy. He paid even less attention to the Republican moderates in Congress, and allowed the Republicans to heal their own deep splits and close ranks against his economic stimulus package. This mattered less for the package itself than for the symbolic effect of his first political setback, and the sign that the gridlock in Washington was set to continue.

"It bodes very poorly for the taxes in the budget resolution and very poorly for the health care legislation," warned the gloomy Democratic senator Dale Bumpers of Arkansas, perhaps Clinton's most devoted ally in the Senate. The opinion polls were gyrating wildly, but all agreed that Clinton had dropped well below 50 percent approval, while ABC and CNN each had his disapproval rating nudging 40 percent. And the time Clinton had devoted to foreign affairs had little enough to show for it. Around two-thirds of Americans were opposed to any further U.S. military intervention in Bosnia or any further aid to Boris Yeltsin's Russia.

The sense of optimism about the economy that lifted the country in February and March, and helped undermine Clinton's argument for his economic stimulus, had been checked. The consumer confidence index, soaring at 78 percent in December, had fallen to 62 percent by the end of April. For the first time since the election, a plurality of Americans, 44 percent against 37 percent, said, "The country is on the wrong track." This mood index, run by ABC and the *Wall Street Journal,* had been the first poll to indicate in 1991 that George Bush was running into serious trouble. Republicans in Congress crowed openly that they were turning Bill Clinton into the Jimmy Carter of the 1990s.

☆ 9 ☆

CLINTON AND THE MEDIA

Throughout the 1980s, Bill Clinton's performance as governor was covered by one of the most aggressive and dedicated press corps in any midsized city in America. A circulation war to the death between the *Arkansas Gazette* and the *Arkansas Democrat* guaranteed furious competition between them, hard reporting, and harder commentaries. Broadly, the *Democrat* criticized Clinton and the *Gazette* supported him. That was politics, but on the matter of Clinton's personality, there was some striking agreement.

"His word is dirt," wrote Democrat columnist Meredith Oakley as he announced in 1991 the presidential bid he had assured Arkansas voters just two years earlier that he would not make, so that he could serve them for a full term. "He is a common, run-of-the-mill, dime-a-dozen politician. . . . The bleaters who care more for celebrity than veracity are basking in a false and empty light. They trumpet the basest form of political expediency, for they revel amid the debris of a broken promise."

The friendlier *Gazette* columnist John Brummett denounced Clinton as "timid, indecisive, wishy-washy, vacillating and a chameleon who tried too hard to get everyone to love him." And Paul Greenberg, editor of the *Pine Bluff Commercial,* the third most prominent paper in the state, was to spread the nickname "Slick Willie" into the national parlance. The term was originally coined, in repeated letters to the editor of the *Arkansas Democrat,* by Jess Crosser of Calico Rock, Arkansas, a reader in his seventies. Clinton had considerable experience governing under an intensely critical Arkansas press, but thriving and being regularly reelected just the same. He was not thin-skinned, constantly chatting with his press critics, telephoning them late in the evening, shrugging off the waspish commentaries.

"He always had a rocky relationship with reporters in Arkansas," noted Ernest Dumas, a veteran columnist on the *Arkansas Gazette.* "He tried to treat reporters like everybody else. He wanted them to be his friends. Remember, everything is personal with Bill Clinton. He never understood the adversarial relationship between politicians and the press. He still doesn't."

After the presidential campaign, he was confident that he could easily ride whatever snipings came from the White House press corps, as he had battled through the scandals that rocked him in New Hampshire. But first he wanted to get his own back. For the Clintons and their campaign staff, one of the highlights of their inauguration celebrations was a four-minute video they had made. It featured pundit after pundit, newspaper columnist after TV commentator, in recorded snippets of their appearances throughout the campaign.

"Clinton is not electable," intoned the first.

"He's going to get out of the race," said the second.

"He won't make it," pronounced a third.

"In November's general election, Clinton will be clobbered by Bush," another talking head declared.

"This guy is not going to be president," came another, and the images began to speed up.

"Bill Clinton is a loser," followed. And then faster and faster the doomsayers dashed to their climax.

"Unelectable."

"He's dead meat."

"Dead in the water."

"He's dead."

"Dead."

And finally, the dizzying parade of gloom faded, giving way to the new president and his wife sitting on a sofa, grinning fit to bust, their arms around each other, and rising on the sound track came the voice of Frank Sinatra crooning "Who's Got the Last Laugh Now?"

They should have listened to Marlin Fitzwater, the outgoing White House press spokesman who had served both Presidents Bush and Reagan, and who had devised a few rules of thumb about surviving in a city that contained over 17,000 journalists, of whom 1,800 were accredited by the White House. "The press can never be destroyed" was one Fitzwater rule. "Grovel if you have to" was another, followed by "Winning means convincing the press to let you live."

By the time Bill Clinton entered the White House, the American media had undergone a structural revolution. Traditionally based around big-city papers that remained resolutely local in their character and much of their coverage, the industry had developed a national media, beyond the weekly news magazines like *Time* and *Newsweek* and the national news programs of the Big Three TV networks. Satellite printing meant that once-local papers like the *New York Times* and the *Wall Street Journal* were now available on breakfast tables in the main cities across the country. *USA Today* had established itself as the first newspaper to be designed from the beginning as a national daily, and was selling over 2 million a day.

The media was also much faster to react. Once governed by the deadlines of the morning and evening papers and the evening TV news, there were now three, perhaps four news cycles in the day—breakfast TV, lunchtime news, the classic evening news, and the late news at eleven. The Bush administration had already learned to grapple with the challenge of reacting to global emergencies in the real-time spotlight of CNN. Like Ross Perot, Clinton had swiftly learned on the campaign trail to court the new segmented media of cable TV, from the Larry King show on CNN to the MTV music channel to playing his saxophone on the late-night talk show of Arsenio Hall. During the campaign, Clinton routinely used the new ploy of giving live interviews to local TV stations across the country by satellite. Properly organized, he could hit a dozen media markets within a single hour, all from one studio equipped with a satellite uplink.

It was a bizarrely disembodied affair. Clinton would speak into the black hole of a TV camera lens, never seeing the interviewer he addressed with such familiarity. A member of Clinton's staff stood behind the camera holding a card bearing the first name of the interviewer and the city where the show was being broadcast. The danger was to assume that the cameras were not rolling during the downtime as the satellite link shifted from the recipient in California to the one in Florida. In Denver, during the primary season, Clinton let loose with some vitriolic reaction to Jesse Jackson after being misinformed that Jackson would throw his support behind Tom Harkin. "A dirty, double-crossing, back-stabbing thing to do," said Clinton, assuming the satellite links were down. But they were not.

But Clinton's increasing familiarity with the new media, and the success of his staff in juggling his simultaneous appearance in dozens of media markets, created a sense of media overconfidence. Clinton did not need the pedestrian services of the traditional White House press corps, went the assumption. He could communicate directly with the public.

Immediately after the inauguration, Hillary and her friend Susan Thomases proposed shifting the press corps out of the cramped former swimming pool in the West Wing basement, to the separate Executive Office Building. This was vigorously protested and voted down, but the press corps's old easy access to the corridor where President Bush's press spokesman had usually kept his door open was suddenly closed by George Stephanopoulos. More frustratingly for the White House press, there were no press conferences with the new president until March 23, although he had held twenty-five sessions with regional press and TV, and appeared again on MTV. Two months into a new administration with no press conference was a record. By contrast, President Kennedy's first press conference came on his fifth day in office, George Bush's on his eighth.

Then, playing golf at the Manassas Club outside Washington, Clinton arranged that the press pool that normally accompanied the president everywhere be excluded from the grounds. The press then scurried to report that his golf partners were the powerful lawyer-lobbyist Vernon Jordan, chairman of his transition team, and his wife's Little Rock law partner who had become the Clintons' man inside the Justice Department, Webster Hubbell.

The simmering animosity between Clinton's handlers and the press corps could hurt him in the long run. The media leapt on the first census of the new administration, performed by the Associated Press, which cast some doubt on Clinton's promise of "an administration that looks like America." Two-thirds of his appointees were white males. And while George Bush's administration was 87 percent white, Clinton's was so far an almost identical 86 percent white. A third of Clinton's team were graduates of the prestigious Ivy League colleges, and 36 percent were lawyers. Clinton's cabinet contained more lawyers, and more millionaires, than the cabinet of George Bush.

Five days before the first press conference, Clinton made a joke that fell terribly flat. Addressing the annual black-tie dinner of radio and TV correspondents, he said, "You know why I can stiff you on the press conferences? Because Larry King liberated me by giving me to the American people directly."

This was true, but was also on occasion to prove a rude surprise. In his first town meeting, in Detroit two weeks after his inauguration, the president faced a skeptical audience, with people saying they voted for him because he had promised a middle-class tax cut, and where was it? Others probed him on the very issues he had left Washington to avoid, gays in uniform and the embarrassing botched nominations of the attorney generals. Interestingly, the American public, or at least the TV audiences in Seattle, Atlanta, Miami, and Detroit, all connected by satellite, turned out to have the same pesky questions on their suspicious minds as the Washington press corps.

The press corps became, in Clinton's mind, part of the antiquated White House way of doing things. He found it all intensely frustrating. "When we took office, I walked into the Oval Office—it's supposed to be the nerve center of the United States—and we found Jimmy Carter's telephone system. Then we went down into the basement, where we found Lyndon Johnson's switchboard. True story. Where there were four operators working from early morning till late at night. Literally when a phone call would come they would pick up a little cord and push it into a little hole."

Technology would let him transform the White House communications system, and in the process outflank the resident press and TV corps camped in his basement. The press secretary was a secondary job, subservient to Stephanopoulos, who was overworked as communications director, policy aide, and often called on to act as congressional liaison man, too. Stephanopoulos did not dislike the press, but he had too little time for the job. The press secretary, Dee Dee Myers, liked the press a lot, but she was kept out of the policy loop, and too often knew too little to give coherent answers. Press complaints about the situation were waved aside; the Washington press corps would take what they were given.

The White House concentrated on its satellite feeds to regional stations around the country, on inviting hundreds of local radio stations to pitch temporary camp on the White House lawn for special announcements. The White House would go online and send out its speeches and policies on the Internet. It would hold town meetings with the public, rather than stand to be nitpicked by reporters. It would set the agenda, and the dinosaurs of the press corps would lumber along behind, keeping up as best they could.

This proved impossible. The new and often lightweight media were no longer prepared to devote so much time to the boring routine of politics, once the thrill of election and the inauguration were over. They left it to the stalwarts, the wire agencies and TV networks and the heavyweight press of the *New York Times* and the *Washington Post* and the *Wall Street Journal.* Papers that were devoured on Capitol Hill and in newsrooms across the country, they set both the tone and the agenda for much of the rest of the media.

As professional reporters, they wanted to be fair. But coming from a proud tradition of independence and adversarial reporting, in which nothing that government said was to be taken at face value, they felt required to be critical. As Leslie Gelb warned in the *New York Times,* "My colleagues and I, like journalistic Dr. Strangeloves, are ready to nuke Mr. Clinton at the slightest provocation." Being human, the journalists felt aggrieved when they were not treated with respect, and they began to suspect that, by Hillary at least, they were actively disliked and distrusted. She did not take long to complain of "the bane of all people in political life, and that is unfair, unjust, inaccurate reporting that goes on from coast to coast, north to south, east to west."

She was angry at reports in *Newsweek* of tantrums inside the White House, of furious standoffs with the Secret Service and lamps hurled across rooms. She wanted privacy for her daughter, and found the press filled with stories of Chelsea telling her school to call her father for permission to give her some medication, because "my mother is too busy." Intent on bustling through her health care plans, she was outraged when the press reported and joined the snipings of health lobbyists that her meetings were held behind closed doors. The jibe by the *Wall Street Journal*'s Paul Gigot that the Clintons ran "the most secretive administration since Nixon" angered her deeply. Above all, she found the press everywhere she turned. The fuss over gays in the military had begun when a reporter pressed Clinton, live on camera, to confirm his campaign pledge to lift discrimination against homosexuals. In the midst of the early fuss over Nannygate, the failure to find a woman attorney general without housekeeping embarrassments, the second choice, Kimba Wood, turned out to be married to a *Time* magazine editor, who wrote a cold report on the White House handling of the matter.

More ominous still for the Clintons in their early months was the striking change in the way the presidency was being described. Hoping to repeat his campaign success on the MTV rock station, Clinton offered himself for an interview, was asked if his choice in underwear was briefs or boxer shorts, answered in good humor, and was stunned by the mockery of the reportage and the sniffs that this was undermining the prestige of the presidency. The Clintons were dismayed by the way the press mocked their chosen innovation of Clinton's televised town meetings.

The tone was perhaps best caught by Tom Shales of the *Washington Post,* probably the sharpest TV critic writing in America. "Bill Clinton was the warm-up act for Michael Jackson last night," Shales began, in his review of Clinton's hour-long town meeting, which was followed by a 90-minute special on the androgynous rock star. "Clinton stood on the stage alone like Elvis at one of his farewell concerts. . . . It was mostly a big bust. What Clinton did on that stage was not presidential. It was Donahue. Throughout the hour, a tone of tackiness prevailed. This looked like bad cable-access programming, only the President of the United States was there. Or was it, the President of the United States, sort of?

"Some people thought Ronald Reagan had a loose grip on reality. Maybe they should take a closer look at Clinton, who is still asking people if they have any ideas about how to deal with the problems he was elected to solve. He promised us a television presidency, but we didn't know it was going to be interactive TV, and that we were going to be asked to do a lot of the work," Shales concluded.

The Clintons were most surprised by the deep and ideological hostility of some of the press. The new media they had courted in the campaign included talk-radio, and there had even been suggestions of appearing on the Rush Limbaugh show to reach his audience of some 20 million listeners. But Limbaugh despised the Clintons as liberal, big-government, tax-and-spend wimps who could not understand the importance of keeping gay troops out of the foxholes because Clinton had dodged the draft. Limbaugh's radio show had greeted the new presidency biliously, reacting with suspicion to Clinton's inaugural speech, which opened with the words "My fellow citizens":

"Wait a minute . . . wait a minute. My fellow citizens? Whatever happened to My Fellow Americans? You think he didn't say Americans by accident? That was on purpose, folks. I guarantee you that's exactly what this administration is all about—their stupid symbolism. You know what the problem with 'Americans' is? 'Americans' is not inclusive enough. No, no, it does not include everybody. It alienates people out there on the fringes whose pain we are all trying to feel. There are a lot of people who aren't proud to be Americans. Native Americans, the people who don't like you to call them Redskins and Braves and all that. This is purposeful. . . . He can't just say 'My fellow Americans.' "

But Limbaugh was only the loudest of the irritants. Far weightier were the editorials in the *Wall Street Journal,* run as a separate and conservative fiefdom from the more objective newspapers. From the early days, they began to question the role and powers of some of the new Arkansans. They began with "Who Is Webb Hubbell?" and their headline "Who Is Vince Foster?" was blamed inside the White House for contributing to his suicide. The *Journal* attacked Clinton's soon-withdrawn nominee to run civil rights at the Justice Department, Lani Guinier, as "The Quota Queen." The *Washington Times,* owned by the Unification Church of Korea, which was run by the Reverend Moon and followers known as the Moonies, was a small, loss-making conservative paper of less than 100,000 in circulation (compared to over 700,000 for the *Washington Post*) that proved a constant critic. The *American Spectator,* a conservative monthly magazine that went from a circulation of 30,000 when Clinton began campaigning, to over 100,000 when he was inaugurated, to nearly 300,000 by 1995, was relentless, stylishly written, and unapologetic in its disdain for the Clintons. It also, like the *Washington Times,* broke a series of stories on Whitewater and on Clinton's sexual escapades in Little Rock, as recounted by his state trooper bodyguards.

In the eyes of conservatives, they had suffered from liberal media bias for decades, and it was time for the pendulum to swing back. There was a rough demographic justice to this surging growth of the conservative press. The Vietnam and Watergate era had seen a wave of new journalists come into the media, reflecting the suspicion of government and of the Vietnam War, which characterized that generation. But in the 1980s of Ronald Reagan and Margaret Thatcher, a conservative movement had developed in many colleges, started its own conservative magazines, and bred a new generation of anti-liberal writers. The *American Spectator* was born of this movement, and hit its stride with a Clinton administration that was, from memories of Gennifer Flowers to its activist government policies, a perfect target.

Nor was the liberal press quite what the right suspected. The Op-Ed pages were filling with conservative columnists. On the *Washington Post,* Robert Novak had always been conservative, George F. Will had been extraordinarily close to the Reagans, and Charles Krauthammer had little time for liberals. On the *New York Times,* former Nixon speechwriter William Safire had become perhaps the single most influential columnist in the press. Disdaining the Bush administration, he took a little time before unleashing his blend of mocking skepticism and hard reporting on the Clintons. But the overall thrust of the prestigious press commentaries was highly critical.

Contempt for the indecision of Clinton's policies, and his backtracking on campaign pledges to be tough on tyrants and to lift and strike in Bosnia, left Clinton with few liberal defenders. Anthony Lewis of the *New York Times* cast high moral suspicion on the new White House. David Broder of the *Washington Post,* a legendarily careful and sober political analyst, reported after the first 100 days that Clinton's stewardship was "a calamity that reached beyond our borders. That this is happening to a man who will remain as president for the next 43 months is an international disaster."

Time ran a cover story on "The Incredible Shrinking Presidency," and *Newsweek* put a dismal picture of the president on its cover to ask "What's Wrong?" Some of the coverage had a personal edge after the decision to sack the White House travel staff, with lurid suggestions of improper handling of money and the statement that the FBI had been called in. The White House press corps had dealt with the travel staff for years and depended on them to organize the trips, hotels, press planes and phone facilities, food at the odd hours dictated by the president's schedule, foreign visas, and baggage handling. They were familiar and trusted colleagues, if not friends, always ready to provide a cash advance in foreign parts. The allegations were hard to believe, and many in the press corps took the affair personally. They began digging hard into the story, which began to look as if the travel staff had been ditched on Hillary's orders to make way for a distant cousin of Clinton from Little Rock and for a new air charter service connected with

Harry Thomason, the president's Arkansan friend and TV producer. Nearly three years later, the head of the travel office, Billy Dale, was acquitted on all the charges of financial impropriety brought against him.

The Center for Media and Public Affairs compared the TV evening news reports on the first three months of the Bush administration in 1989 to the same period for Clinton. They found that for Bush, 74 percent of the evaluative comments made by TV reporters were positive. For Clinton, the proportion was just 21 percent. Reporting this disparity, the *Washington Monthly* suggested that it was a reaction to the clever and deliberate manipulation of the presidential image by the Reagan and Bush administrations: "In the press zeal to avoid being snookered, it has neglected a crucial part of the job: an objective rendering of the news."

The first six months of Clinton in office left him wide open to press sniping, even from liberal reporters like the *Newsweek* team who had covered the campaign with extraordinary insight and sympathy. It was a target-rich environment, from gays in the military to Nannygate, from the starstruck courting of Hollywood to the $200 haircut from Christophe, a celebrity barber. The man from Hope seemed to be developing grand tastes. He suddenly arranged a dinner in New York with his ambassador to the UN, Madeleine Albright, so suddenly that it aroused suspicions that this was a way to use *Air Force One* to take Hillary to a new celebrity hairdresser in Manhattan and their daughter to the ballet. The press outside the White House grew prickly. Asked by one of the president's staff to apply makeup before Clinton was interviewed, a local and perhaps self-important anchorwoman refused, and then made her complaint on camera.

The specialist political reporters outside the White House were adding to the critical tone from their own beats. The diplomatic reporters detailed the policy dithering on Bosnia, and the journalists in Congress analyzed the slow, exsanguinary defeat of the economic stimulus bill in the Senate. Because so many of the reporters in Washington were long-standing friends and contacts of the young policy staff, they knew of the long and rambling and inconclusive seminars in the White House. They also knew that the Clintons disparaged them, even as they reported his unusually fast sag in the opinion polls. The Harris poll's monthly tracking showed a grievous decline, from 54 percent positive in January to 35 percent in June. Worse still were Clinton's negative ratings, from 31 percent in January to 63 percent in June.

Things were looking so bad that even the men he beat were feeling sorry for Clinton. Marlin Fitzwater, Bush's spokesman and press secretary, was shaking his head at the teenage yuppies around Clinton and warning publicly that "what they need is a few old, bald, fat guys in the White House. We reassure people."

Then into the White House came the old bald guy. David Gergen is not fat, but otherwise he fit Fitzwater's job description. A veteran of the Nixon and Reagan White House staffs, he came to know Clinton through the Renaissance weekends held over the New Year holidays at Hilton Head. He was one of many FOBs and informal advisers that Clinton would call late at night to discuss whatever was on his mind—a new book, a new idea, a new problem. As soon as he realized his trouble with the media, Clinton began talking to Gergen. It put Gergen in a difficult position. A regular talking head on the most sonorous of current affairs shows, *The MacNeil-Lehrer News Hour,* and editor of the weekly *U.S. News and World Report,* Gergen may have been a personal chum of Clinton for nearly a decade, and had voted for him in 1992, but he did not sound like a fan.

"Whhoosshhh!! That sucking sound you hear is the air rushing out of Bill Clinton's balloon as he ends his first 100 days in office," Gergen wrote in April, baying with the rest of the press pack. But in private, Gergen had been musing for months about what he called "the burden of the presidency": the fact that four of the last five presidents had been broken by the office; that a single, failed term had become the norm; that the system wasn't working anymore.

Citing patriotism as his reason for riding to Clinton's rescue, the first thing Gergen did was reopen the corridor to his office from the cramped, unsavory basement that was Richard Nixon's revenge on the press corps. Nixon converted the old swimming pool for their use, and legend said he used to mourn the fact that the taps were sealed so he could not drown them all at will. By reopening the corridor, closed by Clinton's baby-boomers as soon as they arrived, Gergen was signaling the kind of open house that let reporters drift in, perch on a chair, float a rumor, and hear an old bald guy lean back and say he's heard a lot of crazy yarns in his time but that one beat even him.

Gergen swiftly organized the first prime-time press conference of the Clinton presidency, on June 17, five months after he had been sworn in. It was not a success. He was so diminished that, of the three main networks, only NBC carried it live, and then only for 30 minutes. The cable news network, CNN, and the PBS public broadcasting channel carried the whole event, with Clinton's carefully prepared joke: "As all of you know, and as a few of you have pointed out in various ways in the past few weeks, I just got here." But he was questioned sharply on his reactions to his press coverage, with a sly reference to President John Kennedy's hard-to-match irony when asked the same question. He had been reading it more and enjoying it less, Kennedy had replied, with his deft and disarming wit. Clinton was more labored.

"I think the most important thing is that we attempt, you and I, to create an atmosphere of trust and respect and that you at least know that I'm going to do my best to be honest with you. And I think you're going to be honest with me, and I expect you to criticize me when you think I'm wrong. The only thing I ever ask is, if I have a response and I have a side, let that get out, and we'll watch this conflict unfold. I mean, this is nothing new. President Jefferson got a rough press, too."

Gergen had no time for the conviction of Clinton's campaign veterans that the new media of satellites and cable TV had made the old press corps obsolete, that they could go over their heads to the people direct. "That works in a campaign when the people are interested. Most of the time they're not. And then you're stuck with the guys who do the trench warfare, covering the grim and grimy business of governing day in and day out. In campaign mode, the new media is fine. In the three and a half years of government before the next campaign, you're stuck with the White House grunts," Gergen said.

"You're an incredibly important part of the democratic process," Gergen confided to the press corps on June 4, his first day on the job. Then came the barbecue, open night for the press and their families on the White House lawn, bonding over the burgers. It got better. The baby-boomers in the press staff interrupted the barbecue to croon: "I hope you'll like us, I know we like you." Then Hillary appeared to say how pleased she was to have "more opportunity to get to know you and your colleagues better."

The Clintons gushed this sort of stuff to all the Washington insiders. At the last barbecue before the press, the president had told the congressmen at their picnic on the south lawn, "This is, after all, your place." Gergen now reassured the White House press that they were honorary insiders, too. But then Gergen himself was a prime member of that modern political faction in Washington, the "Insiders' Party," who were blurring the traditional distinction between Republicans and Democrats.

Gergen wrote speeches for Richard Nixon, was director of communications for his successor Gerald Ford, served on the Bush campaign team in 1980, and then after Bush faltered in the primaries, switched to the winner and defended and justified the policies of Reagan. Suddenly doing the same job for a Democrat, Gergen embodied the permanent government. "No matter who you vote for, Gergen always gets in," said the graffito that suddenly appeared in the toilet of the White House press plane.

Like all places with two-party systems, Washington has always had a permanent government. In Britain, it was composed of the civil service mandarins; in France, of the graduates of the *grandes écoles;* in Japan, of the Tokyo University graduates who went into the Ministry of Finance. Where Washington was different was the way the source of that permanence was changing. Two generations earlier, it had been Wall Street, and then it became the lawyers like Dean Acheson and Clark Clifford. Then it became advertising and marketing experts, from Nixon's H. R. Haldeman and John Ehrlichman to Reagan's Michael Deaver. Gergen's distinction was to illustrate how far the Fourth Estate had grown up. The media was now part of the permanent government, too, which helped explain the way that Bill Clinton was relaunched, as if he were a faltering newspaper. There was a redesign and a face-lift. Fall guys were found and new columnists hired. The advertisers were wined and dined and flattered and treated to enticing dummies. And from the way Clinton swallowed the congressional changes to his budget, the cover price had been cut too.

What had not changed were the three essential characteristics of the Gergen style, basic rules that prevailed for whichever government got in. The first was a degree of ruthlessness, which Gergen learned as research director for Charles Colson, the manipulative PR man in the Nixon White House who was later jailed for his part in the Watergate conspiracy. "You only have one four-star general, but you have got a lot of lieutenants who can give blood," Gergen told John Matese when he was writing *Spin Control,* an illuminating book on White House communications.

So to protect Clinton, the young George Stephanopoulos gave some blood. Not a lot. He remained inside the Clinton fold, kept his access to the key meetings, but was far less on view. The two front-runners for the vacant Supreme Court post, Interior Secretary Bruce Babbitt and Massachusetts Judge Stephen Breyer, both shed some blood in public too, as they were scrutinized, dangled in the wind, and then passed over for Ruth Bader Ginsburg.

Gergen's second rule was that the media can and must be manipulated. As he explained to Hedrick Smith, then writing his primer on Washington's permanent government, *The Power Game:* "We had a rule in the Nixon operation that before any public event was put on his schedule, you had to know what the headline out of the event was going to be, and what the lead paragraph would be."

The third distinctive feature of Gergenism, as he explained it to Frank Ursomaso, his aide in the Reagan White House, was planning. "David used to keep yelling at me, 'Frank, you've gotta be focused on the future.' And I'd say, 'Well, I'm out there ninety days.' And he'd say, 'That's not enough. You gotta be out there six months.' " Gergen's sense of timing was perfect. He came on board just as Clinton bottomed out. The deals had been done with Congress to pass the budget by the time Gergen arrived. The first real transition from one party to another that the United States and White House had known for twelve years, it was always going to take time for Clinton and his team to climb the learning curve.

No sooner did Gergen help them learn than Whitewater began to seep into the White House basement, where the press corps reacted quickly to an entirely familiar story: the White House scandal; the cover-up by an overprotective staff; what did the president know and when did he know it?

Whitewater had become an issue by the very fact that the *New York Times* published the first reports of the ill-fated land deal during the presidential campaign. The relationship with the paper was one that Clinton felt he should consolidate, and shortly after he took office, he invited the new publisher, Arthur Ochs Sulzberger, Jr., to lunch in the private dining room adjoining the Oval Office. The *Times* had endorsed his election, and Clinton wanted to know why the paper was already being so critical. "The best way of describing our relationship with you is tough love," Sulzberger told him. Clinton grinned. "Well, just don't forget the love part."

The *New York Times* was to become one of the administration's most pungent critics. They did not wage the relentless ideological assault of the

Wall Street Journal's conservative editorial pages. The *Times* picked its targets, and as the Whitewater revelations began to shift from the obscure financial dealings in Arkansas in the 1980s to the White House damage control of 1993, Clinton provided targets in plenty. After a *Times* editorial demanding his resignation and a *Washington Post* denunciation of "conduct which most first-year law students would immediately recognize as improper," White House counsel Bernard Nussbaum became the first political casualty of the Whitewater affair, even while he clung to office.

For Howell Raines, the liberal southerner who had become the new chief editorial writer, Clinton's performance was "stupid, irresponsible and improper." It got worse. Under the headline "White House Ethics Meltdown," the Clinton administration was condemned as "easily the most reckless in interfering with the integrity of federal investigative agencies since that of Richard Nixon." By the time the congressional hearings on Whitewater ended in August 1994, the *New York Times* editorials had become openly contemptuous: "Give the Clinton administration witnesses this. They were tireless in their legalistic evasions and prickly self-justifications," it began. "But at what cost to an Administration with a record of recklessly promiscuous conflict of interest and to a President already suspected of being incapable of remembering the whole truth. . . . In the last decade of the 20th century we have a White House that operates by 19th-century rules of political intrigue—hidden files and clandestine tip-offs."

Whitewater undermined everything that Gergen had tried to achieve. His brand of media management could succeed only at the margin, not when the press was in hot pursuit of scandal. "There's a cannibalism loose in our society," Gergen concluded. Whitewater also sapped his own standing inside the White House. Convinced that the Clintons had nothing to hide, and that the only credible defense was complete openness, Gergen pressed hard for the Clintons to offer all available documents to the *Washington Post* and the *New York Times,* with the promise that the Clintons would then be available to answer any questions that arose. Clinton, who had the politician's skill of agreeing without committing himself, left Gergen convinced that his advice was about to be taken. Hillary, who brought a lawyer's protective instincts to what was now an essentially political matter, blocked the advice. She had a single question: Could there be any guarantee that full disclosure would end the controversy? Probably not. The press did not go in for Not Guilty verdicts. And the issue had now gone beyond the media, to the independent counsel and congressional committee.

Whitewater was briefly overtaken by the resignation of Defense Secretary Les Aspin and the search for his replacement. The first candidate to be nominated was Admiral Bobby Ray Inman, a former senior CIA and military intelligence official in the Carter and Reagan administrations, who could thus be presented as a bipartisan and uncontroversial choice. He would probably have faced tough questioning at his confirmation hearings over his private interests in the defense industry since his retirement. Before that began, he was the subject of a swinging attack from William Safire in his *New York Times* column, who called him "a tax cheat . . . manipulative and deceptive." Admiral Inman reacted with an extraordinary outburst, which accused Safire of politically inspired witch-hunting, "a new McCarthyism," and of colluding with Senator Dole, the Republican leader, to step up the pressure on the Clinton administration over Whitewater.

Washington's media and political establishments rocked to Admiral Inman's assaults on the "new McCarthyism" of its combative and incestuous media culture. The *New York Times* stood by Safire, the main target of Admiral Inman's statement, as "a tough-minded journalist and a fair one." And the *Washington Post* in an editorial said that "Mr. Inman is dead wrong to suggest that somehow the power of columnists is such that all must be frightened of responding to their barbs."

"Nothing short of weird" was Safire's pungent response to Mr. Inman's attack. "I don't have to have anybody ask me to turn up the heat on Whitewater. I've been banging my spoon against the highchair about Whitewater ever since Vince Foster's apparent suicide." But Admiral Inman's fate intensified the irritation Clinton had already expressed with the arrogance and rush to judgment of the unelected Washington media elite in their commentaries and in the blizzard of new political talk shows. Clinton had abruptly walked out of press conferences and live TV interviews when the questions turned too hostile for his liking, or insisted on hammering issues like his financial troubles over the Whitewater investment. In an angry statement during a *Rolling Stone* interview he had complained that the press gave him "not one damned bit of credit." The media culture was obsessive and negative, Clinton went on, in the grip of "a compulsion to make big things little and little things big."

The Gergen effect had been negated by Whitewater. But the strategy had been right. A better relationship with the press would depend on a new White House press spokesman. After Leon Panetta had replaced Mack McLarty as chief of staff, he brought in veteran Democratic operative Mike McCurry, who had worked for Senator Kerrey's campaign in 1992 before becoming a highly effective spokesman for Warren Christopher's State Department. McCurry, who was made far more privy to White House decision-making than Dee Dee Myers had been, was affable, efficient, had an engaging sense of humor, and was respected by the press. He set out to target a series of upbeat themes, stressing that Clinton's foreign policy successes were being unfairly ignored, that the economy was performing well, and that Clinton was keeping his promise to create 2 million new jobs a year.

Clinton was still concerned enough about his press relations to read *Out of Order,* by media critic Thomas E. Patterson, a book that explored the long, steady decline of "descriptive journalism." Patterson called this the "Just the Facts, Ma'am" school of journalism in which news and statements and policy papers were reported plainly, without comment. He surveyed the 1960 presidential campaign, and judged that 92 percent of all the news reports had met his criteria of "descriptive journalism." Then he examined the 1992 election coverage, and found only 18 percent of the stories met his standard.

Oddly enough, some of the press agreed. NBC-TV White House correspondent Andrea Mitchell noted that the press corps lived by the code of "Gotcha." Her ABC colleague Britt Hume added, "We live in a time when the worst thing that can be said about a journalist in Washington is that he or she is not tough."

"This is a strange city," commented *USA Today*'s political correspondent Adam Nagourney. "Everyone makes these instant judgments. The conventional wisdom moves way too fast. It's more of a press problem than it is a Clinton problem." A *Washington Post* editorial admitted that "in some instances the field of inquiry into the qualifications and credentials has been expanded to the point of assault on both the privacy and the dignity of the nominee."

That was not the view of the *Post*'s White House correspondent, Ruth Marcus. Unusual for a White House reporter, she published a heartfelt and angry article on the Op-Ed page. "In Washington, White House special counsel Lloyd Cutler likes to say, trust is the coin of the realm. By that measure, the Clinton White House is flat broke when it comes to its dealings with the reporters who cover it. To borrow a phrase from the law of libel, the Clinton White House often seems to be following a pattern of knowing or reckless disregard for the truth," it began. After brief summaries of her evidence, from the sacking of the travel staff to Hillary's trading on the futures markets to Whitewater, she concluded, "Nineteen months of repeated falsehoods and half-truths have corroded the relationship between this White House and the reporters who cover it. The corrosion breeds cynicism among reporters, which in turn contributes to a siege mentality inside the White House."

Apart from the technological changes, which had brought instant and constant TV news coverage and almost-instant comment to political affairs, there were two underlying factors that warped the Washington culture into a kind of blood sport. The first was the distorted character of the city itself, a place that lacked the business tycoons or Broadway stars of New York or the Hollywood stars of Los Angeles or the industrial magnates of a Chicago, and in which the only stars were the politicians and the media who covered them from their telegenic high ground.

The Washington press not only loved to cover itself; its incestuousness had become a perverse pathology. A characteristic Op-Ed page in the *Washington Post,* in the week before the Inman fuss, had one political commentator, David Broder, writing an adoring farewell to another, Paul Duke, the host of *Washington Week in Review.* On the same page, the *Post*'s economics columnist Robert Samuelson was fretting publicly about his profession: "We in the media are often fixated on trivia; we too easily step over the line between essential skepticism and abusive hostility." The previous day, the *Post* had run a long critique of Sidney Blumenthal, Washington editor of the *New Yorker,* for not being nasty enough to President Clinton in a long year-end interview. "*New Yorker* readers deserve more than the profile-in-courage cream puffs Blumenthal is lobbing," said the *Post,* under the headline "Clinton's Man in Washington." This predilection of the Washington press to review itself threatened to become a grotesque and self-important parody of press commentary, as if theater reviewers wrote about one another's notices rather than the performances they were assigned to attend.

The second oddity of the Washington political culture was the way that traditional dividing lines between press and politics had been blurred. Journalists and political aides darted from one job to the other. This was common to both parties. President Clinton's deputy secretary of state, Strobe Talbott, had come from *Time* magazine. His counselor, David Gergen, brought on board during the low point of White House relations with the press, shifted from the Reagan White House to the editorship of *U.S. News and World Report* before shifting back to work for a Democratic president. One of President Clinton's senior aides in the Office of Management and Budget, Matthew Miller, resigned to become economics editor for the *New Republic.* Governor Mario Cuomo of New York took up a radio talk show. Christopher Matthews, a senior aide to former Speaker of the House Tip O'Neill, shone in his new career as journalist and host of a TV political show. Dee Dee Myers left Clinton's White House press office to anchor a TV political talk show with Mary Matalin, the Republican strategist for the Bush campaign.

On the other political wing, the *New York Times*'s Safire used to work as a speechwriter and political aide to Republican president Richard Nixon. (And Hillary Clinton was later to suggest, when he called her "a congenital liar," that he still seemed to be working for Nixon beyond the grave.) Tony Snow went from running the editorial pages of the *Washington Times* to the Bush White House as a speechwriter, and then back to a newspaper column and occasional guest spots hosting the Rush Limbaugh show. Having worked on the Nixon and Reagan White House staff, Pat Buchanan became a pungent right-wing columnist and TV talk-show host before running for the Republican presidential nomination against George Bush. He then returned to his CNN show, *Crossfire,* to be joined by Bush's White House chief of staff John Sununu. Buchanan then ran again in 1996. Journalism and policy-making, commentary and politics, all swirled into one loose but incestuous Washingtonian profession in which not only did everyone know everyone else, but they could even swap jobs.

One effect of this insider culture was to focus media commentary very tightly on the business and gossip and political detail and personalities of Washington itself. This helped embed the concept of a specific frame of mind, which became known as "inside the Beltway," after the ring road that circles the city. Another was to irritate President Clinton to the point of contempt. He paid steadily less attention to the conventional rituals of the media. He learned not to speak off-the-cuff at photo opportunities, not to stay at the podium and answer questions informally after a statement.

The most striking feature of inside-the-Beltway media was its concentration on Washington's political detail, rather than on the wider national picture, or on the deeper historical trends. Clinton's trade skirmishes with Japan and China were reported in admirable detail; his larger trade strategy was seldom explored. The fate of individual weapons systems in the Pentagon budgets were followed closely, but not the striking shift that cut the ready forces of the U.S. Army but increased the manpower, the readiness, and the ability to deploy the U.S. Marine Corps as an instant intervention force. The U.S. Navy's new military doctrine for the twenty-first century, titled "From the Sea," to build the capacity to control and invade the shore and hinterland and dominate the air deep inland, may have been the most underexamined strategic story of Clinton's presidency.

The press is highly fallible; it often misses the big picture or the big story, as it had missed the $200 billion bankruptcy of the savings and loan industry in the 1980s. But Clinton was dismayed by its failure to cover what he saw as legitimate stories professionally, like the Global 2000 education reform, of which he was proud. Hillary was angry at what she saw as laziness in the media reporting on the details of her health reform, too ready to repeat unexamined the criticisms of Republican politicians and partisan experts. "Not one in a hundred of them has actually read it," she complained once to Gergen, thumping her fist on the three-inch-high stack of 1,364 pages. She won a tiny scrap of vindication, after her plan had been humiliatingly withdrawn from Congress, when the *New York Times* quoted Uwe E. Reinhardt of Princeton University: "No one understood this, but the average American patient would have had more choice under the Clinton plan than they now will. If you work for a particular company, your choice of HMOs is whatever that company offers you."

The White House staff was keeping score. Paul Begala ran a search on the Nexis database of all news stories since the health bill had been launched. There were 2,400 stories on the health reform, and over 31,000 on Whitewater. Then he looked at opinion polls that showed that while President Clinton was considered honest by only 37 percent of the public, only 21 percent reckoned the media was honest. "Apparently, consumers of news have come to realize what political professionals across the ideological spectrum have long believed," Begala concluded. "The other party may be the opposition, but the press is the enemy."

Clinton did not see it that way. He had a conspiracy theory of his own and, characteristically, chose to unburden himself in May 1994 before an old press acquaintance and critic from Arkansas, John Burdett. He blamed the Republicans and the political right for all his woes with the media. "It started in the campaign, and for the first time, I guess ever, there was no cessation when I took office. If anything, it just stepped up. The *Wall Street Journal* basically said they were just sort of determined to try and act as if the election hadn't occurred, as if I were some usurper, that there was no legitimacy to the outcome.

"You have got the editorial page of the *Journal,* the *Washington Times,* Rush Limbaugh, Pat Robertson, Jerry Falwell, the Christian Radio Network, the *American Spectator* and the Floyd Brown operation. They are all part of a national thing which has access to unlimited money, and has basically poured it into Arkansas as part of their sort of national strategy. It's a spooky thing, really. The Democrats have nothing to contend with it. Nothing."

It was an extraordinary statement. The president of the United States, the most powerful man in the world, felt powerless against what he saw as a dark political conspiracy to undo him and his election, a plot carried out in the light of day, and in the print media; a plot in which he saw the rest of the media as unwitting coconspirators, duped by their own code of "adversarial reporting" into going along with his persecution.

☆ 10 ☆

THE THREE H PROBLEMS: HILLARY, HEALTH, AND HUBRIS

The most powerful and politically astute woman in America made history by launching the health reform on which her husband's presidency was said to depend, and told a gnarled array of elderly congressmen that she appeared before them "as a mother." This was true. Hillary Clinton had flown back from the United Nations the previous day to attend parents' evening at her daughter's private school. But motherhood was just one of her credentials, the formidably briefed First Lady declared:

"I am here as a mother, as a wife, a daughter, a sister, a woman, as an American citizen concerned about the health of her family and the health of her nation," she began. The thirty-six males (and two women) who made up the Ways and Means Committee of the House of Representatives, the crucial body which writes all of America's tax bills, had never heard anything quite like it. Of forty-two First Ladies, only Eleanor Roosevelt and Rosalynn Carter had ever testified before Congress before, but Mrs. Clinton was the first to penetrate the legislative boiler room of the Ways and Means Committee. Sporting what fashion correspondents reckoned was her seventh new hairstyle since entering the White House eight months earlier, Mrs. Clinton wore a neat suit in telegenic turquoise, gold earrings and necklace. But her real accessories were the files carried by the knot of White House aides, and her own voluminous memory of the 1,364-page health reform plan she helped draft. She never had to look at a note.

It was just the first public appearance in an unprecedented schedule of testifying before five separate congressional committees in a single week.

After the Ways and Means Committee, she went directly to tell the House Energy and Commerce Committee that she was appearing before them "as a mother, as a wife," etc. The next day, she appeared first before Senator Edward Kennedy's Labor and Human Resources Committee, and then before the House Labor and Education Committee. The day after that, she confronted the Finance Committee chaired by Senator Pat Moynihan, who had already called the costing of her plans "a fantasy." This in turn followed 130 separate private sessions before various congressional committees in the previous eight months. The intensity of her personal campaigning reflected the absolute priority given to health reform by Mrs. Clinton and her husband. It was overwhelmingly the issue and the chosen ground on which he hoped to be reelected.

"As a wife, I can imagine the fear that grips a couple whose health insurance vanishes because of a lost job, a layoff, or an unexpected illness," she said. Politicians of the Ways and Means Committee, who themselves faced reelection in the following year, nodded in deferential sympathy, and in respect for a fellow professional who scored a home run with one congressman's question of how he would explain the reforms to his own mother. "If we can't pass the mother test, we're not going to succeed, are we?" Hillary Clinton replied, with polite, deceptive sweetness.

But the Clintons were to fail the mother test, and the congressional test, and see their health reform plan go down to humiliating defeat. They also failed another, possibly more momentous test in its implications, when they found to their dismay that the nation was not yet ready for a thrusting and powerful First Lady in a commanding executive role. This was the third such disappointment to the Clintons. The first had come in Arkansas, when Hillary had resignedly decided to drop her maiden name of Rodham, become Mrs. Clinton, change her style of dress, and play the unfamiliar but dutiful role of wife. The second had come during the campaign, after the fuss that greeted her incautious statement that "I could have stayed home and baked cookies and had teas." She backed out of the limelight, baked (or at least handed out) cookies, and her candidate husband stopped using his rather too cute line that they would be almost a co-presidency—"Buy one, get one free."

This third failure to gain acceptance on her own terms was partly the fault of the office. The First Lady is not elected, and Hillary was not to blame for the generations of sexual politics that ensured that the way to become the most powerful woman in America was still by sleeping with the most powerful man. It was partly the fault of the mishandling of health reform, the issue on which she staked her claim, and put at risk the fate of the Clinton presidency. Blame for this could be shared among many candidates, from her partner in crafting the health plan (Clinton's Oxford chum Ira Magaziner) to the rattled Democrats in Congress; from the astute Republican opposition to the health lobbies who undermined the reform. Nor was she entirely to blame for the clouds of scandal over Whitewater and other Arkansan legacies that settled over the White House for months, destroying morale and credibility.

Nonetheless, she had been the prime mover in the financial ventures of the Clinton family partnership. And conflicts of interest between being both governor's wife and a partner of the Rose Law Firm were her affair. The 10,000 percent profit on her investment in cattle futures was all done in her name. (It was not wholly free of risk. At one point in the frantic year of trading, she was $60,000 down with only $40,000 in her account before the market shifted back in her favor.) Hillary was the prime mover in the Whitewater investment, the one who negotiated the loan for the first speculative building of a holiday home on the site. She was then to become the Rose Firm lawyer who dealt with at least some of the legal business of Madison Guaranty, the doomed bank owned by her Whitewater partner, Jim McDougal. And it was McDougal who expressed her role most succinctly when he noted, "Bill Clinton couldn't balance a checkbook, but he has a wife who sure can."

In the White House, her particular role over the portfolios from Arkansas continued. Her personal White House staff and her old friend Bernard Nussbaum were the ones who searched Vince Foster's office on the night of his suicide, and who took temporary custody of his Whitewater papers. The term "Hillarygate," favored by some Republicans, never caught the national imagination, but it was not altogether unfair. So many of the tangled threads of the Whitewater embarrassments led back to her, which made her a tempting political target.

Even before the inauguration, she was portrayed by the *American Spectator* as "the Lady Macbeth of Little Rock." During the transition, her prominent role in interviewing possible cabinet members provoked suggestions of a co-presidency, labeled *Billary.* "I think that the viciousness of some of the attacks, going all the way back to the campaign and the Republican convention, is because people don't know what to make of women, not just me. There are still so many stereotypes around," she told *People* magazine. "I am who I am, and I know that is a red flag for some on the right wing who have different views about a woman's appropriate role in life or who disagree with the particular political views my husband and I share about providing health care for everybody. They don't believe that, and so rather than attacking the underlying issue and the message, they attack the messenger and try to throw everything—including the kitchen sink—at me."

It was hardly her fault that she became the target for conservatives seeking to exploit the gathering resentments of angry white males against able and assertive women invading the workplace, and expecting the basic human courtesies that on occasion had to be defended with the blunt charge of sexual harassment. "A friend told me I've turned into a gender Rorschach test," she told one interviewer. "If somebody has a female boss for the first time, and they've never experienced that, well maybe they can't turn their hostility on her so they take it out on me." Opinion polls consistently scored her approval ratings at five points lower than that of her husband.

But a central part of the blame was entirely hers, the dreadful mismanagement of her own public image. A handsome rather than conventionally pretty woman, her physical appeal lay in the lively intelligence and character that illuminated her features. But whether persuaded by vanity or by innocence, she became trapped by jarring images of her own, unwise endorsement. The most familiar photographs, each personally approved, betrayed the contradictions. For *Working Woman* magazine she was the confident yuppie, arms assertively crossed, in a brisk business suit, softened at the neck by a discreet silk scarf. For *Vogue,* she vamped in black, dreamily cool and remote in one shot, breathlessly parted lips and bedroom eyes in another. For the *New York Times Magazine,* she preened in pious white for a profile that portrayed her as Saint Joan, hoping to convert a cynical America to her "politics of meaning," and cure it of "a sleeping sickness of the soul."

She was speaking between visits to the sickbed where her father lay dying. But her words, and the beatific pose she chose to adopt for the photographer, invited mockery. The schoolmistress who would lead the way to universal health care was posing also as the high priestess of spiritual renewal. Contrasted with her financial acumen at turning a $1,000 investment into $100,000 on the cattle futures market, this invited ridicule. And compared with the relentless drive that she brought to the health reform project, it invited disbelief. There was a smack of hypocrisy in the Clintons' campaign rhetoric against the 1980s as a decade of greed, when she had invested so profitably in futures. There was a whiff of sanctimony about their promise of ethics in government, after she took her fees from a foundering savings and loan. In her attitudes, as in her mission to run health reform, Hillary made herself the most inviting of targets.

In their single-minded efficiency, their quickness to react and to counterattack, there was something distinctly militaristic about the Clintons. As soon as Clinton realized he was in danger of draining away his honeymoon momentum with the fuss over gays in uniform and the failure to find an acceptable attorney general, he called back his campaign strategists James Carville and Paul Begala to reestablish the "war room." Each evening at 5:30, they gathered in the White House to play through the politics of the next day. And when Hillary was given one hundred days for her new task force to come up with draft legislation for a national health system, she set up a war room of her own, a general staff that would coordinate policy with presentation and ensure that she won on the airwaves and in the media the ground she might not be gaining in the trenches of Congress. She stormed the country, addressing over 1,100 groups. And to one of them, the Chamber of Commerce of Williamsburg, Virginia, she said, "There has been nothing quite like this effort since the planning of the invasion of Normandy."

The effort had to be Herculean. When the Clinton campaign began there had been no health reform plan at all. During the New Hampshire primary, Clinton realized the power of the issue, which was stressed by Paul Tsongas and Senator Kerrey. Clinton recalled that Ira Magaziner had presented a paper on health reform at a Renaissance Weekend seminar and asked him to fax up some ideas. Magaziner sent a memo, which said a credible scheme must include a comprehensive package of health care for all citizens, should be financed mainly by employers, and seek to control costs with an overall budget. For Magaziner, the real anomaly and danger of the U.S. health care system was that it cost too much and delivered too little. The United States spent over 13 percent of GDP on health, while Britain spent 7 percent of GDP, and scored better infant life expectancy.

This was enough to campaign on, but on the summer bus tour through the American heartland, Clinton made two decisions. The first was that since U.S. health costs were so high a proportion of national wealth, reform should be able to save money and ease his budgetary problems. How this was to be done while including the 37 million Americans without health insurance was unclear. The second decision was that he could not get a payroll tax through Congress, and that he could not therefore propose a single-payer system like the Canadian plan, nor a British-style national health service. Clinton asked his pollster, Stan Greenberg, to research the issue, and as a result the phrase "managed competition" was dropped, while more popular themes like "comprehensive care" and "guaranteed private insurance" and "security" stressed. Magaziner, asked to consult more widely among health experts, presented another paper in November. It suggested that the way to include all Americans, and keep the costs down, would be to organize everyone into a range of health insurance purchasing cooperatives. Magaziner also consulted the Jackson Hole group, reform-minded executives in the health and insurance industries who proposed to maintain market competition among insurers within a regulatory framework set by the state.

These were the broad outlines with which Hillary began as she rallied six cabinet members, a host of White House aides, and over 500 outside experts into the special task force. Spurning congressional suggestions that they be sent a bill of broad principles and outlines and they complete the details, Hillary chose to keep control of the process by drafting the plan, and the bill, in the White House. The task force met behind closed doors, which provoked controversy. The issue Clinton had avoided during the campaign—how to include everybody without increasing costs—proved intractable. The 100-day deadline came and went. At the end of May, all three on the President's Council of Economic Advisers reviewed the plan and warned that it would mean $60 billion in new taxes and imperil the economic recovery. The figures were worked over once more. The summer deadline came and went.

Finally, in September, the president addressed a joint session of Congress, vowing at last to give all Americans the guarantee of lifetime health insurance. Speaking at first without a text because the TelePrompTer had somehow been loaded with the State of the Union address he delivered the previous February, and with deep and sometimes passionate conviction, he was eloquent and persuasive, but more than a little vague. Future Americans would find it "unthinkable" that hardworking Americans could be made bankrupt and homeless by serious illness, Clinton said, appealing to the public sense of fairness and community. The polls suggested that his instincts were right; the instant CNN survey found 61 percent of Americans ready to pay higher taxes for universal health care.

Health insurance could not be extended to the 37 million uninsured without cost, and Clinton had already sought to buy off potential critics with some expensive concessions. The AFL-CIO was assured that their hard-won medical benefits from big employers would neither be cut back nor taxed. And the American Association of Retired People was coaxed with promises of cheaper prescription drugs and long-term care. But some Republicans were implacable. "This plan will pass over my cold dead body," drawled the Texan conservative senator Phil Gramm.

Senator Robert Dole and the Republican leadership were not openly critical. Dole said he agreed with the president on the concept and the principle of universal health insurance, but he planned a waiting game to let the costs of the Clinton reform sink in and erode support among key sectors like small businesses and among the individual states, who would have to shoulder much of the administrative burden of the scheme. Most Republicans, reckoning that Clinton had won the broad argument for universal health coverage, were ready for a compromise. So were some in the White House. "While this is a comprehensive plan, it is not put down from the mountains on high," White House Chief of Staff Mack McLarty explained. "There will be a lot of flexibility as we move forward in this process."

The Republicans focused on the higher costs to small businesses, the public's fear that they might lose the chance to choose their own doctor rather than be assigned one, and on the threat to jobs. Two out of every five American workers, some 50 million people, were part-time or short-term employees. Many of them did not get health insurance through their employers, and the Clinton plan said that employers should henceforth pay for part-timers on a pro-rata basis. The Republicans warned that this single provision could derail the great American jobs machine. "A new health care tax would certainly force layoffs and discourage hiring. We are very troubled by the president's plan to mandate the cost of health care on small business," complained Congresswoman Nancy Johnson of Connecticut, author of the Republican alternative health plan.

Clinton, recalling that the initially favorable public reaction to his February speech on his budget was swiftly overwhelmed by the Republicans' ability to label it a new tax bill, was determined this time not to squander his momentum. Although the final congressional vote on health reform was unlikely to take place for nine months, he mounted what the White House called "a new presidential election campaign" to sell it.

The basic package would cost $4,200 per year for a family ($1,800 for an individual), the employer to pay 80 percent of this. But to mollify small businesses—feared as formidable critics—their contribution would be capped at between 3.5 and 7.9 percent of their payroll, depending on average wage levels and numbers of employees. For the unemployed and uninsured, the state would pay the fee. Clinton's plan reckoned this and all his other reforms would cost the taxpayer some $700 billion over five years—about 20 percent of the 1993 total national health bill. This figure, which skated casually over the rising costs of Medicare for the elderly and Medicaid for the poor, could not withstand much scrutiny.

President Clinton was a great procrastinator, tending to put things off until they could only be restored by monstrous effort. This was the pattern of his desperately late but finally effective campaigns to pass the budget and the North American Free Trade Agreement. It was now to be repeated over health reform, but the prospects of final victory were dwindling by the start of 1994. In September, when he launched his historic plan to guarantee health insurance for every American, the opinion polls gave him almost 80 percent support. By December, his plan still enjoyed a two-to-one margin in the polls. In January, it shrank to 50–50 as the Whitewater scandal began to sap his credibility. By February it was not easy to find any responsible figure in Congress who was confident that the plan would be adopted.

"There is not one chance in a hundred that mandatory alliances will survive," said Representative Pete Stark, chairman of the health subcommittee of the crucial Ways and Means Committee. The mandatory health alliances were the heart of the Clinton plan, bringing together small business and individuals into large groups to wring discount prices from the big insurers. The big insurers did not mind this system, which would allow them the lion's share of the market. The smaller insurers feared extinction, and their subtly effective advertising campaigns put the Clinton plan on the defensive. They depicted a good-looking middle-aged couple named Harry and Louise, in a kind of soap opera format, in their home and cars and offices, who became familiar parts of America's cultural furniture. They did not attack the principle of the Clinton plan, but worried about "a new army of government bureaucrats." They fretted about losing the freedom to choose their doctor. But they said the plan only needed fixing, not scrapping. "Congress can change that—and if we send them that message, they will" was the punch line.

From an annual bill of $6 billion in 1960, rising life expectancy and rising medical costs had sent the cost of Medicare to the federal budget spiraling ever upward, to $32 billion in 1980, to $98 billion in 1990, to a budgeted $143 billion in 1994. The budget estimated that Medicare would top $200 billion by 1998, and shortly after the year 2000 it could even exceed the defense budget. Medicare's dominant role in the budget was matched by its dominance in the minds of that powerful electoral constituency, the elderly. The American Association of Retired Persons, which claimed 33 million members, all of them over fifty and almost twice as likely to vote as people under the age of twenty-eight, was one of the most important targets for Clinton's campaign. But the AARP ran a poll of its members and found that just over half of them either opposed the Clinton plan or were uncertain.

Many of them were unable to understand the plan. Clinton was not readily able to illuminate them. One of the Jackson Hole experts complained, "Even those of us who have spent our careers pursuing health care reform cannot fully comprehend it." The complexities of the 1,364-page Health Security bill challenged even the most assiduous policy wonk. One independent conservative scholar who read the entire thing, Elizabeth McCaughey of the Manhattan Institute, whose usual pursuit was French literature, dealt the Clinton plan a sharp blow with a long and detailed textual analysis in the *New Republic,* which provoked an extraordinary howl of outrage and protest from the White House.

Giving chapter and verse, Ms. McCaughey wrote: "If the bill passes, you will have to settle for one of the low-budget health plans selected by the government. The law will prevent you from going outside the system to buy basic health coverage you think is better, even after you pay the mandatory premium. The bill guarantees you a package of medical services, but you can't have them unless they are deemed 'necessary' and 'appropriate.' That decision will be made by the government, not by you and your doctor. Escaping the system and paying out-of-pocket to see a specialist for the tests and treatment you think you need will be almost impossible."

Her critique shook Clinton's supporters in Congress, worried the elderly and those who thought that their current health care might be expensive, but at least was under their and their doctors' control. Ms. McCaughey's hostile assessment, itself riddled with errors that were not quickly exposed, was then followed by a torpedo from a friend. Robert Reischauer ran the Congressional Budget Office, the official watchdog over the budget, and since the Congress had so long been in Democratic hands, Reischauer was no Republican. But his report pointed out that Mr. Clinton's claim of a $58 billion savings on the federal budget over six years was hogwash. The Clinton plan would cost at least another $74 billion, the CBO said. Moreover, what Clinton called a "premium" to be paid by employers was said by Reischauer to be what it really was, for budgetary purposes—a tax. Reischauer knew what he was doing. He revealed that he had prepared for his testimony before Congress by "standing in the kitchen and having my wife throw pots and pans at me."

Clinton had expected attacks on his bill from the right, but not from the left, who sniped at it as a messy compromise that tried to avoid both the single-payer system and the private-insurance structure under which costs were rising out of control and some 37 million people were not covered at all. Having compromised in advance, President Clinton was fighting on difficult ground. Moderate Democrats began to fall in behind the partial and cheaper reform plan offered by Congressman Frank Cooper of Tennessee. Liberal Democrats tried to revive the single-payer concept. Moderate Republicans began drifting from President Clinton to Congressman Cooper.

Hillary defended her creation like a tigress. The Harry and Louise TV ads infuriated her. "They have the gall to run TV ads that there is a better way, the very industry that has brought us to the brink of bankruptcy because of the way that they have financed health care." She denounced the drug companies for their prices, and the insurance companies for their profits and seeking "to exclude people from coverage because the more they can exclude, the more money they can make." Careless of the White House concentration on the NAFTA vote just eight days away and with not a vote to be lost, she attacked the Cooper plan and the conservative Democrats who backed it.

Her fury was related not solely to the criticisms of her health plan, but to a Washington that had suddenly become poisonous. The Clintons retreated to the bracing wintry beaches of Hilton Head for their tenth New Year's Eve in a row in relaxed seminars and talk-ins with the Renaissance Group. One seminar Clinton should have found useful, "Risking Peace: Bosnia, the Middle East, and What Remains of the New World Order," did not detain him long. He left early to play golf. Hillary stayed doggedly throughout a long discussion on her health reform plans.

Nobody had the ill grace to raise the topic on everyone's lips, the return of Whitewater, and the extraordinary nine-day wonder of President Clinton's sex life. On the weekend before Christmas, Washington began to buzz with talk of a new sex scandal, to be unveiled in the next issue of the *American Spectator,* a right-wing magazine whose circulation had risen from 70,000 to over 200,000 since the Democrats had reoccupied the White House.

The story broke publicly on December 20, with two former Arkansas state troopers appearing on the evening news to repeat what they had told the magazine, and what they had been ready to tell the Bush campaign in 1992: that as members of Governor Clinton's security staff they had been expected to connive in a series of extramarital affairs and romantic adventures. They had alerted Clinton whenever his wife was on the prowl, booked hotel rooms for his trysts, lent him unmarked cars, and stood guard while he dallied in parked cars. It was scurrilous and dubious stuff, which sober papers like the *New York Times* initially eschewed. The guilt of the mainstream American media was such that they sought to justify their reports by high-minded guff about the misuse of his perks of office, and whether or not he had tried to silence the disgruntled state troopers with offers of federal jobs. But then the White House felt required to reply, initially through presidential aides, but then with Mrs. Clinton joining in, and finally with the president's end-of-year interviews virtually dominated by it all.

The sex scandal was conflated with the more substantive issue, the *Washington Post*'s probe into the part played by the Whitewater investment in the bankruptcy of the Madison Guaranty Bank of Arkansas. The Resolution Trust Corporation, the body charged with clearing up the vast and nationwide bankruptcy of most of the savings and loan industry, had asked the Justice Department to investigate whether the Madison affair merited criminal proceedings. This related directly to the Clintons, as partners in Whitewater with the owner of Madison Guaranty, and specifically to Hillary, who had represented the bank as a lawyer.

"HRC was 'paralyzed' by it; if we don't solve this within the next two days, you don't have to worry about her schedule on health care . . . doesn't want poking into 20 years of public life in Arkansas," recorded Deputy Treasury Secretary Roger Altman in his diary for January 4. (The diary was made public by congressional subpoena. Altman said he was quoting Margaret Williams, the chief of staff for HRC, as Hillary Rodham Clinton was known in the bureaucracy. Ms. Williams told Congress she had no memory of making the remark.) Altman's note was prescient. Whitewater washed away the political leverage that would have been required to promote Hillary's health reform plan. The bill was a hard sell on its own merits, and once the initial public unveilings were over, Hillary's inexperience in the ways of congressional committees began to show. "I wish you'd run for sheriff once," groaned Ways and Means chairman Rostenkowski, when he tried to explain to her the politics of Capitol Hill.

"I take responsibility for not understanding what was going on," she conceded later, in an interview with a group of women reporters. "There was a lack of politically savvy advice. No one had figured out the dynamics. I regret very much that the efforts on health care were badly misunderstood, taken out of context and used politically against the administration."

Hillary did not give up, and while she professed not to notice them, paid close attention to her opinion polls. They were not disastrous, although her "unfavorable" rating in the Yankelovich poll for CNN-*Time* rose from 20 percent at the inauguration to nudge 50 percent in the first three months of 1994 when the Whitewater affair dominated the press. Her "favorable" rating proved remarkably resilient. At 63 percent in February 1993, it dwindled to a stable 50 percent until the three months of Whitewater, suffered a temporary drop into the mid-40s, and then rose above 50 percent by the end of 1994. The Hart-Teeter polls for NBC–*Wall Street Journal* found a similar sturdiness in her appeal: in response to the question "Do you think Hillary Rodham Clinton is a positive role model for American women?" 66 percent said yes in December 1992, immediately after the election, and 57 percent still said yes in January 1995. There was no massive national rejection of her in person, nor of her role as an activist First Lady.

This may have been because of a strategic shift in her role, with the withering of health reform. The woman who had reinvented herself in 1982 for her husband's campaign to be reelected governor now did so again, at least in the public eye outside the White House. She remained buoyant and cheerful in private and with friends, and even exuberant, dancing to Tamla Motown late into the night after the state dinner for Nelson Mandela. She was at her best with her extraordinarily loyal and tight-knit staff. Her offices remained an intense environment, but also one of the better-humored parts of the White House, the all-woman staff setting a collegial example of exchanges of gifts, small celebrations, and jokes. On the wall of Hillary's conference room hung a framed, blown-up extract from a classified personal ad. It read: "Hillary Rodham Clinton–type sought by single Jewish attorney, 31, who is bright, witty, sincere and cute. There's nothing sexier than an intelligent, powerful and successful female who knows what she wants."

She denied steadily that she was taking a back seat in public life, or reverting to a more conventional type of First Lady, insisting that her concerns for children, health, and education had been constant throughout her life. But the preliminary work on welfare reform done by her staff in 1993, in the hope or expectation that this would be her next charge after enacting the health bill, was to be wasted. By the summer of 1994, when the Clinton health bill had been withdrawn and even the pale Democratic substitutes were withering, there was an eerie sense of "The Lady Vanishes." She took a low profile on Clinton's European trip. In Paris, playing the role of traditional consort, she attended a dance recital at the Opéra, visited Rodin's villa, bought ballet gifts for her daughter.

She was convinced that she was still a political asset for the administration, particularly with core constituencies of women, liberals, environmentalists, and child and poverty groups. She put her toe into the political water, campaigning for her brother's bid for the Florida Senate nomination and for Kathleen Brown's unsuccessful bid to be elected governor of California. She campaigned for mammograms and for children's causes, and she traveled on goodwill tours, as First Ladies had traditionally done, to Norway for the Winter Olympics, to Copenhagen for the United Nations conference on social issues, and to China for the conference on women.

Hillary always spoke more frankly and more politically than most First Ladies of the past, and was blunt in her defense of human rights in Beijing. But the balance had changed. She appeared to be a tamed version of the new woman who had entered the White House. There were goodwill tours with elephant rides in India and pledges of U.S. aid to eradicate measles in Latin America, and an appearance on CNN's Larry King show to take live questions and talk of her concern for "the human issues . . . what do we do to make sure that children have healthy futures and they get the education they need."

"Oftentimes what comes across is just one element of my life," she insisted. "It would be like taking a snapshot of many women at a certain point in that woman's day and saying 'Aha, she is a mom,' because you see her with her children, or 'Aha, she is a career woman,' because you see her at work. The stories come and go and I just remain the same."

In one public aspect of her life, she decided on a change. She took as her model the woman whose photograph adorned her desk, the First Lady with whom she most identified, Eleanor Roosevelt. She began writing a weekly newspaper column, as Eleanor had done with the column "My Day," which ran for over twenty years. "Talking It Over," the title Hillary chose, was deliberately bland, and her themes tended to the cosier sides of domesticity. She wrote of feeding her cat, keeping up her driving skills, telephoning home to make sure her daughter had arrived safely, as if the Secret Service might mislay her. "Whatever minor inconveniences my situation presents, I wouldn't trade it for the world," ran her first column. "I could never have imagined the range of activities that are part of my life today, such as defending public television, planning state dinners, and visiting the CIA with the President."

"How can romance thrive when you live above the office with a round-the-clock staff?" she wrote in a column about her twentieth wedding anniversary. She confided that she and her husband would steal out from the White House on hot summer nights and go dipping in the White House pool. For the anniversary in October it was too cold to swim, and Clinton had given her a book of twenty love poems. She came up with something "equally romantic," she revealed, and went on in tones of most unfeminist coyness: "You might be able to guess what it is. But sorry, I'm not telling."

Almost immediately after the 1994 failure of health reform, she began thinking about a book, and spent much of 1995 working on it in longhand. The theme, on the raising of children, could hardly have been more conventional for a First Lady. But from her initial pioneering work on the law governing children at Yale, to her years with the Children's Defense Fund, this was a theme on which she had legitimate expertise. *It Takes a Village—And Other Lessons Children Teach Us* was a deliberately winsome title, drawn from an African proverb that it takes an entire village to raise a child. She hoped and expected that the book's arguments would cause a public stir, and puncture what she thought was an unfair left-liberal image of herself. She argued that couples should stay together for the sake of the children; divorce should be made legally more difficult; and young people should voluntarily abstain from sex until the age of twenty-one.

This was hardly the agenda of the Christian Coalition, and she overestimated the degree to which these modest homilies could balance a public perception that she was the more left-wing of the Clintons. What she had not expected was the new eruption of Whitewater, at the very moment of her national book tour. Each carefully arranged TV, radio, and press interview brushed aside the book to focus on the new lease on life given the affair by a new round of congressional committee hearings. The first, on Whitewater, was convened by Senator D'Amato, chairman of Senator Dole's presidential election campaign. The second, on the Travelgate matter, was convened in the House, and once again one source of news fed the other in a cascade of controversy in which she was the focus.

The contrast between the 1992 campaign, when her loyalty had saved Clinton, and the years in office, when she was targeted as the more vulnerable and controversial of the two, could hardly have been more dramatic. A balance of power within the marriage had shifted. He had appeared to be the liability before the election; she appeared to be the liability after it. She failed to fulfill the health reform mission. She was not able, and indeed did not try, to make the White House into a glittering social or cultural center. And having deliberately made herself a political figure and an international symbol of the new professional woman, she proved strikingly feeble at fighting back against her critics. She stonewalled, rather than counterattacked. She used legalistic evasions, which may have scored a technical point or two, but by January 1995, 52 percent of Americans told *USA Today* that they did not trust her. Her troubles in Whitewater and Travelgate alike sapped at the presidency, just as her husband was in the fight of his political life over the budget.

He made no recriminations against her, as she had made none when he was the target during the New Hampshire primary. An attack on the one was understood to be an attack on them both, simply part of the rough way that politics were played in a city where to be assigned one's own independent counsel was almost a status symbol. Presidents Bush and Reagan had theirs over Iran-Contra; Speakers of the House Jim Wright and Newt Gingrich each had theirs. Subpoenas and legal fees and congressional committees had become almost routine political harassment. It almost went with the territory, and if Hillary broke new ground as she obeyed the grand jury subpoena to appear and give sworn evidence in the Washington, D.C., courthouse, this was but the logical corollary of her public political role. Such was her own rationalization to her friends and supporters, perhaps in an attempt to dampen the unprecedented enormity of a First Lady taking a limousine from the White House to the grand jury room for a prolonged grilling. The experience was not entirely grueling. One grand juror asked her to autograph a copy of her book, which he had bought. She looked confident, and spoke easily to the crowds of TV cameras as she left the courthouse.

The Clintons' mutual support at least belied the earlier sneers about a marriage of convenience. It was far more than that, from their constant dinners out with friends to special events like Hillary's birthday in October 1995. Hillary plotted with her staff to get a Dolly Parton costume, complete with denim and gingham and gigantic blond wig. There were endless jokes about "Stand By Your Man," the Tammy Wynette song she had incautiously mocked when boasting that she would not stay home and bake cookies. The president could hardly take his eyes off her, followed her around the room, kept touching her tossing blond curls and grinning that his Chicago-born wife was a real Arkansas girl at heart. "Tell you one thing, folks," said the First Lady as the party wound down. "The costume can go back in the morning, but I'm going to hang on to this wig."

There were moments when this playful side of Hillary was allowed to emerge in public. When James Carville, the campaign strategist, launched his partisan and jocular book on politics, *We're Right, They're Wrong,* Hillary turned up at Washington's Palm restaurant to help celebrate. "I'm a pushover for sweet-talking Southern boys," she told the crowd. "I know where they're coming from, but I still fall for it." As America's best-known career woman, Hillary then startled the country, and her friends, with the announcement that at the age of forty-eight she thought it would be "terrific" to have another baby, and that she and the president were discussing an adoption. In glaring contrast to the Republican challenger Senator Robert Dole, about to become a grandpaternal seventy-three, Mrs. Clinton told *Time* magazine that she would be "surprised but not disappointed" to be pregnant again.

Outside the public view, Hillary remained her husband's closest political adviser, the one who insisted after the Republican congressional triumphs that he pick his fights, and give battle only on his chosen ground of Medicare, education, and children. The broad principle of balanced budgets was one thing; the immediate public impact of cuts on the people and the causes least able to defend themselves was the issue she insisted he must define. It was astute politics, rallying the Democrats and aiming at the weak joint between the uncompromising new Republicans in Congress and the more moderate veterans. She urged him to get back in touch with the man she had first called sixteen years earlier, when Clinton went down to defeat in his first reelection bid in Arkansas. Their backs were against the wall, she insisted. It was time to call Dick Morris.

☆ 11 ☆

WHITEWATER

American voters do not expect their politicians to be saints. They have knowingly elected to the presidency drunks, adulterers, and men nicknamed "Tricky" and "Slick." But they do not expect the White House to become the butt of lewd humor, and there was something both comic and demeaning about the *American Spectator*'s account of Clinton's romantic escapades in Arkansas by four, and later five, of his former bodyguards. But the delvings of the Resolution Trust Corporation investigators into the bankruptcy of the Madison Guaranty Savings and Loan in Arkansas were far more serious. The Republicans in Congress carefully followed the old rule of insisting they had no interest in the seamy sexual stuff, but they called for congressional hearings into the financial aspects of the Clintons' colorful Arkansas past. To go from trysts to trust funds was quite a stretch, but the *American Spectator* story of December 1993 managed—just—to connect them.

For well over a year, reporters and investigators had been probing into two separate aspects of Clinton's governorship in Arkansas. The first was his cavalier sex life. Even an American media chastened by the way they destroyed the political career of presidential candidate Gary Hart in 1988 pursued the matter. When faced by a woman like Gennifer Flowers, who said on the record that she had had a long affair with Bill Clinton and played some tape recordings to prove that she knew him well, it became a legitimate story. Clinton himself helped that process of legitimization by admitting, in a national TV interview during his presidential campaign, that he had "caused pain in my marriage."

The second probe was into the complex financial affairs of the Madison

Guaranty Savings and Loan, a small Arkansas banking house that collapsed in 1989, leaving U.S. taxpayers with a $49 million bill to bail out the federally insured depositors. The first reports about the Clintons' connection to the owner of the bank, James McDougal, surfaced in March 1992, during the election campaign, in a story in the *New York Times.* Clinton asked a lawyer friend based in Denver, James Lyons, to compile a quick report, which suggested the Clintons had been silent partners and had lost money in a failed property venture with McDougal, and the fuss faded.

But the Resolution Trust Corporation, the body charged with cleaning up the financial debris of the wave of savings and loan bankruptcies in the 1980s, was legally required to investigate failed banks. The RTC investigators established that a technically bankrupt bank had been paying the mortgage on a property loan to the Whitewater Development Corporation, co-owned by McDougal and the Clintons. The RTC investigators alerted the U.S. Treasury, their parent institution, and referred a possible criminal inquiry to the Justice Department. Alarm bells began to ring inside the White House.

Senior officials from the Treasury, including chief of staff Josh Steiner and the top Treasury lawyer Jean Hanson, discussed the progress of the RTC inquiries with White House counsel Bernard Nussbaum. The meetings took place in October 1993, just after the Justice Department was first asked by banking regulators to investigate possible illegal activity by the failed Madison Guaranty, which Hillary Clinton had represented as a lawyer. Deputy Treasury Secretary Roger Altman, who was acting head of the Resolution Trust Corporation, also discussed with Nussbaum the RTC's own legal strategies. He later admitted this had been "bad judgment." The RTC was weighing its own legal action against the officers, executives, and lawyers of the failed Madison Guaranty—a list that included Hillary Clinton as well as the bank's chief, James McDougal, the Clintons' partner in the Whitewater venture.

Until the end of Clinton's first year in office, those two separate probes—of Governor Clinton's sex life and Whitewater—had never been linked. But the sex and the money began to conflate through Hillary Clinton, the ultimate political wife, who had helped inoculate her husband against sexual scandal by standing by him during the campaign and insisting that in spite of the ups and downs of many modern marriages, their relationship and their family was firm and strong. Tucked away inside the

11,000-word story in the *American Spectator* was the first published suggestion that Hillary Clinton reacted to her husband's dalliances with a romantic liaison of her own.

The incestuous nature of the small southern city of Little Rock and the small state of Arkansas was central to the whole tale. The man she was said to have spent weekends with at a mountain cabin was, like her husband, another country boy made good from the same small town of Hope, her partner at the Rose Law Firm in Little Rock, Vince Foster. The rumors of a romantic relationship between Hillary Clinton and Vince Foster had first circulated in Little Rock in the early 1980s, and then revived again in Washington—as interesting but unproven historical gossip—after a personal tragedy hit the White House.

Vince Foster was an old friend of both Clintons, and he and his wife regularly dined with them at the governor's mansion in Little Rock and at local restaurants. The Clintons would visit Foster's home, sip his proud collection of vintage wines, and use his swimming pool while the outdoor speaker system blared out the Aretha Franklin music he relished. Foster and Hillary Clinton worked in the same office, partners in the Rose Law Firm, lunched together in diners in the five or six blocks that made up downtown Little Rock, worked late together on cases, and never hid the closeness of their professional relationship.

Foster was thus, inevitably, among the Arkansas mafia who came up to Washington when the Clintons took over the White House. Another Rose partner, William Kennedy, joined Foster in the White House counsel's office. Yet another, Webb Hubbell, went to the Department of Justice as assistant attorney general. Along with other FOBs, Arkansas loyalists were spread in key positions throughout the administration. The process was managed by the new White House personnel director, Bruce Lindsey, who had first met Bill Clinton when they were students working in the Washington office of Arkansas senator Bill Fulbright in the 1960s—where another Arkansan, James McDougal, was also going through Fulbright's rite of passage for clever and ambitious boys from his home state.

There was Thomas "Mack" McLarty, the new White House chief of staff and a friend of Clinton since their days in the kindergarten together in Hope. Carol Rasco began working for a children's group that Hillary founded in Little Rock, joined the governor's staff, and ran the Domestic Policy Council in the White House. David Watkins, also from Hope, with wide business interests in telecommunications, became the White House administrative manager. He and Hillary Clinton were partners in a 1983 business deal to start a cellular telephone company in Little Rock. Hillary made a $48,000 profit on a $2,000 investment in that venture. The failure of the Whitewater property company seems to have been an odd aberration in Mrs. Clinton's otherwise stunningly profitable business life.

Vince Foster, another member of the fraternity from the Hope kindergarten, became deputy White House counsel and the personal lawyer for the First Family. His duties were various. Foster had to clear up the mess that emerged when Clinton sacked the old White House travel office staff to replace them with a team from a Little Rock travel agency run by a distant cousin. The sacking was handled by Hope's David Watkins. Foster also had to deal with the embarrassments over Hillary Clinton's personal stock portfolio, which had been trading profitably in pharmaceutical stocks, when she was known to be running the health reform task force.

Finally there was the Madison S&L problem, on which Foster kept files in his White House office. Madison was founded by James McDougal, who had then worked for Governor Bill Clinton as an aide for economic development, and then became one of his most important financial supporters when Clinton went looking for campaign funds. Mrs. Clinton did some legal work for Madison, which was treated with remarkable leniency by Arkansas banking regulators appointed by Governor Clinton.

Moreover, McDougal and the Clintons jointly invested in a property development scheme called Whitewater, a resort complex in the Ozark Mountains. The project was launched in October 1978, the month before Clinton was first elected governor, which may help to explain the eagerness of the local banks to advance him money for Whitewater with little collateral. The Clintons insisted that over the subsequent fourteen years, they had lost a goodly chunk of their savings, as much as $69,000, on their investment, in which they had been initially little more than silent partners. But the questions kept nagging, in part because Whitewater had been very slow to pay its taxes, and because Madison Guaranty found it hard to explain several large payments to the Whitewater account. Since he was steward of all the Clintons' personal financial affairs, Vince Foster kept a file on Whitewater along with his files on the Madison S&L in his White House office.

None of this explained what happened on July 20, when Vince Foster, then forty-eight, left his White House office, drove across the Potomac River to the old Civil War entrenchments at Fort Marcy, walked some 200 yards from his car, leaned against one of the old cannons that dotted the scenic spot, and shot himself in the head.

The work pressures on Foster were intense. He had left his wife and children back in Arkansas, and they had only lately joined him. He was under medical treatment for depression and overwork. The travel office controversy haunted him. He was being pilloried by the *Wall Street Journal,* which had run a lead editorial just three days before his suicide, headlined "Who Is Vincent Foster?" In the week before his death, Foster heard press gossip that the conservative *Washington Times* had assigned a team of reporters to probe his background and to explore the rumors about him and the woman who was now the First Lady. (*Washington Times* spokesmen have insisted this was not the case.)

Apart from the state troopers' claim to have seen Foster and Hillary embracing, and their unsupported allegations of weekend trips to the mountain cabin owned by the Rose Law Firm, there was no evidence that this was anything more than a close friendship. And as Hillary declared, the troopers' evidence was clearly suspect because of their motives of financial gain. Foster, his wife, and their three children had all been family friends of the Clintons, close members of that circle of power and influence in the small state of Arkansas that spread from the governor's mansion through public life and into the centers of private wealth like the Rose Law Firm and the Madison S&L.

In a place as small as Little Rock, a city of 180,000 people and the financial, political, and social center of a small and poor southern state of 2.5 million people, the grand Washington concept of conflict of interest simply did not, and possibly could not, apply. Most of the Little Rock elite came to their positions of local influence through the big high schools of Little Rock, Hot Springs, and Pine Bluff. They had gone to University of Arkansas football games together and squealed the eerie Arkansas hog call of "Sooo-eee" as they cheered on the Razorbacks. They had studied together as the state law school, politicked through the Young Democrats, and networked through Senator Fulbright's office, and through the local power structure around the governor's office.

Everyone not only knew everyone else, they had always known each other. Business and politics and social parties and private lives intermingled through the years, as clever and ambitious young men built their careers and their families. And doubtless some of them, who had dated and flirted and grown up in the same social group before they all married and settled down, slept with one another's wives. It would have been surprising if they had not, in the sexual revolution of America in the 1970s and 1980s.

Three days after the story broke, amid heady talk of a new Watergate and harrumphing Republicans demanding Senate hearings and special prosecutors, Clinton felt constrained to say that he would release his private files on Madison and Whitewater, removed from Vince Foster's office after the suicide, to the Justice Department's investigators. The boil was lanced. The sexual gossip began to fade away. The Arkansas state troopers were found to have misled insurers about a car crash they were involved in. And the fuss began to die down.

The Arkansas mafia in the White House had reckoned that it would. The only threat to Clinton's position would have been some evidence that Whitewater and Madison were used as some kind of illegal slush fund for his Arkansas campaigns. And indeed, McDougal and Madison proved most generous to his 1984 campaign. But this trail appeared to go cold. Under Arkansas law, campaign finance archives need be kept for no more than five years. The documentation kept by the state secretary's office had gone. Whatever Republican gossip may have suggested about campaign finance, the evidence had all been—quite legally—destroyed.

And as Clinton enjoyed the bracing golf links of Hilton Head, he could hope that in 1993, as in his stormy campaign year of 1992, he had shown that American voters had grown out of the puritan tradition that destroyed Gary Hart. Not so. Clinton's new private lawyer had arranged for the Justice Department to subpoena the Whitewater papers, which kept them sealed from public scrutiny, and invited Republicans to ask what was being concealed. Then the new year opened with another sexual allegation, from a former Arkansas state employee, Paula Jones, who complained that Governor Clinton had lured her to a hotel room, dropped his trousers, and urged her to perform oral sex upon him. She then filed a lawsuit against him.

Conservative fingerprints were smeared across the entire affair. Ms. Jones was first mentioned in the celebrated account of what the Arkansas state troopers saw in the *American Spectator* article. Ms. Jones chose the setting of a conservative political conference in Washington in February 1994 to make her first public claim that Mr. Clinton tried to proposition her in a Little Rock hotel room in 1991. She was accompanied by an Arkansas lawyer and longtime Clinton foe, Cliff Jackson, who had first met Clinton when they were at Oxford, where Jackson claims to have used his Republican connections to help Clinton avoid the draft to the Vietnam War. In the 1992 campaign, Jackson publicized Clinton's draft embarrassments, and organized an independent group to run anti-Clinton ads during the primary campaigns.

Ms. Jones's lawyer, Gil Davis, was a veteran Republican activist, a candidate for state prosecutor in Fairfax County, Virginia, in 1975, who helped organize the George Bush presidential campaign in Michigan in 1988. "The only ideology we have is the capacity to be financed, as long as it's a clean matter and these people are not some criminals or disreputable," Davis said. "I guess if I received on her behalf a contribution from Saddam Hussein we'd send it back."

Conservatives rallied to Ms. Jones, starting legal defense funds to finance her campaign and fuel the president's embarrassment. The fundraising effort brought together the most partisan of the various factions of the right, from the Christian Defense Coalition, the anti-abortion group Operation Rescue, and the Legal Affairs Council, which helped finance the defense of Marine colonel Oliver North during his trial arising from the Iran-Contra scandal. Patrick Mahoney, director of the Christian Defense Coalition and a leader of Operation Rescue, opened the first Paula Jones legal fund. The previous year, he had tried to present President Clinton with an aborted fifteen-week fetus, and ran a nine-city "Impeach Clinton in '94" bus tour. The Legal Affairs Council then opened its own appeal for Ms. Jones, and the right-wing talk-show host Rush Limbaugh and the Christian Broadcasting Network of the TV evangelist and former Republican presidential candidate Pat Robertson strongly promoted the cause.

Not unreasonably, Clinton's political aides in the White House suspected a coordinated conspiracy by the right wing to discredit a presidency they had never regarded as legitimate. Mr. Clinton's top-gun Washington lawyer in the sexual harassment case, Robert Bennett, claimed that the Paula Jones operation was "an attempt to rewrite the verdict of the 1992 election."

The Republican leaders, high-mindedly pursuing the Whitewater trail, demanded congressional inquiries as the story dominated the media.

From eastern Europe, in the course of a European trip to a NATO conference and a summit in Moscow, Clinton persuaded Hillary that the best course was to agree that an independent special counsel be appointed to make a full inquiry into Whitewater. This would remove the heat from the Republican demands, he argued, and eventually clear their name. At this time, the law authorizing Congress to appoint an independent counsel had lapsed. But the justice department had the right to nominate an independent investigator. The attorney general appointed a moderate Republican lawyer, Robert B. Fiske, Jr., to the task, and he began by reopening the investigation into the suicide of Vince Foster, already the subject of lurid speculation.

The story continued to spin wildly out of control as the media descended on Arkansas to investigate Rose Law Firm, its former partners now in Washington, and any other story of Arkansas in the 1980s that could possibly be related to the Whitewater affair. They could hardly avoid Hillary's business skill in the futures markets. In releasing the computerized records from Chicago's Mercantile Exchange of Mrs. Clinton's trading in cattle futures, the White House provided the first clear evidence that she was given special treatment by her brokers in turning a $1,000 investment into almost $100,000 in 1978–1979. Her brokers bent the rules to allow her to order ten cattle futures contracts in her first trade. She should have put up $12,000 for those trades, but had only $1,000 in her trading account.

The records indicate that Mrs. Clinton's broker, Robert "Red" Bone, had consistently allowed her to trade in contracts that cost far more than the sums in her account. The Clinton family friend and investment adviser James Blair had a glib explanation for that. "I was a very good customer" of Red Bone's brokerage, paying over $800,000 in commissions," Blair said. "They weren't going to hassle me. If I brought them somebody, they weren't going to hassle them." Blair was and remains a senior executive at Tyson Foods. As President Bush's campaign ads had pointed out, the price of the chicken industry was that the Clinton administration in Little Rock put up with an unwholesome degree of pollution in rivers fouled with chicken waste. Of the personal friendship between the Blairs and Clintons there is no doubt. They had been friends since the Miami convention in 1972. The Clintons stayed at the Blair country home in their visit back to Arkansas the previous summer. But the professional, or financial, relationship between the governor's wife and the business chiefs of Arkansas all looked rather too close for ethical comfort.

Alleging "a White House cover-up," the Republicans took advantage of the old Washington rule that it is less the original error that causes the political damage than the subsequent attempts to control and bury it. They threatened a blockade of all the administration's financial appointments and legislative reforms until the Democratic majority in Congress allowed public hearings into Whitewater.

The very word *water* helped stir echoes of the Watergate paraphernalia of 1973–1974. The mention of special prosecutors and grand juries and then the familiar ritual of senior presidential aides tossed like sacrifices from the White House suggested some dreadful reenactment of the humiliation of Richard Nixon, in which Hillary Clinton had played a modest part. This was not because of any picayune financial fiddlings and delayed taxes and unsavory ways to raise campaign funds in Arkansas politics in the 1980s. Unlike the original Watergate affair, with its covert dirty tricks team inside the White House, using campaign funds to burgle the offices and destabilize the campaigns of Nixon's opponents, the original offense of Whitewater was thin stuff. It is what happened after Clinton's election victory that did the damage: the suicide of Vince Foster; the possible obstruction of justice by senior White House staff in searching Foster's office before the police were allowed in; and their failure to report the removal of files relating to the Clintons' investments in the Whitewater property venture.

The further problem was the understandable efforts by President Clinton's overzealous legal adviser, White House counsel Bernard Nussbaum, to monitor the various inquiries by Treasury and federal banking regulators into the Whitewater mess. It was the implication of an attempted cover-up in three White House meetings with the regulators that provoked special counsel Fiske's subpoenas for a host of senior aides. As the president's lawyer, Nussbaum had a duty to protect his client and his old protégée Hillary Clinton, and to keep an eye on troublesome inquiries that could embarrass them. But as a veteran of the Judiciary Committee's 1973 investigation into Richard Nixon's Watergate scandal (where he first hired the ambitious young Hillary), Nussbaum had a political duty to keep the current White House above suspicion.

The final, grumpy resignation of Nussbaum was unwilling, unrepentant, and had to be forced by President Clinton, just after a self-congratulatory weekly radio talk to the nation about the pace of the economic recovery under his stewardship and the 2,090,000 new jobs created since he had taken the oath of office. Then Clinton decided on the spur of the sunny springtime moment to take his wife and daughter to the presidential retreat, Camp David. Thrilled at the prospect, he did a little jig and flung his arms joyously into the air as he strolled to the helicopter.

The contrast was extraordinary between the president's public insouciance and the grim forebodings of meltdown that gripped the White House staff. As the president waved a cheery good-bye from the White House lawn, the legal wolves began to gather outside the fence. Within the week, seven of the president's men and the First Lady's women were to be interrogated under oath, before a grand jury, by Fiske and his investigating attorneys. The Whitewater damage control strategy, of getting the fuss off the front pages and into the legal oubliette of a special prosecutor's inquiry, had failed. Fiske had proved too feistily independent for the president's comfort. It also meant that the focus of the president's difficulty had shifted fundamentally, from long-ago and financially piddling affairs in Arkansas, in which the American public was never much interested. The investigations were now concentrating on events inside the White House since the Clintons moved in, and at this point the public was taking notice.

A CNN-*Time* poll taken as the Clintons left for Camp David found only 40 percent of voters who said Clinton was "a president you can trust." A majority of 56 percent said that on the question of trust, they "have some reservations." The American public had been down this road so often before. The very language of special prosecutors and subpoenas and grand juries sitting in judgment on the White House carried its own presumptions of guilt. And these phrases triggered reflex memories of all the other presidential scandals with which the country had become so miserably familiar.

There had been so many. George Bush had his Iraq-gate troubles, and was dogged into the last week of the 1992 presidential campaign by his role in the earlier Iran-Contra affair. Ronald Reagan's presidency tottered under Iran-Contra, and before that, President Jimmy Carter's White House never quite recovered from the investigations of his friend and budget manager, the Georgian banker Bert Lance. Lance was subsequently acquitted, but the mud stuck. President Ford was in office too briefly to get into trouble, save for his pardon of Richard Nixon for the Watergate affair, which was memorably described by Daniel Ellsberg as "a slow coup against the U.S. Constitution." Ellsberg, the former Defense Department aide who leaked the Pentagon Papers, was himself a victim of Nixon's plumbers, who burgled his psychiatrist's office in the attempt to get his medical files.

Nixon was the real reference point for modern political scandal, not only because the Watergate abuse of presidential powers sank him, but also because he survived the first modern media scandal. Like Clinton during the campaign, Richard Nixon, as vice-presidential nominee in 1952, faced his tormentors, parading his wife and family and his pet dog, Checkers, on TV. Republicans and conservatives constantly harked back to the original Watergate, exposing the raw wounds they still felt.

"There was not in Watergate anything similar to Vincent Foster's death, nor to the inexcusable way it was handled by the White House: giving the Park Police responsibility for the investigation; the secret removal of files from Mr. Foster's office; the lame statement that the so-called suicide note in Mr. Foster's briefcase had been overlooked earlier," commented Judge (and Professor) Robert Bork. He had been solicitor general under Nixon and was evidently delighted to get his own back on those Democratic liberals who blocked his appointment to the Supreme Court in the Reagan era. "There is far more evidence of a cover-up here than there ever was in Watergate until the tapes were played."

The mood in Washington was poisonous as the Republicans nursed their old wounds from earlier scandals and delighted in watching the Democrats twist in the wind. The vindictive flavor was perfectly caught in an essay written by Mrs. Rachel Abrams, wife of President Reagan's assistant secretary of state Elliott Abrams, who was pardoned by President Bush after pleading guilty to two counts of withholding information from Congress in the Iran-Contra affair.

"I know something about Bill and Hillary Clinton right now," she wrote, in the *Washington Times,* which scored many of the key scoops on Whitewater. "I know how their stomachs churn, their anxiety mounts, how their worry over their defenseless child increases. I know their inability to sleep at night and their reluctance to rise in the morning. I know every new incursion of doubt, every heartbreak over bailing friends, every sting and bite the press gives, every jaw-clenching look at front pages. I know all this, and the thought of it makes me happy."

The Republicans, charging that "we have gone from possible illegal acts prior to assuming office to the possibility of illegal acts by a president in office," saw their revenge for their party's Watergate humiliation twenty years earlier. They also calculated that the Clintons' embarrassments gave them a strong chance of regaining control of Congress in the elections in November. Their rhetoric was partisan and damning. "I don't expect the president to take my advice, but I think if the president wants to serve his term out, he's going to have to begin by leveling with the American people," said Republican senator Phil Gramm of Texas. "This is a case study in self-immolation," charged Republican leader Senator Robert Dole. "Omissions, misstatements of fact, negotiated subpoenas, behind-the-scenes meetings have all created the impression that there's something to hide."

There were reasons why the Whitewater scandal found new oxygen to keep the flames roaring. The first was that the broader Whitewater inquiry was the first opportunity for the U.S. press and public to revisit that great unexplored scandal of the 1980s, the collapse of the savings and loan industry. Shorn of traditional banking controls, these American building societies ran wild in the decade of greed, and their subsequent bankruptcies had to be bailed out by the taxpayers at a cost of over $200 billion. The Madison Guaranty Bank of Arkansas was a classic example. Its failure cost taxpayers some $49 million.

The second new inquiry that Whitewater opened was that other 1980s scandal of the tax-free bonds issued by states and municipalities. The underwriting of those bonds was a safe and lucrative business, usually doled out by state governors like Clinton to important campaign fund-raisers like Daniel Lasater of Arkansas. And with Lasater, the socially incestuous connections of the Little Rock elite began to look politically lethal. He kindly provided a job for Mr. Clinton's wayward half-brother, Roger, and later (like Roger) went to prison for cocaine trafficking. Lasater's bond trading helped topple another, Illinois-based S&L into bankruptcy. The lawyer who successfully negotiated his fine down from $3.3 million to $200,000 was Hillary Clinton.

The two White House aides who helped Bernard Nussbaum search Vince Foster's office after his suicide were Mrs. Clinton's chief of staff,

Margaret Williams, and Patsy Thomason. The person they seem to have been determined to protect was Foster's old Rose Law Firm partner, Hillary Clinton. The phrase "Hillary-gate" began to enter the public vocabulary. But the original sin here had less to do with her, or with Little Rock, or even with the files in Vince Foster's office, than with the perilous vulnerability of all American politicians to their desperate need for campaign funds, and their lack of caution in accepting them.

A former highways commissioner in Arkansas, in the 1980s Patsy Thomasson also worked as top aide to the Arkansas bond dealer Dan Lasater, and took over his business when he went to prison. Patsy Thomasson then went to work for Mrs. Clinton at the Rose Law Firm and followed her to the White House. Lasater, who had given a job on his horse farm to then Governor Clinton's younger brother and paid off his cocaine debt, ran a bond brokerage that handled over $100 million in Arkansas state bond sales. Lasater collected at least $1.6 million in fees for his work. The bulk of these bond sales were on behalf of the Arkansas Development Finance Authority, promoted by Governor Clinton to build the infrastructure that would induce private industry to create jobs in the state. The ADFA charter was drawn up by Webb Hubbell, a partner of Mrs. Clinton in the Rose firm, and all bond deals had to be personally approved by Governor Clinton. One of the companies that received low-interest ADFA loans was owned by Mr. Hubbell's father-in-law and brother-in-law. The Wall Street firm that was sole or joint underwriter in some $400 million of ADFA bonds was Goldman, Sachs, whose vice-chairman Robert Rubin was to become Clinton's secretary of the Treasury.

The inquiry into the affairs of Dan Lasater, who was one of Governor Clinton's key fund-raisers in the mid-1980s, opened two dangerous topics. The first was the use of state bond contracts to reward political supporters, which was widespread in U.S. state politics, and the second was the Arkansas cocaine subculture. While there was no serious suggestion that Governor Clinton ever took the drug, there were allegations that he told the Arkansas state police to turn a blind eye to the use of the local Mena Airport by smugglers who took arms to the Nicaraguan Contras, and were alleged to have brought back cocaine. This was just as tricky an issue for Republicans as for Clinton. Mena Airport was used to supply the Nicaraguan Contras as part of the illegal effort to destabilize the left-wing state of Nicaragua, in a covert operation run from the White House basement by then Marine colonel Oliver North. Clinton was one of the few Democrats to support that effort by the Reagan presidency, sending the Arkansas National Guard to training camps in Honduras.

The Mena airfield in Arkansas was an important part of Oliver North's operation to supply the Contra guerrillas. The arms-carrying cargo plane, whose shooting down by Nicaraguan troops in 1986 launched the investigation into the Contra supply operation, had been based and serviced at Mena. In his memoirs, Oliver North paid tribute to the help of Barry Seal, the former owner of that plane. Barry Seal was a CIA and Drug Enforcement Agency informant, who also on occasion smuggled cocaine for the Medellin cartel. Before his murder, carried out while he was under the federal witness protection program, Seal helped federal prosecutors draw up charges against Arkansas businessmen, including Lasater, relating to the laundering of cocaine money through the state bond market. With the death of the key witness, the case lapsed.

Rose Law Firm, no longer preening at its powerful White House connections, scrambled to restore a reputation that had been battered by the spillover from Whitewater. Rose began to face new scrutiny for its role in helping the discredited Bank of Credit and Commerce International acquire its U.S. banking arm, First American. Rose was the law firm for the most powerful financial group in Arkansas, Stephens, Inc., America's biggest investment firm outside of Wall Street, and its associated Worthen Bank. When Clinton's presidential campaign was faltering for lack of money in February 1992, the Worthen Bank came through loyally with a $3.5 million loan to bail out the state's favorite son.

Stephens, Inc., owned a part of the holding company, Financial General, which controlled the First National Bank of Georgia. This bank was run by Bert Lance, who was forced to resign from his post under Jimmy Carter as director of the Office of Management and Budget. The cause was a 1978 fuss about lax southern financial ethics affronting the more exacting standards of Washington, an interesting forerunner to the Whitewater affair.

Bert Lance, Stephens, Inc., and the Rose Law Firm all helped BCCI to creep into the U.S. banking market through its purchase of shares in Financial General. And in the internecine way of American law and finance, the special prosecutor investigating Whitewater, Robert Fiske, represented former defense secretary Clark Clifford, who was charged with false statements to bank regulators as lawyer and later banking executive for the BCCI-controlled First American. (Little Rock is not the only incestuous small town in America; the world of big-time corporate law is also very tight-knit. So is that of international banking. After BCCI's bankruptcy, Stephens, Inc., bought its Hong Kong branch from the receivers.)

All this, added to speculation on the Rush Limbaugh radio show that Vince Foster had been shot elsewhere and his body moved to the park where he was found, made for an alarming brew. After a furious internal debate, the White House finally decided on a "full-disclosure" strategy. Clinton judged that he had to rebut the accusations of a cover-up. "We are open. We are not closed. There is no bunker mentality," President Clinton insisted, in the course of his second press conference in successive days.

This readiness to cooperate with congressional and independent inquiries calmed the storm. Then the most dangerous aspect of the scandals for the Clintons deflated, when Republican congressional investigators reported that they had found "no surprises" in their review of the police and autopsy reports on the death of former White House deputy counsel Vince Foster. "I found nothing in the report that would disabuse me of the idea that it was suicide, or that would challenge the official verdict of suicide," said Congressman William F. Clinger, Jr., of Pennsylvania, one of a team of Republicans allowed to review the reports in the possession of the special prosecutor, Robert Fiske. But then Congress authorized once more the appointment of an independent counsel, the same device that had been deployed in the Iran-Contra affair, and a loyal Republican lawyer, Kenneth Starr, was appointed to the task by a bench of conservative judges. Robert Fiske was relieved of his duties. Starr began to reopen the Foster suicide yet again, spurred on by a burgeoning subculture of conspiracy theorists.

For an independent counsel asked to investigate a complex tale of conflicts of interest, Kenneth Starr had some jarring interests of his own. Unlike many previous independent counsel, he chose to remain an active member of his private law firm. An inquiry by the *Nation* established that Starr's firm, Kirkland and Ellis, was being sued for professional negligence by the Resolution Trust Corporation, the body which first raised the question of criminal charges over the Madison bankruptcy. Starr's firm eventually settled the suit with a payment of some $325,000, but only after Starr had been pursuing the RTC-related inquiries for seventeen months. Moreover, Starr had been hired by the tobacco company Brown and Williamson to handle its legal battles while the Clinton administration campaigned to curb smoking. Starr also gave legal advice to the Bradley Foundation, which provided financial support to conservative causes, including the *American Spectator,* and the Free Congress Foundation, which finances the conservative National Empowerment Television. Kenneth Starr enjoyed a high reputation for probity in the legal profession, but he was a partisan Republican, a former attorney-general in the Bush administration, who reinforced the impression that the Whitewater affair was the pursuit of politics by other means.

There were more reverberations to come. When the new Republican majority took control of the House and Senate in 1995, they had the license to run their own inquiries, with rights of subpoena, through congressional committees. They sent investigators into a new area of inquiry, the fate of $350,000 of missing funds, taken out as personal loans by then-governor Bill Clinton for his campaigns in the 1980s, but not appearing on local election finance records. Their inquiry benefited from an unexpected discovery in local archives. Until 1990, Arkansas law held that campaign finance records need be kept for no longer than four years, and all state records for elections before that date had legally been destroyed. But the records for Pulaski County, which includes the city of Little Rock and is thus the main fund-raising center of Arkansas politics, existed back to the election of 1984. These records listed twelve personal loans, for sums totaling $400,000, taken out from the small Bank of Cherry Valley, by Governor Clinton between 1983 and 1988.

The bank was run by W. Maurice Smith, also a Clinton fund-raiser, campaign finance chairman, and an Arkansas highway commissioner. According to Maurice Smith, Clinton used these sums to make loans to his election campaign committees, a standard practice by politicians who take out personal loans in the heat of the campaigning, which are later repaid by postelection fund-raising. But the Pulaski County records showed only one such loan from Mr. Clinton, for $50,000, to his 1984 campaign, and none at all for 1986 and 1990. The Senate investigators began probing what happened to the other $350,000. (More than $130,000 of this money had been raised by Governor Clinton to pay off the loans to finance the Blue Ribbon Education Committee. See page 99.)

"Were Whitewater papers destroyed? Were they sent to different places? Who sent them? Who took them, and under whose direction? That's what we are going to have to ascertain," said Senator Alfonse D'Amato, chairman of the Senate Banking Committee. Senator D'Amato and his counterpart in the House, Congressman Jim Leach, postponed further public hearings until after the independent counsel Kenneth Starr concluded his own inquiry.

Two grand juries were sitting in Washington and in Arkansas, weighing the evidence produced by special counsel Starr, with his team of twenty lawyers and twenty-six FBI agents, and with the benefit of the evidence being given behind closed doors by former assistant attorney general Webb Hubbell. The wide-ranging inquiries across Arkansas and the intense focus on the Rose Law Firm found a victim in Webb Hubbell, a former state supreme court judge in Arkansas. Under intense pressure from Kenneth Starr to reach a plea bargain by cooperating with the Whitewater inquiry, he was found to have falsified his expenses and committed fraud, and was sentenced and convicted to a short prison term.

The greatest danger to Bill Clinton was not the testimony of Webb Hubbell, nor the odd circumstances around the death of Vince Foster, nor his cavalier way with the women of Arkansas, nor his wife's financial genius with cattle futures, nor even the overzealous attempts of his staff to protect him. Far less was it the original Whitewater investment, or even the casual ethics that characterized most campaign fund-raising in Arkansas, as they did in U.S. politics more generally. The mortal peril lay in the pride of Congress, and its insistence on its power to act as the highest court of all over any hint of presidential wrongdoing. Add to that congressional prerogative an intensely partisan Republican Party, itching to do to a Democratic president what a Democratic Congress did to the Republican presidents Nixon, Reagan, and Bush, and the stage was set for a drama of constitutional intensity.

But there was a new chorus for that drama, which threatened constantly to become part of the action. It was composed of the new media of the pugnacious radio call-in shows, of the conspiracy theories teeming over the Internet, and of self-appointed truth squads who sent blizzards of info-faxes to journalists and radio stations around the country. This chorus was constantly fed new plot lines by a band of dedicated conservative journalists who were convinced that Bill and Hillary Clinton were wickedness personified. They saw the Clintons as presidential versions of the Godfather, the head capos of an Arkansas mafia that would not stop at serial murder to preserve their power.

The key conspiracy theorists were an interesting crew. There was Sherman Skolnick, a quadriplegic largely confined to his Chicago home, who published the *Conspiracy Nation* newsletter on the Internet. He claimed that Foster was working for the code-breaking National Security Agency and was blackmailed by the Israeli intelligence over his secret Swiss bank accounts.

There was James Dale Davidson, editor of *Strategic Investment,* the newsletter that claimed Foster's body was moved from the Ballston apartment. This was reported by Rush Limbaugh, sending Wall Street into a brief flutter of panic. Davidson, also marketing a video on the death of Foster, claimed that FBI director William Sessions was sacked the day before Foster's death as part of the planned cover-up.

There was Andrew Price, who ran the Clinton Investigative Commission, raising funds for an impeachment campaign on the basis that "I have in my possession compelling evidence that proves beyond all shadow of doubt that Vincent Foster was murdered." There was Floyd Brown, editor of *Clinton Watch,* which claimed that the Dan Lasater cocaine and bond-washing connection still ran through the White House, where Lasater's former executive vice president Patsy Thomasson became Clinton's director of administration. Brown's aide David Bossie was later to join the investigating staff of Senator Alfonse D'Amato. Brown had made his political name with the 1988 attack ads featuring the paroled black rapist Willy Horton, which were used to devastating effect against the Democratic candidate Michael Dukakis. In 1992, he offered a pay-per-call service to hear the tapes of Gennifer Flowers. By 1994, he had built a cottage industry around Whitewater, with forty employees, a mailing list of over 175,000 subscribers to his newsletter *Clinton Watch,* and an annual budget of $3 million. There was the Reverend Jerry Falwell, TV evangelist, who marketed videotapes claiming Clinton's responsibility for multiple murders, including Foster's, to cover up a massive stock manipulation swindle with the Stephens family of Little Rock. There was former Republican congressman William E. Dannemeyer, who claimed that the four federal agents shot in the first raid on the Waco Branch Davidian compound were in fact former Clinton bodyguards who were being conveniently disposed of.

If there was a single mastermind behind all this, it was Richard M. Scaife, multimillionaire heir to the Mellon fortune and owner of the *Pittsburgh Tribune-Review.* Its articles questioning the "suicide" of Vince Foster were regularly reprinted as advertisements by Accuracy in Media and the Western Journalism Center, independent conservative bodies financed by Scaife. "Unless there is a national outcry demanding that the media tell the American people the truth, the cover-up is likely to continue," said Accuracy in Media.

The most relentless reports in the mainstream media came in the *Washington Times,* owned by the Korean cult known as the Moonies; in the editorials, rather than the news pages, of the *Wall Street Journal*; and in the *American Spectator,* the right-wing journal that published the accounts of Governor Clinton's sexual dalliances as recounted by his bodyguards among disgruntled Arkansas state troopers. The *Spectator* also explored the White House travel office affair and the alleged cover-up of Whitewater.

There was a curious British fascination with Whitewater, led by Ambrose Evans-Pritchard of the *Sunday Telegraph.* His reports into the shooting of Luther Parks, the Switzerland travels of Vince Foster, and the Mena Airport cocaine connection have helped others stitch the entire conspiracy theory together. Lord Rees-Mogg, a former editor of the *Times* of London, declared Watergate to be small beer by comparison to "the narco-millionaires of Arkansas [who] bought political protection by bribery and financing political campaigns, including Clinton's. They killed dangerous witnesses, including schoolboys and probably including Vince Foster; his body was moved; his suicide was faked."

Lyndon LaRouche, former Trotskyite and occasional presidential candidate, who claimed that Henry Kissinger was a Soviet agent and that the Queen ran the global narco-trafficking business, counterargued that Rees-Mogg and Evans-Pritchard were part of a British intelligence plot to destabilize the Clinton administration.

"There is an incredible cross-pollination of ridiculous and bizarre conspiracy theories," commented Mark Fabiani, White House associate counsel. "They start up on the Internet, get pushed by privately financed publications like the *Strategic Investment Newsletter,* broadcast on talk-radio, fed across to right-wing newspapers in Britain, and then seep back over here into the conservative press like the *Washington Times* and *American Spectator,* and they pick up steam with each stage. There's an awful lot of smoke, but still no fire."

Each time the big guns of the American media focused on the thickest swirls of smoke, they failed to find any hard evidence of crime. But for the suspicious, that too is evidence of just how far the conspiracy runs. "I say to the powers of the *Washington Post—j'accuse,*" Evans-Pritchard wrote in the *Sunday Telegraph,* an article instantly reprinted in the *Washington Times.* He accused the *Post* of spiking critical stories and of a concerted attempt to "muddy the waters and discredit anybody who has been asking legitimate questions about the death of Mr. Foster."

Contract killings and big-time cocaine smuggling, unusual crashes of private planes in good weather, mysterious fires and burglaries, and attacks on journalists visiting Little Rock to steal their papers—the paranoid subculture of the Whitewater affair reached feverish heights. After months of probing the sexual habits of Governor Bill Clinton in Arkansas, more months sorting through the tightly woven entrails of Arkansas law firms and banking, the president's implacable foes in the conservative press went beyond questioning the suicide of White House aide Vince Foster to suggest a broader Mafia-style pattern of murder and intimidation.

The Murdoch-owned tabloid *New York Post,* which first questioned Foster's suicide, pushed the speculation into weird new terrain when it listed an intriguing series of misadventures under the headline "Mysterious Attacks: Linked to Whitewater?"

On September 26, 1993, Luther "Jerry" Parks was gunned down by ten bullets as he left a Mexican restaurant in Little Rock. His company, American Contract Services, had provided the security both for the Clinton campaign offices in Little Rock and for his transition HQ. The previous week, the Parks home had been professionally burgled, with telephone lines cut to breach a security system, and files on Governor Clinton were stolen. The *Post* quoted Mr. Parks's son Gary, a former submariner, alleging: "I believe they had my father killed to save Bill Clinton's political career."

On March 1, 1994, Herschel Friday, an influential and respected Arkansas lawyer who had been on the Clinton campaign finance committee, died when his small plane crashed on approach to a private airfield that he had used often in the past. The weather was drizzly, it was dusk, and his son was guiding him into land by radio. But the runway was illuminated, the flying conditions were by no means poor, and Herschel Friday was an experienced pilot.

On March 4, 1994, another private plane went down near Lawton, Oklahoma, on a flight from Dallas to Denver, killing a pilot and three passengers. They included an Arkansas dentist, Ronald Rogers, who was about to meet one of the reporters investigating Clinton's Arkansas, apparently to discuss further allegations into Governor Clinton's sexual habits. (It should be noted, although this was not mentioned by the *New York Post,* that accidental deaths in air crashes average about 1,000 a year in the United States.)

The Little Rock Fire Department also dismissed as "routine" the fire that broke out just before midnight on January 24, 1994, on the fourteenth floor of the Worthen Bank HQ in Little Rock. This partially destroyed the offices of the accounting firm KPMG Peat Marwick, which performed the official audit of the Madison Guaranty Savings and Loan, a bank run and eventually bankrupted by James McDougal, the Clintons' partner in the Whitewater development. (Peat Marwick spokesmen said no documents were destroyed in the fire, which took place immediately after the appointment of special prosecutor Robert Fiske, and after the *Washington Times* first reported the shredding of documents at the Rose Law Firm.)

Journalists covering the Whitewater story certainly experienced some unusual difficulties. L. J. Davis, whose long cover story on the Rose Law Firm and the Arkansas bond and financial networks dominated an issue of the *New Republic* in March 1994, was assaulted in his Little Rock hotel room, knocked unconscious, and some of his files were stolen. Davis says that before the incident, he had received some threatening and warning phone calls. (The hotel barman said that the reporter had enjoyed a convivial evening with dry martinis at the hotel bar.)

The *American Spectator* reported three burglaries since its inquiry began. The offices in Arlington, Virginia, were broken into twice in 1993, and other premises in New York were also burgled by intruders who seemed to be searching files, rather than stealing. The classified ads in the *Spectator* offered bumper stickers that read "Impeach the President—and Jail Bill too." If that sounds too moderate, there was a T-shirt that proclaimed "Impeach Hell—Lynch 'Em Both."

In the spring of 1994, the atmosphere in Washington became extraordinary, with Republican congressmen gleefully forecasting Clinton's resignation "by the end of June" over dinner tables, and even some Democrats indulging in black humor jokes about how much they looked forward to fighting the 1996 campaign for the reelection of President Al Gore. The tone was best caught by former marine Colonel Oliver North, the man at the heart of the Iran-Contra scandal, which had rocked the Reagan presidency. "We send the Clintons and their cronies a simple but unmistakable message," he said, when accepting the Republican nomination for the U.S. Senate seat from Virginia. "This is our government. You stole it, and we are going to take it back."

This was not just a matter of conservative revenge for what the Democrats did to Republican presidents over Watergate and Iran-Contra. The compelling image was less of Godfather Clinton growling out orders for contract hits, but of an American pathology, a distrust of government, and a readiness to believe absolutely anything, which harked back to the archetypal conspiracy theory of the JFK assassination and the fabled second gunman on the original grassy knoll. From Dallas to Watergate, from Iran-Contra to Little Rock, a ritual was under way that had become as American as apple pie. Bill Clinton was condemned to follow that sickeningly familiar parade of beleaguered presidents holed up in Paranoia Gulch.

As with so many other storms that had battered him, Clinton rode this one out, and kept plugging steadily at his job. But his credibility was badly shredded just when he most needed it, as his health reform bill began to sink in Congress. The Democrats were demoralized and the jubilant Republicans gained the confidence to block the whole of his domestic agenda. As well as health reform, there was a further casualty of Whitewater—the main author of the health plan, the First Lady. Exhausted, occasionally unnerved, hardly believing the hatred she seemed to provoke, Hillary proposed that her political profile had better be curtailed, at least temporarily. The failure of her laborious plan for reform and her own Whitewater embarrassments combined to end what was once spoken of as the co-presidency.

"What I do not like is the amount of hatred that is being conveyed and really injected into a political system," she confided to a small group of health care reporters. "This personal, vicious hatred that for the time being is aimed at the president, and to a lesser extent myself, is very dangerous for our political process. Those encouraging it should think long and hard about the consequences of such encouragement. We have to draw the line at violence and protests that incite violence."

It was a revealing choice of phrase. She was thinking not so much of her usual complaint about "the overly information-loaded society coupled with cynicism and distrust of government" that she so often bemoaned in private, but from a raw, and for her frightening, personal experience. In Seattle in July 1994, at a health-care rally, she received the worst reception of her life. The Secret Service were on special alert after an intelligence tip that trouble was in store. Police confiscated two guns from one man and a knife from another, as angry demonstrators carried banners that read "Heil Hillary" and howled "Stop the Bitch." Even with the microphones and speakers turned up so high they howled, she barely managed to be heard above the chants and jeers.

After months of assuring her friends that the Whitewater assaults were all part of the fetid atmosphere in inside-the-Beltway Washington, she was jolted by the hostility in one of the most liberal cities in the country. And it was aimed at her, personally, in a way that brought home to her the beleaguered plight of their presidency. Then the cold-blooded murder of an abortion doctor in Florida by what might be called a Christian fundamentalist dismayed her further. She was haunted by fears that this mood of hatred could lead to an assassination attempt on her husband.

In retrospect, the Whitewater affair was a small financial mess in an incestuous Arkansas culture, an embarrassment that surged out of control because of an overprotective White House staff, deeply shaken by the suicide of a friend and intimate. The political opportunities were ruthlessly seized by the Republicans in Congress, able for the first time to sap the authority of a Democratic president, as the Democrats had so often attacked Republican incumbents, and turn it to political advantage. And outside the political arena, in the press and the new media of Internet and talk radio, legitimate inquiry into presidential wrongdoing merged into an opportunist campaign of psychological warfare. It did not succeed in toppling the presidency, nor in destroying Clinton's extraordinarily resilient self-confidence. It very nearly shattered Hillary. And it succeeded in destroying Clinton's central hope of domestic reform, health care, derailing much of the rest of his agenda, and unnerved the morale of the Democrats in Congress and in the country at large. The 1994 midterm elections were always going to be difficult for the Democrats in Congress; Whitewater made them impossible.

The pressure began alternately to ease and to tighten, as old allegations died, but new ones surfaced. Despite their control of both Houses of Congress, the Republicans proved unable to unearth much new evidence on Whitewater in the Congressional hearings they arranged, despite the clear partisan intent of Senator Alfonse D'Amato of New York. The Resolution Trust Corporation concluded that there were no grounds for action against the Clintons, and no evidence that federally backed savings and loans funds were misappropriated to Whitewater or to the Clintons. Vince Foster's widow broke silence to explain her husband's depression, and to condemn loose speculation about this death.

But hideous embarrassment and real menace resulted from the new evidence that was unearthed. The long-sought Rose Law Firm billing records appeared mysteriously on a table near one of Hillary's workrooms in the White House family quarters. Their provenance was never satisfactorily explained. The embarrassment increased when the handwriting of Vince Foster, and one of her fingerprints, were then found on the papers. She had earlier said she thought she had last seen them during the 1992 campaign. The papers showed a modest service—some sixty hours of legal billings over fifteen months, roughly one hour per week. The discovery of the papers provoked an unprecedented subpoena for her to appear before the Washington grand jury. Then the investigations by congressman William Clinger, chairman of the House Government Operations committee, became another complication for Mrs. Clinton over the Travelgate affair. Notes of meetings and phone calls with her by David Watkins, an old Arkansas associate who had come to the White House before resigning over his use of official helicopters, suggested that she had been far more concerned about the travel office staff than she had earlier maintained. A long dispute between Congress and the White House over access to White House papers provoked threats of criminal charges against the new White House counsel Jack Quinn (Clinton's fourth) for contempt of Congress.

But the most menacing aspect of Whitewater had always been the independent counsel, Kenneth Starr, and his dedicated team of lawyers and FBI investigators sifting through the undergrowth of Arkansas business and politics. Although resting heavily on the questionable word of the already-convicted municipal judge David Hale, the prosecution scored a triumph in the fraud trial against James and Susan McDougal and Clinton's successor as governor, Jim Guy Tucker. After three months of trial, over 700 documentary exhibits, and eight days of deliberation, in May 1996 a Little Rock jury convicted them all, despite the videotaped testimony of President Clinton, who denied Hale's claims that Clinton had attended various meetings. The president had not been on trial and the jurors later said Clinton's evidence had been tangential. But his credibility was at stake, and it was damaged by the way jurors from his own state apparently preferrred to believe the word of a convicted felon.

More trials lay in store, for Governor Tucker, and for two bankers charged with improperly steering funds from the Perry Valley bank to Clinton's 1990 governorship campaign. Clinton's closest aide, Bruce Lindsey, was then named as "an unindicted co-conspirator" in the bankers' trial. By July of election year, with Congress investigating a new controversy over FBI files of Republican officials being improperly obtained by the White House, an array of scandals was besieging the presidency. And even while Clinton's double-digit lead in the opinion polls suggested that the voters were still indulgent, something fundamental had changed. The furor over Whitewater could no longer be blamed on their political enemies. An Arkansas jury had ruled that felonies had been committed by the Clintons' partners. With the election looming, it was no longer possible for the Democrats to protest that Whitewater was a scandal without a crime. And from the arcane and tedious details of a land deal nearly two decades old, voters were suddenly confronted with the plain fact that the president's old partners had been tried and convicted as crooks.

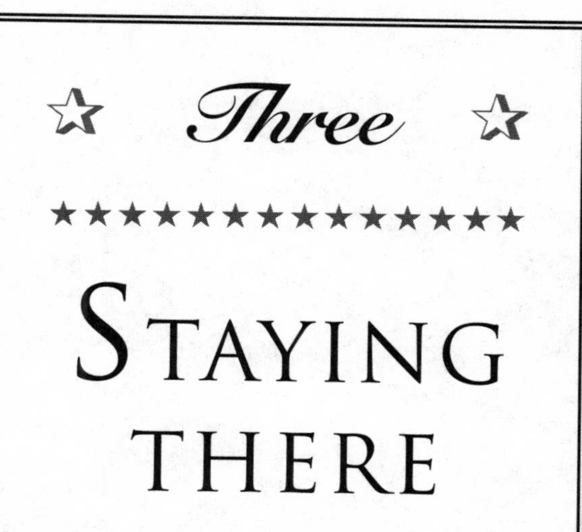

Three

STAYING THERE

☆ 12 ☆

THE WHOLE WORLD WAITING

The new president came into office with more American troops engaged in more countries than any new president since 1945. The U.S. Marines were deployed in Somalia. The U.S. Air Force was pounding Iraqi radar stations and about to start an airlift into Bosnia. The U.S. Navy and Coast Guard were mounting a quarantine of the island of Haiti. Despite his reputation as the foreign policy president, George Bush had bequeathed his successor a series of unresolved crises and vague commitments. Ranging from Baghdad to Port-au-Prince, Pyongyang to Mogadishu, there was no simple theme of the U.S. foreign policy predicaments, just as there was no single enemy against whom a national consensus could be rallied.

Tony Lake, Clinton's national security adviser, tried to define one in the uninspiring word *enlargement,* a strained attempt to capture George Kennan's cold war concept of "containment" of Soviet expansion. The idea was to widen the circle of democracies with free institutions, free markets, and free trade. Rogue states, from Iran and Iraq to North Korea, were to be isolated from the virtuous circle of democracy and prosperity. International institutions, from the UN to the World Bank to NATO, were to be supported to continue the grand process of "enlargement."

The circumstances were very different from the start of the cold war, when the Democratic presidency of Harry Truman had been able to rally bipartisan American opinion and allies around the world into the alliances and economic structures that would endure until after the Soviet collapse. There was, however, one starting point for the Clinton administration, that most of their worries stemmed from the end of the cold war and the fall of the Soviet empire. In the Balkans, in the Caucasus, in Central Asia, and in the Far East, the end of the Soviet dominance and the geopolitical stasis it had imposed paved the way for the wars of the Soviet succession, and for the tensions over its nuclear inheritance. Clinton inherited a dangerous instability across much of the Eurasian landmass, three new nuclear powers of Ukraine, Kazakhstan, and Belarus, and evident nuclear ambitions in North Korea, Iran, and Iraq.

The strategic challenges for the United States were to manage both Russian decline and Chinese empowerment, while dampening the threats to nuclear stability along the great crescent of crisis that stretched all along the old Soviet border from the Baltics through the Balkans and Caucasus to North Korea. The fate of Boris Yeltsin and Russian democracy hung in the balance, and Clinton found his allies wanting. Japan dragged its heels on aid for Russia. Britain and France not only imposed caution in the Balkans, but objected steadily and stingily to Clinton's efforts to construct aid and credit packages for Ukraine. This recalcitrance by European allies was another result of the end of the cold war; less threatened by the Soviet implosion, they were to prove less biddable to American interests and openly contemptuous of American attempts to steer the strategy in Bosnia without paying the tactical price of committing troops on the ground.

These were the high-priority issues of foreign policy, and on the whole and over time, the Clinton team were to handle them with competence, on occasion with masterly success. Belarus and Kazakhstan quickly agreed to scrap their nuclear missiles, or deliver them to Russia to be destroyed under the START treaties. Kazakhstan, in a remarkable display of trust for the United States, agreed to fly its stock of enriched uranium there for safekeeping. Ukraine, whose nervousness at Russian intentions explained its initial reluctance to surrender its own nuclear inheritance, finally agreed to do so in 1994, thanks to Clinton's personal diplomacy after a visit to Kiev. In the same year, the new Ukraine government of Leonid D. Kuchma required World Bank and IMF credits for its economic reform plans. Britain and France balked at providing their share of the new credits, and Clinton filled the financing gap, persuading Yeltsin in a telephone call to defray over $1 billion in oil and gas debts to complete the financing package.

But these successes on the grand scale of diplomacy were to be overshadowed by the hideous embarrassments over the small print of foreign policy. The death of 18 U.S. servicemen in a botched raid in Mogadishu on

October 3, 1993, with accompanying TV film of the naked corpse of a U.S. helicopter pilot being dragged through the streets, was a political disaster. The tactical responsibility was largely that of the Pentagon, sending vulnerable helicopters over a hostile urban area without adequate air cover or armored forces on hand to mount a rescue. The strategic responsibility was shared between the Clinton administration and the UN, who allowed a humanitarian mission to escalate into a counterinsurgency campaign against local militia forces.

Within ten days, another humiliation followed as the USS *Harlan County* turned back from landing 600 lightly armed U.S. and Canadian peacekeepers at Haiti's Port-au-Prince harbor, in the face of an angry mob of Haitians on the dock. In both cases, the responsible official was Defense Secretary Les Aspin, a former chairman of the House Armed Services Committee. He had been appointed in part to manage an orderly reduction in the defense budget, but also as a Capitol Hill veteran to smooth over political rows.

As a politician, Aspin failed his president. He mismanaged the fuss over gays in the military. He allowed his sensible plan to scale down defense spending to be portrayed as "win-hold-win," which meant having the troops win one regional war on the scale of Desert Storm while holding on in another until the victorious reinforcements from the first could arrive. South Korea immediately asked whether it was the low-priority front that would have to hold until relieved. In fact, even with the larger forces of the Gulf War, the United States could not immediately have mounted another operation of similar scale. Win-hold-win had been the unspoken strategy since 1990. Aspin's mistake was to admit it. Aspin botched Somalia, with some help from General Colin Powell, who did not insist on aerial gunships and tanks being sent to support an escalating mission in Mogadishu. Aspin, after a tense exchange with Warren Christopher over the lack of any clear rules of engagement in Haiti, then punctured his reputation as a man who could get along with his old colleagues in Congress. With Christopher in tow, he went back to Capitol Hill to address a restive meeting of the Democrats, and at one point threw out his arms in despair and asked helplessly, "What would you guys do?" It was a moment that doomed Aspin, and helped demoralize the party in Congress.

Aspin's dreadful moment was the lowest point of Clinton's foreign policy—the hapless appeal of a man out of his depth, and the symbol of what seemed a blundering and feeble administration. There were to be similar moments throughout Clinton's first term, as he ducked and weaved over Haiti and Cuba and the threat of waves of refugees, as the United States and the rest of the world community sat by as a gruesome tribal genocide unfolded in Rwanda. Above all there was Bosnia, the first war in Europe since 1945, intractable and brutal and relentlessly televised.

Clinton had campaigned against President Bush's inactivity in the Bosnian war. "We cannot afford to ignore what appears to be a deliberate and systematic extermination of human beings based on their ethnic origin. . . . I would begin with air power against the Serbs to try to restore the basic conditions of humanity," he declared on the campaign trail on August 5. Six days later, he added that he wanted to lift the arms embargo against the Bosnians, because "they are in no way in a fair fight with a heavily armed opponent bent on ethnic cleansing."

Without really thinking the policy through, but with his sympathies fully engaged with the Bosnian Muslims, Clinton had advocated a policy that became known as "lift and strike": air strikes against Serb aggressors, and airlifts of arms and supplies to help the Bosnians defend themselves. Had the war just begun, this could have made sense. But by the time Clinton settled in the White House, the war was nearly a year old, and British, French, and other allied troops were there, wearing blue helmets as a United Nations peacekeeping force. If the United States were to lift and strike, these allied and UN troops would be in the front line, as potential hostages or targets for retaliation. But if the Blue Helmets were to withdraw, the humanitarian effort to keep convoy routes open and feed towns and refugees would halt.

This was one half of the cruel dilemma that was to hamstring American policy for nearly three years. The other half was the vexed issue of the UN itself. During his campaign Clinton had spoken warmly of the UN and its peacekeeping missions, suggesting even that perhaps a permanent UN standing army might be raised, a rapid reaction force on constant standby. The UN and British and French allies were already engaged in Bosnia, with their forces at risk. In order to win international support and a legal mandate from the UN Security Council, they had agreed to operate under UN command. Each time the United States was to press for a firmer response to Serbian aggression with air strikes delivered by NATO, the UN stood on its legal authority as the sole body that could request such strikes.

The UN civilian diplomats in the region, committed to diplomacy, were reluctant to authorize air strikes, whatever the Blue Helmet commanders might say. This dual-key system led to constant irresolution, while the Serbs gained ground. Beset by these constraints, Clinton also dithered as Bosnia revived that debilitating Vietnam syndrome, that fear of American military commitment and casualties that twelve years of Reagan-Bush administrations were supposed to have cured.

"The real question here is, are you prepared to send young men and women from the United States, from my own state of Indiana, to give their lives in the Balkans? I'm not prepared to do that at this point because I can't see a vital American interest," argued the powerful Democratic chairman of the House Foreign Affairs Committee, Congressman Lee Hamilton. "You're not going to solve this problem with air strikes and military action."

President Clinton relied on his "Principals Committee" as the main policy-making body on Bosnia, and this too was divided. Secretary Aspin was for air strikes and lifting the arms embargo. So was Vice President Al Gore, National Security Adviser Tony Lake, and Ambassador to the UN Madeleine Albright. The chairman of the Joint Chiefs of Staff, General Colin Powell, was opposed to any military intervention without the clearest and most tightly defined of short, sharp missions. CIA Director James Woolsey was cool toward the military option. And Secretary of State Warren Christopher had been skeptical of brisk military solutions since his experience in President Lyndon Johnson's administration during the Vietnam War. Along with General Powell, he laid down four strict conditions for military intervention, which would render it almost impossible in the conditions prevailing in Bosnia.

Christopher's conditions were that the goal be clearly explained to the American people; that it win sustained public support; that there must be a strong likelihood of success; and that there must be an "exit strategy." But Christopher was opposed by the professional diplomats in his own department, who urged swift U.S. action, and he was receiving divided counsel from his predecessors. President Reagan's former secretary of state George Shultz called for air strikes, while President Bush's last secretary of state Lawrence Eagleburger and his national security adviser Brent Scowcroft were both against them.

It was a confused debate, in which one side argued that the United

States had no vital interest in Bosnia, and recalled Germany's nineteenth-century chancellor Prince Bismarck's celebrated line that "the whole of the Balkans are not worth the bones of a single Pomeranian grenadier." The other side warned that the war could widen out of control, drawing in Greece and Turkey, the Islamic world, and perhaps even Russia, just as the shot that killed Archduke Franz Ferdinand in Sarejevo in 1914 had launched the First World War. The coherence to the various sides in the debate lay in the way that the foreign policy establishment—diplomats, think tanks, heavyweight media commentators, and senators with strong foreign policy records—were mainly for U.S. intervention, although there was division over the form it should take. The military, the rest of Congress, and the public were all far more hesitant, even while they admitted the powerful moral arguments against continued inactivity.

The real debate was about America's role in the world after the cold war. Clearly the United States was not going to stand as global cop on every dangerous or tragic street corner on the planet. Equally clearly, there were some crises abroad where American interests were so engaged that intervention would be required. Bosnia fell somewhere in the vast and murky gap between, but its capacity to complicate American relations with Europe, Russia, and the Islamic world tilted the balance a long way toward intervention. But there were several kinds of intervention. Diplomatically, through the UN, American foreign policy had been engaged from the start, when the Bush administration supported the UN arms embargo that barred the Bosnians from legally obtaining arms to defend themselves. Again, U.S. diplomacy was engaged when Cyrus Vance, former secretary of state in the Carter administration, and the European Union's representative Lord David Owen, a former British foreign secretary, were authorized as special envoys to reach a peace.

The Vance-Owen plan was a complex solution to a complex problem, suggesting that Bosnia be divided into ten autonomous and separate cantons, three run by Bosnian Muslims, three by Serbs, and three by Muslims, depending on the local ethnic majority; the city of Sarajevo was to be open. Loosely modeled on the Swiss confederation, it was a diplomat's solution, and the Clinton administration damned it with faint praise as endorsing ethnic cleansing by granting the Serbs some of the fruits of their aggression. When he first called on the new secretary of state, Warren Christopher, Lord Owen was convinced that he had not read the plan, nor even the executive summary. Much repeated around Europe, Owen's suggestion fueled the complaints of the amateurism of the new administration. But crucially, Warren Christopher said that if a peace settlement were agreed, the United States would send ground troops as part of an international contingent to help enforce it.

There was little time to weigh options. As Clinton's first hundred days drew to a close, the Serbs were at the gates of Srebrenica, demanding its surrender. The British and French Blue Helmets were taking casualties. Clinton, juggling Boris Yeltsin's warning that he could not back any policy that punished his fellow Slavs of Serbia, with the rebellion among his own career diplomats, who demanded that the United States stop Serb genocide, decided the United States had to do something. He dispatched Warren Christopher to Europe to propose once more the policy of lift and strike, even though both the French and British governments had warned him this was impractical with their troops exposed and the Bosnians months away from fielding a credible defense, however many arms they were delivered. And to lift the UN arms embargo would mean getting past a Russian veto on the Security Council. Better to plug on with diplomacy and the Vance-Owen plan, the British said.

Warren Christopher's mission was not a success. British sources reported that his opening words to Foreign Secretary Sir Douglas Hurd were "I am here in listening mode." At NATO headquarters in Brussels, Secretary General Manfred Worner wanted firm action, led by NATO to replace the ineffectual UN. He suggested that Christopher make his pitch for lift and strike to the assembled NATO ambassadors, Worner would then back him, and they would try to bounce the plan into an agreed policy. "I prefer to have my bilateral meetings first," Christopher replied, and in Brussels the legend developed that Christopher had not pushed lift and strike with anything like the required vigor.

This was partly a matter of personality. Christopher was a mild-mannered and self-effacing corporate lawyer whose understated style was in sharp contrast to that of his assertive and blunt predecessors, James Baker and Charles Shultz. The Europeans, who knew that Clinton was far more concerned with domestic affairs, underestimated Christopher. And he made no converts to lift and strike in London, Paris, or Brussels, in part because he was getting messages from Les Aspin back in Washington that Clinton was "going south" on the policy. The president and his wife had been reading *Balkan Ghosts* by Robert D. Kaplan, a new travel book that described the centuries of Balkan wars, and began to question whether any outside peace-making could ever succeed. Then Clinton read an Op-Ed article by Arthur Schlesinger, Jr., in the *Wall Street Journal* that warned that his domestic strategies could wither in the Balkans as Lyndon Johnson's had in Vietnam.

Always hesitant, Clinton took the obvious way out, and blamed the evident failure of his Bosnian policy on his European allies, who were understandably furious. Britain, at least, had been prepared reluctantly to go along with air strikes if Clinton had insisted. Accustomed by forty years of NATO reflexes to expect American leadership, the Europeans had been waiting for direction. Instead, they received some fairly hesitant ideas from Warren Christopher, which added to the general chorus of hand-wringing. In European eyes, Clinton had consistently hamstrung himself by insisting that no U.S. ground troops would be committed, and that the United States would not act alone. Finally, the White House shrugged and announced that Bosnia was "on hold."

"For an American secretary of state to go and see the allies about a matter on which the president campaigned, and about a matter on which the administration was said to have strong feelings, and then come back and say 'They won't go along with it, so we're going to change our policy,' well, that was without precedent," commented Richard Perle, former assistant secretary of defense under President Reagan. He spoke for many, who judged that Clinton simply did not understand foreign policy and the uses of American power. The criticisms mounted when it emerged that Clinton was not always starting his days in the traditional way with an intelligence briefing, and that on occasion the director of the Central Intelligence Agency had to go through unorthodox channels to reach him. One such channel, the former chairman of the Joint Chiefs of Staff, Admiral William J. Crowe, Jr., was a reliable route; he had rallied a number of fellow officers to endorse Clinton's presidential bid. Accordingly, his phone calls were always returned, at least until he was appointed ambassador to London and found his advice on Northern Ireland routinely ignored.

Clinton could not in his first year summon the fascination with foreign affairs that gripped him as he sat for hours discussing domestic matters like the budget or health care or his national service plan. He did not attend to the details of such operations as George Bush had done, and was staggered to learn what his troops were up to when the news came through that eighteen of them had been killed in a street battle in Mogadishu. He did not attend most of the Principals Committee meetings on Bosnia, but he did absorb the most important issues. Above all, he realized that there was little prospect of pursuing a tough Bosnian policy when Boris Yeltsin wrote in a private letter that he could not countenance U.S. action against the Bosnian Serbs, at least before their proposed referendum on the Vance-Owen plan (which they predictably rejected).

But that was not a point that could be made in public, and the futility of American policy was now being widely condemned in the media and in Congress. The Clinton team were contemptuous of the Europeans, particularly of the British, from whom they had expected more support. Europeans bristled at being lectured on their feebleness by Americans who had none of their troops in danger. A lot of diplomatic energy went into soothing the nasty row in the Atlantic alliance and defusing the violent attack on British and European policies launched in the U.S. Senate.

"The president has sought to bring the allies into participation in a well-conceived Western response. They are refusing, and I foresee grave consequences not simply for Bosnia but for the entire Western alliance," declared Senator Joseph Biden, a senior and influential figure on the Senate Foreign Relations Committee. "They have shown the same vision and same principles that gave us the immortal image of Neville Chamberlain's umbrella. I cannot even begin to express my anger at a European policy that is now asking us to participate in what amounts to a codification of the Serbian victory."

Strong words, and in private both Clinton and his secretary of state had spoken in similar terms. But the transatlantic rift forced Clinton to come up with something else. It was not much, a proposal to send 200 American troops to join a UN monitoring force in Macedonia and to support a Russian proposal to monitor shipments across the Serbian border with Bosnia. But it was the first serious American activity since its food drops, in a region that had already come both to haunt and to paralyze the young Clinton administration in its first real foreign policy challenge. It reflected the scaled-down ambitions of Clinton's new Balkan policy to stop the conflict from spreading into a wider regional war. Above all, it reflected Clinton's sense of priorities. Bosnia was a wretched mess, but as the British and French peacekeepers faced down the Serb threat to Srebrenica, it was a mess he could live with. The deterioration of the political reform process in Russia was far more serious.

In a confidential message to the leaders of the G7, the group of seven leading industrial nations, sent on March 5, 1993, through Germany's Helmut Kohl, Boris Yeltsin asked the West for a blank check. He sought a promise of continued political and economic support even if he had to bring back a Russian dictatorship, suspending parliament and ruling by decree. Suddenly, in his second month in office, Clinton was pitched into an acute foreign policy dilemma made from a perilous brew of his own American budget problems, his relations with Japan and Europe, the lingering threat of nuclear weapons, the fate of the global economy, and the moral question of whether to support Yeltsin's suggestion that he destroy Russian democracy in order to save it.

The stakes were enormous. Failure could mean a return to a kind of cold war with the one country in the world that could still threaten the United States with nuclear attack. It would leave America led by a chastened and hamstrung leader for four years. And it could widen the deepening trade tensions with Japan into a serious strategic dispute that could effectively take the world's second biggest economy out of the G7 process. History gives few second chances, but Clinton now had the opportunity to succeed where George Bush failed. Through parsimony, obsession with Iraq, and a general inadequacy of vision, George Bush failed to nail down the grand strategic bargain that would have thrown the economic weight of the West behind Mikhail Gorbachev's bid to reform the Soviet Union.

Boris Yeltsin returned with an even more acute form of the same fundamental question. From 1945 until 1990, American leadership built the great economic tripod of Japan, Europe, and North America into a distinct strategic entity that became the West, able to coordinate their policies over the long haul under the threat of war and Communist expansion. Could that strategic unity be maintained when the threat appeared so much less mortal, when the challenge was to build something rather than defend themselves, and when the old habits of strategic deference among allies were being overtaken by the commercial squabbles between trading rivals?

The forum to address these issues was the G7. Clinton and his still largely untried national security team were asking themselves whether these annual summits with their traditionally anodyne communiqués were still the right vehicle for international consensus, and whether they could assemble the authority to commit the seven main industrial governments to firm subsequent action. The immediate reaction of Clinton, Major, Mitterand, and Kohl, the West's Big Four, was that their priority must be to sustain the broad principle of Russian democracy without getting trapped into pinning their policies upon the single figure of Yeltsin. That was the mistake Clinton believed Bush had made with Gorbachev.

With both Italy and Canada in the middle of political difficulties and transition, it was assumed that they would follow whatever line the Big Four agreed on. But that left Japan, whose single-party government had plunged into its own crisis of political legitimacy as the country grappled with its first serious experience of economic recession. Japan was seen in the White House as the main danger to the G7 process for three reasons.

The first was Japan's trade policies and surpluses, in themselves another Clinton-era crisis waiting to happen. The second was Japan's insistence at the Houston G7 summit in 1990, a year after the Tiananmen Square massacre, on resuming its aid and trade credits with China as a matter of national priority, which outweighed the need for G7 consensus. The third was Japan's insistence that Russia return the Kurile Islands, occupied in 1945, before Tokyo would join any new international effort to sustain the Russian economy.

The subtext to all this was that Clinton, by instinct and education a Europhile, knew little of Japan and Asia, and was not altogether sure that he liked what he knew. During his election campaign, his toughest international rhetoric was reserved for the Chinese leadership which he associated with Tiananmen Square. When he condemned George Bush for "coddling dictators" he was talking about the gerontocracy of Beijing. And while Clinton's budget proposed reducing the cold war propaganda machines of Radio Liberty and Radio Free Europe, it reserved money for Radio Free Asia, a new one aimed at China.

Japan, with its $50 billion trade surplus with the United States, had a fast-growing rival in China, which enjoyed a $19 billion surplus in 1992. Clinton's first G7 summit at Tokyo in July thus always contained the seeds of a confrontation, as Japan was faced with the fundamental question whether it was committed to the free-trading West and a G7 member in good standing, or whether the corrupt one-party state of Japan's ill-named

Liberal Democratic Party really sought to build a separate Asian condominium of Tokyo and Beijing.

These were potentially apocalyptic questions, but the pace of growth in China was so fast that they had to be seriously considered in the upper reaches of the Clinton administration. After more than a decade of double-digit economic growth, China's GDP in 1993 exceeded that of Britain. It was on course to overtake the German economy well before the end of the decade, to surpass Japan's GDP by the year 2005 and to challenge the U.S. primacy as the world's biggest economy sometime near the year 2020.

This was clearly the time for the West to consider what sort of China that would be, and how far the West could steer it toward the democratic decencies. Optimists suggested that economic growth would produce a prosperous middle class to demand political freedom and a pluralist system. Pessimists looked at Japan and South Korea and concluded that economic dynamism need not be the monopoly of Western democracies. Beijing's choice might rather lie between a continued authoritarian regime and a Japan-style corporate-mercantilism with a democratic facade overlying a corrupt one-party regime.

The G7 consensus was always going to be tested by American toughness with China, and by the Japanese dilemma whether to fall in with Clinton or cut a separate deal with Beijing. But in Clinton's first months, the G7 countries were also confronted with the rather more immediate Russian crisis, and any economic solution would require Japanese support. Clinton, with little experience in foreign affairs, was suddenly learning the interlocking nature of world crises; how Bosnia could not be resolved without Russia, but Russia could not be resolved without Japan, and that part of the U.S.-Japanese relationship that was not dominated by American trade concerns would hinge on the way Clinton dealt with China. And through Hong Kong, that led to more complications with Britain, which brought Clinton back to Bosnia and Russia again.

Clinton counted heavily on the glittering quality of his key aides on Russian policy. Thomas R. Pickering, the ambassador to Moscow, had the reputation of the State Department's best diplomat even before his impressive stint as George Bush's man at the United Nations. Thomas W. Simons, Jr., as the new aid coordinator was another State Department star before a successful term as the last U.S. ambassador to Poland. And Clinton's old Oxford roommate Strobe Talbott, in addition to having Clinton's ear, had the confidence of Yeltsin and the other Russian leaders whom he met repeatedly as a senior *Time* magazine journalist and cold war historian.

Clinton's first real summit, with Yeltsin in Vancouver in April, was a success largely because Clinton decided to follow the traditional American policy of sticking with the man in charge of the Kremlin. Yeltsin wanted assurances of Western support—economic and diplomatic and political—and Clinton gave it. His rationale was that by calling a referendum on increasing presidential powers under the constitution, Yeltsin was following the democratic course. "Win, Boris, win" was Clinton's farewell message. But to give that referendum victory some chance of consolidation, Clinton needed assurances of Western support and debt relief that the United States could not begin to afford alone. Clinton needed to rally the G7, which meant winning over Japan, at his next summit with Japan's new prime minister, Kiichi Miyazawa.

Hanging over the Clinton-Miyazawa meeting was a handwritten note from one of the Russian negotiators at the Vancouver summit, found by a journalist after it was left on a table after the summit meeting. It quoted Clinton telling Boris Yeltsin, "When the Japanese say yes to us, they often mean no." Taken in Japan as a symbol of the new edginess in U.S.–Japanese trade relations, the phrase encapsulated the mood of open suspicion in the Clinton administration. The U.S. trade deficit of just under $50 billion with Japan in 1992, with Japan heading for record trade surpluses in 1993, had sharpened the American line on trade.

"The persistence of the surplus the Japanese enjoy with the United States and the rest of the developed world can only lead to the one conclusion that the possibility of obtaining real even access to the Japanese market is somewhat remote," Clinton complained before Miyazawa arrived. Clinton was far more conciliatory in his direct talks with the Japanese premier. This was emerging as his pattern, similar to the tough words he used about European subsidies for the Airbus before then welcoming John Major with a warm embrace for "the special relationship." Clinton liked to lay down a tough line before a meeting, in the hope of prizing out concessions early. But he was far more conciliatory once the meetings began.

"We need a new partnership, based on mutual respect and responsibility," Clinton said, and went on to praise Japan for living up to those responsibilities by declaring its support for the G7 aid package for Russia. That had been what Clinton required. The two leaders left the difficult details of trade sectors, including semiconductors, auto parts, and supercomputers, to their trade experts, who made little visible progress. But the Japanese alarm at the fall of the dollar against the yen, which had just fallen to a record low of 112 yen to the dollar, put the Japanese on the defensive. The Clinton administration was not unhappy at the dollar's fall, which they saw making Japanese exports more expensive and U.S. exports into Japan steadily cheaper. The Japanese, by contrast, were depressed by an exchange rate, which seemed to make their own economic rebound all the harder to achieve.

Clinton had a way to finesse the endemic United States–Japan trade rows through his plan to make that year's Asia-Pacific Economic Cooperation conference into a genuine summit of the leaders of the Pacific Rim countries. The entire administration talked up the importance of Asia in U.S. foreign policy, with Warren Christopher infuriating Europeans by suggesting that "our foreign policy has been too Eurocentric for too long." The new trade-oriented foreign policy team looked at the raw numbers of U.S.–Asian trade, which in 1993 for the first time topped $350 billion, and declared that America's economic future lay across the Pacific. By contrast, Europe's trade was sunk in recession. A series of arguments over Bosnia policy and over the future size and role of NATO had embittered the Atlantic alliance. NATO itself was endangered, warned former Republican secretaries of state Henry Kissinger and James Baker.

So after the year of wooing Asia, it was decided that Clinton should spend the second year of his administration rekindling the dying fires of America's alliances in Europe. He promised to make three trips across the Atlantic in 1994. After the NATO summit in January, Clinton would visit Britain and France in June for the fiftieth anniversary of D-Day, and then return to Europe in July for the G7 economic summit in Italy. Before the Naples meeting, Clinton would make a brisk tour of Eastern Europe as well.

To prepare the way, Warren Christopher was dispatched to persuade affronted Western Europeans that they remained at the heart of U.S. foreign policy and to reassure Eastern Europeans that the U.S. plan for them to have an arm's-length relationship with NATO was sincere. "Partnership for Peace" offered the Eastern Europeans a loose form of country membership in NATO, so vague that Russia and the Central Asian republics might apply. "P4P," as it became known, stopped far short of extending

NATO membership and its military guarantees against outside aggression. Instead, it invited Eastern European countries to join some NATO military exercises and conferences, to take part in NATO training and develop the interoperability of weapons and command structures, without which any NATO promises of military support would have been hollow.

But what of Russia? Strobe Talbott put the question with great force in a long memorandum, which demanded that NATO be considered from Moscow's point of view. Unless carefully handled, NATO expansion up to the Russian frontier could appear threatening, or even the kind of humiliation that could provoke a nationalist backlash. Yeltsin's Russia remained a great power with its own interests, which would not always be subordinated to those of the United States. Russia's opposition to the entry of Poland, Hungary, and the Czech and Slovak republics into NATO was followed by Russia's request to amend the CFE (Conventional Forces in Europe) Treaty, and allow them to increase the numbers of tanks and guns and men stationed in western Russia. The United States was opposed to this, even while acknowledging that Russia did face a difficult security problem with some of its neighbors of the former Soviet Union.

Talbott argued that the main U.S. interest was to steer Russia to democratic prosperity, to prevent its becoming once more a threat to Europe, and to acknowledge frankly that the United States would rather see Russia as the influence and stabilizing force in Central Asia than Iran. Russia had to be convinced that NATO was not a threat, and that the United States was prepared to accept Moscow as a strategic partner. But such partiality to Russia had to be balanced with even further assurances to the central Europeans, and to the NATO allies.

"Europe remains at the heart of our foreign policy agenda," Christopher said as he left to smooth Europe's ruffled feathers. "Europe is still our most important trading partnership. It provides sixty percent of the profits for U.S. companies operating abroad, over sixty percent of U.S. foreign investment in Europe, and Europeans provide sixty-five percent of all foreign investment in the United States."

The raw figures for trade showed the United States exporting $130 billion of goods and services to Asia in 1993, against $110 billion to Europe. And they showed the United States importing $241 billion from Asia and only $114 billion from Europe. While U.S.–European trade was in rough balance, Asian trade contained an apparently immovable structural deficit for the United States of around $100 billion. Not only were transatlantic trade flows balanced, they were also healthier and more productive for both partners. Europe had $250 billion invested in the United States, in companies which employed 3 million Americans, and paid $20 billion in American taxes. By contrast, Asia's investment of $107 billion in the United States produced fewer than one million American jobs and paid only $7 billion in taxes. The European-owned firms were far more integrated into the American economy.

The Clinton administration displayed its readiness to focus again on Europe with a reshuffle of the high-level staff on European affairs at the National Security Council and the State Department. The low-key assistant secretary of state for European affairs, Stephen A. Oxman, was replaced by the veteran diplomat Richard Holbrooke, summoned back from Germany where he had been ambassador for only eight months. Jennone Walker from the European desk at the NSC in the White House was made ambassador to Prague and replaced by another veteran diplomat, Alexander Vershbow. A Russian expert who also served on the U.S. staff at NATO, Vershbow was a pragmatic professional whose promotion came as a relief to European diplomats in Washington who had been troubled by the overall incompetence of the Clinton foreign policy team in its first eighteen months.

The question on the diplomatic circuit was whether this was the temblor before the earthquake that many expected, the replacement of Warren Christopher and Tony Lake. Having already ditched his first deputy secretary of state, Clifton Wharton, to install Strobe Talbott, Secretary Christopher also replaced his Haitian policy team, his director of policy planning, Samuel Lewis, and then his aid coordinator for the former Soviet Union, Ambassador Tom Simons. There was more than a whiff of scapegoats in the air. Stephen Oxman and Jennone Walker had helped preside over a grim period for U.S.–European relations, marked by bitter rows over Bosnia. But the troubles of Europe went far beyond Bosnia, and the real responsibility rested with Christopher, Lake, and the president.

Relations with Britain were badly shaken by Clinton's controversial and personal decision to grant a temporary U.S. visa to Sinn Fein leader Gerry Adams, against the advice of the State Department, the ambassador to London, and the CIA. The new conservative French government, which had told Washington of its readiness for a much deeper involvement in

NATO, was then dismayed by the vague and dismissive response they received. Clinton's 1994 trip to London and Paris was the opportunity to smooth ruffled feathers, in the nostalgic atmosphere of the D-Day anniversary.

In his speech to the French national assembly on June 7, Clinton finally ditched his policies of staunch support for the Bosnians and he agreed to back the French and British plan to impose a settlement that would effectively partition Bosnia, with 49 percent of territory for the Serbs and 51 percent for the Bosnians and Croats. Squalid as it was, and a reward for Serbian aggression, this was to be the eventual shape of the 1995 peace settlement. But Bosnia had much more agony to undergo before the warring parties could finally be bullied and cajoled into an agreement on such a basis. In the end, the application of raw power was required. Clinton agreed to turn a blind eye to the secret arming of the Bosnians by Iran, via Croatia, after Croatia asked whether the U.S. would object, in April 1994. Slowly, that helped tilt the balance of military power. In 1995, the arguments by UN Ambassador Madeleine Albright that Bosnia could be a political disaster became compelling as the Serbs began to capture the "safe havens" of Srebrenica and Zepa. Clinton approved the use of serious and prolonged air power, and also Tomahawk cruise missiles against the Serbs. He also grasped the nettle of the European allies, who had always complained that air strikes would imperil their peacekeepers. Very well, Clinton retorted. Remove the peacekeepers. That would trigger U.S. troops being deployed to help the allies withdraw. If U.S. troops had to go anyway, they may as well go for a better purpose than riding shotgun on an Anglo-French scuttle. By the summer of 1995, when the Croats counterattacked and sent the Serbs reeling back from most of their conquests, the political and military preconditions were in place for the remarkable diplomacy of Richard Holbrooke, to achieve what became the Bosnian peace agreement. The crucial new factor in the White House was Clinton's political will, and his readiness to deploy U.S. military power.

In effect, Clinton concluded that his relations with his European allies were more important than the morality of a Bosnian settlement. The decision was inevitable, given the weight of U.S. interests involved. The great strength of the Atlantic relationship rested on the cumulative trust and cooperative habits and ways of strategic thinking that came from nearly fifty years of the NATO alliance. That was an asset to be exploited, rather than forgotten or devalued. The absence of such a security structure in Asia cast America's relations across the Pacific in a sharply different light. It was a distinction between a stable trade and security relationship with Europe and a dynamic economic and unstable security relationship with Asia.

It is important to step back and consider these deeper currents in Clinton's foreign policy and his dealings with the major powers, because of the intense and constant criticism over their details and dealings with smaller nations. It was said on all sides that President Clinton was not good at foreign policy. "We've looked like a bunch of wimps for the past couple of years," grumbled former secretary of state Lawrence Eagleburger. Of the resolve to invade Haiti in October 1994 and restore the democratically elected president Aristide, the *New York Times* editorial grandly if tortuously complained that "all this new public posturing does do is squeeze another droplet from the Administration's almost empty vial of foreign policy credibility." Indeed, from the raft-strewn straits of Florida to the still-humming nuclear reactors of North Korea, Clinton's stewardship of the world's last superpower was not a smooth affair.

But some of the lesser known features of the Clinton foreign policy went thumpingly well. And they were his, crafted in the White House and run through his National Security Council, rather than through the conventional channels of the State Department. First, there was the extraordinary role that Clinton played in securing the withdrawal of the last Russian troops from the Baltic states. It was an event which, as Clinton said, "marked the real end to World War Two in Europe."

Clinton had secured from Boris Yeltsin at their Vancouver summit in 1993, and again in their Moscow meeting in January 1994, an undertaking to negotiate the withdrawal of Russian troops. They had been in the Baltic since June of 1940, after the foreign ministers of Hitler and Stalin signed their Ribbentrop-Molotov Pact to carve up Eastern Europe between them. Beset by Russian nationalists inside and outside parliament, and with strenuous objections from the Russian Defense Ministry, Yeltsin did little to fulfill his pledge. Yeltsin cited his concern for the civic and residential rights of the ethnic Russians still living in the Baltic states. In Moscow, Clinton promised to raise this matter with the Baltic leaders, and did so, with a pointed public warning to them that the United States was concerned with human rights everywhere.

Clinton did more than that, thanks to the urging of his young Russian expert in the National Security Council, Nicholas Burns, and the maneuvering of the Swedish ambassador to Washington, Henrik Liljegren, who had established a personal relationship between Clinton and the Swedish prime minister, Carl Bildt, by the useful device of arranging a White House tea party for Mr. Bildt, the Clintons, and the year's crop of seven American Nobel Prize laureates. The Baltic states were a special interest for Sweden, neighbors across a narrow sea, and Bildt pressed Clinton to use his influence with Moscow. Clinton went further, suggesting to Britain's John Major that even though Sweden was not yet a member of the European Union, a special role should be found. Major arranged for Bildt to chair and run an EU working group on the Baltic, which met regularly in Stockholm and added European weight to the pressure from Washington.

Again through Liljegren, the NSC's Nick Burns met Toomas Ilves, the new Estonian ambassador to Washington. Ilves said there was a genuine political problem in the Baltics as well as in Moscow. Many Baltic nationalists were just as resistant to a compromise as Yeltsin. Perhaps Washington could help? Clinton agreed to invite a delegation of 13 Latvian political leaders, including hard-line nationalists who had opposed granting full civic rights to ethnic Russians and wanted no compromises on any "temporary" Russian military presence at the Skrunda radar station, to come to the White House. With Ira Magaziner's health reform task force in full flow, there were no conference rooms available. Clinton said—and there was no precedent for this—they could use the White House situation room in the basement. Vice President Al Gore and National Security Adviser Tony Lake met the Latvians and urged them to give Yeltsin enough concessions to close a deal.

The flattered Latvians then flew back to Stockholm, where Carl Bildt twisted their arms some more, and laid on a Swedish government jet to fly them home. But there was still no movement in a surly Moscow, where Russian foreign minister Andrei Kozyrev was telling a conference of Russian ambassadors that "the greatest achievement of Russian foreign policy in 1993 was to prevent NATO's expansion eastward to our borders." Under the urgings of Nick Burns, Clinton wrote letters to Yeltsin, raised the Baltic issue in every phone call with the Russian leader, and finally, at the G7 summit in Naples in July, hand-delivered to Yeltsin a letter from the Estonian president Lennart Meri asking for a meeting in Moscow.

Clinton pressed Yeltsin to agree, telling him that their troop presence in the Baltic was now more trouble than it was worth, that it was in danger of becoming "a burden to the Russian-American relationship" that threatened to overwhelm Yeltsin's autumn visit to Washington.

Clinton was not joking. The sharply worded McConnell amendment, which threatened U.S. economic support for Russia unless the troops left the Baltic states, had passed the Senate by 89 votes to 8. It was due to go before the House—certain of passage—on July 28. Yeltsin finally agreed, and just in time. On July 25, President Meri turned up in Moscow.

Meri was shown into Yeltsin's presence. On the table, one bottle of Absolut vodka and another of Stolichnaya. Yeltsin had already been sampling, and launched into an angry tirade against Estonia, its ingratitude, its treatment of ethnic Russians, the presumption of this tiny state getting in the way of great powers. Meri, tipped off by Clinton about ways to get along with Boris, calmly replied by congratulating Yeltsin on cutting the Russian ruble inflation rate, and although a near teetotaller, agreed to join Yeltsin in a vodka or two. Or three.

By the end of the night, the bottles were empty, and there was broken china on the floor. Perhaps it was accidentally brushed off by the Russian foreign ministry team, Andrei Kozyrev and Vitaly Churkin, as they dashed in and out of the room to Yeltsin's shouted orders to "get this fixed into a deal." Perhaps the china was hurled to the floor in anger. The sources for this account come from various countries, including Russians, and accounts differ. But by the bleary dawn, it was sealed, and when a badly hungover President Meri got back to the Estonian capital of Tallinn, he told U.S. ambassador Robert Frasure, "Tell Mr. Clinton that Estonia will never forget what he has done for us. Never."

Clinton's second success, the Irish initiative, was a bit better known, largely because it started so badly and seemed to fit his pattern of bumbling. The personal decision by President Clinton to overrule his diplomats and intelligence chiefs and grant a temporary visa for Sinn Fein leader Gerry Adams to visit the United States for 48 hours provoked a major upset in Anglo-American relations at the start of 1994. That decision has since emerged as an important breakthrough in the Northern Ireland political process, which had been a consistent objective of Clinton since his celebrated campaign pledge to send a special "peace envoy" to Ulster.

The Irish policy was driven hard by Senator Kennedy, whose sister was appointed ambassador to Dublin and whose former foreign policy aide Nancy E. Soderberg led the White House effort from her position as staff director, the third-ranking post in the National Security Council. The visa for Gerry Adams was opposed by the CIA director, the attorney general, the director of the FBI, the secretary of state, and by the U.S. ambassador in London. It was urged by Senator Kennedy, Nancy Soderberg, and National Security Adviser Tony Lake, and supported by President Clinton as a chance worth taking to bring Sinn Fein into the negotiating process and the IRA to a cease-fire. "We didn't come here to sit around like potted plants," Clinton told Lake. "If we have a chance to move this thing forward, we have to take it."

In London, Prime Minister John Major was not pleased, but initially prepared to listen to the advice from Sir Robin Renwick, the British ambassador in Washington, that Britain would have to make the best of it and not overreact. Outraged British media reaction made this impossible, but when the dust settled—with a lot of soothing from the Dublin government and from Washington, John Major and Bill Clinton agreed to try something new.

They decided to widen the American involvement and include the Ulster Unionist politicians and thus put the Gerry Adams visa into a much more evenhanded context. The invitation to James Molyneaux, the cautious, seventy-four-year-old leader of the Ulster Unionist Party, with his MPs in the British House of Commons, to come to the White House in April and start a parallel dialogue soothed Unionist fears that the Americans were on the side of the IRA. The British ambassador personally arranged Molyneaux's first visit to the White House. Molyneaux saw Vice President Al Gore and National Security Adviser Tony Lake, and then went up to Capitol Hill to talk to Speaker Tom Foley and Senators Moynihan and Kennedy.

"I believe that the principle of consent in Northern Ireland is now underwritten by American opinion in a very clear way for probably the very first time in history," said Molyneaux as he left the White House. Tony Lake had convinced him that the United States wanted to be evenhanded, and fully supported the position of the two governments in London and Dublin that change in Northern Ireland would only come with the consent of the Protestant majority.

This was not a casual or an isolated gesture. Even further behind the scenes, Clinton's own Irish friends were used as back channels in the process. They included Kevin O'Keefe, a tough Chicago lawyer and old friend of Mrs. Clinton now on the White House political staff, and the Denver lawyer Jim Lyons, who had dampened the first fuss over Whitewater during the 1992 campaign with a report that concluded the Clintons had lost money on the deal. After their report on the Irish mood, Clinton told John Major that a humanitarian gesture would help. Major accordingly moved some IRA prisoners from British jails back to Northern Ireland, easing family visits. And prodded by Clinton, Tony Lake was on the phone to Molyneaux repeatedly on the eve of the IRA's announcement of a cease-fire. Speaking for the White House, Lake reassured the Unionist leader that the United States believed that a cease-fire was coming, and that the constitutional talks that would follow would have U.S. backing. Lake said the process would need Molyneaux's leadership to reassure the Protestants, even if some extremists tried to sabotage it with bombs and bullets.

The fruit of this was an unprecedentedly low-key reaction from the Ulster Unionists, a token grumble that the word *permanent* was notably missing from the phrase *cease-fire* in the IRA announcement. It was to meet that concern that, after some last-minute telephone huddling between British, Irish, and U.S. officials, President Clinton's statement of welcome for the cease-fire included the phrase, "There must be a permanent end to the violence." The U.S.–British relationship, which had been tested by the Adams visa, was significantly restored by the behind-the-scenes contacts with both Dublin and London over Northern Ireland. President Clinton told John Major that the cease-fire was "a testimony to your political courage" in their private phone call, and he meant it.

Clinton slowly but surely learned diplomatic skills. He came to enjoy the telephone diplomacy of long phone calls with other national leaders. They in turn got used to him, even to the jokes he would make about the girth of Chancellor Helmut Kohl, or about the marital troubles of Britain's Royal Family, which fascinated him. They grew accustomed to Warren Christopher's quiet style, to Tony Lake's persistence, as Clinton grew increasingly accustomed to the huge weight of American influence in the world. It was always this way. President Reagan had been derided as a cowboy, until he began dismantling the cold war with Mikhail Gorbachev. George Bush got off to such a slow start as president that the Europeans were dismayed, until he began to display his skills in dealing with Gorbachev after the fall of the Berlin Wall and in rallying the Gulf War coalition.

All American presidents have the resources of the world's biggest military, economic, and diplomatic machinery behind them, which can achieve successes with little direction from the White House. The progress Clinton made in the Middle East was largely thanks to State Department professionals who helped smooth the peace that Israelis and Palestinians were secretly meeting to arrange between themselves. But with the handshake between Yasir Arafat and Yitzhak Rabin on the White House lawn, and subsequent handshakes with the king of Jordan, much of the credit went to Clinton, thanks in part to the careful orchestration by his staff.

By the law of averages, some foreign policy matters will work well. And when Clinton's staff had an event to choreograph, from a Middle East peace ceremony to a set-piece speech at the United Nations, or a summit or a foreign tour where the president's schedule is locked into place far in advance, they usually crafted a powerful performance. But there was little they could do about the perception of incompetence that stuck to him after the failures in Bosnia, in Somalia, and in his first efforts in Haiti. In the course of his second year, Clinton scored solid successes in the Baltics and Northern Ireland, and also succeeded in his gamble of deploying U.S. troops to restore democracy to Haiti. But he won little credit; the reputation of being unimpressive in foreign policy had already been affixed.

In retrospect, this was extraordinary. The American president who barnstormed Europe at the end of 1995 was far older, achingly wiser, and the mirror image of the fresh-faced young governor from Arkansas who was elected to the White House three years earlier. It had begun to fade from public memory that Clinton had won by sneering at George Bush as "the foreign policy president" and promising to focus "like a laser beam" on America's problems at home. But Clinton's domestic agenda, from health and welfare reform to a promise of a college education for every qualified American, lay in wreckage. He had presided over the demoralized collapse of the Democratic Party, and its rout from the Congress they had ruled for forty years.

Instead, Clinton went to Europe as the foreign policy president in his own right, on a victory tour of diplomatic achievements that were to culminate in Paris at the formal signing of the Bosnian peace agreement.

Clinton took credit in Belfast for the Northern Ireland cease-fire, which he broke John Major's heart to deliver, and visited the U.S. troops in Germany as they boarded the planes to enforce the peace in Bosnia, which his administration's diplomacy had almost miraculously achieved. He signed in Madrid a new and grand-sounding accord with the European Union, which was said to reinvigorate the transatlantic alliance beyond the old military ties of NATO.

Clinton traveled looking strangely like the man George Bush had wanted to be: a president visibly confident of reelection, facing a parade of unconvincing campaign rivals, presiding over the world's healthiest economy, and above all, the very embodiment of global leadership. That was the biggest surprise of all. When Clinton took office as the first post–cold war president, America's global role seemed to be almost spent. Looking like a haunting coda to the American century, the inconclusive Gulf War had represented a burden that could no longer be afforded without passing the hat around the sleeker allies. This sense of hesitation was reinforced by the famous reluctance of General Colin Powell to deploy U.S. troops into danger overseas. This was a major factor in the feebleness of Bosnian policy, and Powell's replacement by General John Shalikashvili eased one serious constraint on Clinton's diplomatic options. When he was joined by Admiral Mike Boorda, who had been an ardent hawk for a tougher U.S. policy in Bosnia as NATO's Southern commander, the change in Pentagon advice was apparent and dramatic. General Powell was known for his skill at complaining about what could not be done. General Shalikashvili and Admiral Boorda were far more confident about what could be done. This was to be decisive when the policy changed over Bosnia.

And by 1995, nothing on the planet seemed to get done without the ubiquitous Americans. Four years of Balkan war were resolved on a U.S. Air Force base in Ohio. Israel and Palestine made peace, but only when their leaders shook hands on the White House lawn. A democratically elected president ruled Haiti once more, courtesy of Bill Clinton's soldiers. The pugnacious sects of Ulster plodded sullenly through a non-peace that was better than war, but their serial negotiations took place in the White House office of Tony Lake.

The nuclear arsenal of Ukraine had gone, thanks to Clinton's clinching summit in Kiev. The enriched uranium reserves of Kazakhstan glowed securely in the vaults at the Oak Ridge arsenal in Tennessee, thanks to a secret ferrying mission by Clinton's air force. The Baltic states of Latvia, Lithuania, and Estonia went their bumpy but independent way without the looming presence of Russian troops, courtesy of Bill Clinton's diplomacy. The vast oil reservoirs beneath the Caspian Sea were set for the first time to flow through pipelines that could not be suddenly closed by Russian hands, thanks to discreet presidential task forces that made the decisions in Washington that were carried out by oilmen in Houston and London and by former Politburo members in Baku and Tbilisi.

American pressure and South Korean money had forestalled the emergence of a new nuclear power in North Korea. The constant tension on the nuclear brink between India and Pakistan had been held in check by preventive diplomacy. The prospect of a new cold war with China had flared and died, after public rows over human rights and the protocol of relations with Taiwan. Warren Christopher finally persuaded the Chinese that a long-belated U.S. recognition of Vietnam and a private visa for the president of Taiwan to attend a college reunion in upstate New York did not amount to a new U.S. policy of containment. The United States was not thinking in terms of a new cold war, to hem in yet another emergent superpower on the Eurasian landmass.

The Chinese might have been forgiven for misunderstanding American policy. As in Bosnia, the Clinton administration swung like an irrational pendulum. From refusing to coddle dictators in his campaign, to "comprehensive engagement" that assumed free markets and economic growth would inevitably induce the democratic decencies, to dispatching two aircraft carrier task forces to Taiwanese waters, there was neither consistency nor principle in the U.S. approach. China was allowed a surprising degree of latitude in selling missiles to Iran and nuclear technology to Pakistan, even while it was enjoying a $30 billion annual trade surplus with the United States. The Commerce and Energy Departments wooed Chinese industry, the Pentagon tried to make military friends by helping Chinese technology, and the State Department sought China's help with North Korea, while only the trade representative sought to discipline China's gross and constant breaches of the commercial rules. The National Security Council failed to fulfill its basic task of coordinating policy, until Tony Lake was forced to pay attention during the Taiwan crisis of February–March 1996. The prospect of a military standoff in the Taiwan straits was only resolved when Lake met his Chinese counterpart, Liu

Huaquing, at Pamela Harriman's Virginia farm in the last days of February.

There was still no coherent U.S. policy, but at least a high-level understanding had been reached that the United States understood that China was becoming a great power, entitled to be honored as such. In the end, the United States could claim a modest diplomatic achievement. The U.S. fleet clearly remained the decisive stabilizing force on the Pacific Rim. Taiwan had successfully followed South Korea in negotiating its transition to democracy, despite Beijing's attempts to derail it. The old claim that Asian values were unfriendly to the West's wild and democratic ways had been thoroughly punctured. Given the opportunity, Asians enjoyed the chance to elect and evict their political leaders as much as Americans. This was an important achievement for Western values.

But even the list of successes Clinton could claim, capped by the Bosnian peace agreement, could not still the criticism. The question had always been of his competence and his resolve, of the length of his attention span and his prevarications, until crisis forced him to act. Many in the world outside the United States openly doubted his ability to stick when the going got tough. His foreign policy achievements were all hideously fragile, as unstable as the Mexican peso, as tragically vulnerable as Yitzhak Rabin to an assassin's bullet, or as uncertain as an IRA ceasefire. Bosnia was far from a done deal, as war criminals in Pale strutted their vicious defiance. Repeated killings in Port-au-Prince, and the prospect that President Aristide would not step down as promised for new elections, and that the presence of U.S. troops might have to be extended, suggested that democracy may not be quite the word for what had been restored to Haiti. But Clinton had stood firm and presidential against congressional blowhards who insisted that the United States should only intervene when "our vital interests are at stake." Every country acts when vital interests are at stake. If the concept of superpower meant anything, it defined a state with the ability to choose to intervene for the sake of its preferences. And by this test, in Haiti and Bosnia, in Ukraine and in the Baltic, in the Middle East and in Ulster, Clinton had usually, if belatedly, justified his office.

☆ 13 ☆

TRADE WARS

In October 1995, U.S. Trade Representative Mickey Kantor reported to President Clinton that the gross domestic product of the U.S. economy was expected to exceed $7 trillion for the year. The United States had become the dominant force of the global economy, the biggest trader of them all. In each of the three years of the Clinton presidency, the United States had been the world's biggest exporter. Japan exported less than 10 percent of its GDP; the United States exported 12.3 percent of its much larger GDP. Add together all the imports and exports, and the booming service exports of software and licenses and royalties, and the profits of the U.S.-based multinational corporations that made and sold Coca-Cola and Ford cars and Apple computers and Boeing jets across the world, and more than $2 trillion—almost exactly 30 percent of all the wealth generated in the United States—would come from trade.

When Clinton first went overseas, to take up his Rhodes scholarship at Oxford in 1968, the United States barely needed to trade at all. Imports and exports combined barely amounted to 10 percent of GDP. After the Soviet Union, it was the world's most self-sufficient economy, in energy, raw materials, and consumer goods. The transformation that has taken place as the United States has integrated into the global economy illuminates the real Clinton effect. Beyond Russia or China or Bosnia or Haiti, trade was at the heart of the foreign policy for which history is likely to remember him.

The boldest actions of Clinton's presidency were to defy and split his own Democratic Party in Congress to force through the North American

Free Trade Agreement and the GATT world trade pact. At the end of his first year in office, he convened the heads of state of the whole Pacific Rim at the Asia-Pacific Economic Cooperation conference in Seattle and invited them to consider a giant free trade zone. At the end of Clinton's second year, at the second APEC summit in Indonesia, they signed the APEC accord, pledging themselves to develop a free-trading Pacific Rim over the next fifteen years. Clinton flew almost directly from that summit in Indonesia to Florida, where he had convened all the leaders of the Western Hemisphere, with the exception of Cuba's Fidel Castro. They signed, in Miami, the Free Trade Agreement of the Americas.

The prospects of TAFTA, a Transatlantic Free Trade Agreement, were moving more slowly, largely because the trade and mutual investment flows were already extraordinarily free, except for some politically difficult areas like agriculture, steel, and textiles. In Madrid in December 1995, Clinton signed a new agreement with the European Union to advance the process and to set common product standards for the world's two biggest economic entities that were already deeply integrated. Over half of all Europe's foreign investment was in the United States; over 40 percent of all U.S. foreign investment was in the European Union.

When all these free trading projects, in the Pacific Rim, in the Western Hemisphere, and in Europe were examined together, a clear pattern emerged. The United States had always been broadly committed to a global market based on free trade through the GATT system. But a series of trading blocs were emerging anyway, based loosely around the dollar, the yen, and the deutsche mark. They carried a distinctly alarming echo of George Orwell's awful vision in *1984* of Eastasia, Oceania, and Eurasia, three empires locked in constant rivalry and simmering war.

The elegance of the Clinton strategy was that the Pacific, the European, and Western Hemisphere blocs should all have one thing in common; Clinton's America was locking itself steadily into the heart of each one. If all these new pacts develop as planned, Clinton is likely to go down in history as the true architect of the post–cold war world. Despite the isolationist rumblings and the dislocations of Mexico and the jobs exported to low-wage Indonesia, Americans may one day thank him for it. Clinton had devised the mechanisms to sustain an American global influence far into the next century.

This was all based on Clinton's central insight into the way the world was changing: that the cold war system of geopolitics and geo-strategy was giving way to an era of geo-economics and geo-finance. The arms summits between superpowers that had defined the grand diplomacy of the cold war had already been replaced by international trade pacts and economic summits. Missiles as symbols of global reach gave way to exports, which represented both hard and soft power, from jumbo jets to computing software, from CNN to financial derivatives.

The curious feature of this grand strategic concept was the hesitancy with which Clinton approached it. He only hinted at his convictions in the campaign, began his presidency with a series of rough trade disputes with his main commercial partners, and was always reticent about what became the one big idea of his administration. The reason was political wariness, about a policy most Democratic congressmen opposed, and which affronted the labor unions, a core constituency of his party. Free trade was political dynamite, an issue that sent deep cleavages through both parties, and made for bizarre political alliances. The arch-conservative Pat Buchanan made common cause with Ralph Nader, the consumer advocate who was an icon of the left, in a joint campaign against NAFTA and against the new World Trade Organization agreed to under the Uruguay Round of the GATT negotiations.

There was another reason for Clinton's reticence over his free trading strategy; he could achieve only half of it. In the Clinton vision, the great embrace of the global economy had to go hand in hand with fundamental reforms in the United States, to equip the American work force to benefit, rather than suffer from intensified global competition. Without an overhauled system of education, job training, and improvement of skills, many in the U.S. work force would find it difficult to compete. Without an overhaul of a health system that cost a sharply higher share of GDP than most international competitors, U.S. companies would be at a constant disadvantage, as they loaded the costs of their workers' health insurance onto the retail price of the products. The failure of Clinton's domestic reforms meant that his success in promoting free trade would intensify the pressure on the less-skilled and less-adaptable Americans, while offering them few defenses to help them cope.

Free trade had not begun with Clinton. The process had been getting under way for decades; the great tariff-reducing breakthrough of the GATT system was reached in the Kennedy Round of negotiations in the

1960s, named after the president seven presidencies before Clinton. The free trade pact with Canada had been negotiated under President Reagan, and its extension to Mexico as NAFTA was almost completed by President Bush. In a speech to the Detroit Economic Club in September 1992, President Bush proposed "a strategic network of free trade agreements . . . extending our global economic reach in tandem with our global security presence."

During the campaign, Clinton had challenged this vision. Knowing the deep opposition of the labor unions, Clinton had prevaricated on whether or not he supported NAFTA. Finally he devised a way to support it, but also to mollify Democratic protectionists. He would insist on two sidebar agreements, he promised, one to safeguard U.S. labor protections and occupational safety rules, and another to ensure that U.S. environment regulations were not undermined by unscrupulous Mexican companies prepared to cut costs by ignoring pollution dangers.

Clinton was then to take over the Bush inheritance on free trade, to expand it and push it into a core principle of his administration. But there were few signs of this in his first months in office. While claiming to be a free trader, Clinton picked a combative team of trade negotiators who launched his administration into a series of early disputes with the former cold war allies who were now seen as commercial rivals. The new trade team included former executives from American Express, from the accountants Coopers and Lybrand, and from the Cray supercomputing group, who all shared experience of resistant Japanese markets. "It's frustrating as hell. It drives you crazy," commented the accountant, W. Bowman Cutter, now deputy director of Clinton's National Economic Council. John A. Rollwagen, of the Cray group, had defined the United States–Japan relationship as "economic war." Ira Wolf, assistant U.S. trade representative for Japan and China, had been Motorola's representative in Tokyo.

The U.S. trade bureaucracy followed strict legal procedures to impose penal tariffs of up to 110 percent on European and other steel imports. The French government retorted that it could not swallow a GATT deal after such behavior. The Europeans were in disarray, and the United States proceeded to exploit their differences. Germany broke ranks with its partners to reach a separate deal with the United States on telecommunications, and the German central bank dutifully lowered its interest rates in advance of the 1993 G7 summit in Tokyo, when Clinton asked them to do so.

Clinton also prepared an uncompromising demand for managed, rather than free trade with Japan at G7, the annual economic summit of the leaders of the industrialized world: the United States, Japan, Germany, France, Britain, Italy, and Canada. Before the G7 met, the Clinton administration announced a new trade policy demanding that Japan cut its trade surplus in half and increase its imports by one-third. There was no threat of automatic trade retaliation if Japan failed to comply. But President Clinton's new team of trade negotiators with Japan, drawn mainly from U.S. businessmen with direct and frustrating experience of trying to export to Tokyo, insisted that they wanted results "within three to four years"—in time for Clinton's reelection bid in 1996.

As usual with Clinton's diplomacy, the tough talk before the meeting was the prelude to a deal. The Japanese had noted with satisfaction Clinton's appointment of Mickey Kantor as U.S. trade representative. Kantor had been a partner in the law and lobbying firm of Manatt, Phelps and Phillips, which was the registered lobbyist in Washington for Japan's NEC electronics giant, and he had lobbied personally for the motor manufacturer Suzuki. Kantor, a fierce competitor whose rages when losing at tennis were to become legendary in Washington, had been Clinton's campaign manager. But he lost the chance to head the transition team after he gave a special briefing on the incoming Clinton administration to clients of Manatt, Phelps.

In the event, Kantor was to become an extraordinarily effective manager of the trade portfolio, forging a personal relationship with the European trade commissioner Sir Leon Brittan, which resolved the GATT disputes, and forcing the Japanese to reconsider their assumption that fat lobbying contracts were the way to insert Trojan horses into the U.S. establishment. Kantor, an old friend of Mrs. Clinton, gave Clinton his unreserved loyalty, even offering to drop NAFTA from the legislative schedule if that would help Clinton press his budget and health reform plans. As a result, his trade counterparts elsewhere knew that Kantor had the president's ear and his backing, and that his deals would be honored.

At the Tokyo G7, the Japanese agreed to aim for the broad trading targets the United States wanted, while suggesting a series of working groups of officials to discuss the various trade sectors. This was standard Japanese negotiating strategy, which guaranteed good relations in principle but long delays in practice. Joseph Massey, the assistant trade representative for Japan and China, fluent in Asian languages and known in Japan as "the black prince" for his toughness and experience in negotiation, saw it as a classic Japanese tactic, drawn from Japan's history of medieval siege warfare. Japanese castles were designed around a concentric ring of moats and defenses. Take one, and another loomed. Take that, and the next moat lay in wait. There would be no swift breakthroughs, Massey warned, but long, hard slogging—unless the fort, the Japanese bureaucracy in the Ministry of Finance and the Ministry of International Trade and Industry, could be suborned from within.

One way to achieve that was to convince the Japanese *keiretsu,* the giant corporations, to argue the American case for opening the Japanese market against their own bureaucracy. One ploy was to encourage Japanese manufacturing investment in the United States, and by the time Clinton arrived in Tokyo, the biggest-selling imported car in Japan was a U.S.-manufactured Honda Accord. The second way to make the keiretsu support U.S. goals was to deploy an exchange rate strategy. In 1985, the Japanese yen had stood at over 250 to the dollar. When Clinton arrived in Tokyo, it was down to 120, which made U.S. exports to Japan far cheaper, and Japanese exports to the United States far more expensive. By 1995, the yen was dipping as low as 80 to the dollar, at which point it became almost impossible to make a profit on Japanese exports to the United States. The third way to suborn the Japanese bureaucracy was to wait for the soft power of U.S. culture, from hamburgers to rock music to Levi's jeans to Toys "R" Us stores, to steadily swell Japanese consumer demand for imports.

Japan was not like other countries, where government-to-government negotiations could produce a deal that the bureaucracies could be ordered to enforce and that the businessmen would have to live with. The Japanese bureaucracy was different, far more entrenched and powerful than the politicians. And Japan's own political crisis, which was to topple Prime Minister Kiichi Miyazawa and lead eventually to the weak coalition of a Socialist prime minister Tomiichi Murayama dependent on Liberal Democratic votes, was to strengthen the bureaucracy's hand.

The prospect of a political earthquake was in the air when Clinton arrived in Japan in July 1993 with elections only two weeks away. Understanding the political pressures this imposed on Prime Minister Miyazawa, Clinton was content with the appearance of a deal, which would make it easier to swing the Japanese behind his wider strategy of locking America into the emerging trading zone of Asia. For a tantalizing few months, the deeper strategy of counting on change within Japan seemed to be working. Morihiro Hosokawa, leader of the New Party and dedicated to reform of the moribund political system, emerged as prime minister.

"All discussion of a Japan–United States global partnership, burden sharing and shared values, ring hollow unless Japan reforms it antiquated nineteenth-century system and the national bureaucracy at its core" was Hosokawa's political statement. "We don't have a government of the people, by the people, or for the people, but of the bureaucracy, by the bureaucracy, for the bureaucracy." Hosokawa, who constantly referred to his admiration of Clinton, was for the new White House the Japanese leader of its dreams. His scheduled summit with Clinton in February 1994, was seen as the real chance to seal a new United States–Japan relationship. Sadly, Hosokawa was not to last long in office, brought down by a political establishment over a campaign finance scandal.

But first, the NAFTA battles had to be fought at home. As the vote loomed in November, Clinton was fighting the bulk of his own party and its leadership in Congress, and battling the trade unions, still the best-organized and best-financed component of the Democratic Party. The stakes were high: "The psychological impact of such events on the world economy could be traumatic," argued C. Fred Bergsten, director of Washington's Institute for International Economics, and one of the main architects of the free trade strategy. "The collapse of the institutional structure of the postwar trading system, and the broader implications for international economic cooperation and American leadership—markets everywhere could react sharply. Private investment and consumption could fall precipitously. A severe world recession could result."

Clinton also took the risk of defeat at the hands of his own party and the humiliation that would follow on the eve of his flight to Seattle for the first Asia-Pacific summit with the leaders of China, Japan, South Korea, Taiwan, Australia, Canada, and the Southeast Asian countries. For Clinton, there was no real gap between these events. NAFTA and the Asia-Pacific summit and the GATT world trade talks were all part of the same overriding foreign policy, most clearly seen through the change in the American concept of isolationism. Neo-isolationism, once pinned to the overseas military role and deployments of the United States, had come to refer to an economic posture, almost a synonym for protectionism. Clinton couched the NAFTA debate in precisely these terms.

"This vote on NAFTA comes at a defining moment for our nation," he argued. "This country is now the most productive country in the world, across a broad spectrum of manufacturing and service industries in this economy. We can win. And we have to decide whether we are going to reach out and win or try to withdraw."

NAFTA would combine the 250 million Americans and the 90 million Mexicans and the 27 million Canadians into a no-tariff trading block with a combined GDP of some $7 trillion a year. Of this combined wealth, Mexico contributed just 5 percent, Canada just under 10 percent, and the United States the rest. NAFTA put an elephant in bed with two mice. Most of the fears of jobs fleeing to low-wage Mexico were heavily overstated by Ross Perot, the unions, and the Democratic rebels. Most economic studies reckoned that although some 200,000 or so low-wage U.S. jobs could go, NAFTA would create more American jobs in return. And in a U.S. economy that was generating 150,000 new jobs a month, the NAFTA effect on employment was likely to be picayune. If a low-wage environment with tariff-free access to the United States were the key to economic success, then the U.S. colony of Puerto Rico, which also offered substantial tax advantages for U.S. corporations to open factories, would be the El Dorado of the hemisphere. It was not. Ross Perot's impassioned arguments against NAFTA found little support in Puerto Rico, whose 2.6 million inhabitants had a per capita income of $6,000 a year—less than one-third of the U.S. level.

The NAFTA vote in Congress was finely balanced. David E. Bonior, the able Democratic whip who was rounding up the votes against his own president, claimed already to have the 218 votes needed to defeat NAFTA. Clinton was helped by a sturdy and combative performance by Vice President Al Gore in a TV debate on NAFTA with Texan billionaire Ross Perot. Instant opinion polls conducted by CNN declared the debate a clear victory for Gore, by a margin of 59–32. After the show, public support for NAFTA jumped from 34 to 57 percent, while those opposed dropped from 38 to 34 percent. Gore's achievement, impressive for an often wooden debater, was to help the undecided make up their minds his way. Remarkably for CNN, which normally attracted less than 1 percent of U.S. viewers, some 11 million people tuned in.

In spite of the bitter debate in Congress, most of NAFTA's goals had already been achieved. Canada and the United States reached their own free trade pact in 1988, and Mexico began slashing its import tariffs in 1987. In the six years since, the United States had gone from a $5.7 billion trade deficit with Mexico to a $5.2 billion trade surplus in 1993, as trade between the two countries more than tripled. The real benefits of NAFTA lay in the future, in Clinton's policy to extend NAFTA to include Chile and Argentina, the two most developed Latin American economies, into the nucleus of an eventual Western Hemisphere free trade system. And beyond that lay the prospect of extending that free trading area into the world's fastest-growing region of Asia and the Pacific. That historic shift in trading patterns had already been overtaken by another, equally revolutionary change. In 1992 for the first time, the United States exported more ($170 billion) to Latin America and to those parts of Asia that exclude China and Japan than it did to Western Europe and Japan combined ($160 billion). So the White House, hoping for a win in the NAFTA vote, prepared a draft paper for the Asia-Pacific summit in Seattle that suggested the Pacific Rim nations were moving forward to a new PAFTA (Pacific-American Free Trade Area) of their own. This in turn put pressure on the Europeans to reach a quick GATT deal and then move on to the broad, sunlit uplands of global free trade.

Despite a U.S. deficit in manufacturing trade that would exceed $100 billion in the year of NAFTA, Clinton believed that free trade must benefit the market leader. The United States was the world's biggest exporter, with 12.3 percent of global exports in 1995 (compared to 11.8 percent for Germany and 9.3 percent for Japan). That deficit in manufacturing trade was not what it seemed. First, there was the 1992 U.S. surplus in services of $64 billion, which was growing at 20 percent a year. Then the U.S. Commerce Department admitted that while imports were precisely counted by U.S. Customs, many exports carried no tariff and were at least 5 percent underreported. The underestimate in U.S. exports to Canada was so large that in 1994 the Commerce Department began to use Canada's import statistics to measure U.S. exports to its biggest trading partner. And the conventional trade statistics massively under-represented the real weight of U.S. business in the global economy. The fact that Ford and General Motors were the largest and second-largest auto manufacturers in Britain, for example, simply did not figure into the U.S. trade statistics.

Although the United States itself accounted for only 12 percent of world exports in manufactured goods, U.S.-owned multinationals operating overseas accounted for another 17 percent of manufactured exports. Altogether, the United States turned a handsome profit from the global economy.

But the NAFTA debate opened a class fissure in America, between the elites who supported it and the populists, unions, and Democrats in Congress who feared it. This was NAFTA's dirty little secret. It would benefit the 100 million Americans in a household headed by a college graduate, who were doing very well out of the global economy and the new U.S. export miracle. But it would not help the 50 million or so in the underclass, and would also threaten the 100 million blue-collar and lower-middle-class white-collar workers in the middle. These were the very people who elected Bill Clinton, but had seen their household incomes stuck in real terms since 1972. Intent on the pursuit of his new foreign policy of geofinance, Bill Clinton was putting at risk his political base.

Still, Clinton scored a stunning personal success in winning the congressional vote for the NAFTA by the convincing margin of 234–200 votes. With a combination of pressure, outright bribes, and intense personal effort that recalled Lyndon Johnson's ruthless mastery of the Senate, Clinton stamped his authority on Congress and the nation. And by putting the prestige of his presidency on the line, he stilled the doubts about the depth of his political principles. The hard-faced men of the Congress had assumed that they had the measure of the new president as a man who could be easily intimidated, and he proved them wrong.

From the drama and tension of the vote in Washington, a jubilant Clinton flew to Seattle for the first Asia-Pacific summit, the gathering of fifteen nations of the world's fastest-growing trading region. In background briefings, White House officials made it clear that Clinton saw the NAFTA vote, APEC, and the looming deadline on the Uruguay Round of the GATT world trade talks as three tightly connected aspects of a single U.S. policy to promote global free trade—but on American terms.

Clinton found the other fifteen nations at the Asia-Pacific Economic Cooperation conference resisting his plan to use the threat of a new Pacific free trade area against the Europeans. But for once, the Japanese delegation was led by a reformist, Prime Minister Hosokawa, who was prepared to back Clinton when he could. Asian officials finally accepted U.S. insistence that the APEC summit issue a joint statement opposing any attempt by the French or European nations to reopen the Blair House agreement on agricultural subsidies. Clinton thus succeeded in tightening the pressure on the EC to reach a GATT deal, and in creating the perception of a Europe facing isolation as the two other great trading blocks of Asia and North America combined against it. The tough U.S. negotiating stance toward the European Community in this last lap of the GATT negotiations was emphasized when the United States blocked the European application to attend the APEC summit with observer status. Trade attachés from individual European countries then flew to Seattle to monitor the event and found that the only way they could get even to the fringes of the conference was by securing temporary accreditation as members of the press, a crude but effective way of delivering a political message to the European governments.

But it was not plain sailing for Clinton's vision to become the godfather of a new U.S.–Asian partnership. Traditional diplomatic issues of security and human rights constantly recurred. While enthusiastic about prospects for trade expansion, the Asians were distinctly cool to U.S. suggestions of a more formal structure. Japan, Hong Kong, and South Korea were all insistent that global free trade was their objective, rather than any Asia-Pacific system, and that their new forum should be seen "not as a trade block, but a building block to global free trade. . . . We prefer to reach multilateralism through GATT, with the ultimate aim of a global trade block," said Thomas Chau, Hong Kong's secretary for trade.

Malaysia's prime minister, Dr. Mohamad Mahathir, who pointedly declined to attend the APEC summit, was so suspicious of American motives that he urged an Asia-Pacific grouping that excluded the United States and Canada. "They want us to practice the kind of democracy that brings about instability, economic decline, and poverty. With this, they can threaten and control us."

The fruition of the APEC initiative was to come one year later, as the second APEC summit in Indonesia agreed to develop a Pacific Rim free trade zone. The immediate task for Clinton was to mend his fences with the anti-NAFTA Democrats and win back the support of the American trade unions. Clinton promised to prepare new legislation, most of it stemming from ideas promoted by his old friend and labor secretary, Robert

Reich, for a radical overhaul of the U.S. unemployment insurance system. "As we enact NAFTA, we must recognize that we have a solemn obligation to make our involvement in international trade serve the interests of our people. That means they have to be able to adjust to change. . . . So what the labor secretary is now trying to do is to set up a system where people who lose their jobs immediately—and even before they lose their jobs—begin training programs, begin job placement programs, begin thinking about what the future really holds instead of living with a system that was yesterday's reality and is today's sham," the president promised.

The unions were to be disappointed. What finally emerged was a modest consolidation of existing schemes, with no new funding. Clinton had a way of testing to the limit the loyalty of his supporters, and his inability to get his ambitious domestic reforms approved in Congress was worse than a disappointment—it left him enacting an essentially Republican agenda, plunging ahead with trade while doing little to alleviate its impact on Democratic voters. He also plunged ahead with trade despite the human rights concerns that Democrats had traditionally upheld. Another result of his APEC trade policies threatened rebellion among the liberals in Congress and among human rights supporters when Clinton agreed to grant China Most Favored Nation trading status, which slashed tariffs on China's exports to the United States.

"This decision will confirm for the Beijing regime the success of its policy of repression on human rights and manipulation on trade," complained the Senate Democratic leader, George Mitchell of Maine.

"Sometimes a president has to disagree with strong supporters," Sandy Berger, deputy national security adviser in the White House, said rather apologetically. "We did not believe that essentially severing our relations with China was the best way to support human rights. Opening China in the long term to the international community is the better way."

All this was wholly consistent with the trade and export priority that Clinton had placed at the heart of his foreign policy. But that new relationship began with a thumping diplomatic success for Beijing, and with yet more evidence that Clinton was a president who could be tempted or intimidated into ditching his. Beijing successfully defied the U.S. president, publicly humiliated his secretary of state Warren Christopher by arresting more dissidents during his visit to China, and outmaneuvered Clinton in his own forum of U.S. politics by recruiting the lobbying power of corporate America. On the day that Clinton announced his retreat, the Boeing corporation confirmed that China was "within weeks" of signing a $5 billion contract for fifty new airliners. Other such carrots were dangled, including U.S. access to a ten-year telecommunications market in China valued at $500 billion.

These contracts were enthusiastically promoted within the administration by Ron Brown, the commerce secretary, and his undersecretary for international trade, Jeffrey Garten, who devised a new export strategy called BEM. It stood for "big emerging markets," ten targeted countries that Garten expected would double their share of world trade over the fifteen years and absorb more imports than Japan and Western Europe combined by the year 2010. The BEMs were China, Indonesia, South Korea, India, Turkey, South Africa, Poland, Argentina, Brazil, and Mexico, and Garten established a special task force for each one. American businessmen were asked to provide their wish lists for what the U.S. government might do to help, from scrapping regulations, easing customs requirements, helping with export credit, and so on.

Brown and Garten also established a "war room" inside the Commerce Department to coordinate the winning of big export orders. The sale of Boeing commercial jets to China and to Saudi Arabia, AT&T's telecommunications to Indonesia and China, and General Electric's power stations to Brazil and Indonesia were all run from the war room. Interagency task forces of staff from the State Department, U.S. Customs, the Export-Import Bank, and any other part of the government that could help were recruited and put to work in the war room to help win the contract. If President Clinton was needed to phone the Saudi king, the war room made the recommendation. The operations ran under strict conditions of commercial secrecy. When journalists were once allowed into the war room, all charts and papers had been cleared to preserve the anonymity of the latest contract. A major concern of the war room was bribery and corruption, and the generous credit terms that rival countries might offer to win big orders. The European Airbus consortium was a constant worry. The assets of the Central Intelligence Agency were available to the war room when required, and the CIA was to be deeply embarrassed when it was found tapping the phones of Japanese trade negotiators and when agents were expelled from the Paris embassy, accused of commercial espionage.

After his NAFTA victory, President Clinton had to face another congressional battle, and again depend on the support of the Republicans as his own Democrats deserted him in droves, to enact the new GATT agreement. Senator Dole exacted one key concession, the right for the United States to review its membership of the World Trade Organization's rules if it lost three successive cases in the WTO court, and it passed both House and Senate in a lame-duck session after the ringing Republican victories in the November election. Despite the triumphantly large majorities in House and Senate to agree to the GATT treaty, the Democrats' hostility to GATT was far from dead. On the day President Clinton flew to Miami for his Summit of the Americas, the new Democratic leader in the House, Congressman Dick Gephardt, gave him a nine-page letter that said that Clinton's free trade enthusiasm was part of the reason for the thumping Democratic defeat in the midterm congressional elections.

"We must do all we can to ensure that we do not have another NAFTA-like debate that divides the Democratic Party," Gephardt warned. Future trade agreements must make their priority "improving the economic lives of working people." Were the phrase not so unfashionable in American political discourse, Gephardt might have said that there was a class problem with free trade. Free trade boosted imports and exports and created a larger economic pie, but it divided that pie in ways that disproportionately benefit the wealthy, the educated, the skilled, and the adaptable. It exacerbated that growing disparity, apparent in U.S. income statistics since 1972, between the incomes of those with a high school diploma or less and those with college degrees.

"There is a centrifugal force, splitting our and other countries' work forces, a historical shift of the balance of industrial and social power towards people with skills," Secretary of Labor Robert Reich told a summit audience in Miami. His remedy was orthodox enough; more education, more training and retraining, more "upskilling" of the labor force. President Clinton tried to fend off his internal critics by arguing in Miami that this was already happening, that the bulk of the new jobs created in the past year were in high-skilled and high-paying work. Certainly 62 percent of the year's new jobs were in the category defined as managerial and professional. But that figure concealed a lot of laid-off corporate executives who now called themselves "consultants."

"We hope we are seeing the beginning of the end of a twenty-year trend of stagnant wages," Clinton said, which strained credulity, like much of his rhetoric in Miami about free trade as a panacea and bulwark of democracy. The 35 nations of the Western Hemisphere produced in 1994 a total GDP of some $8,000 billion, of which the United States alone provided over 75 percent, with a GDP of more than $6,000 billion. Mexico and Canada, the two U.S. partners in NAFTA, provided another $900 billion. Brazil, with a GDP of $425 billion, Argentina with $200 billion, Venezuela with $60 billion, Chile with almost $50 billion, and Colombia with $45 billion made up the great bulk of the remainder. And a host of poorer countries, from Paraguay and Bolivia, with GDPs of some $5 billion each, and the small economies of Central America and the Caribbean islands, were the nervous minnows in this pool of gross disparities.

But, countered Clinton and the free traders, Latin America was rivaling East Asia in rates of growth and of commercial expansion. The imports of U.S. neighbors to the south, which grew from $40 billion in 1988 to just over $100 billion in 1994, would collectively buy more U.S. exports, Clinton assured the Miami summit, than the European Union and Japan by the year 2010. The high-flown rhetoric and abundant promises concealed some serious questions, about the ability of most Latin American countries to deal with U.S. competition. Few had yet fully recovered from the lost decade of debts and recession in the 1980s, which left average real incomes little more than half of what they were in 1983. And with a total loan exposure of $450 billion, and interest rates rising again, Latin America's debt burden had never been greater. The continent remained wracked by social and political divisions and by monstrous disparities of wealth. The angry peasant uprising in the Chiapas province of Mexico rumbled on. The ex-president of Brazil was being tried for fraud as the summit met in Miami. Chile was hailed as the model of free market development; Chile's former president, Patricio Aylwin, gave a speech on the eve of the Miami summit warning that only the wealthiest 20 percent had benefited.

"The Latin leaders feel in a way that they have been double-crossed," said Sebastian Edwards, the World Bank's chief economist for Latin America, just before the summit opened. "Their trade liberalization has been the most dramatic in history. But these guys opened up in exchange for nothing." So, even as they met in Miami, some Latin leaders were publicly fretting whether free trade was delivering quite what it had promised, and whether the United States was playing entirely fair. "We have adopted the free market, low-tariff model of commerce that the United States has promoted. But all of a sudden, Colombia cannot sell its roses in the United States, nor Ecuador its bananas, nor Panama its tuna, nor Chile its apples—all because U.S. producers lobby against our competition," complained Colombia's president Ernesto Samper. He had a simple word for the real U.S. trade policy: "neo-protectionism."

Nonetheless, Clinton became the third U.S. president to address a summit of the Latin countries and to hold out the prospect of free trade and a vision of hemispheric cooperation to its 500 million neighbors in the Americas, from Canada to Chile. But unlike President Franklin Roosevelt in Buenos Aires in 1936 and President Lyndon Johnson in Uruguay in 1967, Clinton claimed to have already begun to fulfill the promise, by restoring democratic rule to Haiti.

The tactics of political opportunism inevitably jostled with the grand strategy of free trade. The Democratic defeat in the U.S. midterm elections increased Clinton's need for a striking political success at Miami, and his administration suddenly scrambled to provide it. The result was a final communiqué that was cobbled together with little serious thought for the commercial realities behind the sweeping homilies on the marvels of free trade. One sign of this was the absence from the presummit negotiations of U.S. trade representative Mickey Kantor. Another was the behind-the-scenes sniping by the State Department's Latin experts at the way the White House suddenly pushed for bold initiatives in a region of which it knew little. And there were risks involved, which meant that American taxpayers could be conscripted to rescue the global economy when it suffered one of its predictable hiccups.

The crisis of the Mexican economy at the end of 1994 was a direct result of the policies followed by the free market orthodoxies of Harvard-educated president Carlos Salinas in the pursuit of NAFTA. The Mexican peso was deliberately overvalued, and the balance of payments allowed to spiral into crisis, to maintain the allure of Mexico as a market for U.S. goods and investors. The collapse of the peso and of the Mexican stock market sent tremors through emerging markets around the globe, from Poland to Thailand. It also provoked President Clinton to mobilize a swift emergency credit to stabilize the peso.

In Congress, new Speaker Newt Gingrich and Senate leader Robert Dole supported the first Clinton plan, for the United States to extend a loan guarantee of up to $40 billion for the Mexican government to float some new and longer-term bonds to get through an essentially short-term funding crisis. Like co-signing a bank loan agreement, this would not have cost the United States a penny, unless Mexico defaulted, and then the United States would have had the collateral of Mexico's oil revenues. But such was the economic illiteracy of many congressional members that this was somehow seen as a $40 billion payout to Mexico, when, as one congresswoman put it, "Detroit can use that money."

Speaker Gingrich marched boldly out to support the Clinton plan, and found himself almost alone. The rank and file and the 73 freshman Republicans, who had hitherto treated Gingrich as the Moses who would lead them to the promised congressional land, decided to stay on the bank and watch the Red Sea flood in over their abandoned Speaker. Gingrich was hit by that same populist revolt of which he had hitherto been the prophet. At least he was not entirely isolated. The talk show host Rush Limbaugh was also seized by a fit of responsibility to support the Mexican bailout, largely because the wily Federal Reserve chairman Alan Greenspan had paid Limbaugh the compliment of giving him a private briefing on the perils to the global economy of a Mexican collapse. Rush Limbaugh stumbled bravely across the airwaves, as his devoted listeners wondered whether he had taken leave of his populist senses.

As Gingrich floundered, President Clinton decided to ignore Congress and mount a bailout on his own authority. He took $20 billion from the currency stabilization fund, stretching his legal powers to the very limit to do so. He then bullied the IMF into stumping up $17.8 billion—with scant consultation of the affronted Europeans. Alan Greenspan wheedled another $10 billion from the Bank of International Settlements in Basel, and the deed was done. It was a bold display of leadership by Clinton, operating in the new strategic arena of global finance in the way that other presidents had acted decisively in the geopolitical crises of the cold war. It was also a moment when the swirling currents of history, the rivalries and the self-interest of great powers, and the deeper logic of high finance suddenly came together at a single point to define the shape the world would take in the future.

A similar moment came on October 4, 1995, in London, when the great oil and energy corporations of the West, under intense pressure from the White House, gathered to decide the fate of the oil of the Caspian Sea. A modern version of the nineteenth-century struggles for influence in this same Asian heartland between the czarist and British empires, this was the new Great Game. Riding on this meeting was an immediate $10 billion of Western investment, the first installment for an eventual commitment of $50 billion to the pipelines and oil and gas fields of central Asia, the crucial resource of economic growth for the coming century. And if intelligence sources were to be believed, also at stake was the life of Eduard Shevardnadze, the legendary Soviet foreign minister during Perestroika, who had become the embattled leader of the small, war-torn, and still just independent republic of Georgia. Shevardnadze himself was convinced that the car bomb that had wounded him on the eve of the London meeting was a warning ordered from Moscow.

Led by British Petroleum (BP) and Amoco, the participants on the Azerbaijan International Oil Consortium had to decide at the London meeting whether to bow to U.S. pressure and agree to export the oil from the Caspian Sea through two pipelines. One pipeline had already been long built, and ran through embattled Chechnya and north to the Russian Black Sea port of Novorossiysk. The Russians, seeing their control of the pipeline routes as the key to their future influence over the former Soviet republics, insisted that the oil should flow north.

The other pipeline, which the governments of the United States, Turkey, and Georgia were urging, had yet to be built, at a cost of some $2 billion. It would go from the Caspian shore at Baku across Georgia to the Black Sea port of Supsa, and break Moscow's stranglehold over the pipelines. BP, for whom this initial $8 billion investment in the Caspian oilfields was but the start of a much greater interest in Russian energy supplies, had favored the northern pipeline route through Russia. "Whatever is good for BP is fine by us," said Thomas Young, Britain's ambassador in Baku, a cheery comment that skated over an extraordinary saga of maneuvering and discussion between London and Washington as they sought to support the interests of their oil giants.

The Great Game had begun in September 1994, when the National Security Council obtained the stunning results of the oil exploration surveys conducted by Amoco and British Petroleum in the Caspian Sea. The known and proven reserves of the Chirag and Azeri fields were 4.5 billion barrels. But the White House now knew that the estimated reserves were several times larger. "The Caspian and Kazakh basins are going to be the major source of world energy in the twenty-first century. The reserves are up there with the Persian Gulf," a senior NSC official confided. "We want a pipeline agreement with Russia within the next two weeks. The president is really pressing Yeltsin on this." The Clinton-Yeltsin summit that followed was a partial success, but then Russia's strategic calculations in the region were thrown into disarray by the eruption of war in Chechnya.

The oil rush of the twenty-first century had been under way ever since. The U.S. companies Amoco and Pennzoil joined British Petroleum in the $8 billion development project for the Caspian signed with the former Soviet republic of Azerbaijan. Under that deal, BP and Amoco each got 19 percent of the consortium; the republic of Azerbaijan got 30 percent; Pennzoil, Unocal, and Norway's Staatoil each got 9 percent. There were other smaller investors, including Turkey's Petroleum Corporation, the Saudi-based Delta group, and Britain's Ramco. With 39 percent of the consortium, American oil companies had the lion's share. So the Clinton administration set up a special task force to watch over U.S. interests. Chaired by Deputy Secretary of State Strobe Talbott, it included NSC and CIA staffers, and senior officials from the Energy and Commerce Departments.

The U.S. oil companies were initially alarmed by the unusual level of government interest, fearing that their commercial decisions could fall victim to geo-strategic concerns. The first guidance from the White House was a virtual order: in no circumstances would there be a pipeline that ran south through Iran. Clinton objected strenuously when cash-short Azerbaijan tried to sell 5 percent of the deal to the Iranian national oil company, and insisted that deal be reversed. The White House objected again when Conoco signed a $1 billion deal with Iran to develop two fields in the Persian Gulf, despite the U.S. official policy of "double-containment" of Iraq and Iran as two rogue states. That was stopped, too.

There was little unusual about a divergence between U.S. government policy and the corporate practice of Big Oil. A fuzzy and hypocritical understanding long permitted U.S. oil corporations to buy and market some 30 percent of Iran's oil exports, so long as they were not sold to U.S. consumers. But Iran and the Persian Gulf were old hat. The new game had become that twilight zone of Central Asia, no longer securely tucked behind Soviet skirts. To ensure that Russian interests were clearly understood in Azerbaijan, Russia backed the 1993 coup that replaced the fiercely nationalist government of Albufaz Echibey with a former Soviet Politburo member, Geidar Aliyev, and 10 percent of the consortium was shifted from

Azerbaijan to Russia's Lukoil. There were more coup flurries in 1995, in which Russia's hand was harder to prove, although both U.S. and British intelligence reported that they had few doubts that Moscow was involved.

The Caspian oil deal was not only important in itself. It was the crucial precedent, whether or not Russia would be able to monopolize the pipelines for the oil from the Caspian and the even larger oilfields of Kazakhstan and gas fields of Turkmenistan. Chevron had a $20 billion contract to develop the vast Tengiz oilfield in Kazakhstan, but that was barely chugging along as Russia refused to allow any more than a million barrels a year through its pipelines. The Chevron operation stalled, pending negotiations for a new pipeline across Kazakhstan and Russia to the port of Novorossiysk.

British Gas and Italy's Agip signed a similar deal to develop the Karachaqanak natural gas field of Kazakhstan, which had proven gas reserves of 100 trillion cubic feet. Again the Russians were involved, through the vast state gas monopoly called Gazprom, which Russian prime minister Viktor Chernomyrdin used to run. To the south, in the former Soviet republic of Turkmenistan, there were known gas reserves of 90 trillion cubic feet, and again the only pipeline ran through Russia. To try to break out of the Russian stranglehold, Turkmenistan president Saparamurad Niyazov staged a bizarre ceremony in November 1994. He invited the leaders of Turkey, Pakistan, Iran, and Azerbaijan to join him in digging a ceremonial hole, in which two short lengths of pipeline were welded together. That was it. There was no more pipeline, and none has been added since. The plan to get Turkmen gas out through Iran and Turkey to the world markets, and Pakistan's hopes of a pipeline through Afghanistan to its own port at Karachi, stalled on the joint U.S.–Russian opposition to any pipeline route that Iran could control.

The published figures for the oil and gas reserves were for proven resources. The estimates of what could be in that vast region from Baku to Kazakhstan range far, far higher, suggesting that it could rival the Persian Gulf as a source of energy in the twenty-first century. And it was on the basis of those estimates that U.S. strategy was being made. The implications of all this were raised in startling form by Senator Robert Dole in a foreign policy speech designed to establish his credentials as a presidential candidate. Dole gave a new definition of the globe's energy supplies as a crucial strategic interest of the United States, and its implications for U.S. military deployments.

"The security of the world's oil and gas supplies remains a vital interest of the United States and its major allies," Dole said, recalling the Gulf War to liberate Kuwait from Iraq as the key symbol of American concern for the Persian Gulf. "But its borders now move north, to include the Caucasus, Siberia, and Kazakhstan. Our forward military presence and diplomacy need adjusting."

The Great Game had immediate political implications. The reason for the Clinton administration's low-key comments on Russia's disastrous war in Chechnya was that the United States had looked at the pipeline maps and understood their crucial strategic importance. The main pipeline from Baku ran north along the Caspian Sea to Makhachkala, and then headed east into Chechnya. Just outside the demolished city of Grozny was the refinery complex and switching station where the Baku oil was split into two new pipelines. One went east to Novorossiysk, and the other line ran north to Astrakhan, joining the pipeline system to Kazakhstan. The pipelines meant that Chechnya was Russia's Kuwait.

This was not just a matter between Russia and the West. China was already jostling to become a player. Indeed, another 140 billion barrels of oil (about sixty years of Saudi oil production) lay in China's Karamay and Tarim basins, adjoining the Kazakhstan border. Clinton's task force did not take seriously China's proposal to break the Russian monopoly with a 5,000-mile pipeline to take Kazakh gas and oil to the energy-hungry coastal cities of China and on to Japan. The costs would be astronomic. Yet China was the force that was really driving the new Great Game, because China's remarkable growth rates required energy resources and promised to revolutionize the economics of oil all over again. Already the world's sixth-leading producer of oil (ahead of Venezuela), China in 1994 became a net importer.

In 1995, there was a world glut of oil. Indeed, the strongest motive of the United States and its Saudi ally in maintaining the oil embargo on Iraq was to prevent a further plunge in the oil price, should Iraq start offering its million barrels a day back on the world markets. Adjusted for inflation, the world price of oil in 1995 was close to what it had been in 1973, before the great OPEC price rise. China's looming oil demands looked likely to change all that. The International Energy Agency, based in Paris, reported that the growth in oil consumption of developing countries alone would, over the next decade, be the equivalent of the entire oil consumption of Western Europe.

China in 1994 consumed about 5 barrels of oil per head (compared to 30 barrels a head in Germany, and 53 barrels a head in the United States). The lower estimates for China's growth suggested this would double to 10 barrels a head within ten years. That meant an extra 6 billion barrels a year, or 16 million barrels a day—twice the production of Saudi Arabia. Combine that soaring demand with the declining production in the North Sea and Alaska's North Slope, and oil demand and oil prices were set for some dramatic growth. Put that together with the meeting of the oil executives in London, and the brew became intriguing. The new strategic cockpit, the energy source on which the great industrial economies will depend in the coming century, lay not just in the Persian Gulf but in the heart of Eurasia.

This was the region where Russia, China, and the Islamic world, and the religious-cultural traditions they each represent, all met and jostled for influence. The most powerful American and European energy corporations had their deals, their drills, and their personnel in place while the Russians commanded the essential infrastructure, in the form of pipelines. This is where the cold war era of geopolitics came into collision with Clinton's dawning new world of geo-economics. And it was significant that the first wars of the post–cold war world, the Gulf War against Iraq, and Russia's battle for its pipelines in Chechnya, had been about oil. Danger, profits, and power all swirled together. As the Azerbaijan International Oil Consortium agreed in London to go with Clinton's policy of two pipelines, breaking the Russian stranglehold, the new Great Game was under way. Clinton's perception that the cold war world was being transformed into a new era of global finance was only part of the truth; in the Great Game, geopolitics and geo-economics were indistinguishable.

☆ 14 ☆

CLINTON'S RELAUNCH AND THE REPUBLICAN RECOVERY

Despite President Clinton's promise of "an explosive hundred-day action period," the date brought little to celebrate. He held a defiant press conference, to brush aside the defeat in the Senate of his economic stimulus package, and claimed, "We have already fundamentally changed the direction of American government." But then, at a meeting with his domestic policy staff, the president arrived with a sheet of notepaper on which he had scribbled the words *New Democrat,* followed by a list, which went: National Service, Welfare Reform, Health Care, Job Training, Children, and Police.

This, Clinton explained, was the agenda that had got him elected by defining him as a different kind of Democrat, free of the old ideological debts and with innovative ideas to address the social problems that underpinned the country's economic crisis. Where was it now, he asked. Why was his administration being hammered in Congress and the media as just another bunch of tax-and-spend Democrats, as Washington insiders in debt to traditional lobbies and special interests? The evidence of lost momentum was plain. A CBS News poll had found 50 percent of Americans disapproving of his handling of the economy. Only 40 percent said his new economic and tax plans were fair to people like themselves, and 48 percent found them unfair.

The battle to pass his budget brought more trouble. There were two separate rebellions under way among moderate Democrats, one in the House and another in the Senate. But the headquarters of each was in Oklahoma, the home of an interesting breed of conservative Democrats, who confused their northern liberal colleagues by playing politics as hard as southerners and relishing a sturdy independence like westerners. The first Oklahoma rebel was Congressman Dave McCurdy, one of Clinton's most fervent supporters in the election campaign. He was the leader of some seventy Democratic congressmen who demanded far deeper spending cuts and accused Clinton of winning the White House as a moderate "New Democrat" but governing and spending like a traditional liberal. Organized by McCurdy into a new group called the "Mainstream Forum," the Democratic rebels wanted to defeat the president's proposed energy tax, which would hit oil-producing states like Oklahoma particularly hard. They also wanted to take the political risk of capping the sacrosanct entitlement benefits like pensions and Medicare.

The 70 members of the Mainstream Forum had a far more general concern, based on the message from their constituents that Clinton's five-year budget plan would only control the rise of the deficit, not reverse it. Even under Clinton's rosiest assumptions, the national debt would increase by $1,000 billion by 1997. "The White House seems to be in a closed loop with the liberals," McCurdy complained. "They are listening to a small group of people who don't support a New Democrat agenda and weren't with Bill Clinton in the beginning." There was a personal edge to the tussle. McCurdy, one of the first congressmen to endorse Clinton's candidacy and one of his nominators at the Democratic convention, had hoped to be named secretary of defense. He was passed over, and then Speaker of the House Tom Foley engineered McCurdy's demotion from the chairmanship of the Select Committee on Intelligence. A member of the Air Force Reserve, who made a point of serving for a week with his unit in the Persian Gulf during the war against Iraq, McCurdy was not a man to be lightly crossed.

Oklahoma was next door to Arkansas, and McCurdy and Clinton were once staunch political friends who worked closely together in the Democratic Leadership Council. The president dashed over to Congress to twist arms and use the appeal of old friendships to put out McCurdy's prairie fire. The wily Oklahoman was happy to be reasonable, because he knew that the sparks had already spread elsewhere. From their native Oklahoma, and from their dominance of the House and Senate committees on intelligence, Representative McCurdy and Senator David Boren were accustomed to working together. They were both under considerable pressure from the oil interests at home to fight the new energy tax. And while Mc-

Curdy was collecting various presidential promises for being reasonable, Senator Boren was about to drop the second Oklahoma bomb upon his fellow Rhodes scholar, Bill Clinton. (If the Battle of Waterloo was won on the playing fields of Eton, much of the drama of the Clinton administration had its roots in British education; McCurdy went to the University of Edinburgh.)

Senator Boren sat on the Senate Finance Committee, whose support was essential to pass Clinton's budget. The committee contained eleven Democrats and nine Republicans. By defecting to the Republican side on the budget vote, Boren could block the process. Moreover, Boren gathered another centrist Democrat from another oil-dependent state, J. Bennett Johnson of Louisiana, and two moderate Republicans, Senators William S. Cohen of Maine and John Danforth of Missouri, into a gang of four who presented their own alternative budget plan.

It would kill off the proposed energy tax, court the Republicans by cutting capital gains taxes, and hit the popular target of cutting government spending by $2 for every $1 that was raised in new taxes. The figures looked hastily compiled, and the real target was Clinton's energy tax. A far more serious political defeat now loomed for the White House than the rejection of the $16 billion economic stimulus package. For a president's entire budget to be defeated by a Congress his party dominated would be a political humiliation unprecedented since the dog days of Jimmy Carter. This was also a crucial moment for Clinton, because this battle inside the Democratic Party was perhaps best understood as a war between the left and the right sides of the president's brain. Genuinely a New Democrat, Clinton believed that the liberal and welfare reforms of the 1960s were well intentioned, but had rotten results. He sincerely wanted to end the dependency culture of welfare, to espouse fiscal discipline and cut the deficit. He genuinely believed in the need to bring back the spirit of national service, to make college education available to all in return for two years of work in the community, the police, or his planned new ecology corps.

But he was also a liberal, or rather, a social democrat at heart. He believed in government, in the role of the state as activist, as investor, as the institution that set great national priorities. He wanted to pump public money into job training, into high-tech research, and use U.S. economic power to bend the traditions of free trade to America's commercial benefit.

McCurdy and Senator Boren knew Clinton well enough to understand this constant debate inside the president's head. The Republicans saw it in rather different terms, as a battle between Clinton's centrist instincts and his wife's liberal convictions. Between them, the Democratic centrists and the Republicans began to put in doubt the whole ambitious agenda of New Democrat reform.

For Clinton, this was the classic Washington gridlock and defense of special interests, and he took to the campaign trail again to rally some public momentum. His campaign strategists had advised him to do so. On the road again, Clinton rejoiced in the adrenaline of the permanent campaign. Diminished and frustrated by the stubborn political culture of Washington, Clinton loved to plunge back into the massed rallies in the summer sunshine with a sound system blaring out mainstream rock before the local high school band belted out the national anthem.

"I want this, I want this," he cried as he reluctantly left a crowd of some 20,000 people at Los Alamos. He had spotted a group of young cheerleaders in red-white-and-blue-striped T-shirts, each bearing a capital letter, and when they stood in line their shirts spelled *C-L-I-N-T-O-N-!* He rallied them into line, plunged into the middle, and commanded photographs as the high school band launched into "Louie, Louie." He waited and grinned for the group photo as aides waited to get the names and addresses of each cheerleader to send them final prints. Bruce Lindsey gazed contentedly over the Los Alamos sports field and reckoned this was the biggest crowd Clinton had addressed since his inauguration. "It's good for him," said Lindsey. "He needs this energy, this touching of the base. It puts Washington into perspective." Paul Begala gulped in the crowd's cheers and enthused, "The worst day in America is better than the best day in Washington."

The electioneering was also a form of escape. The tragedy of Bosnia, and Clinton's agonized ditherings over what to do, were hurting not only the White House but that mood of American self-confidence in the world that Clinton inherited from George Bush and Ronald Reagan. As one of the forest of posters that greeted him in San Diego read, "It's leadership, stupid." It was also careless arrogance. It was on this jaunt that he held *Air Force One* on the tarmac at Los Angeles Airport while he had his hair cut by Christophe, the $200-a-cut Hollywood coiffeur. The Federal Aviation Authority later denied that other commuter flights were held up by *Air Force*

One's delay. No matter. The perception was that the Man from Hope had turned into the jet-setter from Hollywood. Then the investment fund that managed Mrs. Clinton's personal share portfolio was found to have sold short some health-care stocks. Since Mrs. Clinton ran the health reform task force, this caused a stir, although she was blameless in the fund's investment decisions. But Hillary as the calculating yuppie began to join Clinton's $200 haircut in the media, particularly on talk-radio. The haircut provided a convenient label to pin on a fundamentally baffling president, who was both campaigning machine and policy wonk.

His very flexibility suggested a readiness to compromise in principle and a readiness to fold under pressure. In deciding to withdraw the nomination of his Yale Law School colleague Lani Guinier as assistant attorney general with responsibility for civil rights, Clinton even cast doubt on his loyalty to his old friends. Lani Guinier was close enough to the Clintons that they attended her wedding. Like so many of the FOBs, she was a believer in his political cause. When Clinton had his well-publicized spat with the Reverend Jesse Jackson during the campaign, Lani Guinier was one of those who helped persuade other black politicians to grit their teeth and stick with Clinton.

When he first put her name forward, Clinton said that he had always hoped that the civil rights division of the Justice Department would one day be run by an experienced civil rights lawyer like Lani Guinier. She had impeccable legal credentials, with federal judges competing to recruit her as their clerk when she graduated from Yale Law School. As well as a practicing lawyer of note, Ms. Guinier had been an academic and a leading legal theorist. And that was where the trouble lay. Her articles for serious law journals, hitherto places where legal pioneers had been expected to think aloud about the future of the law, were scoured by the Republicans for ammunition to defeat her. And in her musings on the way that the system of voting majorities could result in clearly democratic decisions that had grim effects for racial minorities, they smelled blood. Ms. Guinier had criticized "simple-minded notions of majority rule," and suggested ways to give legal protection to minorities, much as the Senate sometimes required more than just a simple majority to pass legislation.

"At the time of the nomination, I had not read her writings. I wish I had," President Clinton confessed as he dropped her. "The problem is that this battle will be waged based on her academic writings. And I cannot fight a battle that I know is divisive, that is an uphill battle, that is distracting to the country, if I do not believe in the ground of the battle," Clinton added. "That is the only problem."

In effect, he decided to cut his losses and duck the kind of televised inquisition of a controversial nominee that had become the hallmark of the Senate Judiciary Committee. Because of Clinton's delicate relations with Congress, and the need to placate conservative Democrats in the Senate, it probably made political sense to avoid this fray. But he paid—yet again—a stiff price among his liberal constituency, his feminist supporters, and much of the black lobby, which counted Lani Guinier, who had a black father and a Jewish mother, as one of their own. She also served a distinctive term as the chief legal officer for the National Association for the Advancement of Colored People. Representative Kweisi Mfume, chairman of the Congressional Black Caucus, said Clinton had "succumbed to fear and innuendo and a whispering campaign by a few faceless and spineless senators who masquerade as Democrats." More ominously, Congressman Mfume added that he and his 38 colleagues in the Black Caucus on Capitol Hill would now "reassess and reevaluate its relationship with the administration."

The problem was not that Clinton had yet to identify what kind of president he sought to be. He had dallied with several roles: the industrial strategist; the economic galvanizer; the political fixer; the social engineer; and the great reformer. None quite fit, except for that curious role that became the highlight of his campaigning trips—the TV host at one of his carefully staged town meetings. Clinton usually entranced audiences who were accustomed to the superficial charms and glib clichés of the talk show host. But he had come into his presidency with more ambition and more vision, and until 1996 the real electorate he had to seduce were the 435 congressmen and 100 senators in Washington.

"He'll figure it out. He always does," said Betsey Wright, his chief of staff in Arkansas, after his first defeat in the Senate. She was right. Afficionados of the art of politics at its most raw were treated to a feast of deals and horse-trading, arm-twisting, and seduction, as Clinton pushed his budget bill through a House of Representatives dominated by his own Democratic Party with the narrow margin of 219 votes to 213. The voting tally underestimated Clinton's success. Once it was plain that they had won, the party managers allowed some fence-sitters with serious fears of electoral retaliation to cast a symbolic vote against their president.

At the start of the final day of the House vote, President Clinton was still ten votes short of the 217 he needed. But he was more than confident that enough members of his party would grit their teeth and pass what the Republicans dubbed "the biggest tax increase in the history of the world." (They were both right and wrong on this. In constant dollars, President Reagan's tax increase ten years earlier was much higher. In inflated dollars, Clinton had indeed won the unenviable new record.)

The entire Clinton cabinet and the party leadership put the rest of the world on hold and went hunting for votes. Each member of Clinton's cabinet was given a list of between five and twenty congressmen to lobby in person. Usually old political allies or local friends, or congressmen seeking favors from a particular government department, they were wooed by cabinet members who dropped most other business for the supreme administration priority of winning the budget vote. All avenues of leverage were pursued. White House communications director George Stephanopoulos arranged a "Coke and cheese" party for congressional aides, promising them that in return for loyalty the president would visit the editorial boards of their local newspapers and give live interviews to local TV stations before the next congressional elections.

It was instructive to watch the process at work. New congressman Ron Klink from Pittsburgh, unhappy at the impact of the proposed energy tax on his district's few remaining steel mills, was telephoned on the floor of the House by the president on the day of the vote. They spoke for twenty minutes. Mr. Klink had earlier been phoned by Vice President Al Gore, and the roads and bridges and summer jobs programs of Pittsburgh were promised benefits from presidential gratitude once he was persuaded to follow his party line. Treasury Secretary Lloyd Bentsen had a hard sell, to win over those 15 of the 21 Texas Democrats who were against the budget plan. He invited them to lunch, and as a veteran of Texas politics Bentsen used his wiles to win over the two key members, the Texas delegation leader Jack Brooks, who also chaired the Judiciary Committee, and Kika de la Garza, chairman of the Agriculture Committee. With their support, other congressmen seeking judgeships and agricultural favors for their supporters began to fall into line.

In the end, the fate of the budget came down to Clinton's readiness to compromise on the impact his energy tax would have on oil-producing states, and his promise to embark on annual reviews to hold down the growth of the entitlement programs of pensions and Medicare. Entitlements accounted for some 40 percent of the $1.5 trillion budget. Capitol Hill veterans realized that the president had won when the Texas Democrat Charles W. Stenholm assured Congress that he had been promised "improvements" to Mr. Clinton's unpopular new energy tax. This would also help steer the bill over its next hurdle in the Senate.

Clinton had arrived in Washington at the start of the year as a congressional novice. When he then lost his economic stimulus package in the Senate, his inexperience showed. It was the president's baptism of fire in Washington, the education of the Arkansas outsider in the arcane process of winning a crucial vote in Congress. He took to it eagerly, visiting Capitol Hill, hosting the Black Caucus of minority congressmen at the White House, wooing Hispanics, arranging jogging and golfing dates with waverers, and learning when to concede and when to hold firm. The stakes were very high. For a president to see his budget voted down to defeat by a Congress in which his party controlled both House and Senate would be a political humiliation without precedent in living memory.

"One of the problems we have had is that toward the end of the campaign and for a few months thereafter, we were all so exuberant about the process of change that we have lost sight of how long change would take," confessed Begala. But the victory in the House alone could not make him once more "the Comeback Kid." Another, even tighter vote in the House lay in wait over the reconciliation bill, the final compromise package of the varying budget bills passed by the House and by the Senate. That finally squeezed through, by a margin of 218–216. The Senate still lay in wait, where the Democratic majority was much thinner, and was cut even further when Bob Krueger lost his special election to inherit Lloyd Bentsen's seat in Texas. The defeat reduced the Democratic majority in the Senate to 56, against 44 Republicans, making it more difficult to peel away Republican moderates, while giving more power to Democratic dissidents. Success in the House was, however, the essential precondition to keep the budget alive, and every nerve was strained to achieve it.

In the Senate, it all came down to a single vote, that of Clinton's 1992 campaign rival Senator Kerrey. The personal tension between them was stretched taut, and so were the politics, with Kerrey's insistence on more budget discipline. He and the president exchanged shouted expletives on the phone. The top White House staff arranged to woo Kerrey at a hasty lunch, but got the wrong name and wrong address, and time for talk was brief because Kerrey wanted to see a film that started at two. Finally the next day, from the Senate floor, his eye on the TV camera and convinced Clinton was watching, he declared, "I would not and should not cast a vote that brings down your presidency." Finally, the dramatic pre-dawn vote in the Senate, passing more than 95 percent of President Clinton's budget by the narrowest of margins that depended on the casting vote of Vice President Al Gore.

"What this means is incalculable," Clinton said, almost reveling in the $500 billion cut in the deficit over the next five years. "It sends a clear signal to the markets that interest rates should stay down. And for the first time in years, an American president is in a position of economic strength, trying to lead a revival of growth and opportunity all over the world."

Inevitably, Clinton had to swallow some compromises to get his budget through the Senate. His hope for a broad-based energy tax was replaced by a more narrow gasoline tax of 4.3 cents a gallon. But the populist core of the Clinton budget remained, with almost 80 percent of the new tax revenues coming from households with incomes over $200,000 a year. The $500 billion in deficit savings came almost equally from new taxes and from spending cuts. He also secured the earned income tax credit, a measure strongly backed by the DLC because it rewarded work. It was designed to ensure that any family who worked would not fall below the poverty line. If they had too little income to qualify to be taxed, they received a payment, called a tax credit. A single worker earning less than $9,000 a year received $300. A couple with two children earning less than $27,000 a year could receive up to $3,584 a year. At a cost of $18 billion a year, it ensured that the poor would be better off working than on welfare.

Having passed his budget and squeezed out his victory, Clinton became buoyant again. His appointment of David Gergen as counselor seemed to improve relations with the media. His poll ratings rose with his holiday on Martha's Vineyard, where he hobnobbed with Jackie Kennedy Onassis and went sailing and caught a little of the Kennedy glow. He relaxed, and began thinking of new challenges. The economy was starting to look very healthy indeed. Consumer spending and personal incomes rose by nearly a full percentage point in October. House purchases hit their highest point for a decade and retail sales in general were up by 6 percent over the year. Unemployment sank to 6.4 percent, and in the year since Clinton was elected, 2.4 million new jobs were created, more than in the entire four years of the Bush administration. The consumer confidence index jumped by an extraordinary eleven points. He was sure health reform would be a triumph, that he could pass NAFTA, and even win back the liberals by passing the Brady bill to control handguns. So he did, and the National Rifle Association never forgave him, nor the congressmen who passed the bill, storing up their names for punitive targeting in the 1994 elections.

All seemed to be going according to plan, and his address to Congress in September on the health reform plan was hailed as a triumph. His positive ratings in the Harris poll jumped from 34 to 45 within a week. The month of October was set aside by his schedulers to barnstorm the country to sell the health plan, but as he prepared to leave for California to address a labor union conference, news came from Moscow of the occupation of the Russian parliament by anti-Yeltsin forces, led by Vice President Aleksandr Rutskoi. Clinton immediately declared his support for Yeltsin in a brief press statement from the Rose Garden, as Yeltsin's tanks began to bombard the parliament building. He then flew to California as planned, phoning Yeltsin from *Air Force One* to say, "You get stronger and better." But even before Clinton took off, the first dire news was coming into the White House situation room from Mogadishu.

It took almost thirty hours for the full scale of the disaster to emerge, of eighteen dead U.S. troops and two Black Hawk helicopters shot down. Clinton had no idea that the raid was to take place, or that the original humanitarian mission in Somalia had degenerated so far into a low-intensity war. He thought he had spelled out his new and more cautious policy toward the UN and peacekeeping missions when he addressed the General Assembly at the end of September, warning that "if the American people are to say yes to peacekeeping, the UN must know when to say no." Five days later, and unknown to Clinton, the U.S. Rangers in Mogadishu were boarding the Black Hawks to launch their raid, without air cover against ground fire and without armored support on standby.

The White House machine had simply not been paying attention. No meeting of the Principals Committee, of the secretaries of state and defense, of Tony Lake and General Powell was called on Somalia until after the humiliation of American arms. Clinton gave his health care speech, which disappeared from a news agenda now overwhelmed by Moscow and Mogadishu, came home and ditched the rest of the sales campaign for his health plan. Fielding the Somali crisis, he was suddenly overtaken by what looked like another humiliation as the USS *Harlan County,* with its shipload of lightly armed U.S. and Canadian peacekeepers under a UN mandate, turned back rather than face a possibly hostile reception from armed thugs.

Battered abroad, unable to campaign for health care at home, and looking at voting tallies in Congress that spelled defeat for the NAFTA vote, Clinton was back in crisis. Almost immediately, Republicans scored a clean sweep in the November off-year elections to win the mayoral race in New York and governorships of New Jersey and Virginia. The elections were dominated by local issues, but as the nearest electoral verdict to an interim referendum on the Clinton administration, the results dismayed the White House. Clinton had been elected with strong support in the South and in the big cities of the North and West, and the results suggested that those bases were now imperiled. It took an earthquake in urban politics to have America's two biggest cities, New York and Los Angeles, run by white male Republicans. The results were a personal reverse for Clinton, who had campaigned repeatedly to save Mayor David Dinkins in New York and Governor Jim Florio in New Jersey—his personal campaign strategist James Carville had been assigned to the Florio reelection effort. The Republicans also scored a convincing 58–41 percent margin in Virginia, where a white conservative defeated a moderate Democratic woman with considerable help from the right-wing Christian Coalition. "First, I want to thank God" was the instant reaction of the newly elected Virginia governor George Allen.

Once again, in a political crisis, Clinton pulled through, rallying former Presidents Bush and Carter and mounting another intense personal lobbying effort to pass the NAFTA bill, again by a narrow margin and dependent on Republican votes. The Clinton scorecard at the end of the year looked impressive. He might win by a whisker, but he was winning, particularly in Congress, which passed 88 percent of the measures he sent up to Capitol Hill. That was a better performance than the legendary congressional veteran Lyndon Johnson secured in his first year, and a record beaten only by President Eisenhower. Many of these were minor reforms, but the Family Leave Act was important for workers with sick relatives to care for, and the Earned Income Tax Credit was a genuine breakthrough in social policy. More significant politically was the Motor Voter Act, making it easier to register to vote when collecting a driving license. Within two years, it had increased the number of registered voters by nearly 5 million, most of them poor and potentially Democratic voters, if they could be rallied to voting booths. But the success with the big bills, the budget and deficit reduction, and NAFTA caused intense strain and splits inside the Democratic Party in Congress.

There were also angry complaints about the way the Democratic National Committee, the main party organization, was being run by David Wilhelm, Clinton's personal nominee. The bulk of the $19 million spent by the DNC in the year went to support the president's programs like NAFTA, health care, and the budget, rather than to the party's candidates elsewhere. Much of the money went to Clinton's campaign consultants, with $2 million to Stan Greenberg's polling expenses. In baseball parlance, they said that David Wilhelm was batting "oh for six": the Democrats lost all of the big six elections—the mayoral races in Los Angeles and New York, the Senate races in Texas and Georgia, and the governorships in Virginia and New Jersey. There was serious alarm among Democratic senators and congressmen up for reelection the next year that the DNC had its priorities all wrong and that the party could lose control of the Senate unless it shifted its priorities away from the White House and back to the party at large.

Clinton's powerful State of the Union address in January sailed over the Arkansas sex scandals and the rising tide of Whitewater to display a ruthless determination never to be vulnerable to Republican charges that he was soft on crime. The slogan was: "Three strikes and you're out." Three convictions for violent crimes would mean life in jail. The applause from the Democrats overwhelmed the sound of gnashing teeth from the Republican benches. That had been their line.

"Let's be honest," Clinton went on, in a breathtaking reiteration of the Reagan creed. "Our problems go way beyond the reach of any government program. They are rooted in the loss of values, the disappearance of work, and the breakdown of our families and communities." Then Clinton used yet another of the lines the Republicans had been honing ever since they thought that "family values" might replace "national security" as a way to convince voters that the Democrats were dangerous liberals. "We cannot renew our country until we realize that governments don't raise children—parents do," Mr. Clinton said. Then he pulled off a stroke that even Reagan must have admired. "Parents who know their children's teachers, turn off the TV, help with the homework, and teach right from wrong can make all the difference. I know. I had one."

With a catch in his voice, a sudden drop in timbre to signal the personal emotion, Clinton reminded the nation that he had come from humble origins, raised by a mother who had died earlier in the month. Until this silver-tongued Arkansan, only Ronald Reagan among recent American presidents had dared plumb this depth of public sentimentality. It took the delivery of a trained actor and nerves of steel to try it on nationwide TV, before the joint houses of Congress. Clinton pulled it off with elegance and conviction. One almost forgot that telling warning from Haley Barbour, the Republican national chairman, that Clinton was "an Elmer Gantry president, who can mount the bully pulpit and say anything he thinks you want to hear." (Elmer Gantry was a fictional silver-tongued evangelist and fraud; the Sinclair Lewis novel and subsequent 1960 movie starring Burt Lancaster embedded the type into American mythology.) Clinton was a far more solid figure, but his southern origins and Baptist roots, his ability to talk and campaign his way out of trouble, his fluency that often flirted with the glib, carried a certain Gantry-esque echo.

He plundered the speeches of past presidents to recraft an inspirational rhetoric of politics. "American renewal," the theme of his speech, was pure Reagan. And his peroration on the way in which neighbor had helped neighbor and Americans had come together in the face of the almost biblical plagues of fires, floods, earthquakes, and ice storms that had lately been visited on the land went back to Abe Lincoln. They showed, Clinton said, "the better angels of our nature." More than most presidents, Bill Clinton possessed a historical sense, backed by an impressive range of reading in political biography and American history. And knowing full well the public skepticism of all politicians, and the impact of that nickname "Slick Willie," Clinton deliberately draped himself in the mantle of the presidency as a national dynasty. He not only echoed the presidents past, he cited their names like a mantra.

"For sixty years, this country has tried to reform health care," he said.

"President Roosevelt tried. President Truman tried. President Nixon tried. President Carter tried. Every time, the powerful special interests defeated them. But not this time." From the Great Tradition, this heir to all the presidential ages advanced to hurl down his challenge, brandishing that talisman of presidential power, the veto. "Hear me clearly. If the legislation you send me does not guarantee every American private health insurance that can never be taken away, I will take this pen, veto that legislation, and we'll come right back here and start again," he vowed.

Clinton was at his best in set-piece speeches such as this, and took extraordinary care to craft and rewrite them. He knew they were his opportunity to address the nation directly, unique opportunities to drive up his poll ratings, to impose himself as president above the tittle-tattle of Troopergate or the rumblings over Whitewater. In the NBC–*Wall Street Journal* poll, his approval ratings nosed above 60 percent. It did not last. Whitewater demoralized the Democrats, and the investigations and then the formal charges against veteran congressman Dan Rostenkowski of Chicago undermined the Democrats' power in the real heart of Congress. It was as if Colonel Clinton's regiment had lost its sergeant major. Rostenkowski, chairman of the powerful House Ways and Means Committee, where taxes were written and the fate of bills was sealed, was a graduate of Mayor Richard Daley's tough school of Chicago politics. He made deals that rewarded his friends and punished his enemies and turned vague policy ideas into hard laws. He could have retired earlier with $1 million from his built-up campaign fund, but Rostenkowski chose to stay on and work with a Democratic president. He was brought down by petty misuses of funds and expenses and official cars, involving postage stamps and part-time jobs for relatives, and Clinton lost an indispensable ally.

Clinton had a roller-coaster year in 1993, plunging up and down in the polls, but pulling out key victories on the budget and NAFTA from the teeth of defeat. There were to be no such dramatic successes in 1994, when he was knocked constantly off-balance, at home and abroad. The old year had ended with the unpleasant surprise of Vladimir Zhirinovsky, a bizarre and wild-eyed Russian nationalist. In the December elections, he became leader of the largest party in the Russian parliament, threatening a difficult summit for Clinton in Moscow in January. The process of Russian reform was in evident jeopardy, and as soon as Clinton left Moscow, President Yeltsin dismissed the reformist prime minister Yegor Gaidar whom Clinton had just been praising. Constantly jolted by new Republican demands for congressional hearings on Whitewater, Clinton came home to the hideous and televised carnage of the mortar bomb in the Sarajevo marketplace in February, which forced him to deal with Bosnia again. He rallied NATO to send token air strikes, sufficient to silence the Serb guns and impose a cease-fire that lasted for most of the year. More important, his diplomats brokered an agreement between the Bosnian government and the Bosnian Croats to end the grisly second front of the Bosnian war and form an improbable confederation. He also, while flying back from President Nixon's funeral, agreed to turn a blind eye to the secret arming of Bosnia by the Iranian government. The arms were flown into Croat airfields; the Croats took 30 percent. Clinton's ambassador to Croatia, Peter Galbraith, was given "no instructions" when he asked for guidance. While this could have been seen as a conspiracy to evade the UN arms embargo, the arms saved Bosnia while avoiding an open clash with the European allies. Barely was that achieved than the spring brought new waves of Haitian and later Cuban refugees toward American shores.

Beset by the Republicans inside and outside Congress over Whitewater, the butt of the hostile radio talk shows, Clinton found himself involved in battle after battle with his Democratic allies. Human rights liberals were appalled by his decision to grant China most favored nation trading status. Social liberals worried about his plan to reform welfare, which called for a two-year limit on welfare payments combined with skills training, and then the recipient had either to find a job in the private sector, or take a state-subsidized one. There was no serious funding or provision for the skills training, nor for the state jobs, and the White House hardly bothered to urge the bill upon Congress. Several congressional committees held hearings, but none acted or voted on the bill.

The White House had lost control of both the political initiative and of the agenda. One of its better reforms, to use federal funds to impose national goals and standards in high school education, was unveiled, approved, and funded by Congress to the tune of $400 million a year. Named "Goals 2000," it was barely reported or hailed in the media. The coverage it did attract was the one brief argument thrown up by the religious right over prayer in schools. This was unfair. Goals 2000 was an attempt to install a national curriculum, not just of the education basics, but to instill an understanding of the tools of learning.

The goal was not just to achieve a 90 percent graduation rate from high school, but to ensure that all graduates could interpret and use tables, charts, and graphs; an atlas, maps, and a globe; a dictionary, calculator, and encyclopedia. Interesting benchmarks were set, to demonstrate competence in English, math, science, history, and civics, at the ages of nine, thirteen, and seventeen. The seventeen-year-olds were expected to know the difference between a symphony and chamber music; to show some understanding of the functions of NATO, the United Nations, and Amnesty International; to identify the Magna Carta, Bill of Rights, and Declaration of Independence; and were expected to "develop a position and argue the case" whether the Civil War was inevitable. Of the various education reforms being developed around the world, this was probably the most imaginative in blending the traditional rigors of basic learning with an attempt to produce rounded young citizens. If it worked as planned, America's high school graduates in the twenty-first century would be an interesting bunch. But the Clinton administration and Education Secretary Richard Riley got hardly a whiff of credit, even in their own party. The noisy arguments over high-profile bills were too compelling.

The Black Caucus was appalled by Clinton's irresolution over Haiti and by much of his crime bill, which concentrated on more police, more prisons, and more time spent in prison. Blacks and Hispanics made up half of a prison population that was now over a million, the highest rate of incarceration in the Western world, and over 45 percent of the sentences were related to drugs. Resolved to be seen as tough on crime, Clinton had only token sympathy for the Black Caucus's insistence that addiction treatment made more long-term sense than prison terms, and that drug sentencing and capital punishment were dismayingly racist in their effects. They had a point. Sentences were much harsher for crack cocaine, used by blacks, than for powder cocaine, preferred by whites. Blacks convicted of murder were far more likely than whites to get the death sentence.

Offending his liberal allies, bereft of Rostenkowski's skills in Congress, watching Hillary's vast and complex health reform plan slowly languish, very little seemed to go right for Clinton. And the increasingly confident Republicans began to defy and block him in Congress at every opportunity. "We see that clearly the president is effectively diminished in the eyes of the American people. That gives us an advantage in the upcoming election," said Senator John McCain of Arizona. "The Democrats in 1992 basically blocked the entire Bush agenda. We are doing no less, in my view."

The monthly Harris poll ratings for 1994 recorded the erosion of Clinton's presidency. The same question was asked each time: How would you rate the overall job Clinton is doing as president—excellent, pretty good, only fair, or poor? Only *excellent* or *pretty good* counted as positive. Only *fair* and *poor* counted as negative, so negative rating may have overestimated the real animosity of those who thought *only fair* was a neutral judgment. But there was no disputing the trend. In December 1993, Clinton enjoyed a positive rating of exactly 50 percent, and remained at that figure in January and February 1994. By April, he had dropped to 48 percent, to 42 percent in May, down again to 40 percent in July, and lower to 34 percent approval in September. His negative ratings rose inexorably, from 48 percent in February to 64 percent in September.

Clinton resorted to the standard White House response to such a plight; on June 27, he changed his chief of staff. McLarty was pushed aside to a vague counselor title but to a precise role as personal envoy to corporate chieftains and moderates of both parties in Congress. Budget director Leon Panetta was promoted to chief of staff, and imposed administrative rigor on the Oval Office and the capricious, half-disciplined man within. This was part of what seemed like a second attempt to form an administration. Perhaps the crucial change had come at the Pentagon with the appointment of Dr. William Perry, defense secretary, and the promotion of General John Shalikashvili to replace the overly cautious General Colin Powell. With the Pentagon in both more authoritative and more supportive hands, the CIA also came under new management, the Pentagon's Dr. John Deutsch, who was able to gain far more of the President's time and confidence than the first director, Dr. James Woolsey. Inside the White House, the campaign consultants were eased out, cut off from their direct access to the president, forced to report to deputy chief of staff Harold Ickes, and then to Clinton. What had been the ever open door of the Oval Office acquired a watchdog. Except in direst emergency, to get to the president, Tony Lake, Stephanopoulos, and even Bruce Lindsey (looking like the last of the Arkansas Mohicans at Clinton's side) had to go through Panetta. The days were structured, starting with the 7:30 senior staff meeting, and an attempt to impose a single message for the day. Meetings were given firm time schedules, and a firm list of those who would attend. The free-floating talk-ins of the first year ended. "The change was like going from college into your first real job, with a boss and discipline and a structure of hierarchy," commented one of those who survived the process.

The shake-up came barely in time. Suddenly, in August, it became a battle for survival. The defection of 58 congressmen of his own party on the crime bill confronted Clinton with the immediate and devastating prospect of a failed, and indeed a humiliated, presidency. If he could not get the $30 billion crime bill through Congress, with its new array of death penalties, its vast new prison building schemes, its pork barrel funds for local police authorities around the country, then he probably could never pass anything at all. "We are at the turning point for the administration and for the country," said Clinton's labor secretary Robert Reich, after the president convened a post-vote four-hour emergency session at midnight with his top political advisers. A crisis meeting of his cabinet followed in the morning.

"Your president is just not that important to us," sneered the chairman of the House Republican Conference, Congressman Dick Armey, as the crime bill went down to defeat. He was also a president from whom power had ebbed visibly away. He had become a political figure who inspired little loyalty among Democrats, and even less fear among Republicans, because he had lost so much of that automatic deference and respect that was traditionally the president's due.

The new crime bill, without doubt the most draconian ever drafted, should have won easy Republican acclaim. It funded 100,000 new police officers and another 100,000 new prison places and "boot camps" for young offenders. It extended the federal death penalty from two to sixty crimes, including car-jacking and drive-by shootings, and required life imprisonment for a third felony if it involved violence. Children of thirteen and fourteen could now be prosecuted—and punished—as adults for violent crimes. It also included a ban on nineteen types of assault weapons and funds for crime prevention through social programs, sufficient to win grudging support from liberal Democrats. Women's groups backed the change that made sex-based violence a civil rights violation and imposed federal penalties for spouse abuse and stalking a woman across state lines.

The Republicans, convinced that they had Clinton on the run, declared open war when the Republican National Committee threatened to withhold party funds from any congressman who voted for the gun control provision in the crime bill. This gave Clinton an opportunity that he was swift to seize, dropping all other business to fly to Minneapolis to address a national conference of police chiefs.

"Last night, we had a vote on democracy's most fundamental responsibility, and law and order lost," he said. "Two hundred and twenty-five members of Congress participated in a procedural trick orchestrated by the National Rifle Association and intensely promoted by the Republican congressional leadership. A trick designed with one thing in mind—to put the protection of partisan and special interests over the protection of ordinary Americans. It is the same old Washington game," he declared. "Yeah, it was a defeat yesterday, and I felt terrible about it. But this morning I woke up feeling good because that's a vote I'd much rather be on the losing side of than on the winning side. I'm glad I will never have to explain to my wife, my daughter, my grandchildren, and the people who sent me to Washington why I did something like what was done to the American people yesterday."

Houdini had escaped again. Clinton finally won his crime bill. But health reform was dying in Congress, which insisted on its vacation. It left the final rites for health reform to be passed in the autumn, before the November congressional elections that Democrats awaited with dread, the Republicans with hope and excitement and an extraordinary mood of aggression.

"Left-wing ideologues in the White House and a bunch of machine politicians are trying to run over the rest of the country," declared the intensely partisan Republican whip Newt Gingrich, targeting Hillary Clinton in particular as a "committed left-winger."

The attack on the First Lady and the rejection of traditional bipartisanship was a deliberate strategy by Gingrich, a former history professor from Georgia. He believed that sharp political confrontation had put the Republicans within reach of their first majority in the lower house of Congress since 1954. Gingrich also embodied a fundamental shift in the nature of the Republican Party, and in American political geography. The Republicans, as the party of Abraham Lincoln that mobilized against slavery and the South in the Civil War era, barely enjoyed a political presence in the South in the 1960s. By the 1990s, it was becoming their heartland.

In 1960, when their regional base was the Northeast and Midwest, only one Republican congressman in fourteen was a southerner. In 1994, as the party that had consistently dragged its heels over civil rights and attacked the Democrats as the party of the left and the minorities, one in three Republicans in Congress came from the South.

The new breed of Southern Republicans were far more conservative than their dwindling band of colleagues from the North and Midwest. They were much closer to the Christian fundamentalist groups, more likely to oppose gun control and abortion, and far more intransigent in their political approach.

The 46 Republican congressmen and 6 senators who voted with the Democrats to pass the crime bill in a bipartisan spirit came largely from the party's old base of the North and Midwest. All but 1 of the 14 House Republicans from Connecticut, Massachusetts, New Jersey, Maine, Rhode Island, and Delaware voted for the bill. The 33 Republicans from Georgia, Virginia, Texas, Arkansas, Alabama, Louisiana, and North and South Carolina all voted against it. The nervousness of the remaining Southern Democrats at the rising Republican threat explained why President Clinton had so much trouble in delivering the votes of his own party in Congress. Of the 132 congressional seats from old Confederate and border states, the Democrats' total of 71 seats was to drop sharply in November and give the South a Republican majority for the first time in U.S. political history. It was for this goal—winning Republican control of the House through an essentially regional transformation—that Congressman Gingrich ignored the particular merits of crime bills or health reform.

Gingrich had become Republican Whip after winning a risky but effective personal vendetta against the 1980s Democratic Speaker Jim Wright, forcing his resignation on ethics charges. Impatient at the gentlemanly delaying tactics that had become the Republican rule in the House after decades in opposition, Gingrich won a dedicated following among younger Republicans for his passion and aggression. But Congress was not his only arena. In 1986, he took over a sleepy political campaign group called GOPAC, which became the vehicle for his regeneration of the grassroots of the party, grooming a new generation of Republicans as candidates for local and eventually national political office.

GOPAC gave Gingrich an unprecedented personal power base throughout the party. By 1995, more than half of the Republican congressmen had gone through GOPAC's training courses. Among the training tapes and services GOPAC provided to its recruits was a paper, "Language: A Key Mechanism of Control," which gave a Republican a list of 75 negative words and the advice "Apply these to the opponent, proposals, their record, and their party." Among the key words were *corrupt, sick, hypocrisy, shame, disgrace, cheat, steal, greed, self-serving, pathetic,* and *permissive.*

Gingrich sought to do to the Republicans what Clinton had done with the Democrats in 1992: capture the party, transform its ideology, and invigorate it with campaigning passion. "I will not rest until I have transformed the landscape of American politics—I am not interested in preserving the status quo, I want to overthrow it," he declared in 1991. His objective was to abolish the liberal welfare state and replace it with a conservative opportunity society, and to energize his party with a rhetoric of revolutionary fervor.

His tactics were inspired. As Congress returned in September, he rallied the Republican members and the candidates for the November elections at the Capitol, and 367 of them solemnly signed the ten-point "Contract with America" that was to be their manifesto. Term limits for congressmen; a balanced budget amendment; no U.S. troops under United Nations command; cuts in capital gains taxes; a $500 per child tax credit to reinforce the family; no more welfare for teenage mothers—it was a bewitchingly simplistic list of remedies that contained a deep core of ideology. Each item had been carefully tested on focus groups organized by Gingrich's pollster, Frank Luntz. "There's not a single one [of the ten points] that pulls less than sixty percent. We wouldn't write a contract that didn't have great standing with America," said Congressman Dick Armey, who was about to become House majority leader.

The Democrats mocked it as extremist, but had pitifully little to offer as an agenda of their own. Their successes, from the crime bill to Goals 2000 to the success in persuading North Korea to suspend its nuclear development project, simply came and went without the slightest public impact. Even Clinton's boldness in resolving to restore the democratically elected president of Haiti by military force was diluted by the success of the last-ditch mission of former president Jimmy Carter and retired general Colin Powell to persuade the military junta to go peacefully. Clinton's diplomatic skill in getting a UN mandate and the promise of international military and economic support to help the U.S. effort in Haiti could not energize his party.

"Our base was demoralized. Our members were frustrated and running scared, as opposed to aggressively defending. There was a psychology in place that we were having a hard time containing," said Tony Coelho. A former congressional star who had left under an ethical cloud, Coelho had been conscripted back from Wall Street to overhaul the shattered structure of the Democratic National Committee after Clinton finally allowed Panetta to sack David Wilhelm. The task proved impossible. Democrats were preparing for their campaigns in the usual way, as a series of local and personal races. The Republicans, Coelho saw, had changed the game. "The Republicans were trying to elevate the election to a national anti-Clinton referendum, and make all our candidates run as Clintonites."

The reform agenda Clinton had proposed was mainly dead or dying in the waning weeks of the 103d Congress. When a bill had a chance of passing, the pit bull of the Republican Party attacked again. Lacking the votes to defeat the new anti-lobbying bill, Gingrich called on conservative talk show hosts like Rush Limbaugh. They whipped up concern that the bill might limit the ability of religious and local groups to put pressure on their congressmen, and a blizzard of phone calls and telegrams and e-mail to Washington later, another piece of Clinton's reform legislation lay dead on the floor of Congress.

As the remaining working days of the wretched 103d Congress whittled down, stalling was the equivalent of political extinction. The retiring Senate majority leader, Maine Democrat George Mitchell (who gave up the chance of a Supreme Court seat to stay in the Senate and pass health reform), called it "total obstructionism of a kind we have never seen before." The casualty list of bills in the closing weeks went far beyond health reform. Campaign finance reform, lobby reform, telecommunications reform to facilitate the "global data highway," a reform to make gold and silver miners pay more than the token $2.50 an acre to exploit federal land, reform of the Superfund pollution cleanup law—all fell to the Republican blockade.

The congressional elections triumphantly vindicated Gingrich's strategy. The Republican landslide swept aside the Democratic majorities in the Senate, the House of Representatives, and the fifty states' governors' mansions. The Republican gain of 9 Senate and 53 House seats was of a similar order of magnitude to the defeat of President Truman's Democrats in 1946, and the post-Watergate humiliation of the Republicans in 1974.

Democratic attempts to argue that this sweeping verdict was simply a vote against incumbents, a generalized discontent with politicians rather than a rejection of Democrats, collapsed in the face of the fact that not a single Republican incumbent was defeated. The election was a deeply personal verdict, against a president who had campaigned himself hoarse, who had clawed back some much-needed foreign policy successes, and whose achievements in cutting the deficit and delivering economic growth could not mollify an angry electorate. Nor could they mollify many Democrats, who told the White House that they preferred not to have Clinton come and campaign on their behalf.

"Bill Clinton won this election for us," crowed the conservative Republican senator Phil Gramm of Texas. The implications of the midterm elections went beyond the personal repudiation of Clinton and Democratic potentates from Ann Richards in Texas to Mario Cuomo in New York to Speaker Tom Foley in Washington. Even Clinton recognized the degree to which the voters had turned against the concept of big and activist government that had loomed so overwhelmingly in American lives since Roosevelt's day. They wanted, he acknowledged, "a smaller government that gives them a better value for their dollar."

Dismissing the Clintons as "the enemy of normal Americans . . . counterculture McGoverniks" and sneering at the "left-wing elitists" of the White House, Gingrich declared victory in the cultural war. "This was a conservative tide, not just a partisan election," he said, adding that his mission was to reverse "the long aberration" in American culture that began in the 1960s. "Until then, there was an explicit, long-term commitment to creating character. It was the work ethic. It was honesty, right or wrong. It was not harming others. It was being vigilant in the defense of liberty. It was very clear and we taught it."

Culture wars aside, it was an extraordinarily divisive election. America's great swing to the right was overwhelmingly a male phenomenon. A majority of women voted Democrat, by a margin of 53–47, while men voted Republican by a huge margin of 57–43. In Tennessee, fewer than one man in three voted Democrat. The Republican sweep was also a white tide; whites voted against the Democrats by a margin of 58–42. The Republican vote among whites rose by 8 percent over the 1992 elections. By contrast, 60 percent of Hispanics and 91 percent of blacks voted Democrat. Putting these two phenomena of race and sex together, white males voted Republican by a stunning margin of 63 to 37, a testosterone challenge that the Democrats would have to confront if they were ever to win office again.

Most important for the long term was the final collapse of that traditional Democratic redoubt, of the South. For the first time in over 120 years, a majority of the South's senators, congressmen, and governors were Republicans. There were three clear reasons for this. The first was the new power of the religious right, which for the first time deployed its faithful as a political machine to get out the vote with 33 million voter guides distributed through 60,000 churches. The second reason was the disgust of southern white males with a president who had evaded the Vietnam draft and then tried to give gays an honorable place in the U.S. military. Fewer than one southern white male in three voted Democrat, an extreme form of the nationwide gender gap (or Hillary factor) that had 8 to 12 percent more women voting Democrat than men. And the third reason for the southern disaster was that, except to beat Ollie North in Virginia, the black vote stayed home.

The new Republican majority entered office divided between the impetuous House and the more deliberative Senate; between the Dole and Gingrich generations; between cultural conservatives and social moderates; and most immediately between those who wanted to grant the voters instant tax cuts and those who would first save the money by cutting the budget. But like a well-drilled army whose assault goes to plan, the triumphant new Republican majority swept into both chambers of Congress, cleared the old Democratic trenches of the committees and the staffs, and began to zero in their guns on the next target of the budget. Their general, Newt Gingrich, was elected Speaker of the House on cue, the 11 new senators and 83 new congressmen were sworn in, and the officers and new committee chairmen were briskly elected. Then they addressed the action agenda for the first day—eight items of rule reform, and a new bill to make the Congress subject to all the laws it passed for the rest of America.

"In terms of World War Two, we are at 1942," Speaker Gingrich said. "We have begun to mobilize the forces. We have begun to launch bridgeheads. We are a long way from D-Day." The January 4 opening was dubbed "the Longest Day" by Gingrich, to pass the new rules that dismantled the congressional power centers the Democrats had built up in their forty-year control of the House. It ran to a strict schedule, with only twenty minutes permitted for debate on each issue, and the Democrats firmly warned not to get in the way. President Clinton wisely took the advice and took some time off from politics, going home to Arkansas to be photographed in hunting gear, carrying two ducks he had shot. In the new Washington of Speaker Gingrich, master of the angry white male vote, Clinton was prepared to look like a life member of the National Rifle Association.

Despite his first reaction of near panic, Clinton understood one essential feature of the 1994 election—the turnout had been less than 40 percent. It had been 56 percent when Clinton was elected. And if the midterm vote had been a referendum on him, it had therefore drawn to the polls every Clinton-hater in America. He now knew the size of his most implacable opposition, and it was about one in five of the voters. Less than 20 percent of the electorate had voted Republican, and just over 19 percent had voted Democrat, despite the party's woes. In many of the closest fought seats, the final vote tally was so close that, had a total of 22,000 votes across the country gone a different way, the Democrats would have held the majority in the House. Between the 40 percent who had voted in 1994 and the 56 percent who had turned out for the presidential election was a vast potential pool of 26 million voters, the undecided and the apathetic, that Clinton could yet win back. It was, indeed, time to go hunting.

☆ 15 ☆

THE COMING OF THE NEW CONSENSUS

The United States has traditionally been governed by a double consensus in which both parties broadly agree on the main goals of both foreign and domestic policy. There has been vast room for argument and party rivalry within this steadily evolving consensus, but there have always been times when the tectonic plates of national interest and economic environment suddenly shift and the political process is thrown into disarray until a new consensus forms. The Clinton presidency marked just such a period. He was the first president since Roosevelt to watch the simultaneous crumbling of fifty years of agreement on the fundamental principles of policy both at home and abroad. He was also to become the first president since Roosevelt to craft the framework of a new consensus for foreign and domestic strategies alike.

Under siege during the Reagan presidency, but largely preserved by a Democratic Congress, the old New Deal and Great Society consensus on domestic matters finally collapsed in the Clinton years. Clinton's role in that process was initially shrouded by his deep faith in the potential of activist government. But his election manifesto of 1992 was uncannily close to what became the Republican "Contract with America" in 1994. Clinton campaigned on a middle-class tax cut and a promise to halve the deficit within four years. At one incautious moment, he even promised to balance the federal budget within five years. He demanded "an end to welfare as we know it," and a reinvented government that would be smaller and more entrepreneurial. Clinton explicitly challenged the Great Society model, which had been the core of the modern Democratic Party's identity. He lifted whole phrases from Ronald Reagan's text ("Governments don't raise children; parents do") and pledged to be tough on crime in a classically authoritarian way, from 100,000 extra police on the streets to "three strikes and you're out"—lifetime imprisonment for repeated felonies.

Clinton insisted that he was a New Democrat. With little caricature, this could be defined as one who rejected the traditional wimpishness of the bleeding-heart liberals and recognized that those blue-collar patriots who abandoned their Democratic loyalties to vote for Ronald Reagan were essential to Democratic hopes of regaining the presidency. A New Democrat was tough on crime, tough on welfare, resolute for the death penalty, and insisted on personal responsibility rather than state handouts. A New Democrat believed that state benefits must be earned, that college scholarships should be financed by a form of national service, and that there was a difference between the deserving and the undeserving poor. The state should prefer the poor who were prepared to work to those who were not.

The issue is less whether Clinton meant his rhetoric, but the degree to which he explicitly repudiated the traditions of the Democratic Party and renounced the old consensus. Consider, by contrast, the electoral platforms and the practice of the Republican presidents of the New Deal era. Eisenhower had presided over the most classically Keynesian strategies of public investment in postwar America: the building of the interstate highway network and the crash program of higher education after the shock of Soviet technological superiority with the first *Sputnik* satellite of 1957. Richard Nixon declared himself a Keynesian, imposed unprecedented peacetime controls over prices, wages, and imports, and sought to expand the welfare state with a bill for a national health insurance system and another for a minimum family income. By contrast with Clinton, Nixon was a big-government liberal.

"Putting People First," Clinton's 1992 campaign manifesto, declared: "Our policies are neither liberal nor conservative, neither Democratic nor Republican. They are new. They are different." He denounced the "brain-dead politics of both parties" and charted the outlines of a new consensus, located in what he called "the dynamic center." In his first two years, he was to be frustrated by the Democratic Congress, although some successes were scored. The "reinventing government" project run by Vice President Al Gore shrank the federal work force to its smallest since the Kennedy administration—before the Great Society was launched. One reason why Clinton shrank from attacking corporate America for downsizing its work-force was that by 1996, Clinton had become the downsizer-in-chief. The federal bureaucracy had been cut by 11 percent—200,000 jobs—in the Clinton years. In Clinton's third and fourth years, he was confronted by a Republican Congress that ironically proved far more ready to join him in the emergent new domestic consensus. There was much shadow boxing for party political purpose between the Republican House and Senate and the Clinton White House. But in the arguments over balancing the budget within seven years or in nine, or whether to increase Medicare premiums to a Republican $84 a month or a Clintonian $76 a month, there were distinctions without serious difference.

The principles of the new domestic consensus, which could be summarized as a leaner and meaner government, were broadly shared by Clinton and by Gingrich. The size of the bureaucracy and of the deficit had to be shrunk, and the budget balanced, but funding for the Pentagon should remain close to cold war levels. Medicare and Medicaid had to be reformed before the rising demographic tide of old people bankrupted the system. Crime had be fought with more police and more prisons, and welfare had to end "as we know it." More and more federal government responsibilities had to be shared with or offered to the states, and tenants should be encouraged to buy their public housing. Individuals should be responsible for their own lives and for their families.

The national security consensus of active internationalism, which had prevailed since the Second World War and throughout the cold war, also began to crumble apace under Clinton's presidency. Embodied in large foreign garrisons and in loyalty to foreign alliances and institutions from NATO to the UN, it depended on the broad agreement of both parties that the nation faced a mortal danger. The collapse of the Soviet Union and the subsequent enfeeblement of Russia had taken the enemy away. The new consensus that Clinton devised, with the strong support of Republicans led by Congressman Newt Gingrich, was for the United States to take the lead in promoting the new global economy based on free trade. It remained an internationalist vision, albeit based far more on exports and overseas investments than on military alliances and security commitments.

These clear underlying movements toward a new double consensus took place below the superficial levels of political argument, and were further shrouded by the extraordinary chorus of personal vituperation mounted against the Clintons by the Republicans. The sweeping Republican success of 1994 in gaining control of both houses of Congress for the first time in forty years was hailed by triumphant supporters in the United States and Europe as a historic political shift that would fulfill Speaker Newt Gingrich's promise "to replace the welfare state with the conservative opportunity society." Only two years earlier, the electoral victory of Bill Clinton in defeating an incumbent president and installing the first Democrat in the White House in twelve years was hailed as a similarly historic success for a revitalized Democratic Party, invigorated by a modernized concept of an American social democracy brimming with ideas for industrial strategy, public investment, and a national health system.

The zeitgeist, or at least the fashionable interpretation of deeper political currents, can change fast in the information age. And yet, as one might expect from two baby-boomers from broken homes who managed to avoid the Vietnam War, whose only jobs were university lecturing and elected office, and who each owned the same private car (a 1966 Ford Mustang convertible), the Clinton and the Gingrich visions had some striking features in common.

Neither one could abide the classic foreign policy presidency of George Bush. Each built his political appeal on the promise of a middle-class tax cut, to be financed through a diminished government bureaucracy, with Americans educated and challenged to compete in the bracing new world of the global economy. Each believed in an activist government. In the Clinton view, government had a duty to equip the public with the educational tools to succeed; in the Gingrich view, to steer them toward the moral values without which success would have no meaning. Clinton would intervene in the schools and economy, Gingrich in the private lives of welfare mothers and the history curriculum of the schools. Those common threads linking Clinton and Gingrich suggested that something more fundamental was at work than a conventional shift in the balance of power from left to right, or from an activist concept of government to a shrunken one.

In his policies, as distinct from his personal life, it was not easy for the Republicans to define Clinton as a man of different values. He had learned many of the lessons of the Democratic defeat of 1988, sufficient to impose in Arkansas rules that withdrew a driving license from high school dropouts and required parents to attend teacher conferences in schools. He allowed himself to be knocked off balance over gays in the military, permitting the issue to be defined as one of military virility rather than social fairness. But in sacking his surgeon general, Joycelyn Elders, and in his churchgoing and in Hillary's call for sexual abstinence for teenagers, the Clintons fought against Speaker Gingrich's attempt to label them "counterculture McGoverniks."

Indeed, Hillary Clinton appeared on the Oprah Winfrey show in May 1995, to say, "I'm all in favor of bringing back some old-fashioned hypocrisy. I think the kind of dysfunctional behavior that we are subjecting our children to gives them no role models, gives them the feeling that anything goes, that they can do anything with no consequences, and get on television which—my goodness—validates everything."

In what was probably the finest single speech of his presidency, Clinton took the pulpit of Dr. Martin Luther King, Jr., at the Mason Temple Church of God in Memphis, Tennessee. In the place where Dr. King had preached "I have been to the mountaintop" the night before his murder, Clinton invoked his name to address "the great crisis of the spirit that is gripping America today. He would say, I fought to stop white people from being so filled with hate that they would wreak violence on black people. I did not fight for the right of black people to murder other black people with reckless abandon. . . . I fought for freedom, he would say, but not for the freedom of children to have children and the fathers of the children to walk away and abandon them as if they don't amount to anything."

It was a stern and moralizing admonition that only a black leader, or a president in full command of his bully pulpit, could have delivered. And it was given more force by Clinton's unyielding defense of the principle of affirmative action, against a Republican Congress that sought to make political capital by describing it as reverse racism. "White racism may be the black people's burden, but it is white people's problem. . . . I want to mend affirmative action, but I don't think America is at a place where we can end it," Clinton said at the University of Texas on the day that Nation of Islam leader Louis Farrakhan rallied in Washington twice as many black men as were ever convened by Dr. King.

In an America where racial debate was polarizing between Republicans' condemnation of a black pathology and the Nation of Islam's demand for a separate black state, Clinton's message was unashamedly traditional. He reaffirmed the liberal goals of public education and social improvement to further racial assimilation in an American melting pot where "we have more in common than we sometimes admit. . . . The great potential of this march is for whites to see a larger truth, that blacks share their fears as well as their hopes, and that most black people share their old-fashioned American values."

Racial politics was one of several striking stands taken by Clinton in the course of 1995, as if to challenge the sneers from Democrats and Republicans alike that he had no backbone and was always prepared for a compromise. "I think most of us learned some time ago that if you don't like the president's position on a particular issue, you just have to wait a few weeks," suggested Democratic congressman David R. Obey of Wisconsin. Clinton also displayed, no doubt belatedly, both leadership and resolve in seizing the diplomatic opportunity for a Bosnian peace settlement after the defeats of the Bosnian Serb armies in the summer of 1995. Rallying NATO behind a serious campaign of air strikes and leading an energetic diplomatic offensive, Clinton then took the extraordinary political risk of committing U.S. troops to enforce the peace agreement, despite the near certainty of U.S. casualties being ferried sadly home throughout his reelection year.

Clinton also displayed a tactical firmness over the budget to challenge the new Republican ascendancy in Congress. Having already conceded his agreement to a balanced budget, he fought an astute rear guard action over its terms. He was able to personalize the battle, taking as his target Speaker Gingrich, the one leading politician whose negative ratings rose far higher than his own. The wicked Gingrichites were plotting to destroy American values by undermining the Medicare system for the elderly, the Medicaid system for the poor, the college loan program for the ambitious, and the network of rules and regulations for protecting the natural environment. But the president, as if mentally screening his favorite movie *High Noon,* declared that he would go alone into the dusty street and do righteous battle against the bad guys. Clinton appeared, from the beginning of 1995, to be hopelessly outmatched by the Republican majorities in the House and Senate, and the demoralized Democrats viewed him with suspicion and even a touch of contempt. Some of this he brought on himself. After the slaughter they had suffered in the midterm elections, the Democrats had a right to be outraged by his incautious admissions to fund-raising audiences that he thought he had raised their taxes too much in his 1993 budget. Perhaps the lowest point came at the second prime-time press conference of his presidency, when he was asked about his own role when the Republicans so dominated the agenda, and his reply was a self-pitying bluster that "the president is relevant here."

That was the lowest point because within twenty-four hours, the federal building in Oklahoma City was destroyed by a terrorist bomb, killing over 180 people. It is an unwritten part of the presidential job to act, on occasions of great national sentiment, as medicine man, monarch, and minister to the hapless flock. Ronald Reagan sealed his own grip on the presidency as mourner-in-chief after disaster befell the *Challenger* space shuttle. Clinton became presidential, perhaps for the first time, when he fulfilled his sacerdotal duty at the day of national mourning in Oklahoma.

That was the mystic explanation for the return of the Comeback Kid. Clinton himself had another, so rational that it carried a deliberate echo of an Einstein formula. The president called it "E-squared M-squared," and it stood for the issues on which he chose to make his stand and fight against the Republican Congress. Environment and Education were the two E's; Medicare and Medicaid were the two M's. The opinion polls of Stan Greenberg at the DNC matched those being presented directly to Clinton by Morris; the public was not against all public spending, and was not an enthusiastic supporter of the Republican rhetoric about a conservative revolution. The more extreme forms of that rhetoric also carried an uncomfortable resonance after Oklahoma City. It was not that Dole and Gingrich were in any sense linked with or responsible for the lunatic fringe of antigovernment militias. But just as Democrats in the 1970s were wary of being linked to the extreme left, so the Republicans of 1995 had suddenly to watch their right flank with great care.

It would be difficult to overpraise the tactical skill with which Clinton blunted, diverted, and finally defeated the surging momentum of the new Republican majority. He began by agreeing with their budget goals, but proceeded to argue over the timing and the details. Although he was casting the vetoes, he so arranged matters that the Republicans took most of the blame in the opinion polls for the interruption of government services. He cleverly deployed the perks of his office, from *Air Force One* to the power of veto, from meetings in the White House to the ability to invite one heroic federal worker, who had rescued others from the Oklahoma City bombing, to be an honored guest at his State of the Union address. When 1995 began, the Democrats and Clinton's White House team were demoralized, and the Republicans were crowing that a historic political realignment was under way. By the start of 1996, the government was still functioning, the Senate Republicans were arguing with their colleagues in the House, and there was a movement to replace Speaker Newt Gingrich with his deputy, Congressman Dick Armey.

The Republican agenda gave Clinton the chance to define himself by standing guard over those core achievements of the New Deal and the Great Society that still enjoyed broad popular support. He seized the opportunity, cast veto after veto, allowed the government to start closing down as 800,000 federal workers were sent home for three days, then for three weeks, and made speech after speech about "the violation of our values." All along, however, he was prepared to concede the fundamental Republican target of balancing the budget within seven years.

Beneath the surface of this battle over the budget, a parallel drama was unfolding within each political party. The dispirited and much-diminished Democrats in Congress, reduced by the 1994 midterm elections to a largely liberal core that constantly shed southern conservative defectors to the Republicans, grappled for an identity. In the White House was a New Democrat who insisted on being tough on crime, on reforming welfare, and exposing American workers to the stormy competition of free trade. In the Congress was an unwieldy coalition of Democrats. Its main currents were pro-labor protectionists; minority legislators who saw welfare reform as a code phrase for abandoning the underclass; and liberals, some of whom deplored America's grim precedence in incarcerating more of its citizens than any other country, while others worried most about defending Medicaid and Medicare.

In the Republican Party, the fissures were even more confusing. There were the cautious veterans of the Senate led by Robert Dole and the firebrands of the House led by Speaker Gingrich. There were the Christian Coalition supporters who battled to outlaw abortion and the liberal Republicans who thought that a sleeping dog was better left undisturbed. There were isolationists and internationalists, passionate free traders, and that reborn America First protectionist Pat Buchanan. Rallying for a repeal of the Sixteenth Amendment to the Constitution, which authorized the income tax, were the fiscal zealots of the House with their passion for flat taxes.

In the year that he had to mobilize for his reelection campaign, Clinton faced a tumultuous political realignment in which conservatives stopped conserving very much, and tried, in Speaker Gingrich's terms, to become revolutionaries. But Speaker Gingrich had lost the aura of visionary leadership that he had won by marshaling the new Republican majority. He whined at being treated with insufficient respect aboard the presidential plane, and said that he had reached his target of seven years to balance the budget through "intuition." The House Ethics Committee, after much delay, appointed an independent counsel to investigate his murky financial affairs, and the Federal Election Commission filed legal charges that his GOPAC organization had broken the campaign finance rules.

Having suffered desperate damage from the new venom of negative campaigning against his alleged womanizing and his Whitewater embarrassments, Clinton now saw the most charismatic leader of the opposition embroiled in a similar mess. But Clinton had already learned to roll with the punches and to plod on regardless, knowing from 1992 that the American voters respected a politician who took the heat and refused to buckle.

As 1996 dawned, and against all the odds, Clinton was well positioned for reelection. He had been lucky, which Napoleon always said was the most important quality in a general. In the matter of General Colin Powell, Clinton had seen his most formidable and most popular rival decline the contest. He faced a less than compelling band of Republican rivals in 1996, who were led in the opinion polls, in campaign funds, and in organization by seventy-two-year-old senator Robert Dole. As the caucuses and primaries got under way, Clinton faced no Democratic challenger of the kind who had sapped President Johnson in 1968 and President Carter in 1980, and enjoyed a clear ten-point lead over Senator Dole in all the opinion polls, a lead that widened steadily as summer wore on.

This was a most dramatic recovery from the humiliation of his second year in office. Clinton had seen the keystone of his domestic agenda crumble into ruin in Congress, and then presided over the collapse of his party and its eviction from the congressional majority it had enjoyed for forty years. And yet, that collapse was almost an act of liberation for Clinton. The Democratic majority had fought his free trade agenda, refused to stand by his health reform, and almost sank his crime bill. The coming of a Republican majority gave Clinton something to stand against in a political landscape of extraordinary fluidity. An America in which the Democrats had lost their century-long grip on the South, had seen the Republicans become mayors of the big cities of New York and Los Angeles, and in which the Republican Party had made a Faustian bargain with the particularist lobby of the Christian Coalition, was a very different American polity from the one that had prevailed for the sixty years after the New Deal.

By 1995, the Christian Coalition controlled thirteen state Republican parties, and was the dominant influence in at least twelve more. It promised to become to the Republicans what organized labor had been to the Democrats in the years after the New Deal. The Christian Coalition had built a grass-roots organization of unusual strength. It claimed 1.6 million members, with chapters in 1,600 counties and over 60,000 affiliated churches. Its goal was to have ten activists in each of the 175,000 voting precincts in America, ready for the 1996 presidential election. If achieved, it could probably claim to be the dominant political party machine in the country. Neither the Democrats nor the Republicans, which had largely degenerated into rather creaky systems for channeling corporate funds to TV companies, would be able to claim such a nationwide organizational reach.

The Republican Party, however, was still a far broader coalition than the Christian Coalition would like. It contained powerful supporters of abortion rights, some prominent advocates of gay rights, and a large core in its traditional base of the affluent suburbs and the country clubs who were palpably uncomfortable with the stridency of the new Republican leaders. In his support for affirmative action and gay rights, Massachusetts governor William Weld was one of several leading Republicans, like Governor Christine Todd Whitman of New Jersey or Senator Arlen Specter of Pennsylvania, who seemed ideologically closer to President Clinton than to Speaker Gingrich. And in his rhetoric of balanced budgets and middle-class tax cuts, of death penalties and an end to traditional welfare, Clinton sounded far more attuned to these liberal Republicans than to the bulk of his own party in Congress. That had been Clinton's political appeal from the beginning, not only on the 1992 campaign trail with his talk of "a third way," but in his original identification with the New Democrats of the DLC.

In the course of 1995, Clinton won back the New Democrats from their earlier dismay. In Clinton's first summer in the White House, Al From had sent him a stiff memo that read: "The bottom line is this: By the end of your campaign, most Americans believed you when you said you were a New Democrat. Today, too many of them believe you are governing like an old one." By the end of 1995, the DLC leaders were proud to call him one of their own, claiming that at last he has recaptured the political initiative. His successor as DLC chairman, Senator John Breaux of Louisiana, declared, "The president has been reborn."

It was never easy to say exactly what Clinton did stand for. His desk at the Oval Office betrayed his taste for a range of inspirations. Most presidents make do with the bust of one inspiring predecessor. Clinton has five: Abraham Lincoln, Theodore Roosevelt, Harry S. Truman, and two of Franklin Delano Roosevelt. There was also one of comedian Will Rogers. He was always prey to sudden and surging enthusiasms on the basis of the most recent interesting conversation, or the latest speed-read book. He became briefly spiritual after he read Stephen Carter's *The Culture of Disbelief: How American Law and Politics Trivialize Religious Devotion.* Then he read *Awaken the Giant Within* by the new age self-improvement guru Anthony Robbins, and invited him up to give personalized seminars at Camp David. Clinton developed an instant fascination for third world birth control after reading a despairing essay in *Atlantic Monthly* about the disintegration of West Africa. He read David McCullough's biography of President Truman to inspire himself with the prospect of an electoral comeback after defeat in the midterm congressional elections. Then he read John Morton Blum's *The Progressive Presidents,* and in the following week spent five days touring the four important electoral states of Pennsylvania, Florida, Colorado, and California, raising a brisk $5 million for his well-funded reelection campaign, and talking about the Progressive era at the beginning of the twentieth century.

It was not a politician's stump speech, but more that curious blend of the preacher and teacher that was the Clinton hallmark, and another feature he shared with his contemporary, Newt Gingrich. The speech was designed to reinvent himself again as the New Progressive, or, as he sought to imply, the kind of leader Americans were lucky enough to elect once in a century.

"I believe this is the most profound period of change we have faced in a hundred years. If we do this election right, if we make these one-hundred-year decisions right the best is yet to be," was the new theme. "We have a set of one-hundred-year decisions to make," he said in Philadelphia. "We've got a big stake in the future and a great deal of how we live for the next twenty years will be determined by the outcome of this presidential election," he continued in Florida. "This is one of those get-off-the-dime elections," he assured them in Colorado. "Since we got started as a country we've had about four periods of really profound change: obviously, leading up to and then after the Civil War, and then when we changed from a rural to an industrial economy between about 1895 and 1916; and then the Great Depression, and World War Two and the cold war; and now coming out of that, this new global economy and the information age."

To the bafflement of the mainly elderly audiences to whom he was speaking on health and Medicare reform, Clinton was giving history lessons, and also poaching the rhetoric of Republican Speaker Gingrich about the coming third wave of the new information age. "About a hundred years ago, a lot of the ties that bound people together were uprooted, families were uprooted, whole communities began to disappear. We also saw children working ten, twelve, fourteen hours a day, six days a week, in the mines and factories of this country. We saw an absolute disregard for the preservation of our natural resources. . . . And for about twenty years we had this raging debate, and we decided that the national government should promote genuine competition, if it meant breaking up monopolies; should protect children from the abuses of child labor that were then present; should attempt to preserve our natural resources; and should in common promote the personal well-being and development of our people. . . . And what happened after that was the most dramatic, breathtaking period of economic and social progress in the United States ever experienced by any country," he went on in Philadelphia. "We can do it again if we make change our friend."

As always with Clinton, the latest book and the newest enthusiasm were seized upon because they reinforced a tactic or a policy he already had in mind. The New Progressive theme was a way, palatable to most Democrats, to explain Clinton's own response to the changing political landscape and the way he felt he could place himself within it to win reelection.

The vogue word in the Clinton reelection team was *triangulation*—to distinguish the president from the old guard Democrats in Congress, but also from the new right-wing Republicans. Conceived by the political consultant Dick Morris, who had worked exclusively for Republicans since his last campaign for Clinton in Arkansas in 1990, triangulation sought to run a campaign on the four E's: economy, education, environment, and Re-

extremism. Morris's relationship with Clinton had always been nvolving one Clintonian punch to the Morris jaw in the 1990 governorship campaign. But ever ready to answer his old friend's call, Morris returned to his side to provide the political rationale for Clinton's gamble that the Republicans might pass more of his domestic agenda than the old Democratic Congress had done.

It was Bill Clinton's unilateral declaration of independence from the Democratic Party in Congress. Against the pleadings of his party and almost all of his White House political advisers, he announced his own plan to balance the budget over ten years, rather than the seven years of the Republican project. In the course of seventy-two hours in June, between his collegial and determinedly well-mannered exchange with Speaker Newt Gingrich at a New Hampshire town meeting and his five-minute TV address to the nation on his budget plans, Clinton tried to reinvent himself as Dwight D. Eisenhower. The historical parallel is compelling. In his first two years in office, President Eisenhower enjoyed (if that is the word) a Republican majority in Congress. The Democrats then regained control in the 1954 midterm elections. But Eisenhower went on to reelection two years later, having forged an effective bipartisan relationship with the Democratic Speaker Sam Rayburn.

In effect, Clinton accepted that the Republican victory in the November elections was a moment at which history changed, with a firm new American consensus to cut government spending and balance the budget. He prepared to go along with Speaker Gingrich, portraying himself as the one to protect the poor and elderly from the harsh effects of Republican cuts and to insist on the government's strategic role in investing public funds in the future through education and job training. In making this decision to abandon what has been called the "reactionary liberalism" of the congressional Democrats, President Clinton's strongest support in the White House and cabinet came from that other southern centrist, Vice President Al Gore. It was not enough to be against the Republicans, Gore insisted. The president had to stand for something positive, to erect a banner around which his supporters could rally.

To achieve it, Clinton was prepared to end a tradition of welfare that went back to the New Deal, of using public funds to help poor and solitary mothers stay with their children. "I had no idea how profoundly what used to be known as liberalism was shaken by the last election," mourned New York's Senator Moynihan. The sixty-year consensus was over, and a new one was emerging with Clinton's essential backing. It was widely interpreted as shifting the center of balance in American politics to the right. That was only partially true. The process was far more complex and deep-rooted. It also reflected a shift of the geographical center of gravity in American politics, from the North and East to the South and West. It reflected a transformed socioeconomic system. When the New Deal consensus was devised, there was an identifiable mass working class, employed in large factories and organized into mass unions, who lived in the cities. By the time it ended, the American social system was marked by a mass middle class, in which barely one employee in ten in the private sector was a union member, and they lived in suburbs.

When the New Deal welfare system was put into place, Americans retired from work at the age of sixty-five, and usually died having collected Social Security for less than five years. When it reached its crisis in the mid-1990s, the welfare state of America, and those of Europe and Japan, were all groaning under the demographic weight of an aging population who customarily collected their pensions for ten years, often for fifteen, and sometimes far more. A great medical achievement, and a human triumph, this broad extension of the life span was a fiscal nightmare. Perhaps, in the way that it had required the Republican anti-Communist Richard Nixon to open U.S. diplomatic links with China, a Democratic president was needed to tackle the financial consequences of the demographic revolution. Clinton had made one brave stab at the issue with his bill for universal health reform. He was then to compromise with the Republicans when they took up the challenge.

Bill Clinton was almost genetically designed to comprehend these deeper currents of demography, geography, and economics, which required that America find a new consensus in the years after the end of the cold war. His own life embodied so many of the changes that America had undergone to make the old New Deal consensus redundant. He came from the South, a part of the country that had gone from backwardness to unprecedented prosperity, from chronic population loss to population growth within his lifetime. His mother had worked and educated her way into the new mass middle class, and he had won scholarships and university credentials that catapulted him into the ranks of the American elite. He was a meritocrat at a time when American society was uniquely tailored to reward merit.

He was one of the most typical of all American presidents, in that his own life paralleled so much of the nation's own growth. He was born into that baby-boom generation of children conceived by the fathers who came home from World War Two, a generation which became the dominant age cohort of the next seventy years. His small-town boyhood and intense family ties spoke to that hunger for roots in an America that was the most relentlessly mobile of societies, and the education and achievements of his youth embodied that American passion for self-improvement and attainment. Bill Clinton was always to be found at that endlessly moving spot where the bulk of his generation wanted to be at a particular time. He was passionate for Elvis and for John Kennedy. He was devoted to the cause of civil rights, and then, like the bulk of his contemporaries, he both avoided the Vietnam War and opposed it, while not letting that stand on principle obscure his deeper commitment to his own qualifications and career. He and his wife chose the law as their careers, when the law was becoming the predominant career aspiration of the ambitious. He and his wife then sought to make serious money in that period when the baby-boomers were prepared to be known as yuppies.

Bill Clinton contained all of the characteristics of his generation, distilled to an intensity that matched his ambition. Those characteristics were not solely defined by self-interest. He always maintained an almost mystic faith in education, as both civic duty and moral good, convinced that his route to distinction should be even wider and easier for his successors. He never compromised on his absolute commitment to the cause of civil rights as defined by Martin Luther King. There was racism in America, and it had to be confronted. Success was harder for black Americans to achieve, and they deserved society's help. But at the same time, if society was going to offer its help through affirmative action, then poor and black Americans had to do what the Clinton family and tens of millions of other upwardly mobile Americans had done: work hard, stay in school, play by the rules, offer a personal commitment to match the social opportunity.

Nor did Clinton ever abandon his faith in the role and the duties of the state as a great machine for social improvement. The evidence of government's capacity to do good has shaped his life. The federal government had brought the investments and the roads and the military bases to the South, which had helped haul the region out of a century of backwardness. The federal government had forced the South to end segregation and give black Americans the vote. The state had ended the long nightmare of poverty for the aged and had financed the educational system that allowed Clinton's generation to blossom. "Government's responsibility is to create more opportunity. The people's responsibility is to make the most of it," he said when announcing his presidential bid, as succinct a statement of his creed as he ever made.

Bill Clinton was the archetypal postwar American, his life unfolding to the rhythms of the vast social revolution that was gathering speed around him. The first in his family to go to college, he was also the first in his family to go abroad in anything but military uniform, the first governor of his state to go abroad to open trade missions, the first president whose summits were on trade pacts rather than arms treaties.

The contradictions in his life defined him, from redneck roots to Rhodes scholar polish. He was raised by strong women, yet one of the defining moments of his youth came when he had to defend his mother against a drunken stepfather. He was the boy who worked assiduously to be teacher's pet and to be voted class president, and then put on shades to play in a jazz trio. Single-minded in political ambition, he was thoroughly undisciplined in much of his personal life, from keeping time to running meetings to gratifying his vast personal appetites. He was not, in the America of the sexual revolution, an unusually promiscuous man, nor was he a faithful husband. In this, too, he was hardly atypical of his generation in America at large, nor in the political milieu he had chosen. He was, in his flaws and sensual weaknesses, his readiness to put off hard decisions until it was almost too late, his fondness for spending, and his casual approach to debt, utterly typical of the America of his day. He was, in that sense, the president America deserved.

He was at his political best in the smallest of small-town gatherings, a catfish supper or a convivial summer barbecue, and in its television equivalent of the talk show. To an American transfixed by the garrulous confessions of daytime TV, he was the confessional president, intimate and yet so glib that he began to devalue the coinage of appearances so easily caricatured. But he was also a master of the set-piece theater of the grand public speech. His State of the Union addresses were invariably the occasion of a jump in his opinion polls. Yet, for a president who spent more on polls than any predecessor, and devoured them and set his political course by them like some ancient Roman reading the auguries of the sacrificial beasts, he often used them as a spur to fight, rather than pander. If there was one constant characteristic of Bill Clinton's political career, it was an utter refusal ever to give up. Evicted from his governorship of Arkansas, he came back to win again and again.

Eclipsed by scandal in the New Hampshire primary, he plowed on with his campaign. Torpedoed in his first three months as president by his own inexperience and rotten advice and a recalcitrant Congress, he slogged on to lose health reform and a Democratic Congress, and he slogged on yet again. In the core of the man, there was something very nearly invincible. For a president so eager to be loved by all, there was a determination to keep on talking and dealing, and if he could not get his way, then he was prepared to settle for half of it.

This was his real mastery, the dealing of politics. In Arkansas, he had learned to compromise with the rich and powerful whose campaign funds could be the difference between election and defeat, and whose investments might mean grim and dirty and polluting jobs, but they were better than no jobs at all. In Washington, he proved to be better at dealing with Republican zealots than with Democratic pragmatists. On the international stage, he learned when and how to deploy the great asset of presidential prestige. In persuading Boris Yeltsin to withdraw the last troops from the Baltic states; in nudging his British allies to deal on Northern Ireland; in levering the great reluctancies of the Middle East; in seizing the moment to impose a peace settlement in the Bosnian war, he applied the political skills of an Arkansas backroom fixer to the great international issues of his day, and helped them all along.

To keep the process moving, to keep the talks in session, never to accept a failure as final—this was the essence of his politics. With Bill Clinton, a deal was never complete and a victory could always be qualified with the makings of another deal somewhere down the road. He would always come back for more, and there would always somewhere be that characteristic Clintonian wire coat hanger that could be poked beneath a door to hook back one final decision in order to substitute it for another. As with all politicians, the most important next date in his calendar was the next election, but he had an unusually flexible sense of political time, always ready to turn this year's setback into next year's agreement.

In the end, whether he is a one-term president or not, Bill Clinton will be remembered for what he did for the long haul. He came to the White House to lead an America deeply uncertain of its global role, increasingly wary of its global commitments. And in the most consistent single strategy of his presidency, he shifted the nature of that debate away from the militarized slogans of the past to the commercial realities of the future. He had become the free trade president, who had locked America into the dominant place in the new institutions of the global economy. At home, the failure or hopeless dilution of so many of Clinton's individual reforms was in the end balanced and even outweighed by his part in finally sinking the untenable old consensus of the New Deal, and the crafting of a new one.

The leaner, meaner government was not what Clinton had set out to achieve, nor was it a new domestic order to be proud of. But it was wholly consistent with the campaigning promises he had made in 1992, and it gave him something that he might otherwise have lacked, a compass to steer by in a second term. The new tasks of politics would be to define just what could be done within that leaner, meaner model; to establish what Americans would accept as sensible long-term investment, rather than immediate handout. For his texts, he could turn back to his campaign speeches of 1992, to lifetime education and job training, to equipping the American people for the intensity of global competition into which he had already thrust them.

Without such a return to the promises of domestic reform, Clinton would leave a clouded legacy of an America whose social system was breaking down from that mass middle class of his youth into a curiously European, even Victorian social system. Bracketed by an underclass of which lean, mean government had virtually washed its hands, and by an overclass of Clintonian meritocrats, the American middle class was sullen, insecure, and far from sure that their children would do any better. The tragic irony of Clinton's presidency was that it had done little to make politics work for these "forgotten hardworking middle-class families of America" on whom he had based his presidential appeal. He had been a rewarding president for America's bondholders and for its exporters, for its stock market investors and its industries of policing and prisons. But they had not elected him.

The ordinary Americans who had put him into the White House, with a 43 percent mandate, faced a difficult dilemma as they weighed their votes in 1996. His four years in office had delivered over 9 million new jobs, but they came with a very different economy of part-time employment and downsized corporations, of job insecurity and constant vulnerability to global competition. He had presided over unprecedented rates of incarceration in the prison system and the highest number of executions since the 1930s, but violent crime was sharply reduced. His term in office had seen an export boom, and the United States delivered the best economic performance in terms of productivity, inflation, and job creation of any of the major industrial economies. The difficulty was that while the U.S. economy as a whole was performing well, the U.S. economy as the sum total of the experience of more than 250 million individual Americans was very much more problematic.

Unlike Bush, Clinton had a defense. He could claim to have confronted the great constraint of the deficit. By April of election year, it was clear that growth and buoyant tax revenues and lower spending were combining to cut the year's deficit to $135 billion, the lowest figure for over a decade. Clinton's initial decision, at his administration's first meeting on economic strategy, was to insist that the deficit should be cut to $200 billion by his reelection year. He had done very much better than that, and had maintained economic growth and cut both inflation and unemployment.

To an extraordinary extent, Clinton's first term had resembled what might have been in George Bush's second term. America had reasserted its leadership of NATO; and in the Middle East, in Bosnia, in Northern Ireland, and in cajoling Russia into a kind of partnership, it had reaffirmed the obvious—that little could be achieved internationally without the engagement of the world's only superpower. Clinton had continued and far expanded Bush's original perception of a central U.S. role in crafting a "new world order" of free trading democracies. And yet Clinton's failure in much of the domestic agenda, from reforms of the health, welfare, and unemployment systems, left him open to the same kind of populist attack he had deployed so effectively against President Bush.

Americans still grumbled that the recovery had been feeble, and that most family incomes had been stagnant. But the United States was an island of prosperity amid the rest of the industrialized nations. When Clinton was campaigning to win the White House, his rivals used to say that the cold war was over, America had lost, and Japan, or perhaps the new united Germany, had won. By the time Clinton faced reelection, the Japanese and European models were looking far less attractive. Japan's economy was smaller at the end of 1995 than it had been in 1990. Germany was in serious straits, with unemployment above 10 percent, and the budget deficit and national debt were so high that Germany could not meet the criteria it had set for its European partners as the minimum proof of economic stability that would allow the move to a European currency.

From the perspective of his reelection year, most of the rest of the world would judge Clinton as an initially troubling and feckless, but finally admirable president. Most Americans might have preferred to withhold judgment of a man whose achievements in government were those of a traditional liberal Republican president. But in setting the course for the new international consensus of free trading internationalism, and for the new domestic consensus around leaner and meaner government, he had strong grounds to claim his right to reelection. Only a second term would define whether Clinton could make that leaner government work for most Americans, by giving them the education, the job training, and the psychological security that would make that furious new world of global competition into a challenge that was rewarding as well as bracing. Having acquiesced in the great shrinkage of the New Deal and Great Society, he had still to show that activist government could be made to work. His strength was that nobody else on the political landscape seemed much inclined to try.

CLINTON ADMINISTRATION CHRONOLOGY

1993

January 20	Inauguration
22	Zoe Baird nomination withdrawn
25	Hillary Clinton given health reform task force
February 10	Promise of U.S. troops to enforce Bosnia peace
17	Clinton presents economic plan to Congress
April 3	First summit with Yeltsin
19	FBI assault on Branch Davidian compound at Waco, Texas, followed by fire and 83 deaths
29	Clinton loses economic stimulus bill in Congress
May 19	Christophe's $200 haircut at LAX
June 4	David Gergen appointed
July 5–6	G7 Tokyo summit
19	Vince Foster found dead
September 13	Arafat and Rabin sign peace accord at White House
27	Health reform plan unveiled to Congress
29	White House first hears of possible Justice Department criminal investigation into bankruptcy of Madison Guaranty
October 3	18 U.S. Rangers killed in Mogadishu
11	USS *Harlan County* turns back from Haiti
November 17	Congress passes NAFTA
20	Asia-Pacific summit in Seattle
December 15	Defense Secretary Aspin "resigns"
19	*American Spectator* publishes "What the Troopers Saw"
21	*Washington Times* says Whitewater files removed from Vince Foster's office after his death

1994

January 6	Senator Dole demands special prosecutor
12	Clinton, from NATO summit in Europe, asks Janet Reno to appoint an independent counsel to investigate Whitewater affairs
30	U.S. visa granted to Sinn Fein's Gerry Adams
February 5	68 die in Sarajevo marketplace mortar attack; NATO promises to protect Muslim "safe havens"
March 5	White House counsel Bernard Nussbaum resigns
18	U.S. diplomacy establishes Bosnian-Croat Federation
April 10	NATO jets hit Serb ground targets at Gorazde
June 27	Leon Panetta appointed White House chief of staff
28	2,656 Haitian boat people picked up by U.S. Navy
July 6	G7 economic summit in Italy; Yeltsin pressed to withdraw last Russian troops from Baltic states

July 21	Clinton health reform plan dropped by Congress
August 12	Crime bill defeated
17	Deputy Treasury Secretary Roger Altman resigns after congressional hearings into "improper" referrals to White House
21	Crime bill passed
31	Cease-fire announced in Northern Ireland
September 18	Haitian military agree to leave office
27	GOP congressmen sign "Contract with America"
October 7	U.S. reinforcements rush to Persian Gulf after Iraqi threat
November 8	The Republican landslide victory in Congress
11	U.S. stops enforcing UN arms embargo in Balkans
December 1	GATT trade pact passes Congress
6	Lloyd Bentsen resigns as treasury secretary
9	Miami summit on Western Hemisphere free trade pact
29	Mexican economic collapse

1995

January 4	Republicans take over Congress
February 4	$1 billion sanctions threat against China
March 2	Republicans lose balanced budget amendment in Senate
April 18	Clinton says, "The president is relevant here"
19	Oklahoma City terrorist blast
May 8	Moscow summit; Clinton demands "more robust" policy on Bosnia
17	Clinton's first veto, on $16 billion budget cut
June 14	Clinton promises to balance budget in ten years
July 11	Fall of "safe haven" Srebrenica
25	Fall of "safe haven" Zepa
August 4	Croatian offensive begins against Bosnian Serbs
11	Clinton vetoes Congress attempt to lift arms embargo
19	Death of Ambassador Robert Frasure and two other members of U.S. negotiating team on Mount Igman in Bosnia-Herzegovina
30	Start of NATO air strikes, led by U.S., against Bosnian Serb air defenses
September 7	Outline of Bosnian peace agreement announced
October 5	Bosnian cease-fire announced
16	Million-Man March; Clinton sticks with affirmative action
November 8	General Colin Powell says he will not run for president
14	First U.S. government shutdown in budget battle; lasts three days
21	Bosnian peace agreement reached at Dayton, Ohio
30	Clinton's triumphant reception in peaceful Belfast
December 1	Clinton signs treaty of intent for free trade with European Union
15	Second U.S. government shutdown begins; lasts two weeks

December *15*	Last day for New Hampshire primary deadline; Clinton will face no serious Democratic opponents

1996

January 8	First Lady is "congenital liar," writes William Safire in *New York Times*
9	Budget talks with Congress break down; U.S. Appeals Court says Paula Jones's lawsuit may proceed
23	"The era of big government is over," says Clinton in much-praised State of the Union address; Dole's response falters
26	Hillary Clinton appears before grand jury
February 9	IRA breaks cease-fire with bomb in London; two dead
20	Pat Buchanan wins New Hampshire primary
27	Steve Forbes wins Arizona primary
March 2	Dole wins South Carolina primary
12	Dole sweeps Super Tuesday primaries
14	Clinton orders two carrier groups to Taiwan waters
25	Dole secures Republican nomination by winning California primary
April 28	Clinton gives video testimony in Jim McDougal's fraud trial
May 15	Dole steps down from senate
August 12–15	Republican convention, San Diego
26–29	Democratic convention, Chicago
September 2	Electronic convention of Perot's Reform Party
November 5	Election Day

INDEX

Note: HRC refers to Hillary Rodham Clinton.